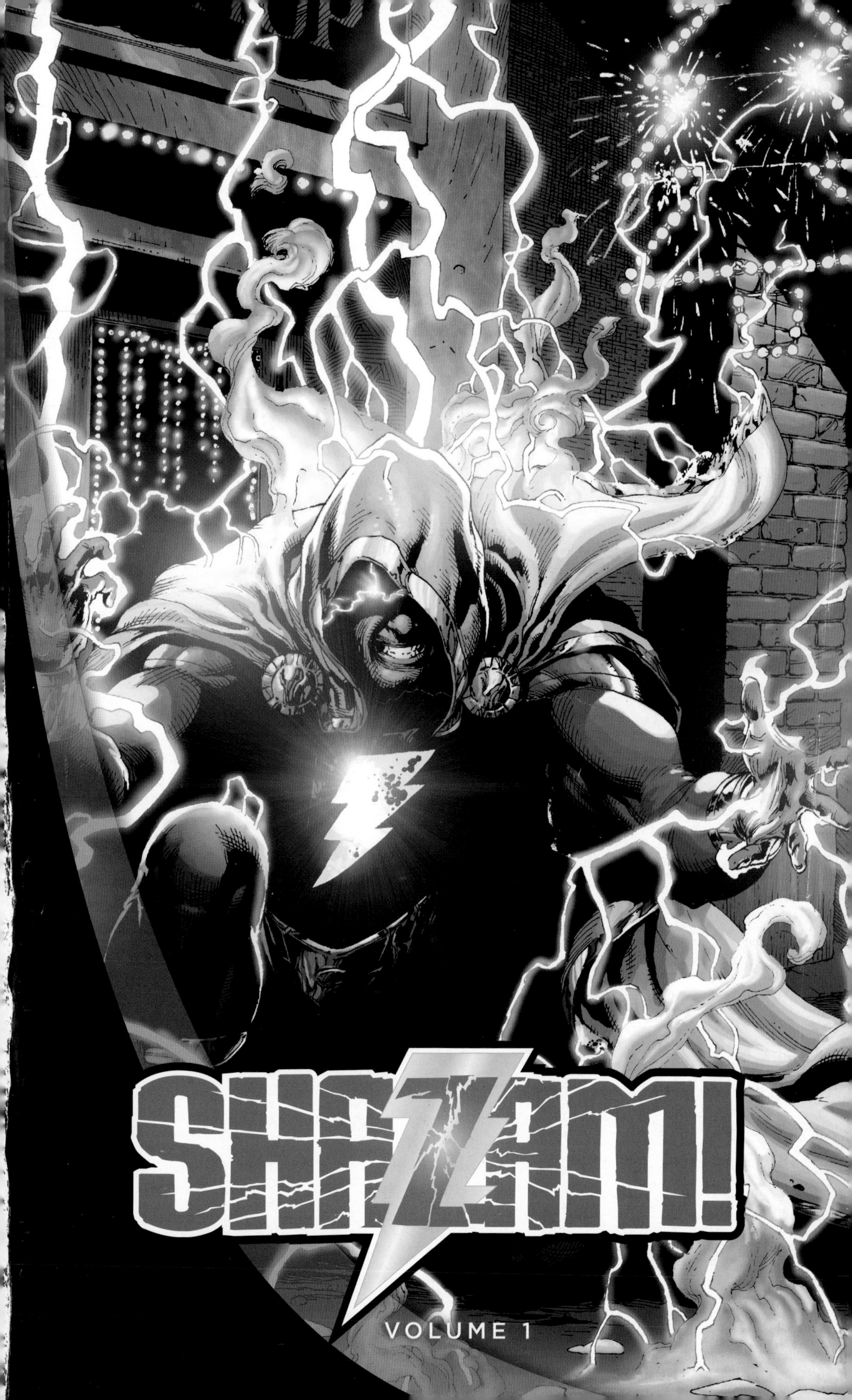
SHAZAM!
VOLUME 1

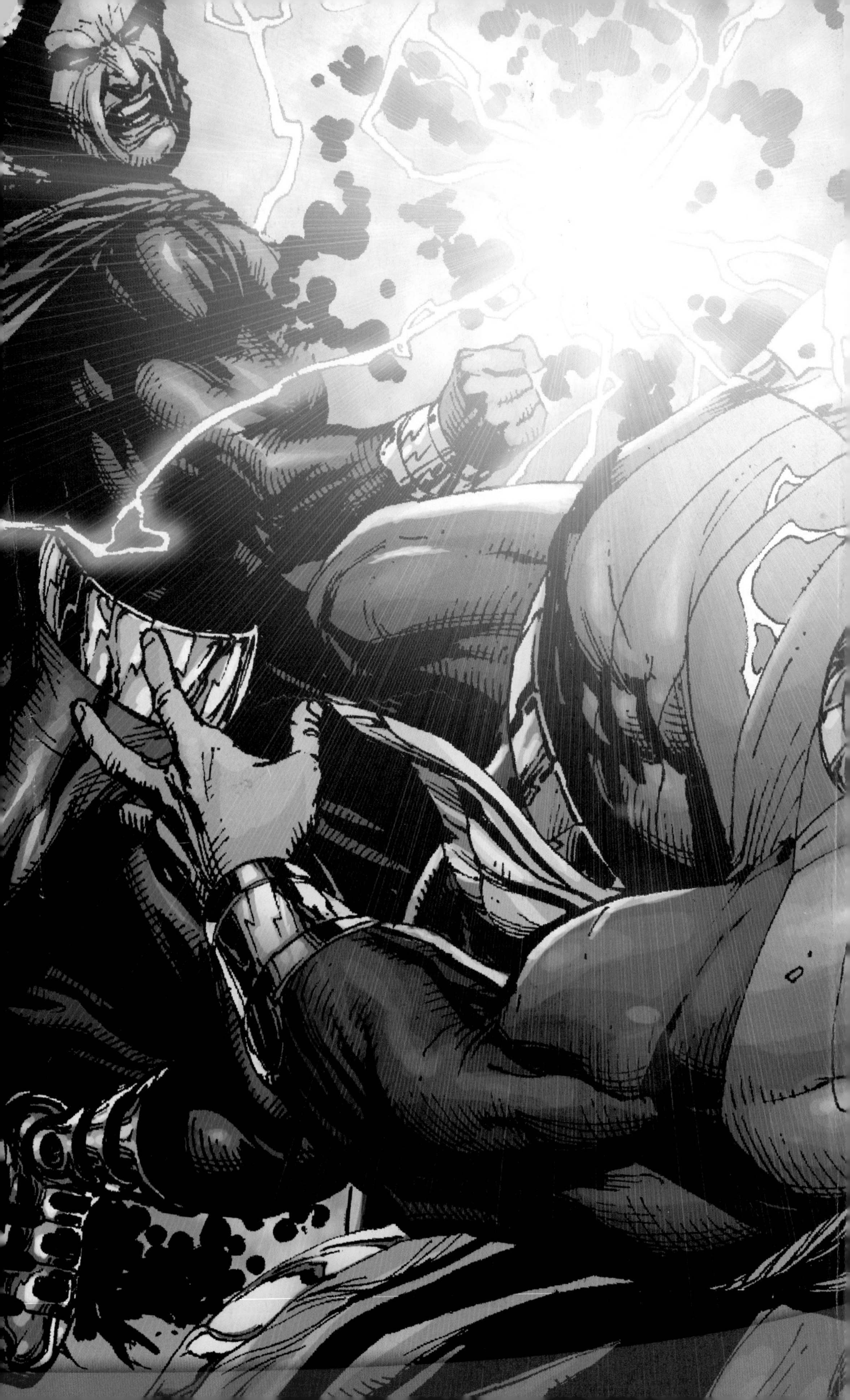

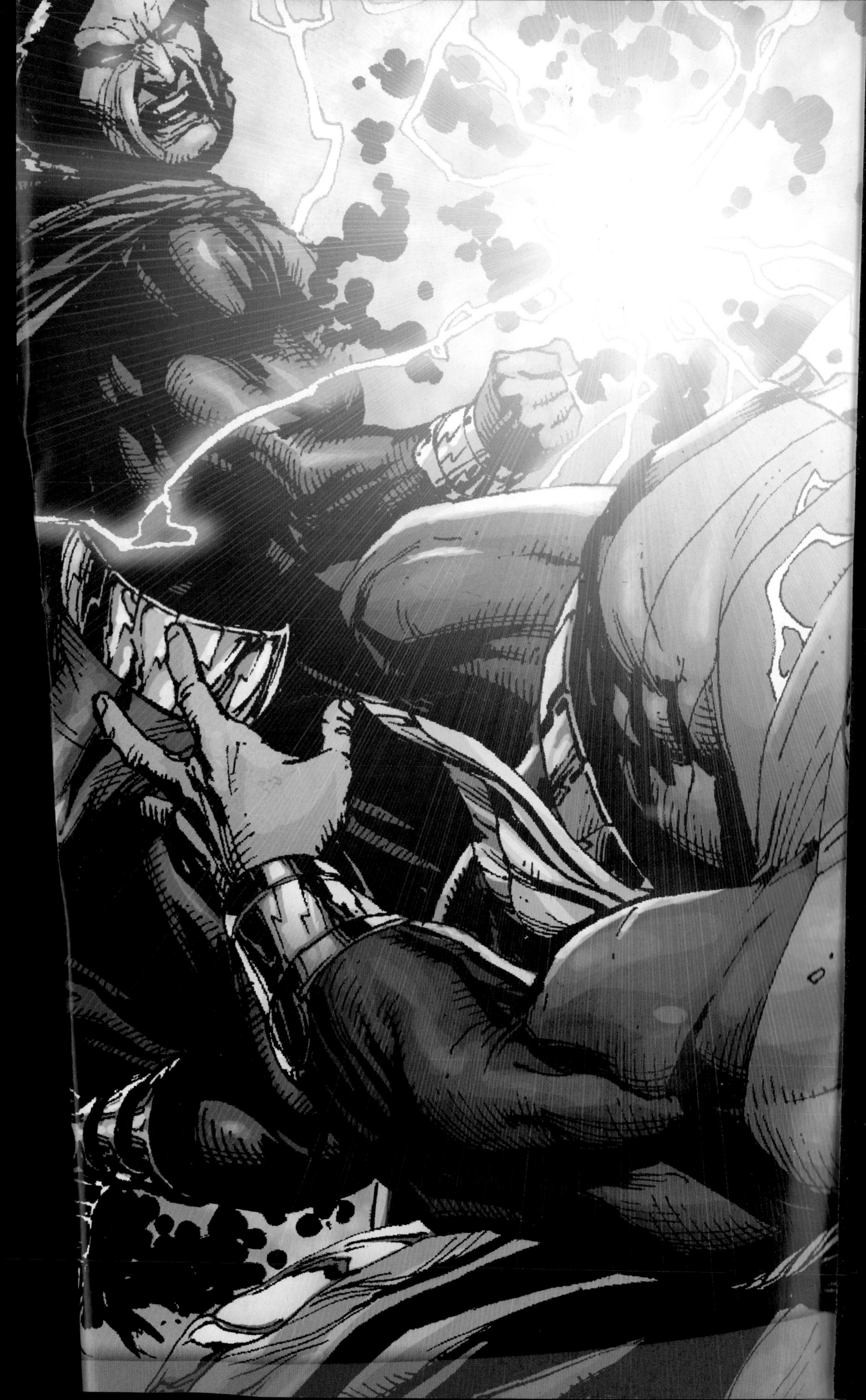

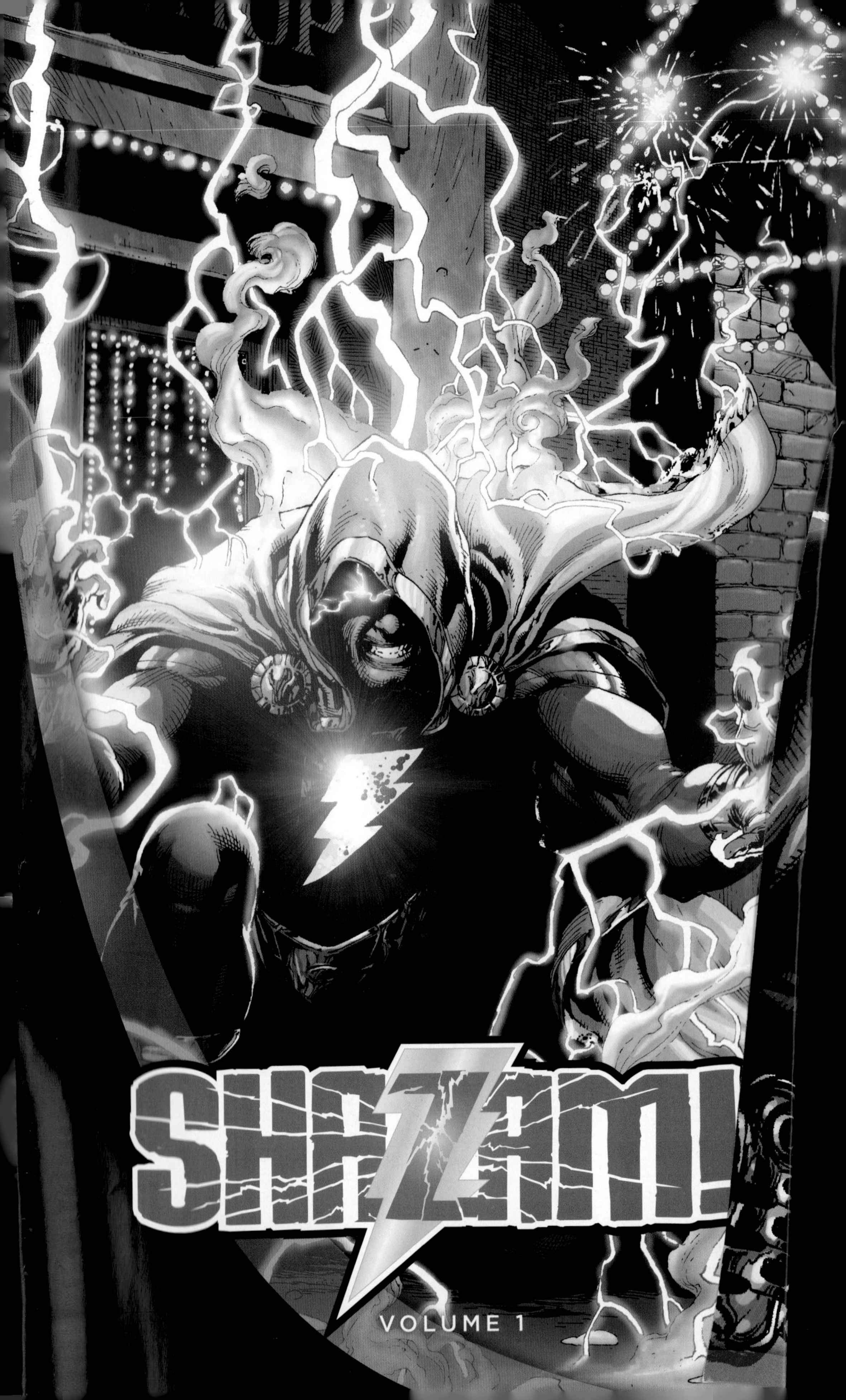
SHAZAM!
VOLUME 1

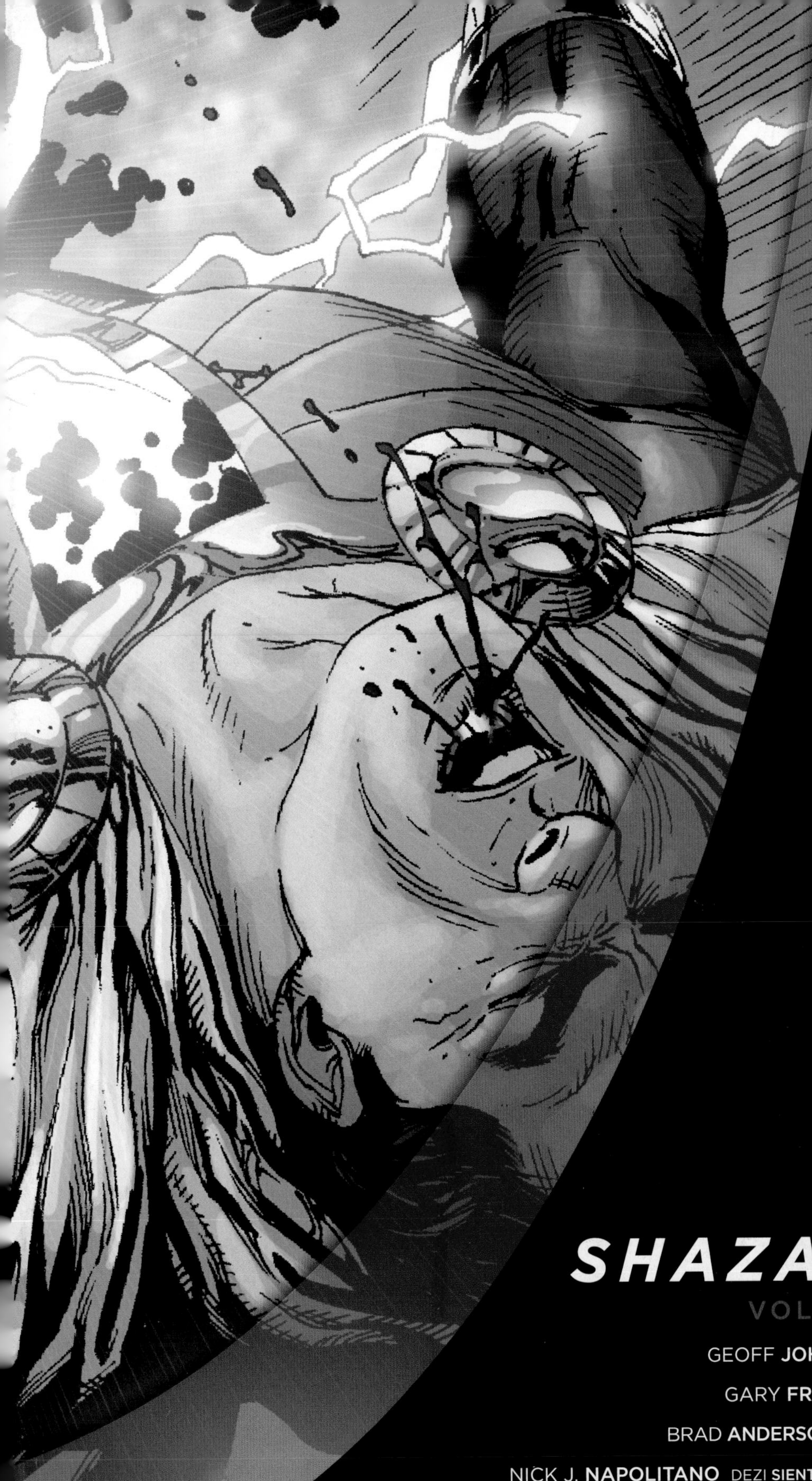

SHAZAM!

VOLUME 1

GEOFF **JOHNS** writer

GARY **FRANK** artist

BRAD **ANDERSON** colorist

NICK J. **NAPOLITANO** DEZI **SIENTY** letterers

GARY **FRANK** & BRAD **ANDERSON** collection cover

BRIAN CUNNINGHAM Editor – Original Series KATIE KUBERT Associate Editor – Original Series
DARREN SHAN KATE STEWART Assistant Editors – Original Series PETER HAMBOUSSI Editor
ROBBIN BROSTERMAN Design Director – Books ROBBIE BIEDERMAN Publication Design

BOB HARRAS Senior VP – Editor-in-Chief, DC Comics

DIANE NELSON President DAN DIDIO and JIM LEE Co-Publishers
GEOFF JOHNS Chief Creative Officer
JOHN ROOD Executive VP – Sales, Marketing and Business Development
AMY GENKINS Senior VP – Business and Legal Affairs NAIRI GARDINER Senior VP – Finance
JEFF BOISON VP – Publishing Planning MARK CHIARELLO VP – Art Direction and Design
JOHN CUNNINGHAM VP – Marketing TERRI CUNNINGHAM VP – Editorial Administration
ALISON GILL Senior VP – Manufacturing and Operations HANK KANALZ Senior VP – Vertigo and Integrated Publishing
JAY KOGAN VP – Business and Legal Affairs, Publishing JACK MAHAN VP – Business Affairs, Talent
NICK NAPOLITANO VP – Manufacturing Administration SUE POHJA VP – Book Sales
COURTNEY SIMMONS Senior VP – Publicity BOB WAYNE Senior VP – Sales

SHAZAM! VOLUME 1

DC Comics, 1700 Broadway, New York, NY 10019
A Warner Bros. Entertainment Company.
Printed by RR Donnelley, Salem, VA, USA. 8/23/13. First Printing.

HC ISBN: 978-1-4012-4244-2
SC ISBN: 978-1-4012-4699-0

SUSTAINABLE FORESTRY INITIATIVE

Certified Chain of Custody
At Least 20% Certified Forest Content
www.sfiprogram.org
SFI-01042
APPLIES TO TEXT STOCK ONLY

Library of Congress Cataloging-in-Publication Data

Johns, Geoff, 1973- author.
Shazam! volume 1 / Geoff Johns, Gary Frank.
pages cm
"Originally published in single magazine form as Justice League 7-11, 0, 14-16, 18-21."
ISBN 978-1-4012-4244-2
1. Graphic novels. I. Frank, Gary, 1969- illustrator. II. Title.
PN6728.S46J64 2013
741.5'973—dc23
2013020543

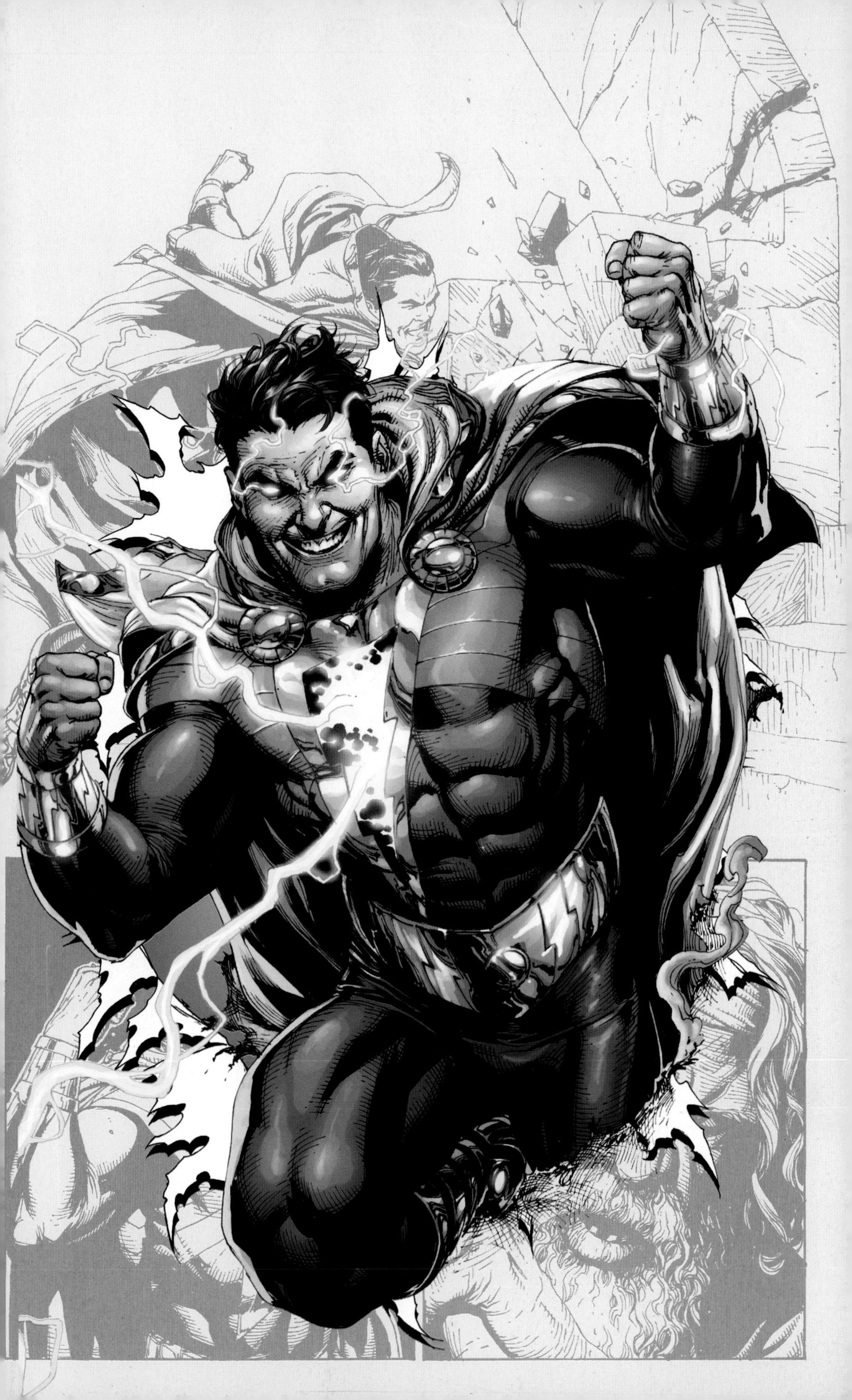

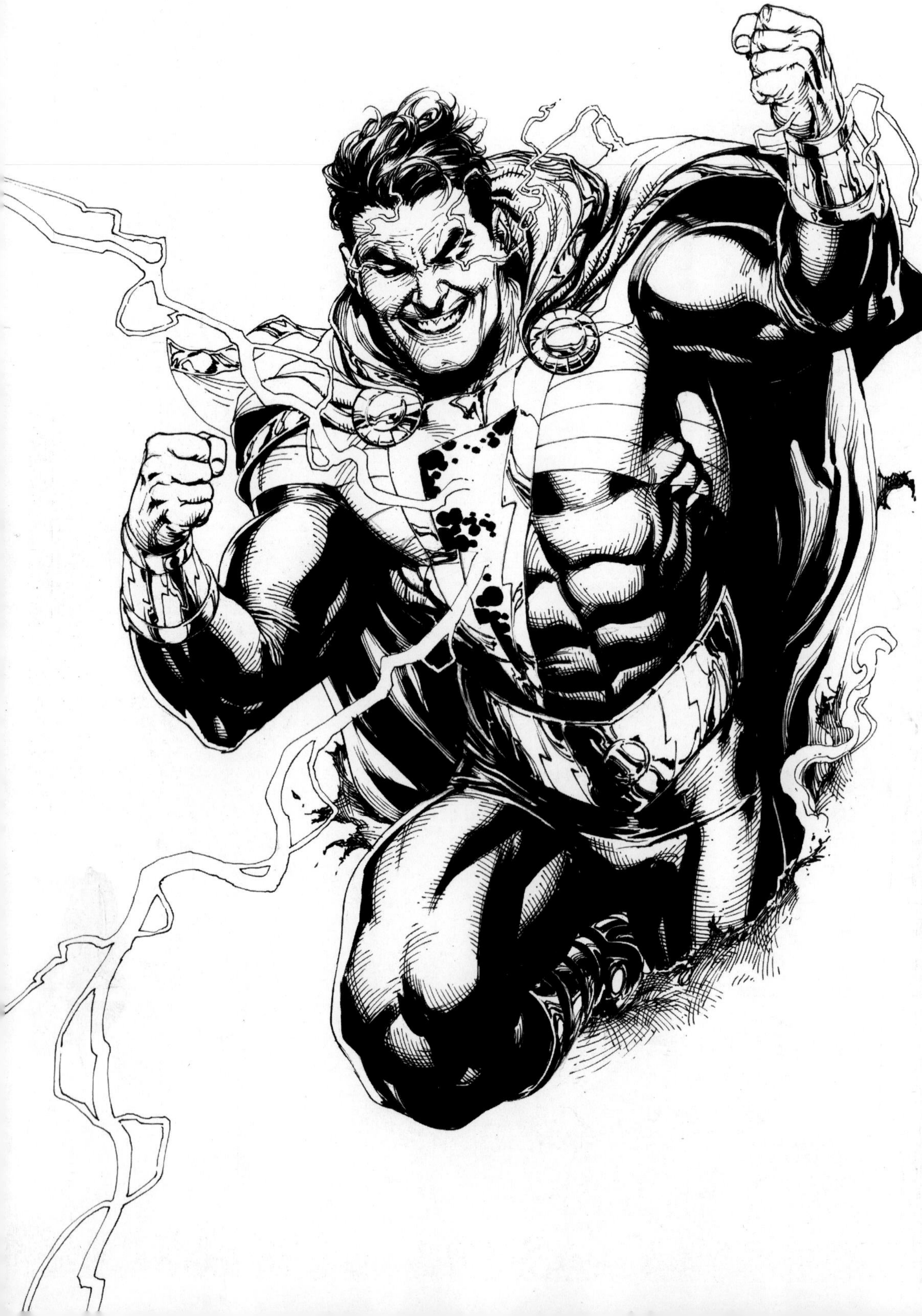

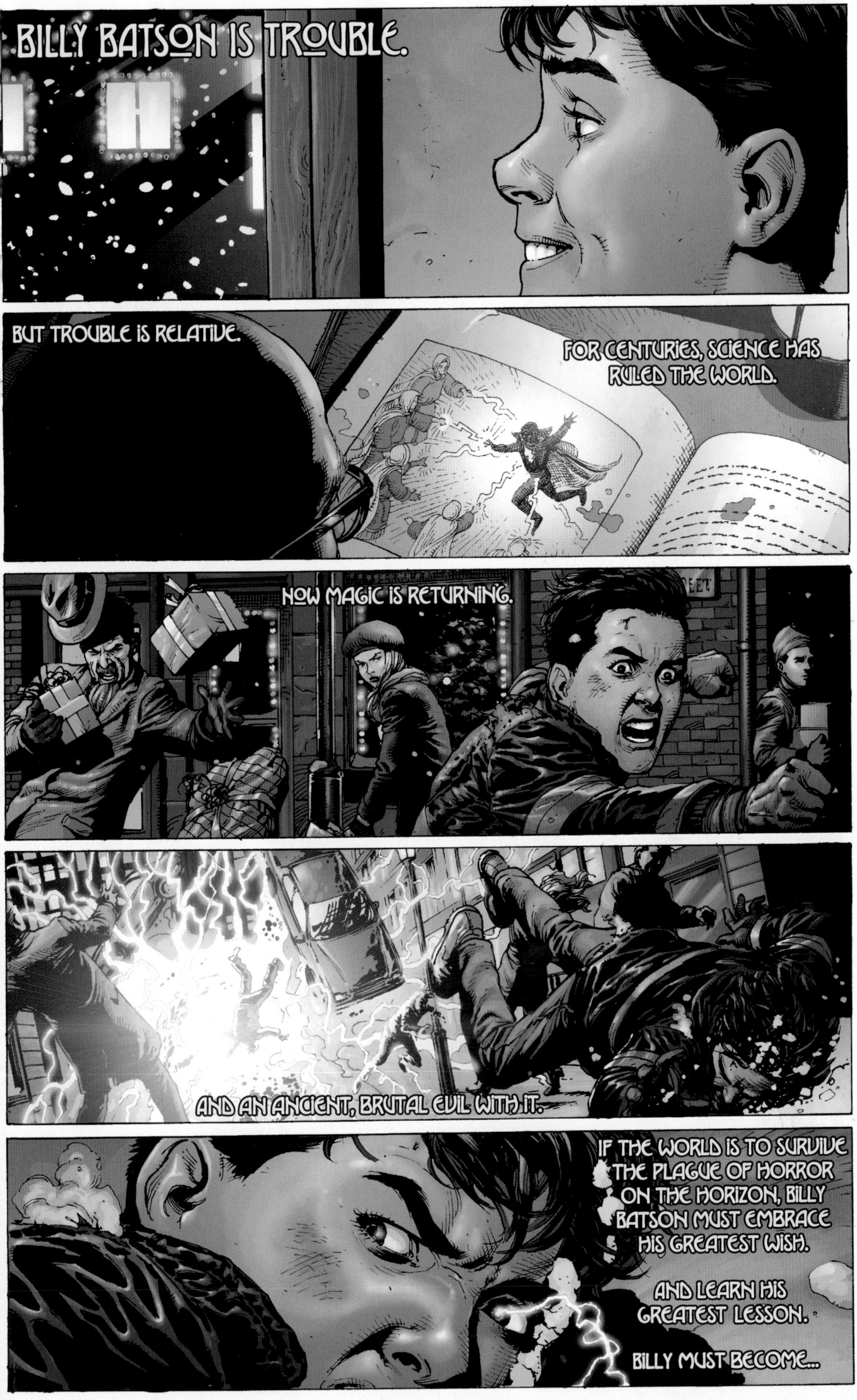

BILLY BATSON IS TROUBLE.
BUT TROUBLE IS RELATIVE.
FOR CENTURIES, SCIENCE HAS RULED THE WORLD.
NOW MAGIC IS RETURNING.
AND AN ANCIENT, BRUTAL EVIL WITH IT.
IF THE WORLD IS TO SURVIVE THE PLAGUE OF HORROR ON THE HORIZON, BILLY BATSON MUST EMBRACE HIS GREATEST WISH.
AND LEARN HIS GREATEST LESSON.
BILLY MUST BECOME...

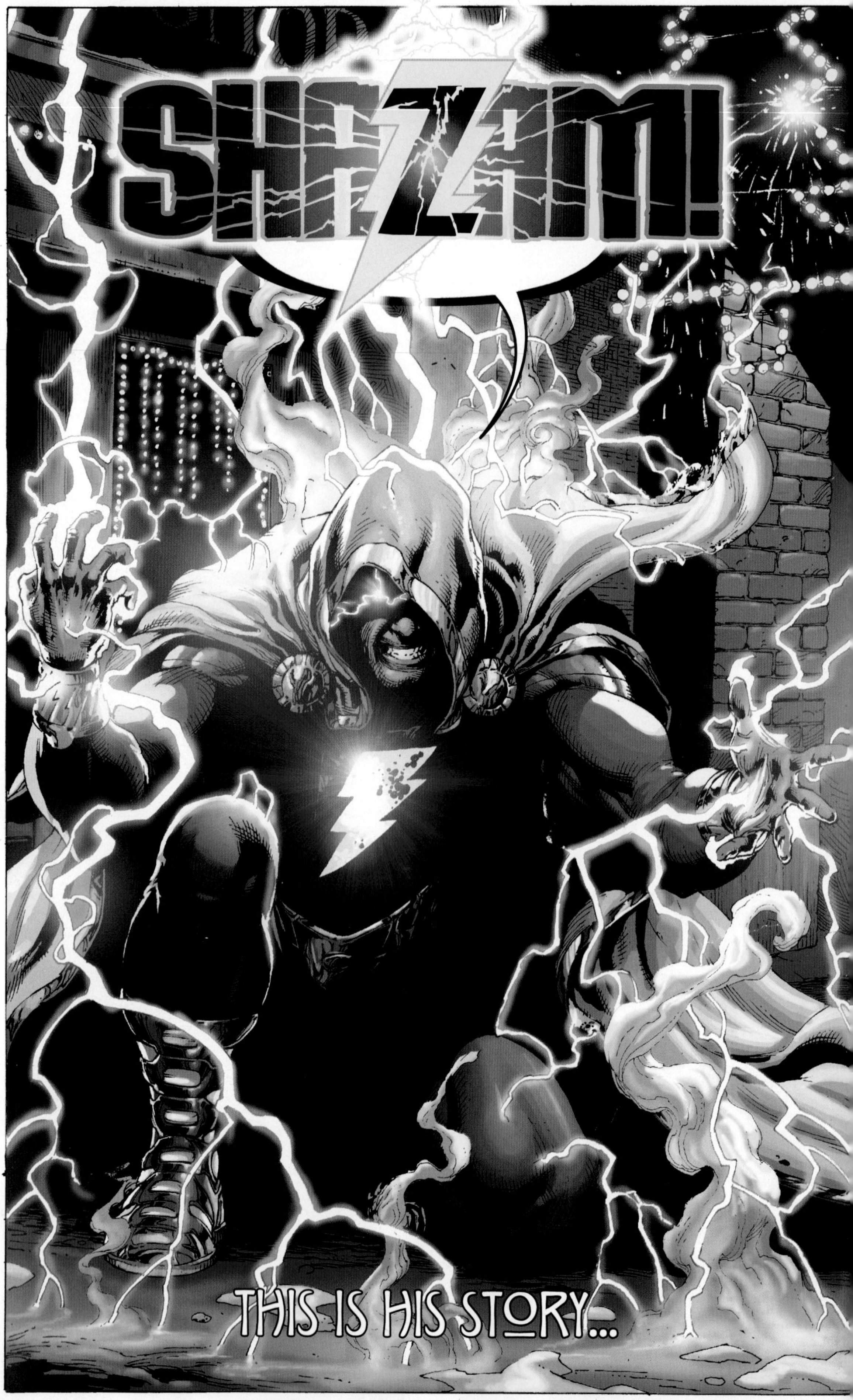
SHAZAM!
THIS IS HIS STORY...

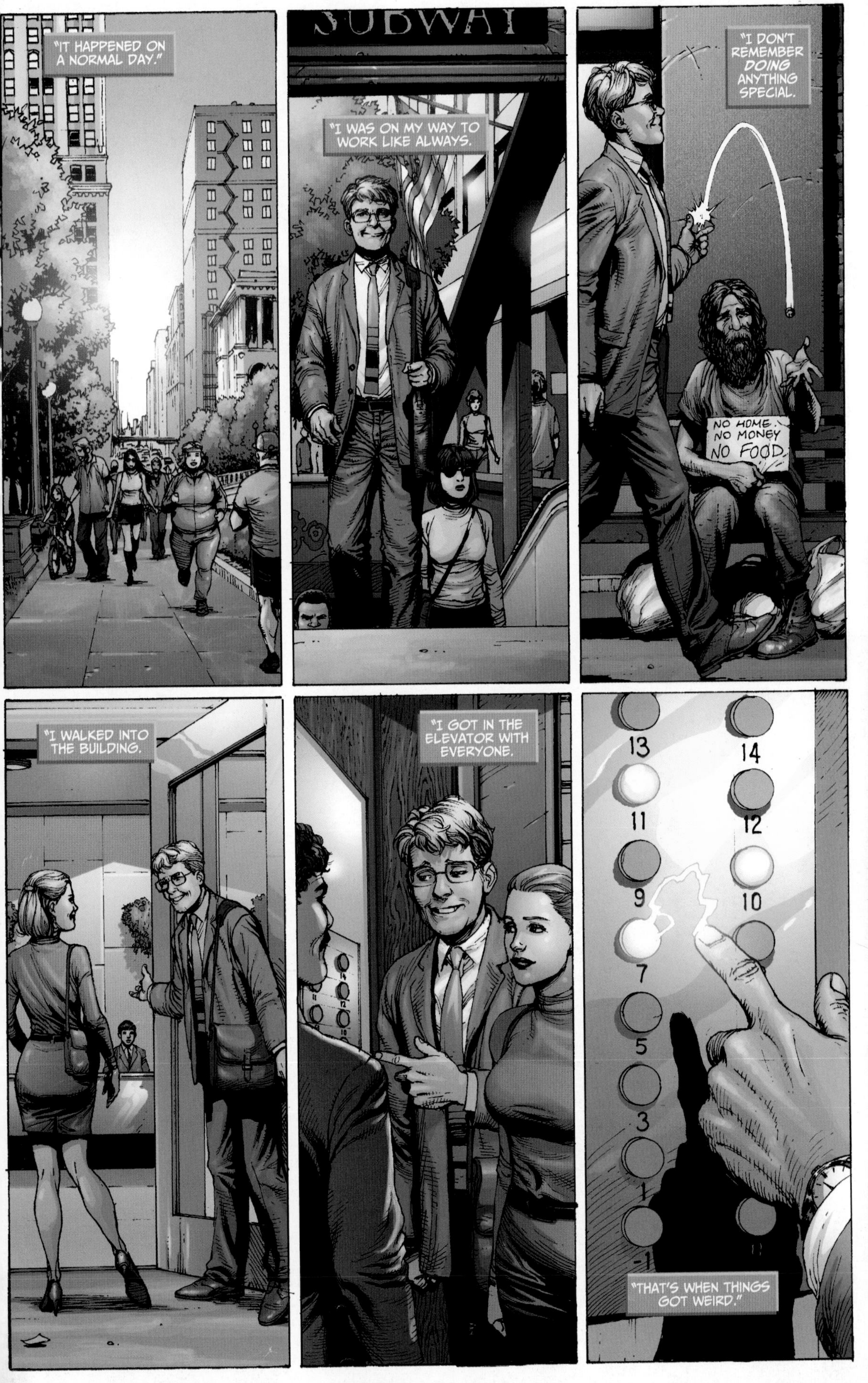
"IT HAPPENED ON A NORMAL DAY."
SUBWAY
"I WAS ON MY WAY TO WORK LIKE ALWAYS.
"I DON'T REMEMBER *DOING* ANYTHING SPECIAL.
NO HOME NO MONEY NO FOOD
"I WALKED INTO THE BUILDING.
"I GOT IN THE ELEVATOR WITH EVERYONE.
13 14 11 12 9 10 7 5 3 1 -1
"THAT'S WHEN THINGS GOT WEIRD."

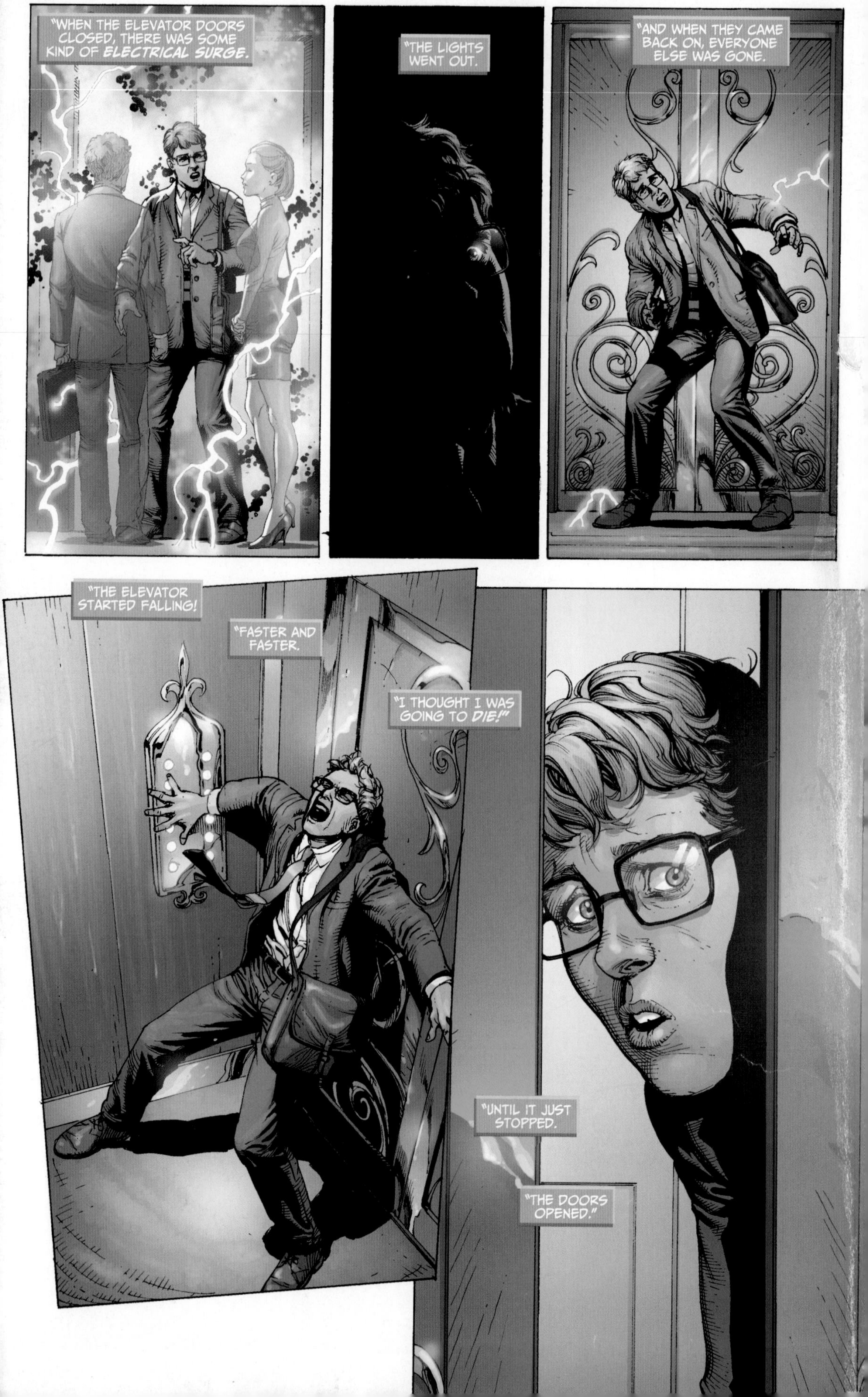
"WHEN THE ELEVATOR DOORS CLOSED, THERE WAS SOME KIND OF ELECTRICAL SURGE.
"THE LIGHTS WENT OUT.
"AND WHEN THEY CAME BACK ON, EVERYONE ELSE WAS GONE.
"THE ELEVATOR STARTED FALLING!
"FASTER AND FASTER.
"I THOUGHT I WAS GOING TO DIE!"
"UNTIL IT JUST STOPPED.
"THE DOORS OPENED."

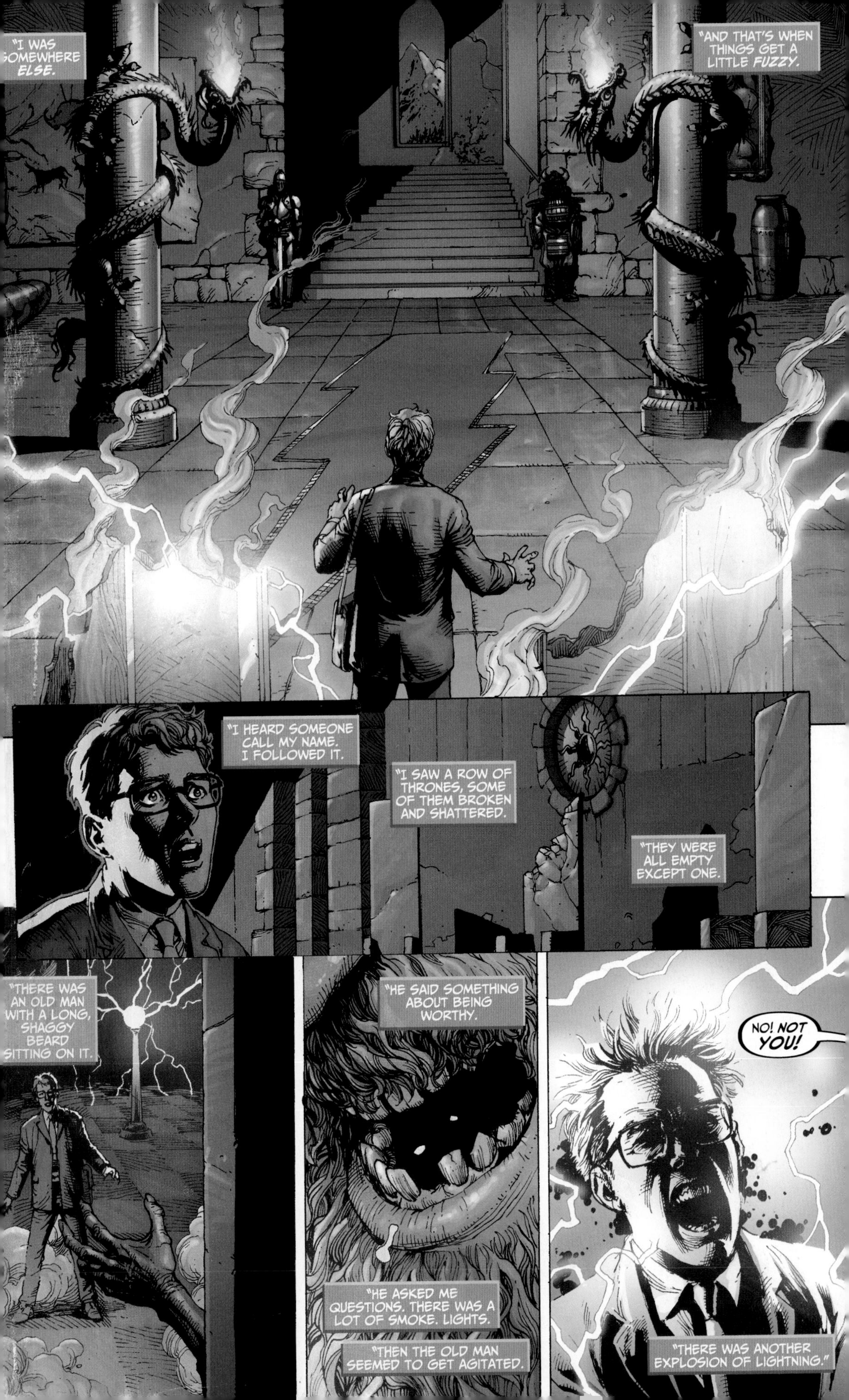
"I WAS SOMEWHERE ELSE.
"AND THAT'S WHEN THINGS GET A LITTLE FUZZY.
"I HEARD SOMEONE CALL MY NAME. I FOLLOWED IT.
"I SAW A ROW OF THRONES, SOME OF THEM BROKEN AND SHATTERED.
"THEY WERE ALL EMPTY EXCEPT ONE.
"THERE WAS AN OLD MAN WITH A LONG, SHAGGY BEARD SITTING ON IT.
"HE SAID SOMETHING ABOUT BEING WORTHY.
"HE ASKED ME QUESTIONS. THERE WAS A LOT OF SMOKE. LIGHTS.
"THEN THE OLD MAN SEEMED TO GET AGITATED.
NO! NOT YOU!
"THERE WAS ANOTHER EXPLOSION OF LIGHTNING."

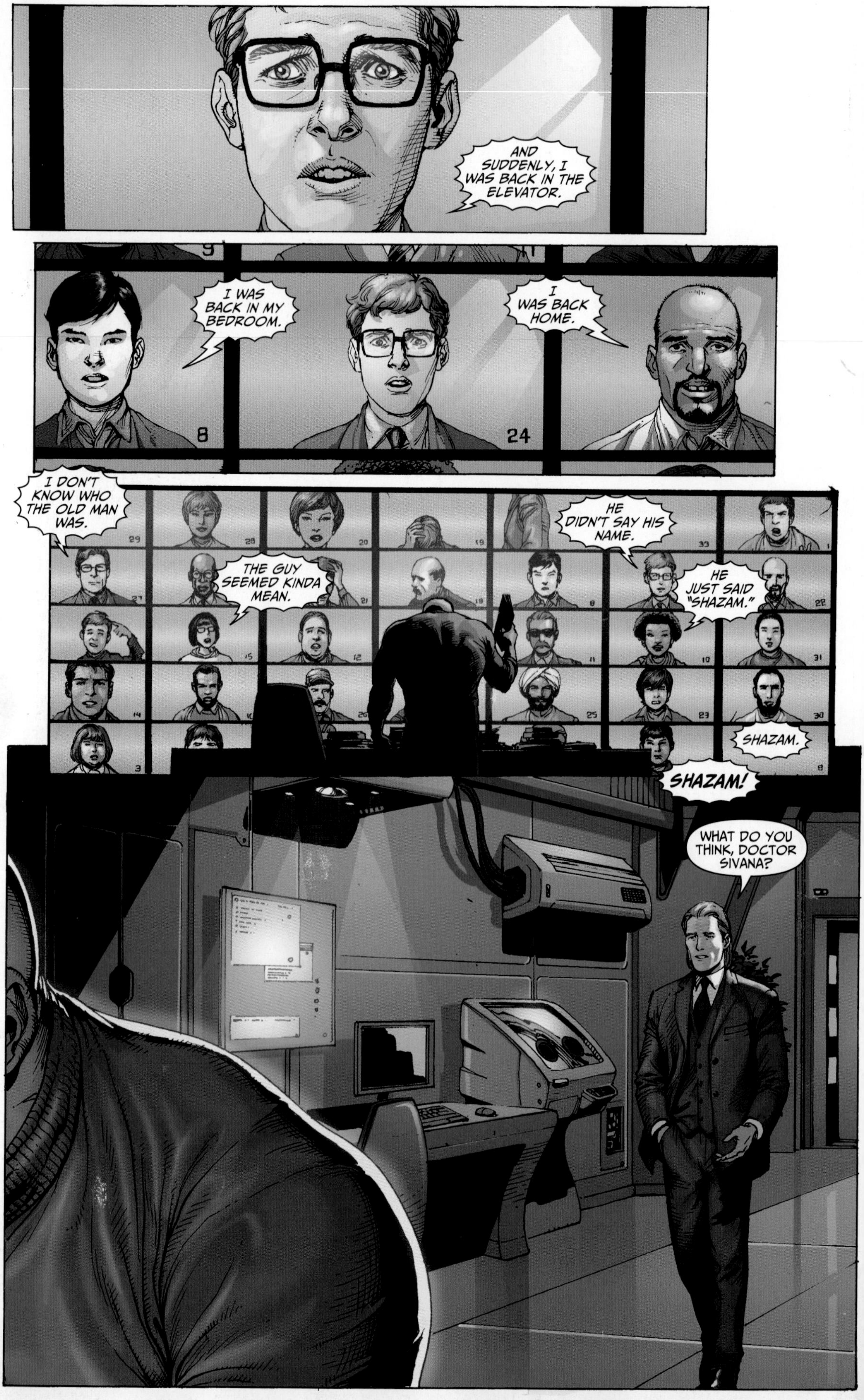
AND SUDDENLY, I WAS BACK IN THE ELEVATOR.
I WAS BACK IN MY BEDROOM.
I WAS BACK HOME.
I DON'T KNOW WHO THE OLD MAN WAS.
THE GUY SEEMED KINDA MEAN.
HE DIDN'T SAY HIS NAME.
HE JUST SAID "SHAZAM."
SHAZAM.
SHAZAM!
WHAT DO YOU THINK, DOCTOR SIVANA?

I THINK THIRTY-SEVEN PEOPLE FROM *ACROSS* THE *WORLD* WITH NO CONNECTION WHATSOEVER ALL SEEM TO SHARE A *SIMILAR EXPERIENCE.*

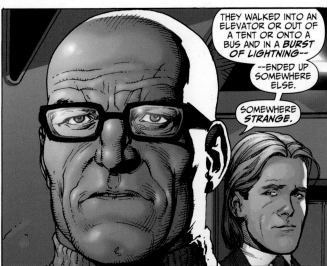

THEY WALKED INTO AN ELEVATOR OR OUT OF A TENT OR ONTO A BUS AND IN A *BURST OF LIGHTNING--*

--ENDED UP SOMEWHERE ELSE.

SOMEWHERE STRANGE.

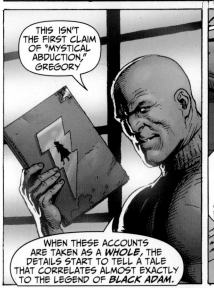

THIS ISN'T THE FIRST CLAIM OF "MYSTICAL ABDUCTION," GREGORY.

WHEN THESE ACCOUNTS ARE TAKEN AS A *WHOLE,* THE DETAILS START TO TELL A TALE THAT CORRELATES ALMOST EXACTLY TO THE LEGEND OF *BLACK ADAM.*

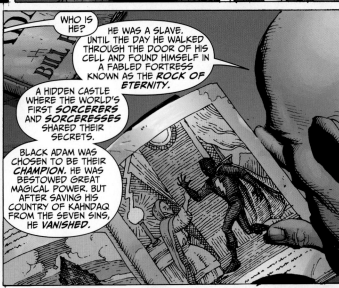

WHO IS HE?

HE WAS A SLAVE. UNTIL THE DAY HE WALKED THROUGH THE DOOR OF HIS CELL AND FOUND HIMSELF IN A FABLED FORTRESS KNOWN AS THE *ROCK OF ETERNITY.*

A HIDDEN CASTLE WHERE THE WORLD'S FIRST *SORCERERS* AND *SORCERESSES* SHARED THEIR SECRETS.

BLACK ADAM WAS CHOSEN TO BE THEIR *CHAMPION.* HE WAS BESTOWED GREAT MAGICAL POWER. BUT AFTER SAVING HIS COUNTRY OF KAHNDAQ FROM THE SEVEN SINS, HE *VANISHED.*

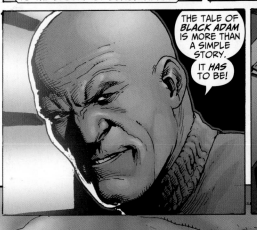

THE TALE OF *BLACK ADAM* IS MORE THAN A SIMPLE STORY.

IT *HAS* TO BE!

I SPENT MY *LIFE* TRYING TO UNLOCK THE *SECRETS* OF *SCIENCE* TO SAVE MY FAMILY.

BUT SCIENCE *FAILED.* THEY NEED A *MIRACLE.*

THEY NEED *MAGIC.*

MAGIC EXISTS.

AND AT LAST I KNOW HOW TO *FIND* IT.

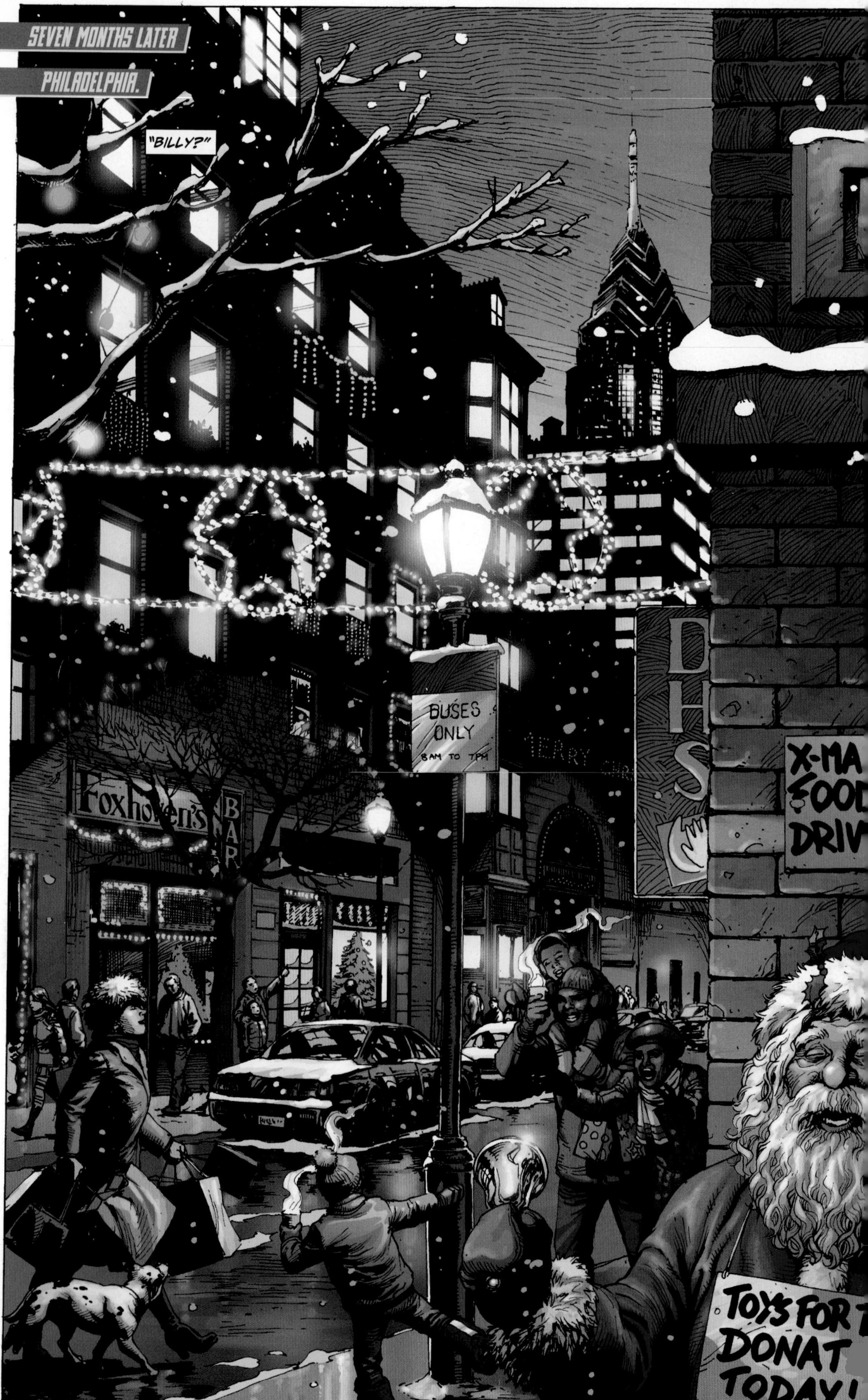
SEVEN MONTHS LATER
PHILADELPHIA.
"BILLY?"
BUSES ONLY
8AM TO 7PM
Foxhoven's
BAR
X-MA
FOOD
DRIV
TOYS FOR
DONAT
TODAY!

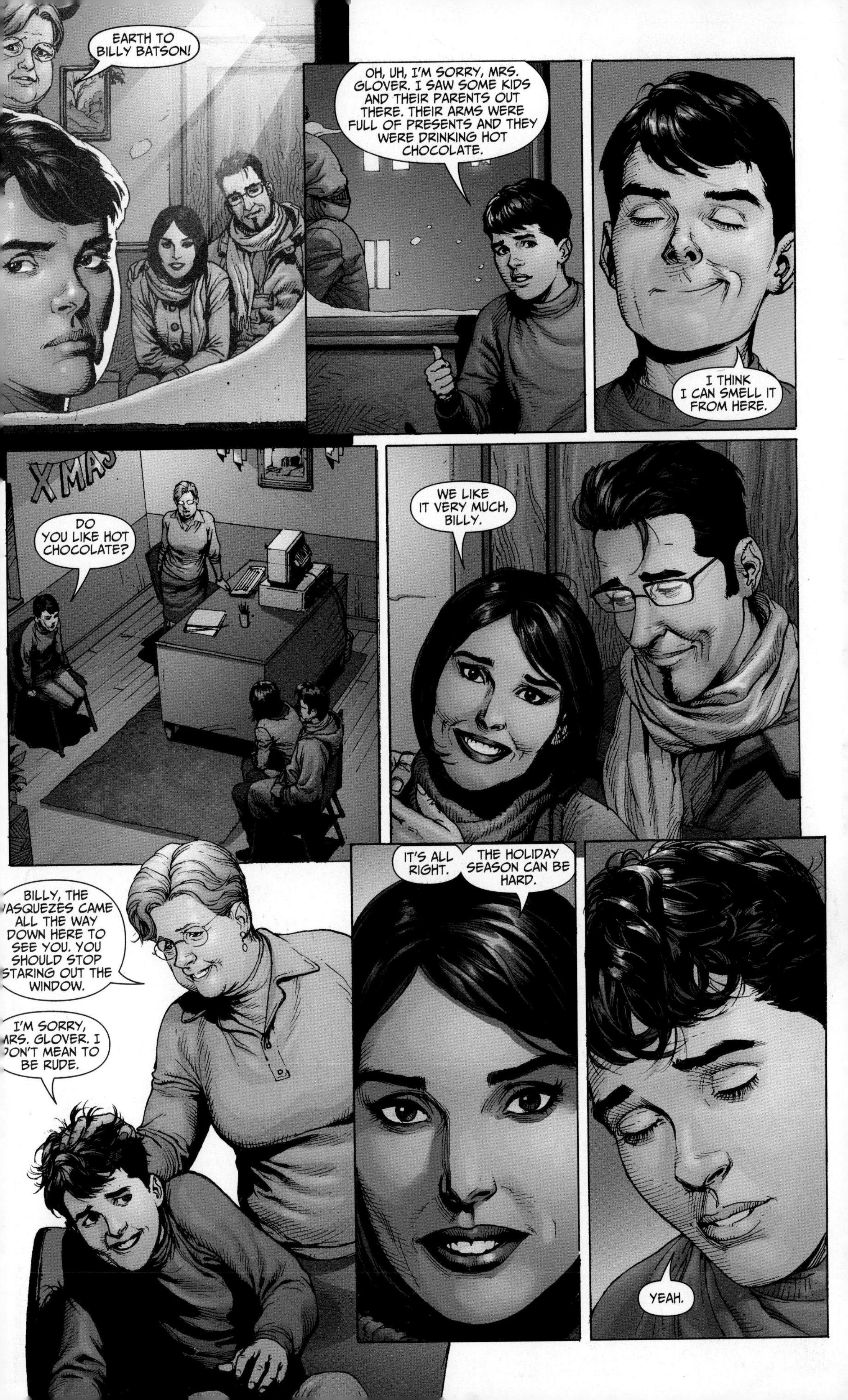
EARTH TO BILLY BATSON!
OH, UH, I'M SORRY, MRS. GLOVER. I SAW SOME KIDS AND THEIR PARENTS OUT THERE. THEIR ARMS WERE FULL OF PRESENTS AND THEY WERE DRINKING HOT CHOCOLATE.
I THINK I CAN SMELL IT FROM HERE.
XMAS
DO YOU LIKE HOT CHOCOLATE?
WE LIKE IT VERY MUCH, BILLY.
BILLY, THE VASQUEZES CAME ALL THE WAY DOWN HERE TO SEE YOU. YOU SHOULD STOP STARING OUT THE WINDOW.
I'M SORRY, MRS. GLOVER. I DON'T MEAN TO BE RUDE.
IT'S ALL RIGHT.
THE HOLIDAY SEASON CAN BE HARD.
YEAH.

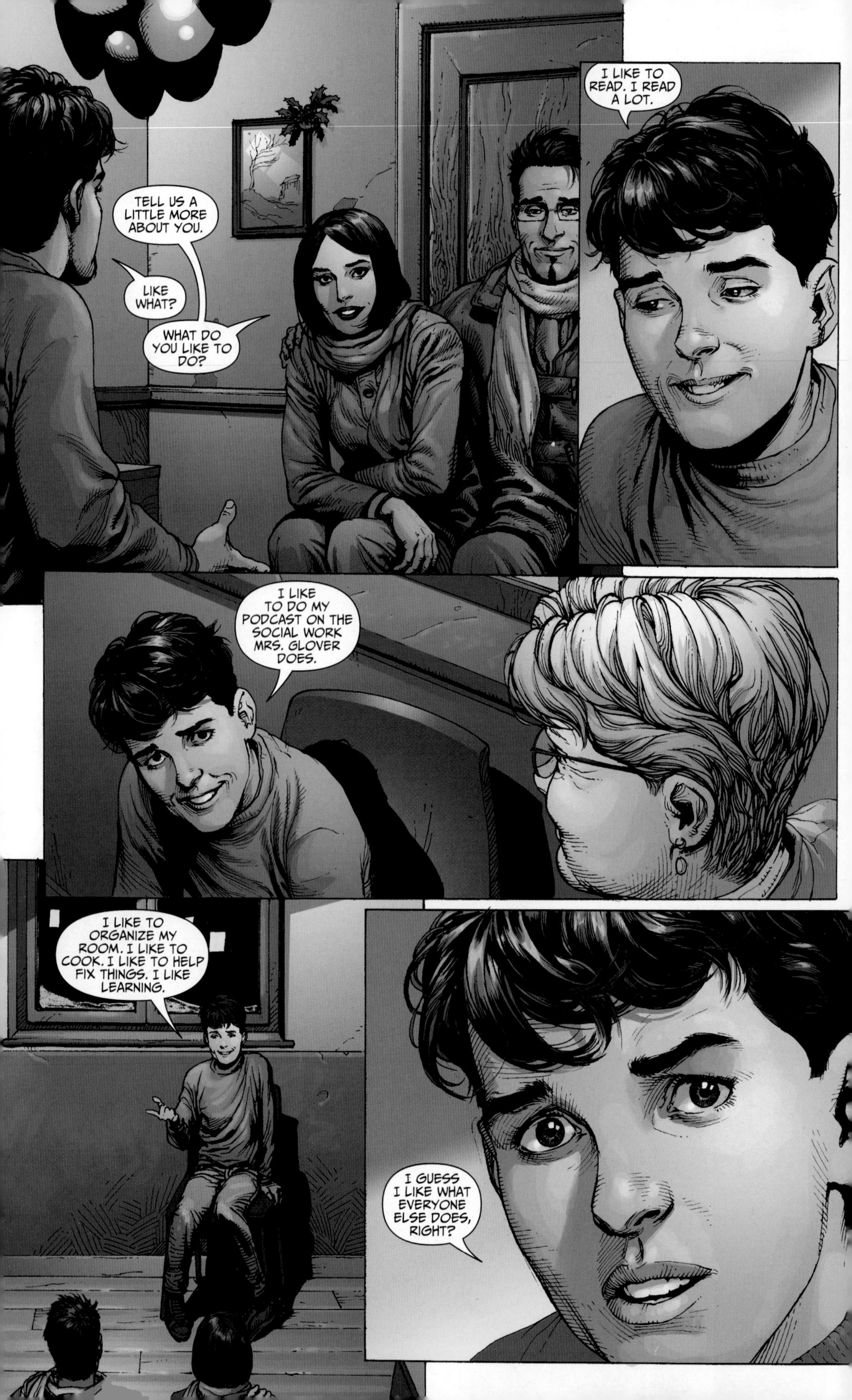
TELL US A LITTLE MORE ABOUT YOU.
LIKE WHAT?
WHAT DO YOU LIKE TO DO?
I LIKE TO READ. I READ A LOT.
I LIKE TO DO MY PODCAST ON THE SOCIAL WORK MRS. GLOVER DOES.
I LIKE TO ORGANIZE MY ROOM. I LIKE TO COOK. I LIKE TO HELP FIX THINGS. I LIKE LEARNING.
I GUESS I LIKE WHAT EVERYONE ELSE DOES, RIGHT?

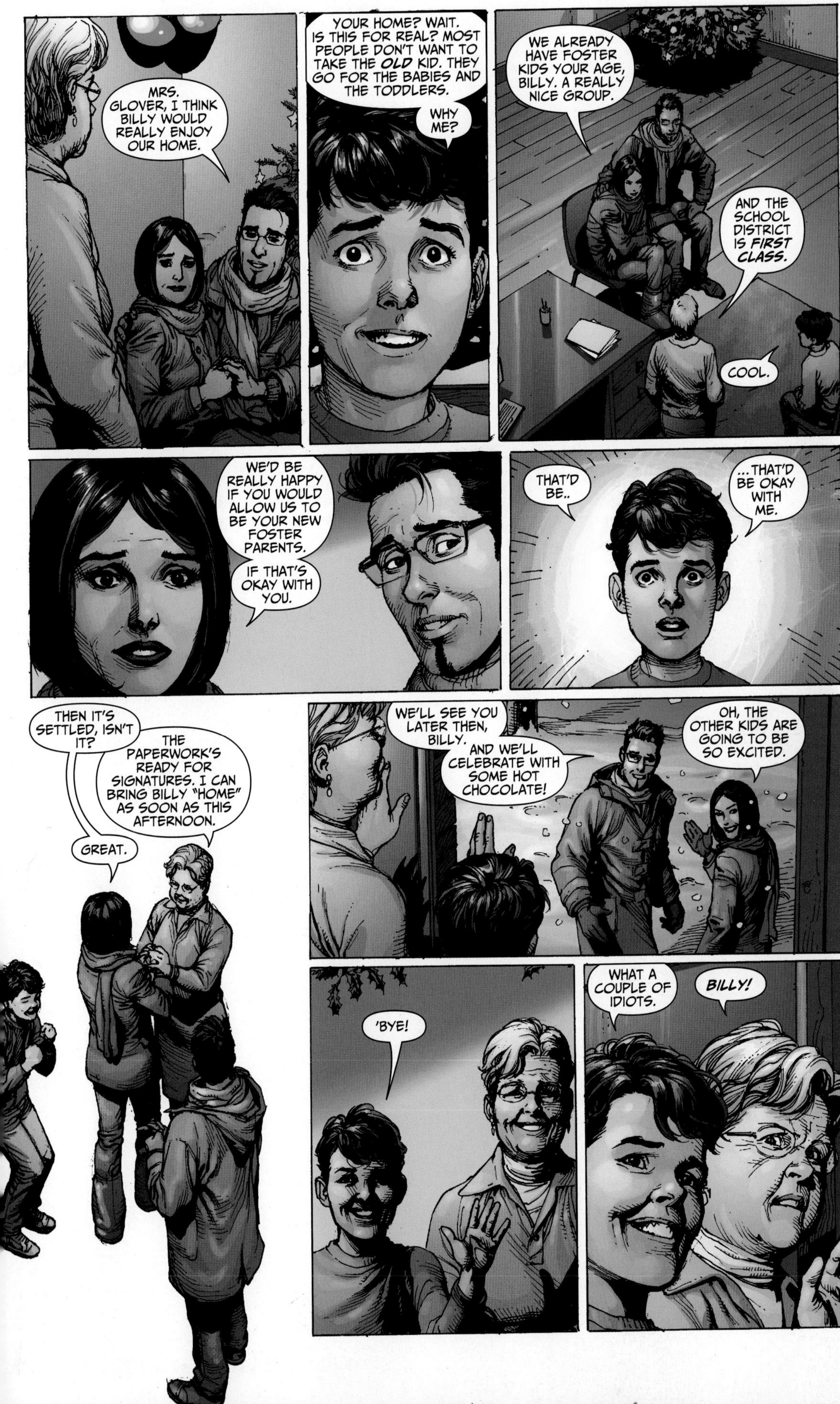
MRS. GLOVER, I THINK BILLY WOULD REALLY ENJOY OUR HOME.
YOUR HOME? WAIT. IS THIS FOR REAL? MOST PEOPLE DON'T WANT TO TAKE THE OLD KID. THEY GO FOR THE BABIES AND THE TODDLERS.
WHY ME?
WE ALREADY HAVE FOSTER KIDS YOUR AGE, BILLY. A REALLY NICE GROUP.
AND THE SCHOOL DISTRICT IS FIRST CLASS.
COOL.
WE'D BE REALLY HAPPY IF YOU WOULD ALLOW US TO BE YOUR NEW FOSTER PARENTS.
IF THAT'S OKAY WITH YOU.
THAT'D BE..
...THAT'D BE OKAY WITH ME.
THEN IT'S SETTLED, ISN'T IT?
THE PAPERWORK'S READY FOR SIGNATURES. I CAN BRING BILLY "HOME" AS SOON AS THIS AFTERNOON.
GREAT.
WE'LL SEE YOU LATER THEN, BILLY.
AND WE'LL CELEBRATE WITH SOME HOT CHOCOLATE!
OH, THE OTHER KIDS ARE GOING TO BE SO EXCITED.
'BYE!
WHAT A COUPLE OF IDIOTS.
BILLY!

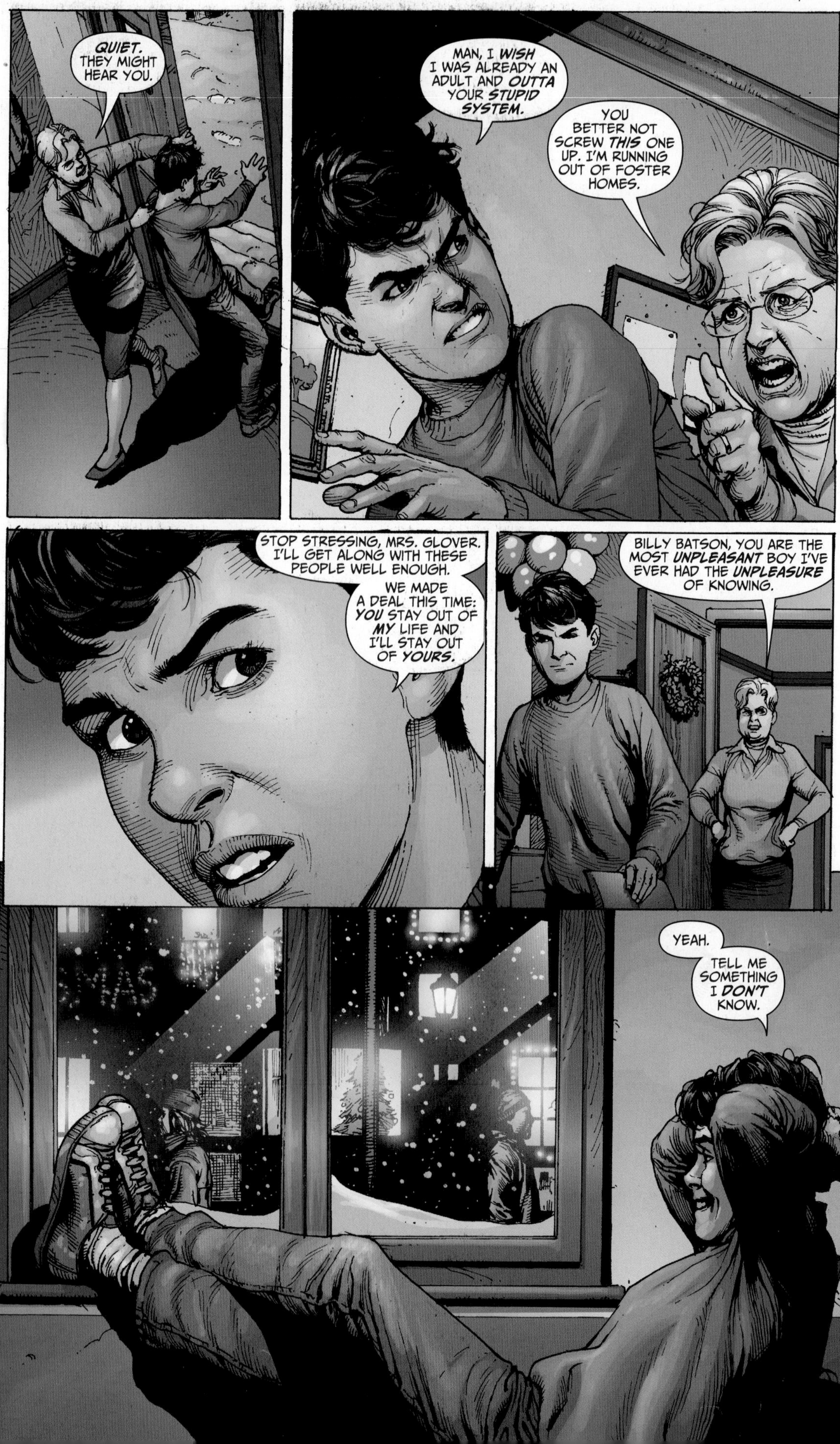
QUIET. THEY MIGHT HEAR YOU.
MAN, I WISH I WAS ALREADY AN ADULT AND OUTTA YOUR STUPID SYSTEM.
YOU BETTER NOT SCREW THIS ONE UP. I'M RUNNING OUT OF FOSTER HOMES.
STOP STRESSING, MRS. GLOVER. I'LL GET ALONG WITH THESE PEOPLE WELL ENOUGH.
WE MADE A DEAL THIS TIME: YOU STAY OUT OF MY LIFE AND I'LL STAY OUT OF YOURS.
BILLY BATSON, YOU ARE THE MOST UNPLEASANT BOY I'VE EVER HAD THE UNPLEASURE OF KNOWING.
YEAH.
TELL ME SOMETHING I DON'T KNOW.

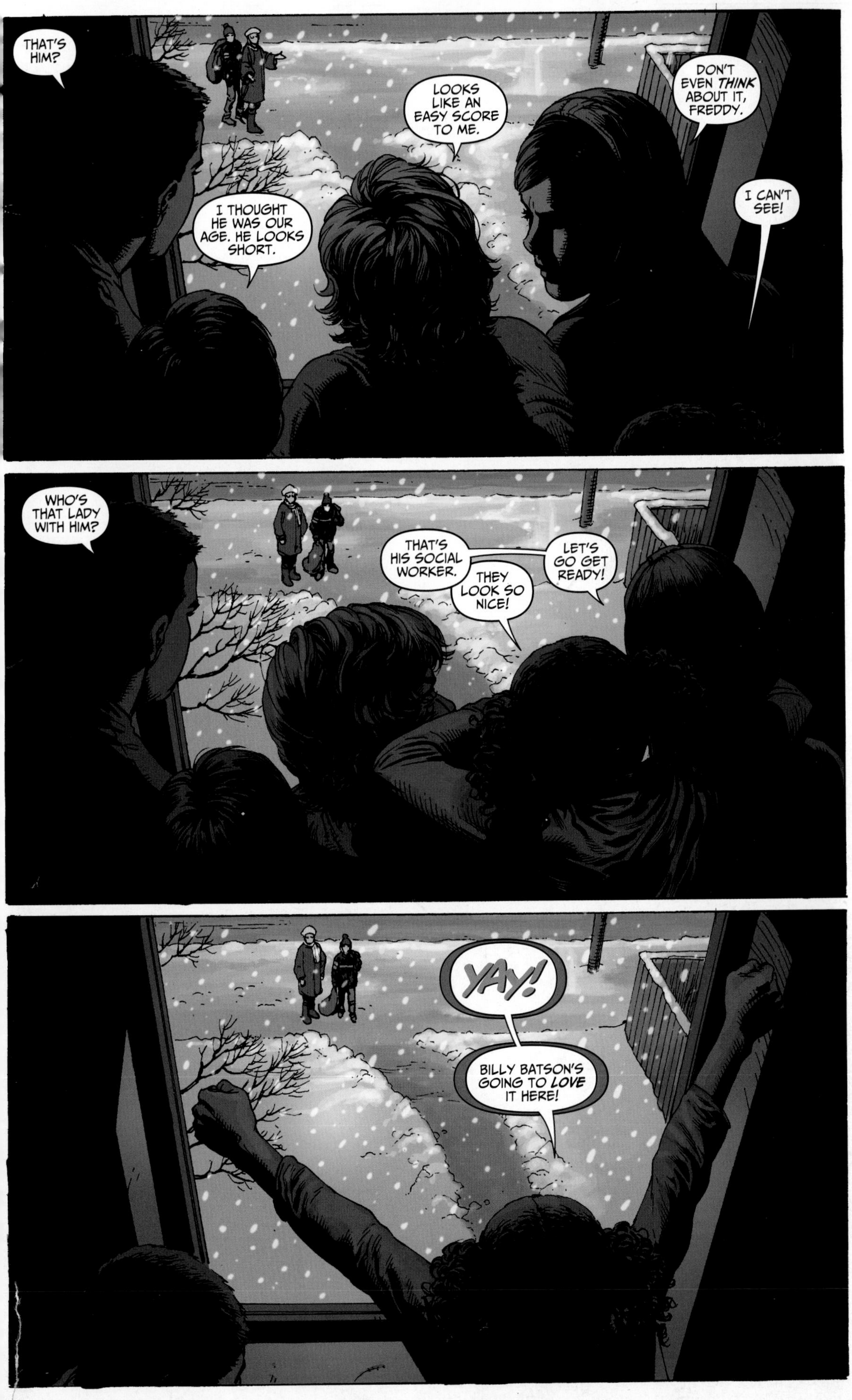
THAT'S HIM?
LOOKS LIKE AN EASY SCORE TO ME.
DON'T EVEN THINK ABOUT IT, FREDDY.
I THOUGHT HE WAS OUR AGE. HE LOOKS SHORT.
I CAN'T SEE!
WHO'S THAT LADY WITH HIM?
THAT'S HIS SOCIAL WORKER.
LET'S GO GET READY!
THEY LOOK SO NICE!
YAY!
BILLY BATSON'S GOING TO LOVE IT HERE!

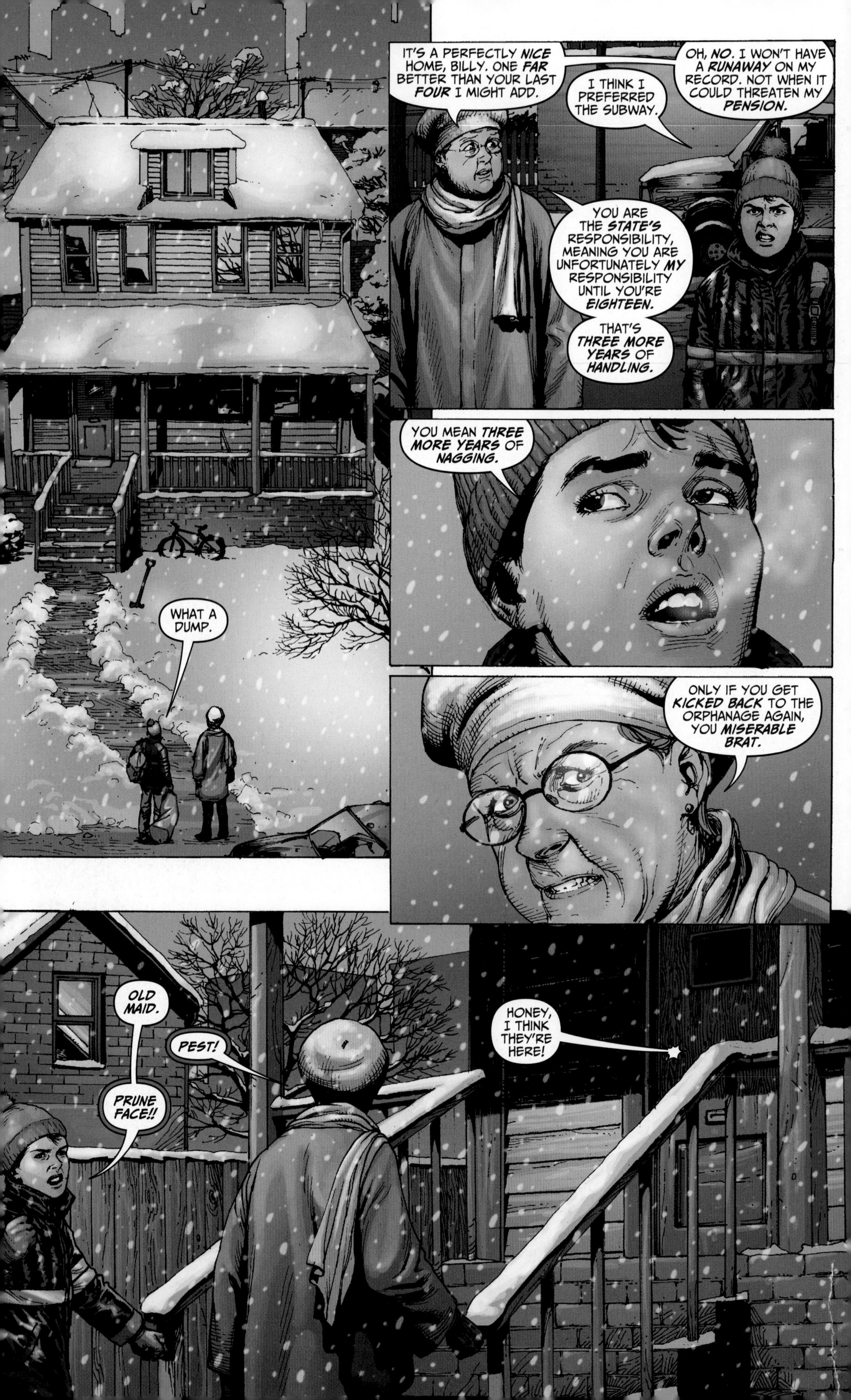
WHAT A DUMP.
IT'S A PERFECTLY NICE HOME, BILLY. ONE FAR BETTER THAN YOUR LAST FOUR I MIGHT ADD.
I THINK I PREFERRED THE SUBWAY.
OH, NO. I WON'T HAVE A RUNAWAY ON MY RECORD. NOT WHEN IT COULD THREATEN MY PENSION.
YOU ARE THE STATE'S RESPONSIBILITY, MEANING YOU ARE UNFORTUNATELY MY RESPONSIBILITY UNTIL YOU'RE EIGHTEEN.
THAT'S THREE MORE YEARS OF HANDLING.
YOU MEAN THREE MORE YEARS OF NAGGING.
ONLY IF YOU GET KICKED BACK TO THE ORPHANAGE AGAIN, YOU MISERABLE BRAT.
OLD MAID.
PEST!
PRUNE FACE!!
HONEY, I THINK THEY'RE HERE!

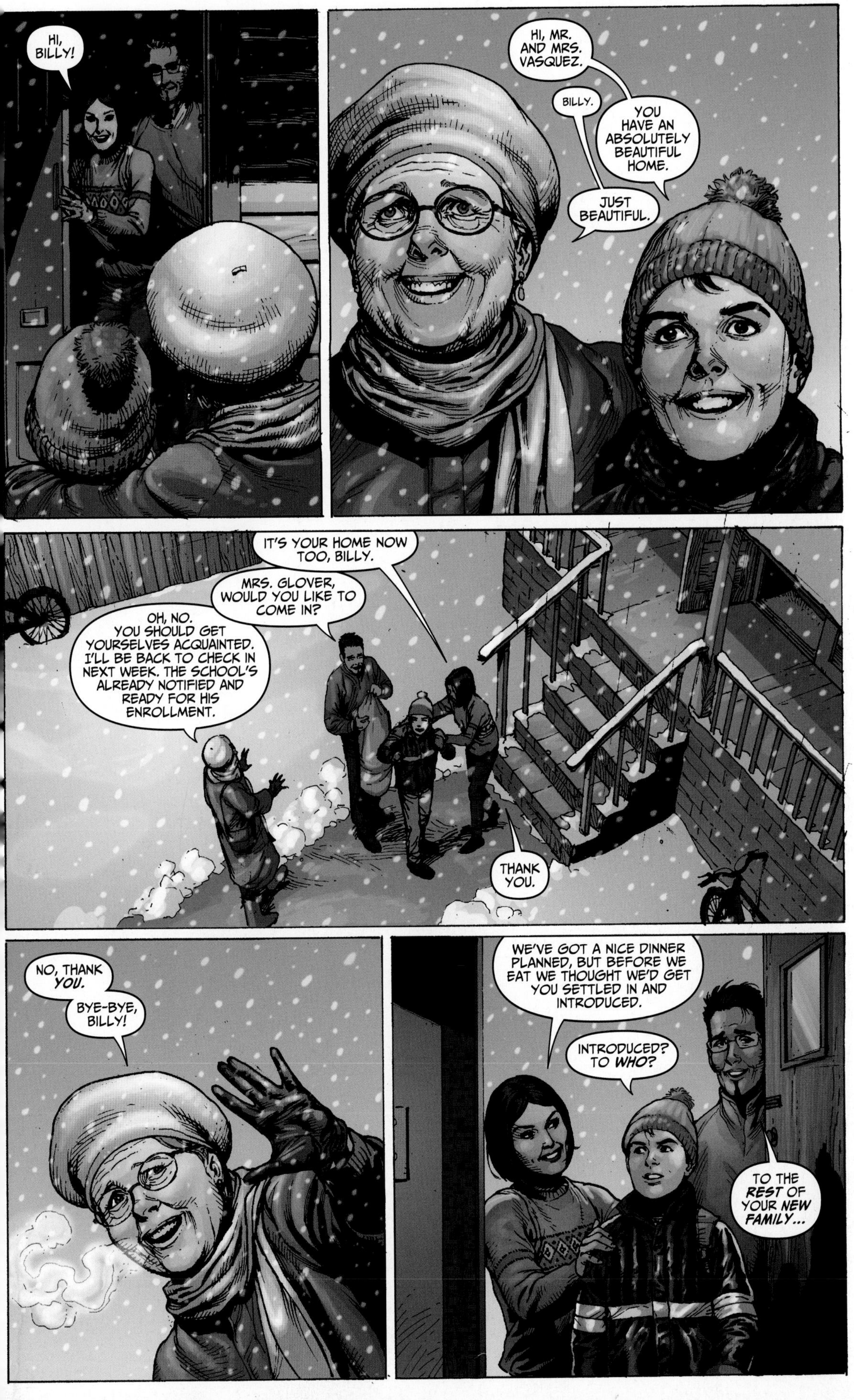
HI, BILLY!
HI, MR. AND MRS. VASQUEZ.
BILLY.
YOU HAVE AN ABSOLUTELY BEAUTIFUL HOME.
JUST BEAUTIFUL.
IT'S YOUR HOME NOW TOO, BILLY.
MRS. GLOVER, WOULD YOU LIKE TO COME IN?
OH, NO. YOU SHOULD GET YOURSELVES ACQUAINTED. I'LL BE BACK TO CHECK IN NEXT WEEK. THE SCHOOL'S ALREADY NOTIFIED AND READY FOR HIS ENROLLMENT.
THANK YOU.
NO, THANK *YOU.*
BYE-BYE, BILLY!
WE'VE GOT A NICE DINNER PLANNED, BUT BEFORE WE EAT WE THOUGHT WE'D GET YOU SETTLED IN AND INTRODUCED.
INTRODUCED? TO *WHO?*
TO THE *REST* OF YOUR *NEW FAMILY...*

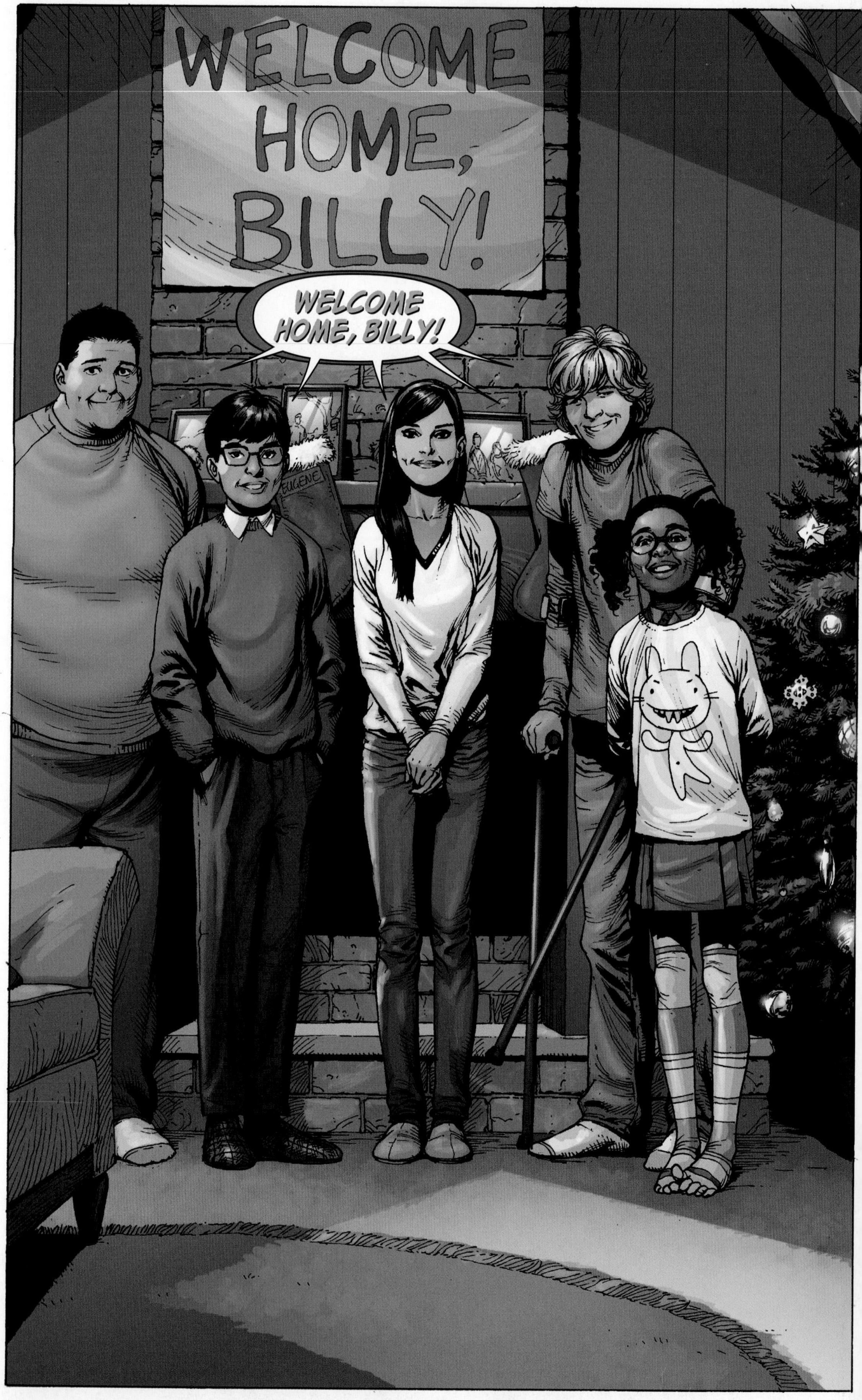
WELCOME HOME, BILLY!
WELCOME HOME, BILLY!
EUGENE

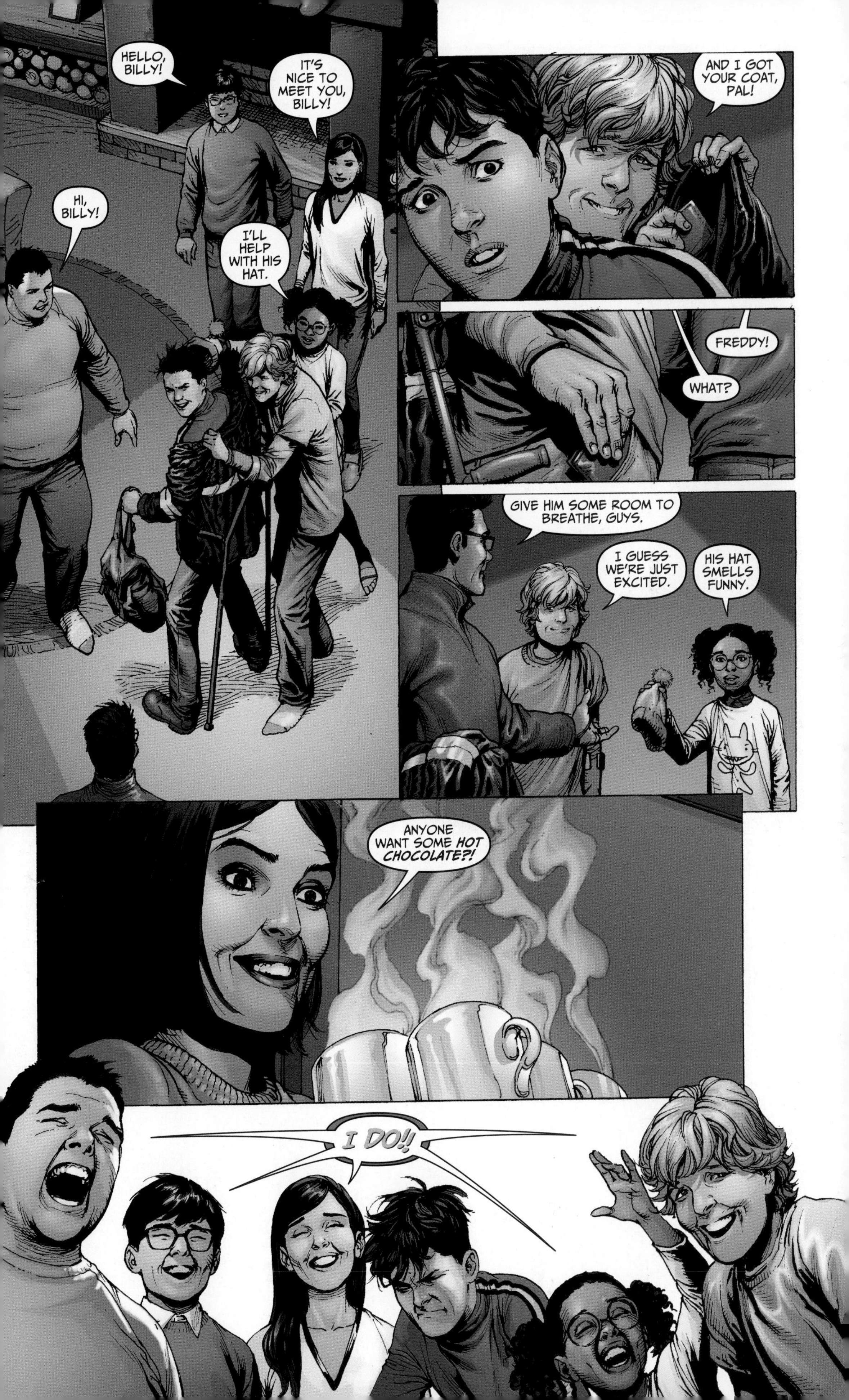
HELLO, BILLY!
IT'S NICE TO MEET YOU, BILLY!
HI, BILLY!
I'LL HELP WITH HIS HAT.
AND I GOT YOUR COAT, PAL!
FREDDY!
WHAT?
GIVE HIM SOME ROOM TO BREATHE, GUYS.
I GUESS WE'RE JUST EXCITED.
HIS HAT SMELLS FUNNY.
ANYONE WANT SOME HOT CHOCOLATE?!
I DO!!

HOW ABOUT SOME INTRODUCTIONS?

KIDS?

UM...

MARY SHOULD GO FIRST!

TRY AND STOP HER.

YES, WELL, I'M *MARY*. I'VE BEEN LIVING HERE FOR AS LONG AS I CAN REMEMBER, SO IF YOU HAVE ANY QUESTIONS YOU CAN ASK *ME* FOR HELP.

AND THIS IS MY RABBIT *HOPPY*. HE WAS ON HIS WAY TO BECOMING ANOTHER CASUALTY OF COSMETIC TESTING UNTIL I RESCUED HIM FROM THE PUPPY MILL PET STORE.

BUT *I* WAS THE ONE WHO DISTRACTED THE OWNER.

FREDDY FREEMAN HERE. NEVER SEEN A FIRE ALARM I DIDN'T PULL.

FREDDY!

TAKE IT AWAY, AMIGO!

UM, I'M...I'M PEDRO AND, UM...

I'M PEDRO.

THIS IS EUGENE. HE LIKES TO READ, JUST LIKE *YOU*, BILLY.

I ONLY READ *NON-FICTION*.

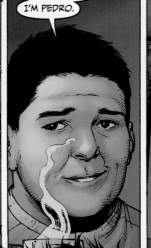

AND I'M *DARLA!*

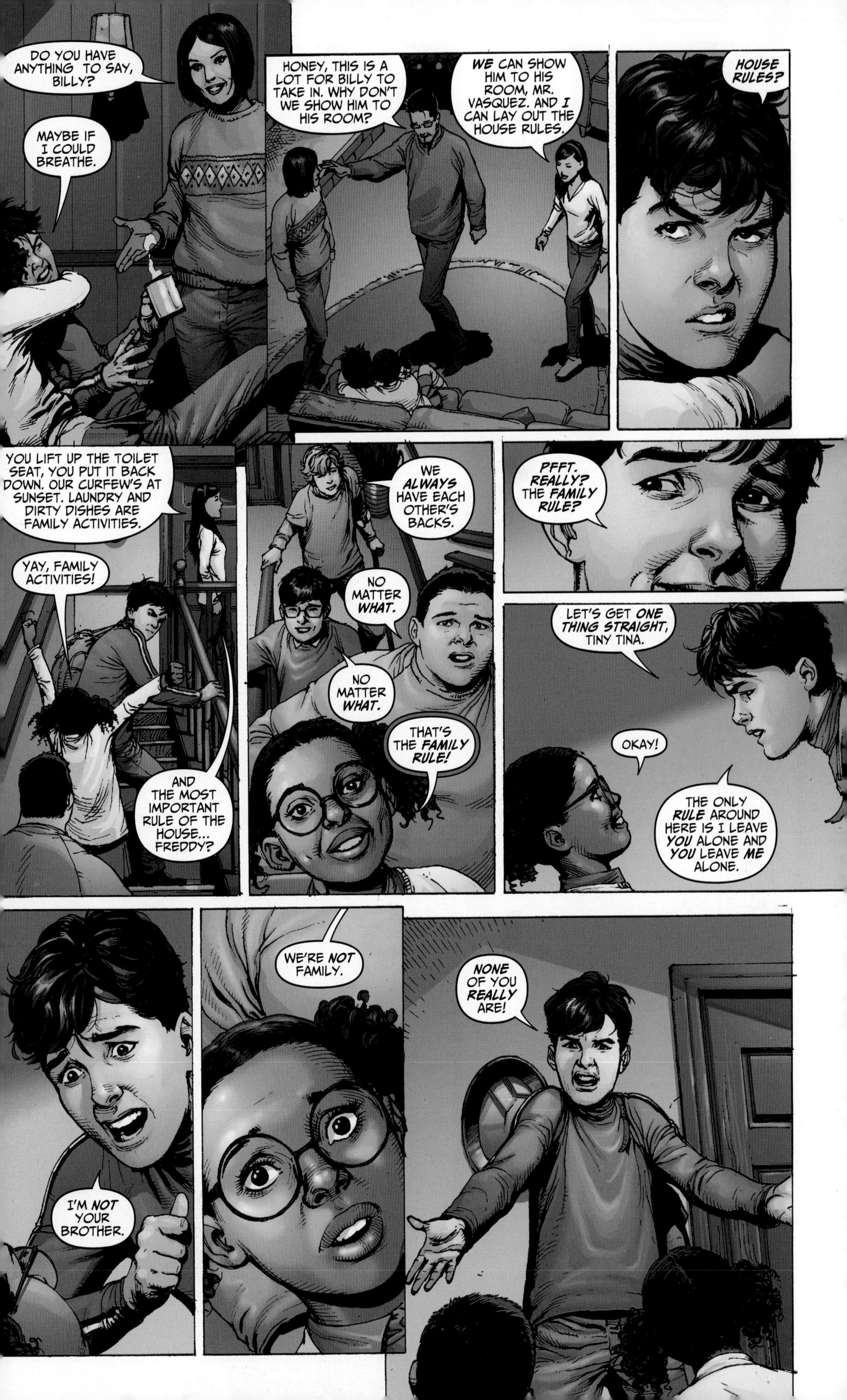
DO YOU HAVE ANYTHING TO SAY, BILLY?
MAYBE IF I COULD BREATHE.
HONEY, THIS IS A LOT FOR BILLY TO TAKE IN. WHY DON'T WE SHOW HIM TO HIS ROOM?
WE CAN SHOW HIM TO HIS ROOM, MR. VASQUEZ. AND I CAN LAY OUT THE HOUSE RULES.
HOUSE RULES?
YOU LIFT UP THE TOILET SEAT, YOU PUT IT BACK DOWN. OUR CURFEW'S AT SUNSET. LAUNDRY AND DIRTY DISHES ARE FAMILY ACTIVITIES.
YAY, FAMILY ACTIVITIES!
AND THE MOST IMPORTANT RULE OF THE HOUSE... FREDDY?
WE ALWAYS HAVE EACH OTHER'S BACKS.
NO MATTER WHAT.
NO MATTER WHAT.
THAT'S THE FAMILY RULE!
PFFT. REALLY? THE FAMILY RULE?
LET'S GET ONE THING STRAIGHT, TINY TINA.
OKAY!
THE ONLY RULE AROUND HERE IS I LEAVE YOU ALONE AND YOU LEAVE ME ALONE.
I'M NOT YOUR BROTHER.
WE'RE NOT FAMILY.
NONE OF YOU REALLY ARE!

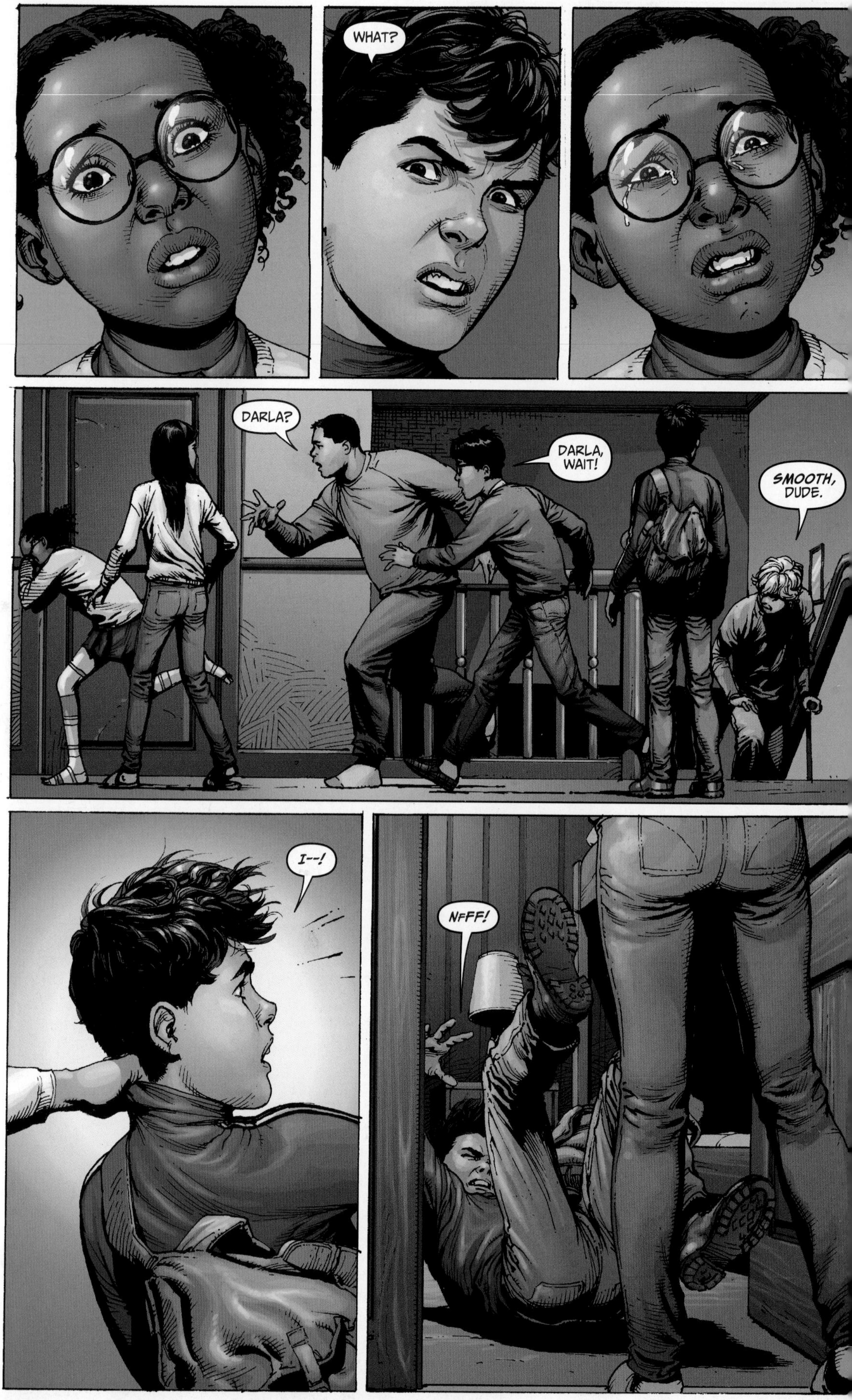
WHAT?
DARLA?
DARLA, WAIT!
SMOOTH, DUDE.
I--!
NFFF!

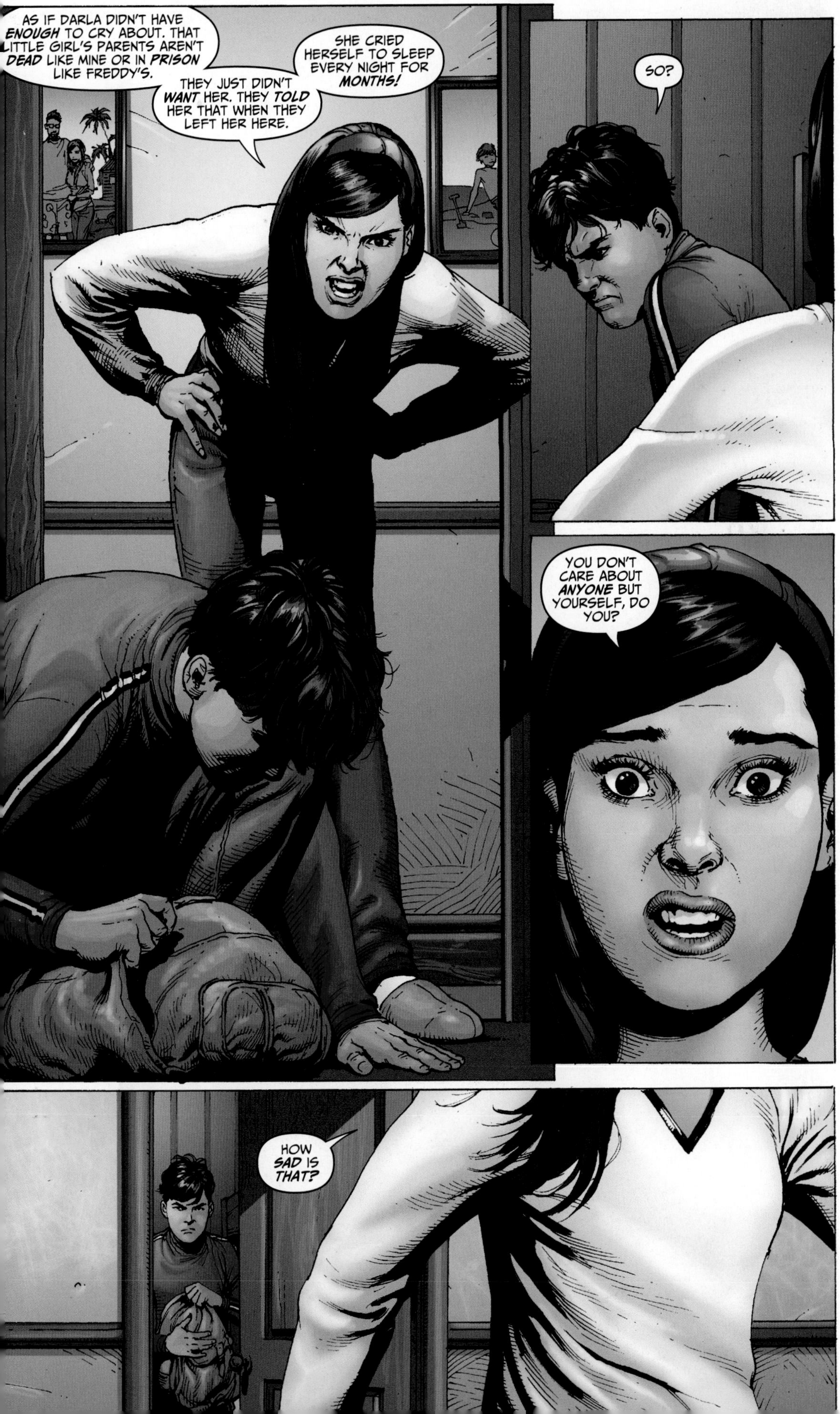
AS IF DARLA DIDN'T HAVE ENOUGH TO CRY ABOUT. THAT LITTLE GIRL'S PARENTS AREN'T DEAD LIKE MINE OR IN PRISON LIKE FREDDY'S.
THEY JUST DIDN'T WANT HER. THEY TOLD HER THAT WHEN THEY LEFT HER HERE.
SHE CRIED HERSELF TO SLEEP EVERY NIGHT FOR MONTHS!
SO?
YOU DON'T CARE ABOUT ANYONE BUT YOURSELF, DO YOU?
HOW SAD IS THAT?

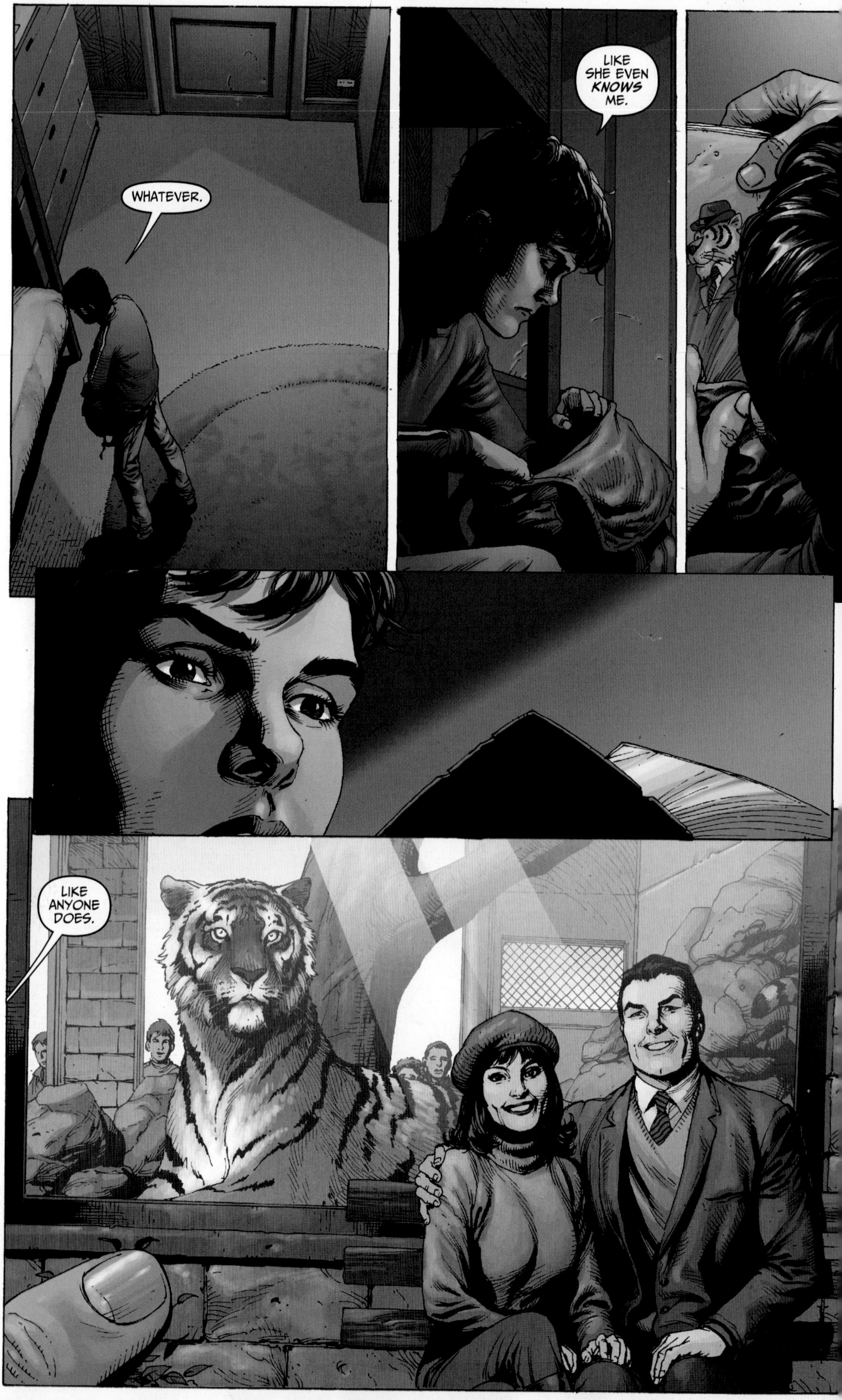
WHATEVER.
LIKE SHE EVEN *KNOWS* ME.
LIKE ANYONE DOES.

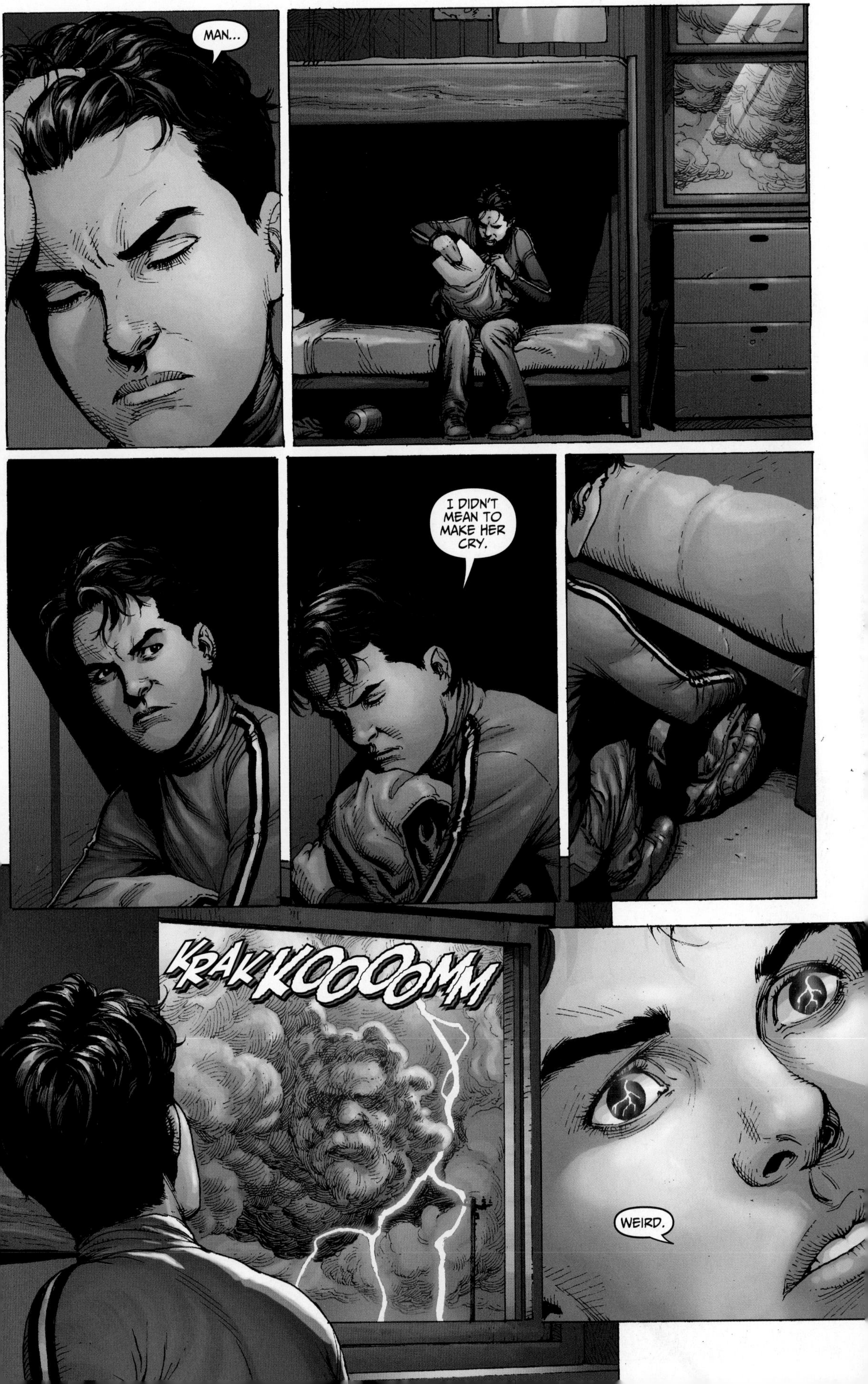
MAN...
I DIDN'T MEAN TO MAKE HER CRY.
KRAKKOOOOOMM
WEIRD.

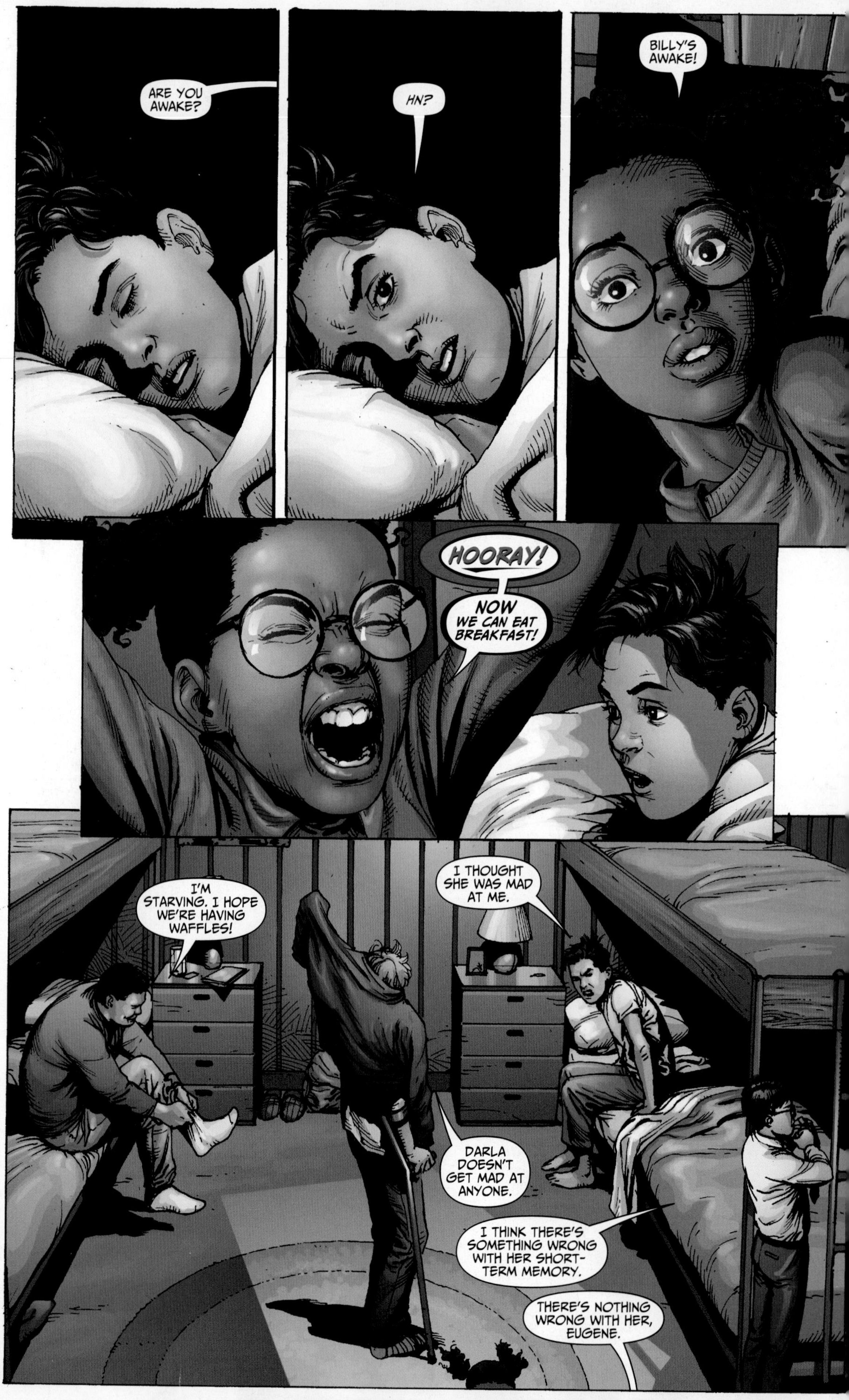
ARE YOU AWAKE?
HN?
BILLY'S AWAKE!
HOORAY!
NOW WE CAN EAT BREAKFAST!
I'M STARVING. I HOPE WE'RE HAVING WAFFLES!
I THOUGHT SHE WAS MAD AT ME.
DARLA DOESN'T GET MAD AT ANYONE.
I THINK THERE'S SOMETHING WRONG WITH HER SHORT-TERM MEMORY.
THERE'S NOTHING WRONG WITH HER, EUGENE.

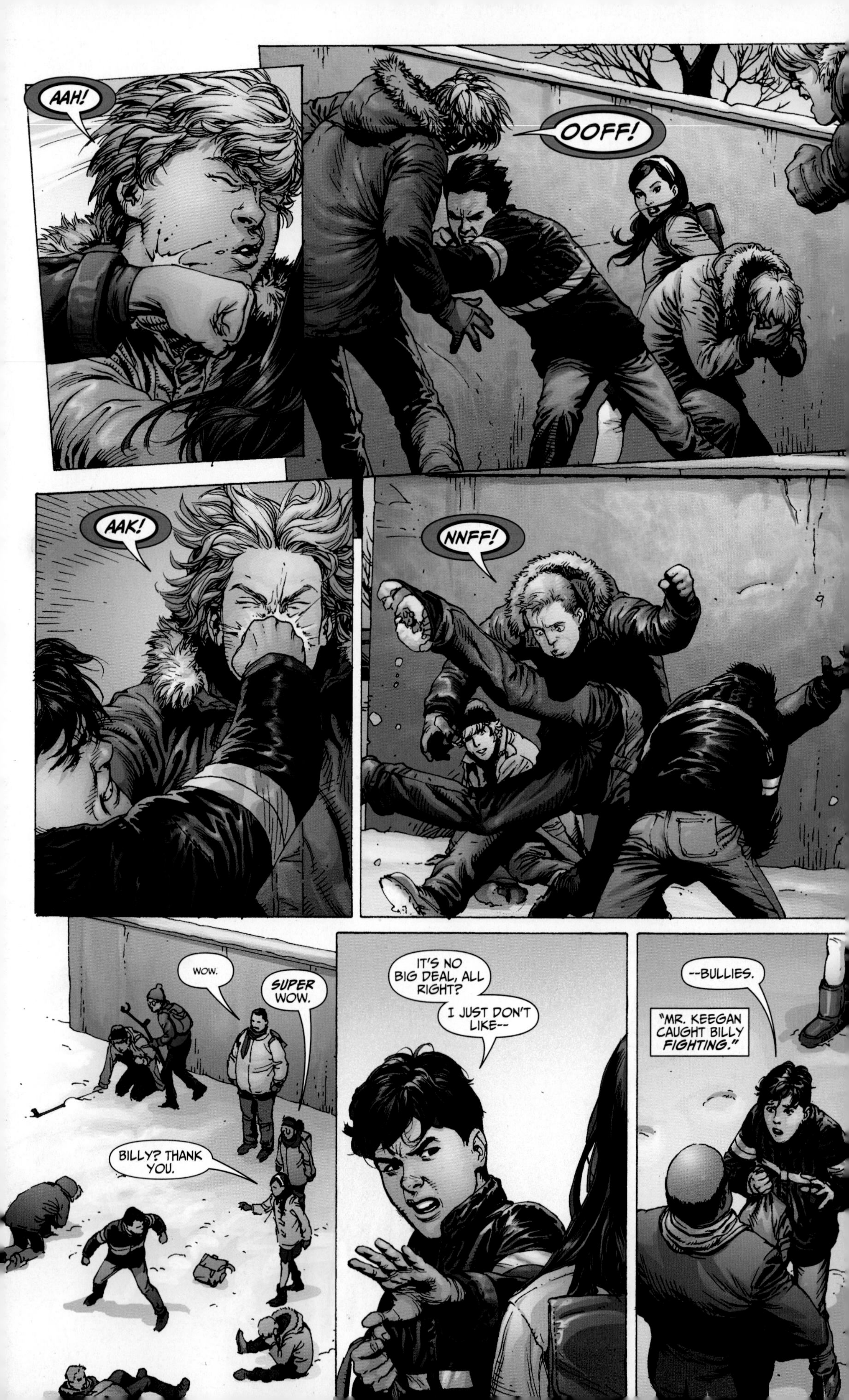

AAH!
OOFF!
AAK!
NNFF!
WOW.
SUPER WOW.
BILLY? THANK YOU.
IT'S NO BIG DEAL, ALL RIGHT?
I JUST DON'T LIKE--
--BULLIES.
"MR. KEEGAN CAUGHT BILLY FIGHTING."

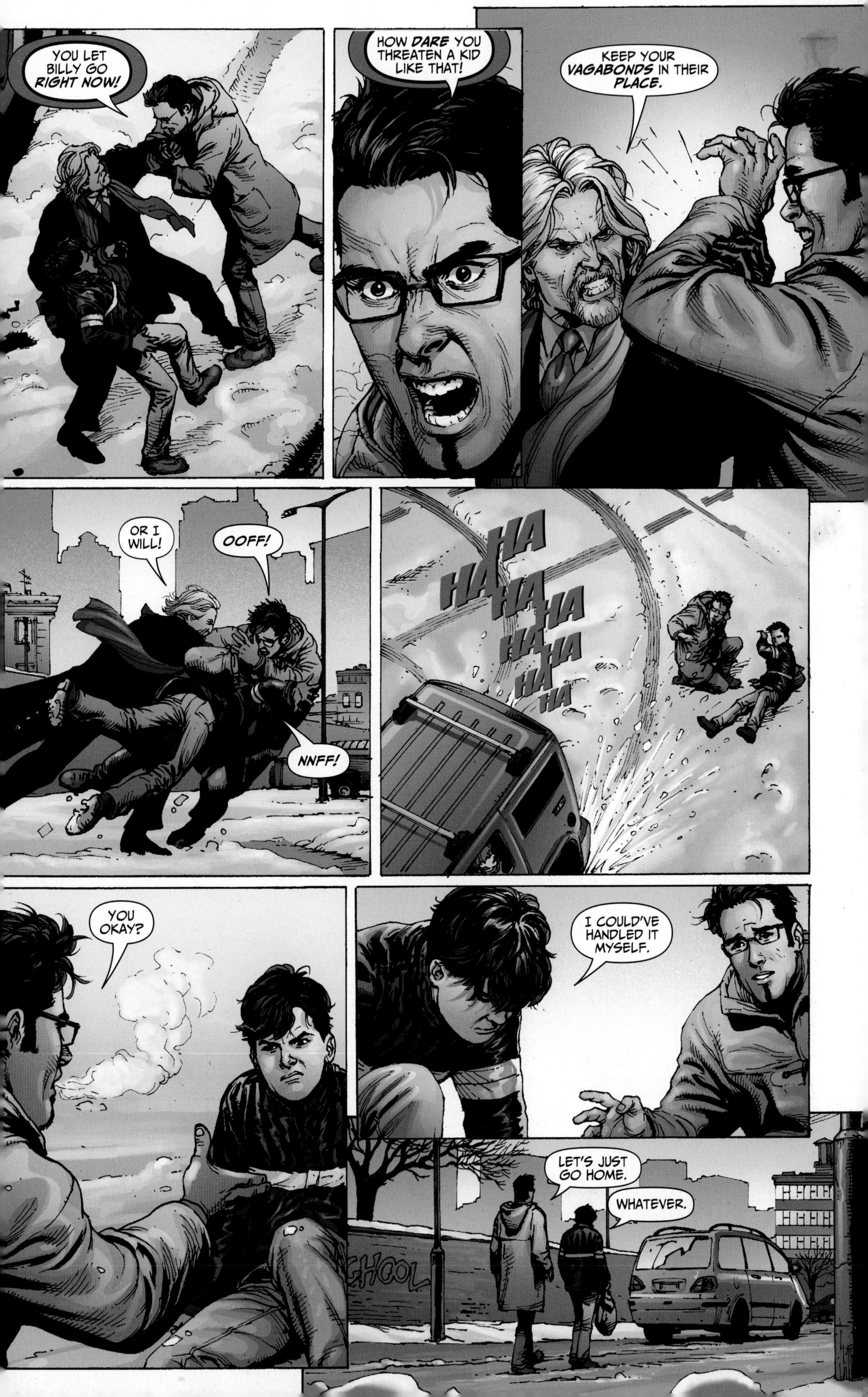
YOU LET BILLY GO RIGHT NOW!
HOW DARE YOU THREATEN A KID LIKE THAT!
KEEP YOUR VAGABONDS IN THEIR PLACE.
OR I WILL!
OOFF!
NNFF!
HA HA HA HA HA HA HA HA
YOU OKAY?
I COULD'VE HANDLED IT MYSELF.
LET'S JUST GO HOME.
WHATEVER.

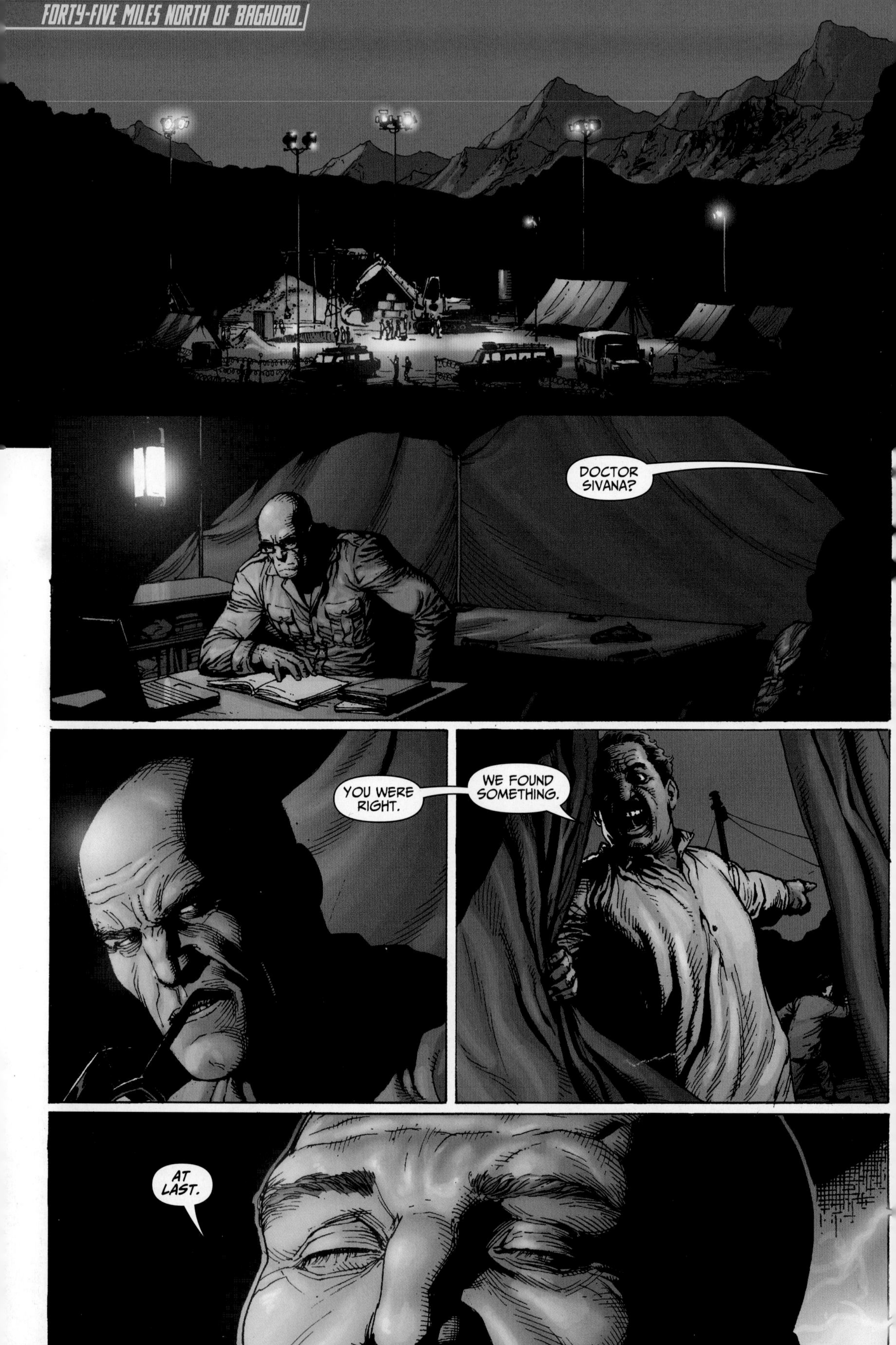
FORTY-FIVE MILES NORTH OF BAGHDAD.
DOCTOR SIVANA?
YOU WERE RIGHT.
WE FOUND SOMETHING.
AT LAST.

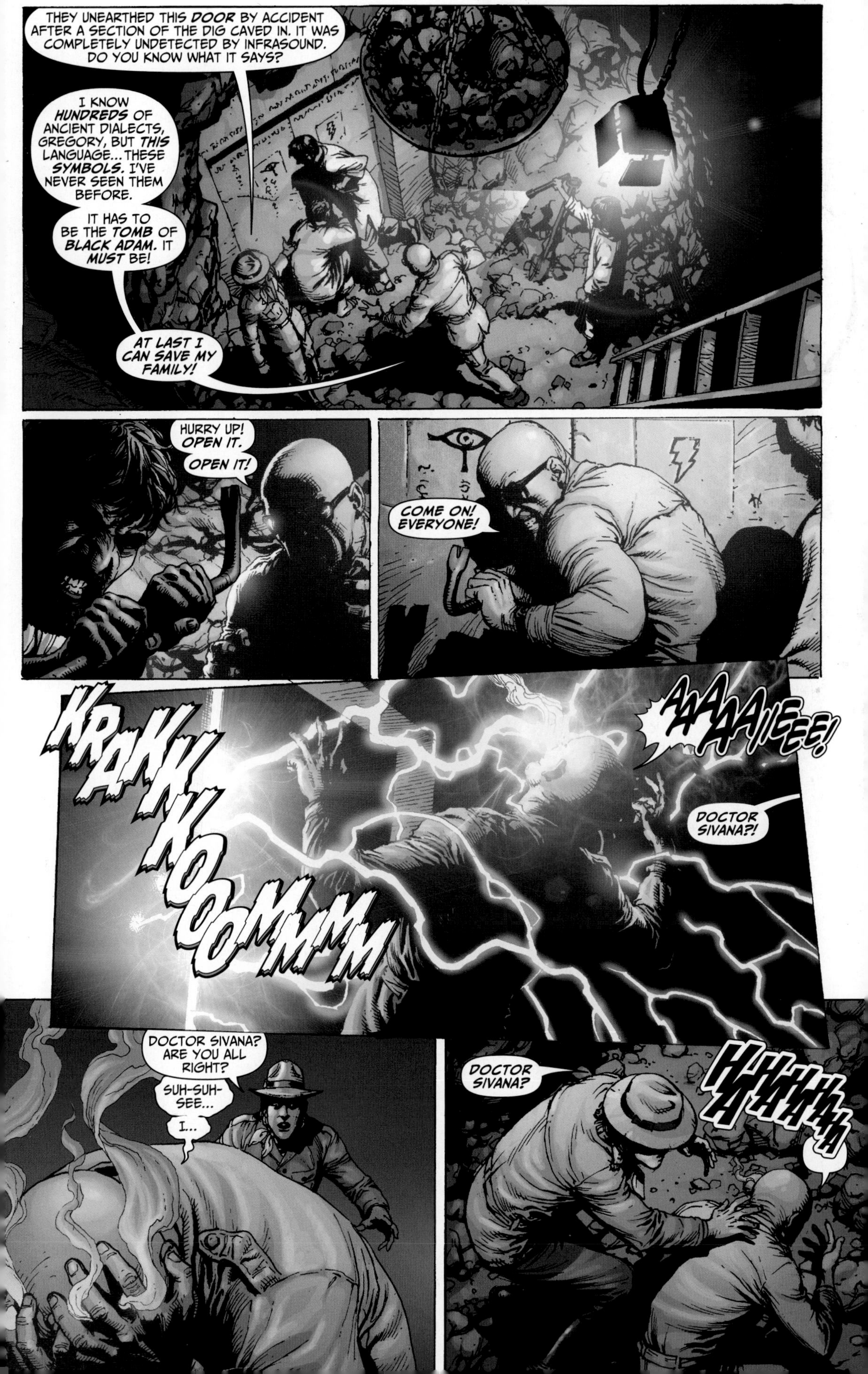
THEY UNEARTHED THIS DOOR BY ACCIDENT AFTER A SECTION OF THE DIG CAVED IN. IT WAS COMPLETELY UNDETECTED BY INFRASOUND. DO YOU KNOW WHAT IT SAYS?
I KNOW HUNDREDS OF ANCIENT DIALECTS, GREGORY, BUT THIS LANGUAGE... THESE SYMBOLS. I'VE NEVER SEEN THEM BEFORE.
IT HAS TO BE THE TOMB OF BLACK ADAM. IT MUST BE!
AT LAST I CAN SAVE MY FAMILY!
HURRY UP! OPEN IT.
OPEN IT!
COME ON! EVERYONE!
KRAKKKOOOMMMM
AAAAAIEEE!
DOCTOR SIVANA?!
DOCTOR SIVANA? ARE YOU ALL RIGHT?
SUH-SUH-SEE...
I...
DOCTOR SIVANA?
HAHAHAHA

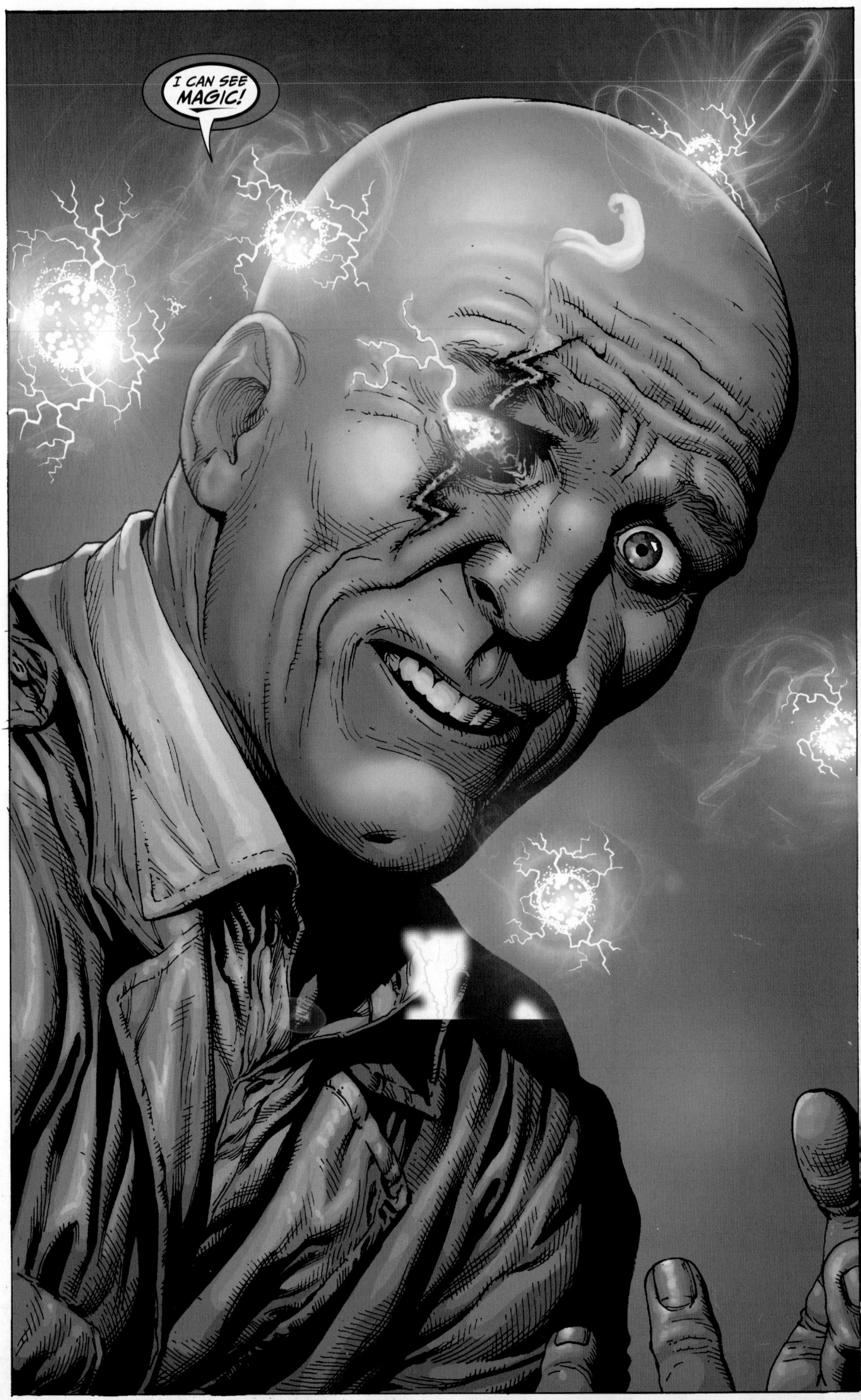
I CAN SEE MAGIC!

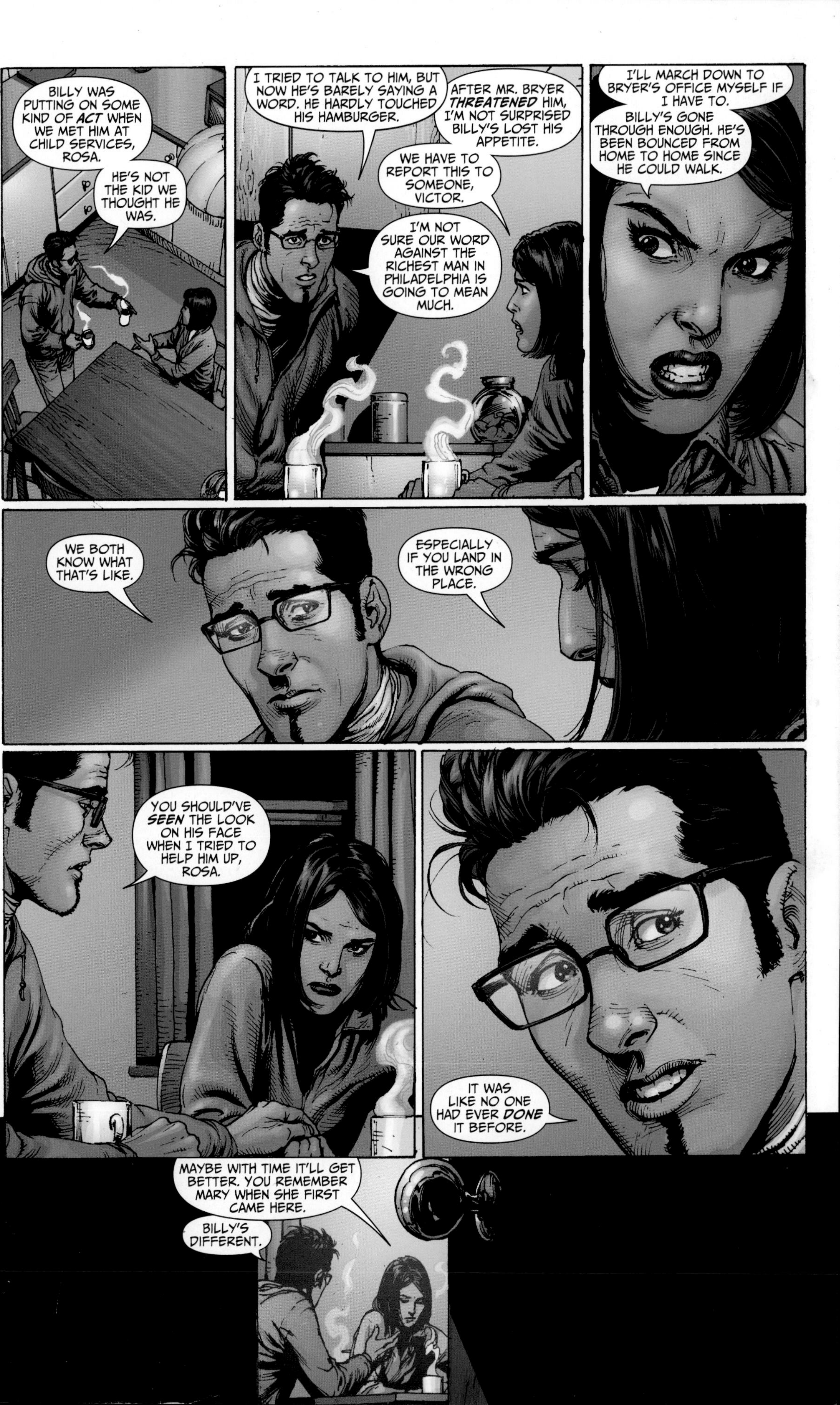
BILLY WAS PUTTING ON SOME KIND OF ACT WHEN WE MET HIM AT CHILD SERVICES, ROSA.
HE'S NOT THE KID WE THOUGHT HE WAS.
I TRIED TO TALK TO HIM, BUT NOW HE'S BARELY SAYING A WORD. HE HARDLY TOUCHED HIS HAMBURGER.
AFTER MR. BRYER THREATENED HIM, I'M NOT SURPRISED BILLY'S LOST HIS APPETITE.
WE HAVE TO REPORT THIS TO SOMEONE, VICTOR.
I'M NOT SURE OUR WORD AGAINST THE RICHEST MAN IN PHILADELPHIA IS GOING TO MEAN MUCH.
I'LL MARCH DOWN TO BRYER'S OFFICE MYSELF IF I HAVE TO.
BILLY'S GONE THROUGH ENOUGH. HE'S BEEN BOUNCED FROM HOME TO HOME SINCE HE COULD WALK.
WE BOTH KNOW WHAT THAT'S LIKE.
ESPECIALLY IF YOU LAND IN THE WRONG PLACE.
YOU SHOULD'VE SEEN THE LOOK ON HIS FACE WHEN I TRIED TO HELP HIM UP, ROSA.
IT WAS LIKE NO ONE HAD EVER DONE IT BEFORE.
MAYBE WITH TIME IT'LL GET BETTER. YOU REMEMBER MARY WHEN SHE FIRST CAME HERE.
BILLY'S DIFFERENT.

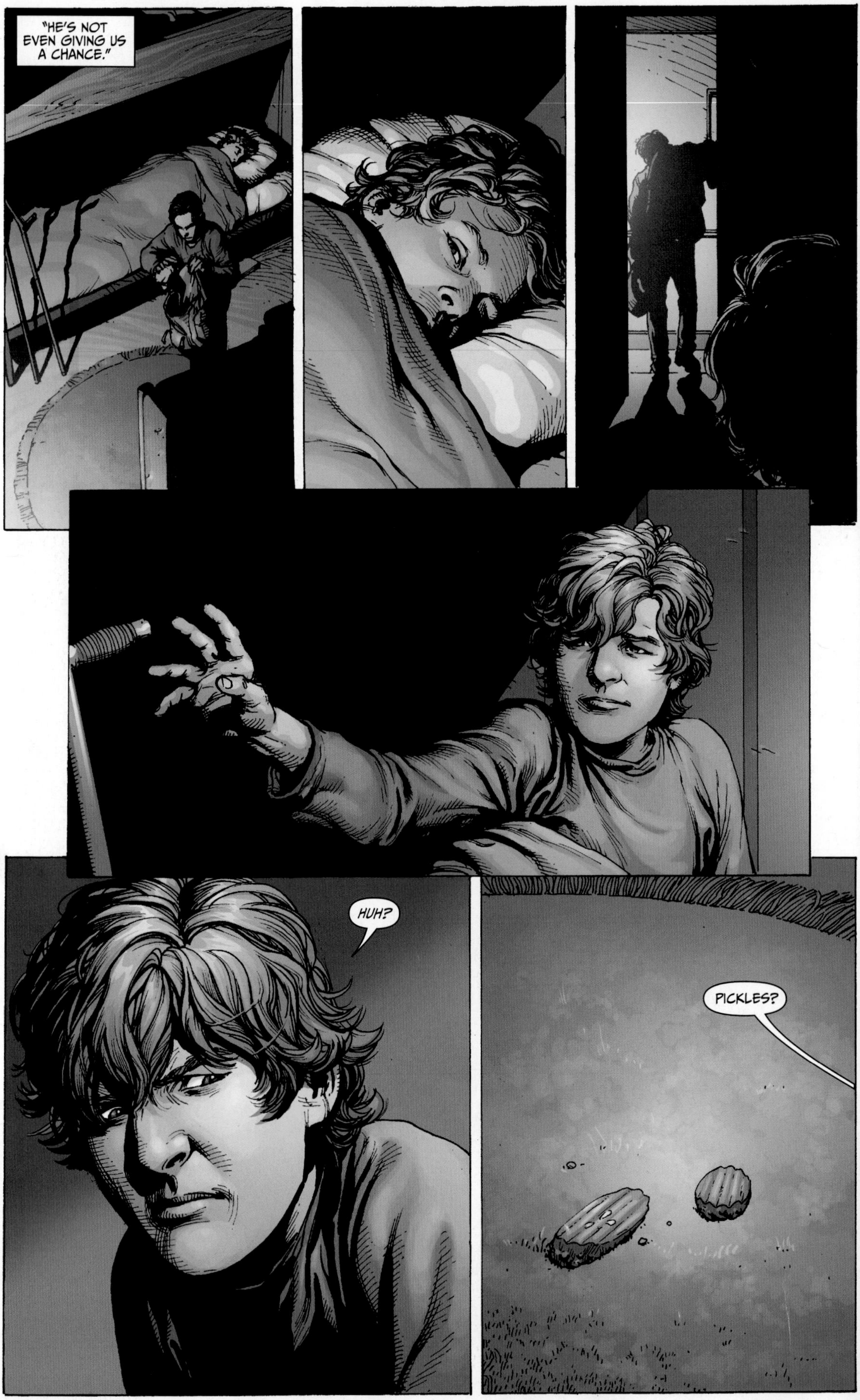
"HE'S NOT EVEN GIVING US A CHANCE."
HUH?
PICKLES?

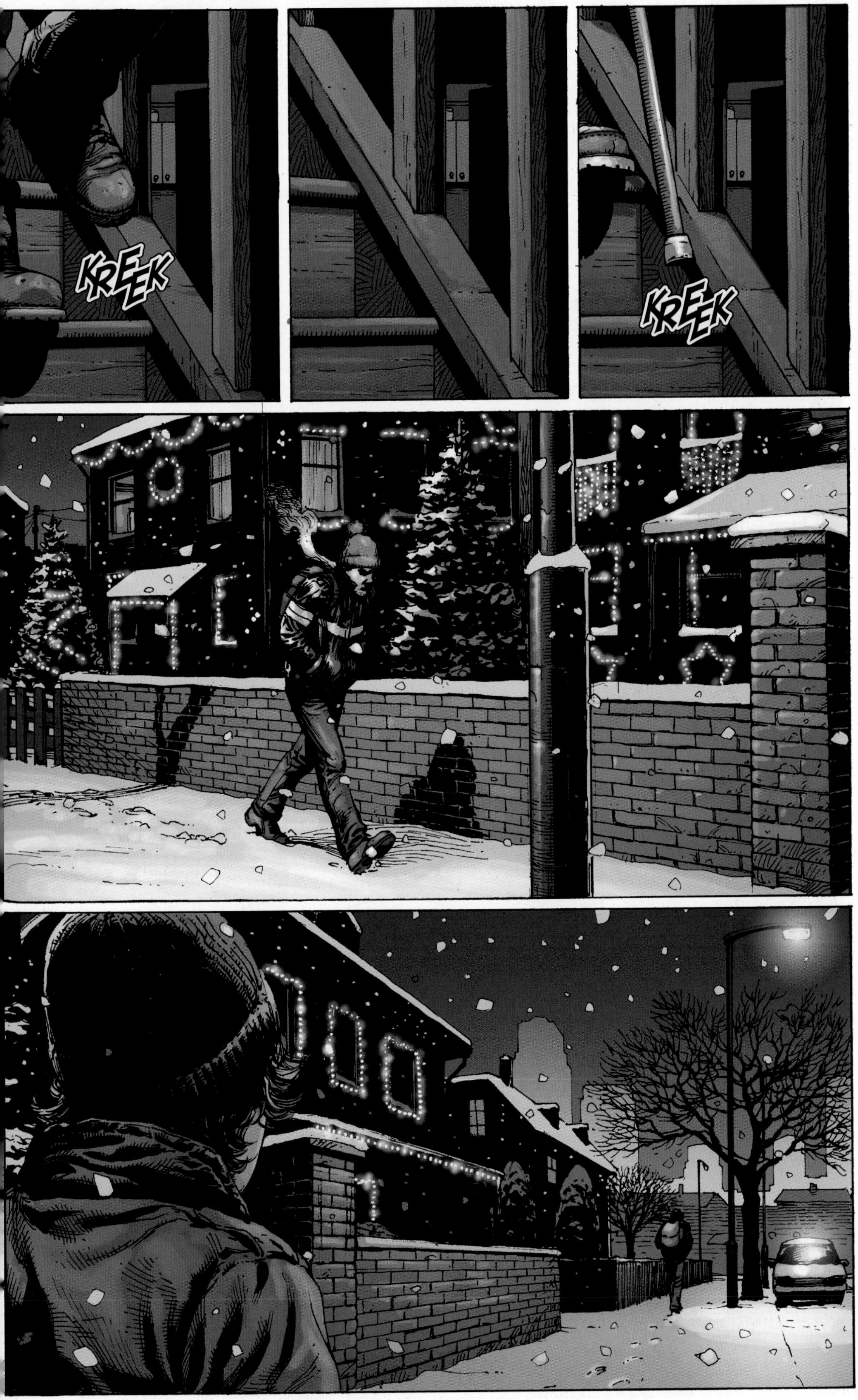
KREEEK
KREEEK

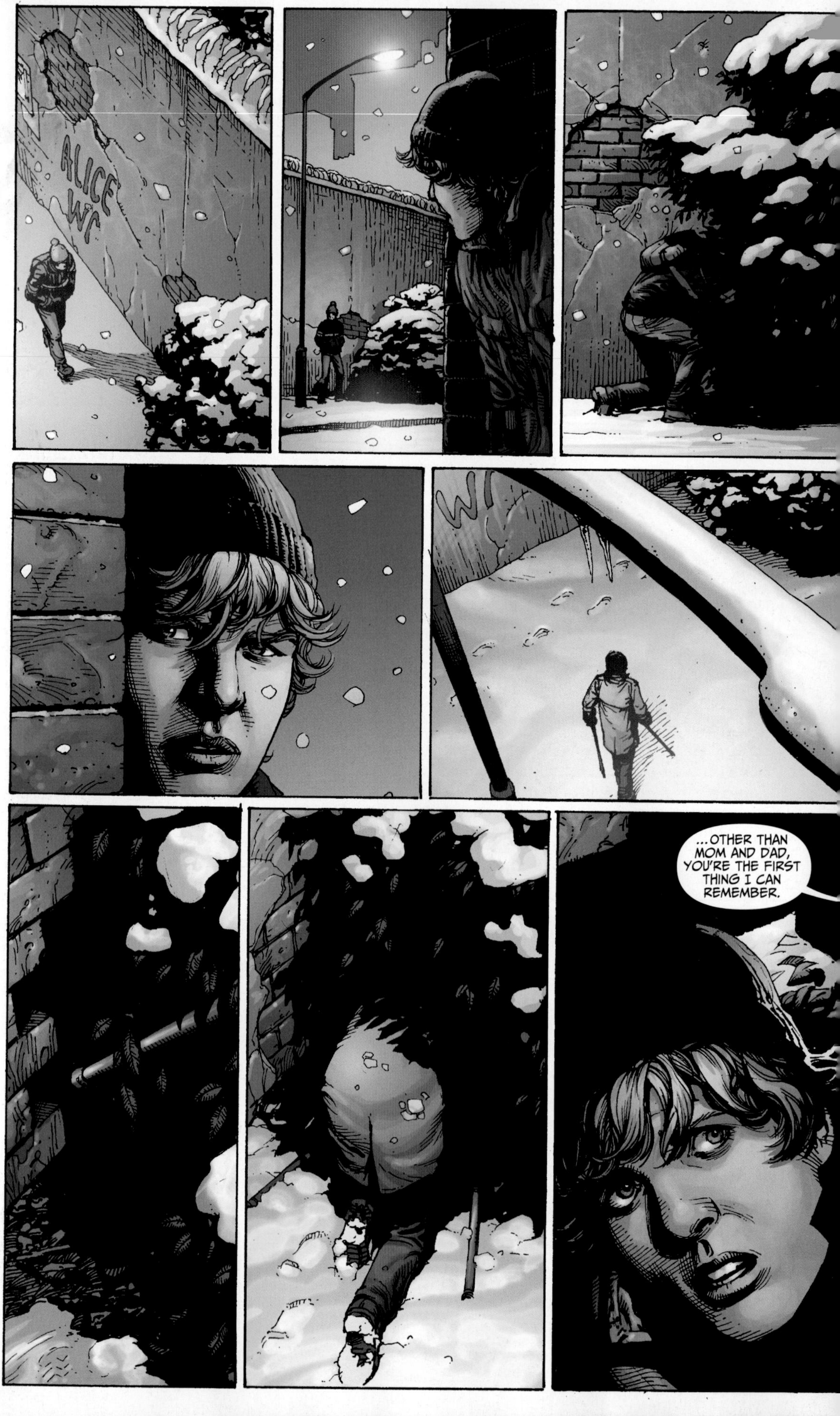
...OTHER THAN MOM AND DAD, YOU'RE THE FIRST THING I CAN REMEMBER.

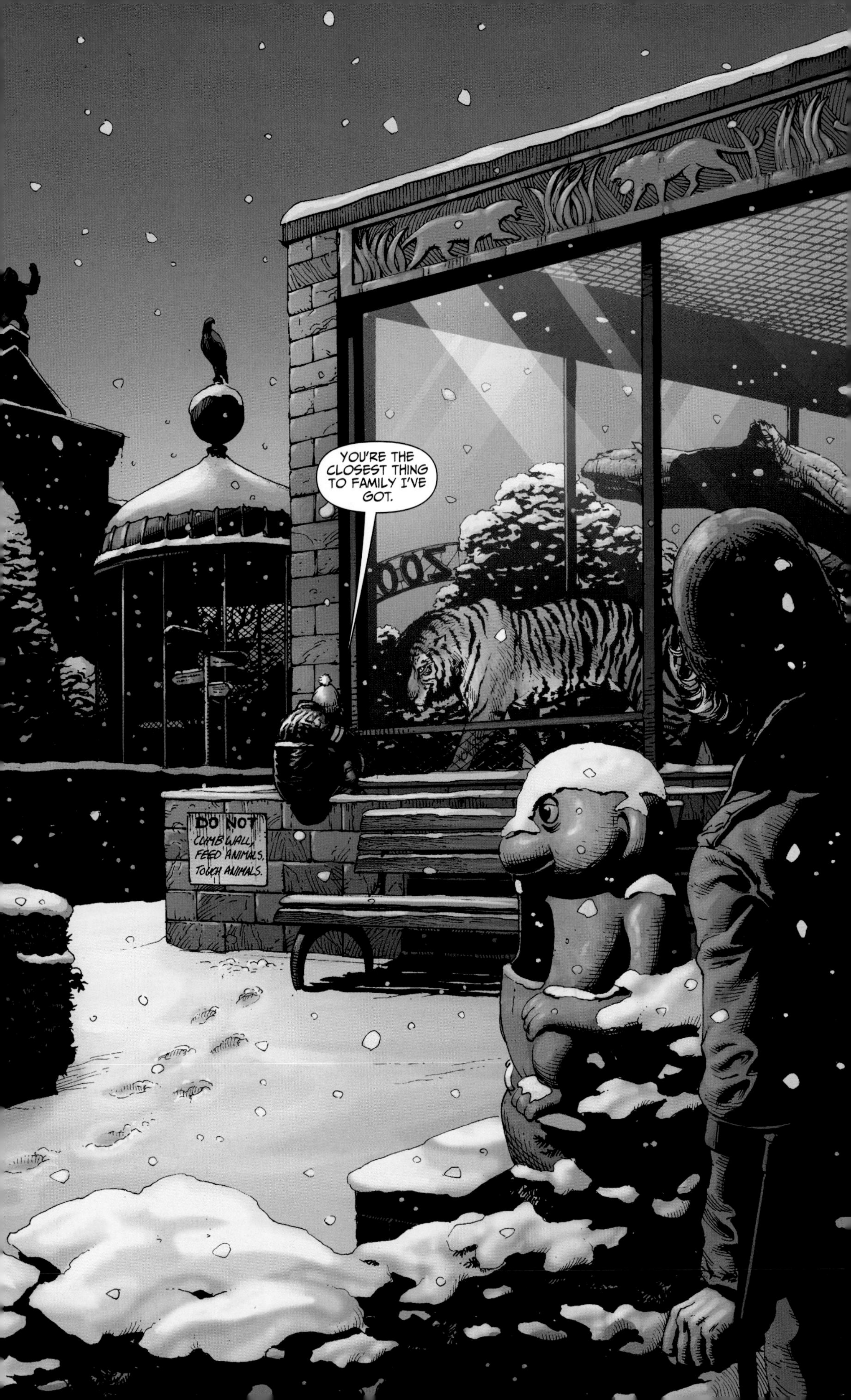
YOU'RE THE CLOSEST THING TO FAMILY I'VE GOT.
DO NOT
CLIMB WALL,
FEED ANIMALS,
TOUCH ANIMALS.

NO PICKLES. JUST HOW YOU LIKE IT.

WHAT IS IT, TAWNY?

WAIT!!

CLIMB WALL
FEED ANIMALS
TOUCH ANIMALS

OOFF!

OW.

FREDDY?! WHAT THE HELL ARE *YOU* DOING HERE?

WHAT THE HELL ARE YOU DOING TALKING TO *TIGERS?* AND WHY DO YOU HAVE A PICTURE OF HIM IN YOUR *WALLET?*

MY WALLET?

YOU *TOOK* MY WALLET?

RELAX, DOCTOR DOLITTLE. I WAS JUST CURIOUS. IT'S ALL THERE. THREE *WHOLE* DOLLARS.

AND YOUR MEMBERSHIP CARD TO THAT *FAMILY FINDER'S* WEBSITE. YOU LOOKING FOR YOUR *BIRTH PARENTS?*

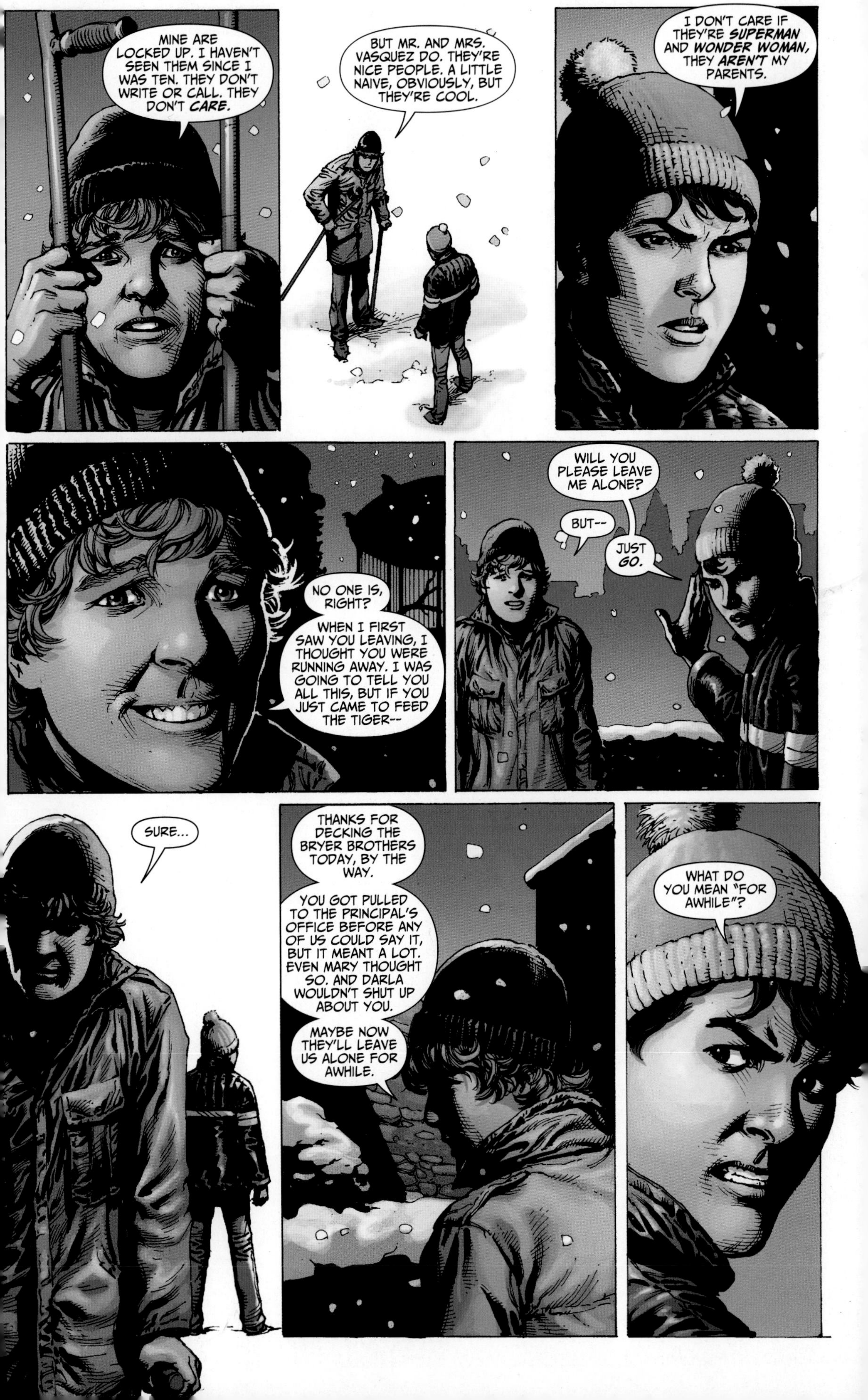
MINE ARE LOCKED UP. I HAVEN'T SEEN THEM SINCE I WAS TEN. THEY DON'T WRITE OR CALL. THEY DON'T CARE.
BUT MR. AND MRS. VASQUEZ DO. THEY'RE NICE PEOPLE. A LITTLE NAIVE, OBVIOUSLY, BUT THEY'RE COOL.
I DON'T CARE IF THEY'RE SUPERMAN AND WONDER WOMAN, THEY AREN'T MY PARENTS.
NO ONE IS, RIGHT?
WHEN I FIRST SAW YOU LEAVING, I THOUGHT YOU WERE RUNNING AWAY. I WAS GOING TO TELL YOU ALL THIS, BUT IF YOU JUST CAME TO FEED THE TIGER--
WILL YOU PLEASE LEAVE ME ALONE?
BUT--
JUST GO.
SURE...
THANKS FOR DECKING THE BRYER BROTHERS TODAY, BY THE WAY.
YOU GOT PULLED TO THE PRINCIPAL'S OFFICE BEFORE ANY OF US COULD SAY IT, BUT IT MEANT A LOT. EVEN MARY THOUGHT SO. AND DARLA WOULDN'T SHUT UP ABOUT YOU.
MAYBE NOW THEY'LL LEAVE US ALONE FOR AWHILE.
WHAT DO YOU MEAN "FOR AWHILE"?

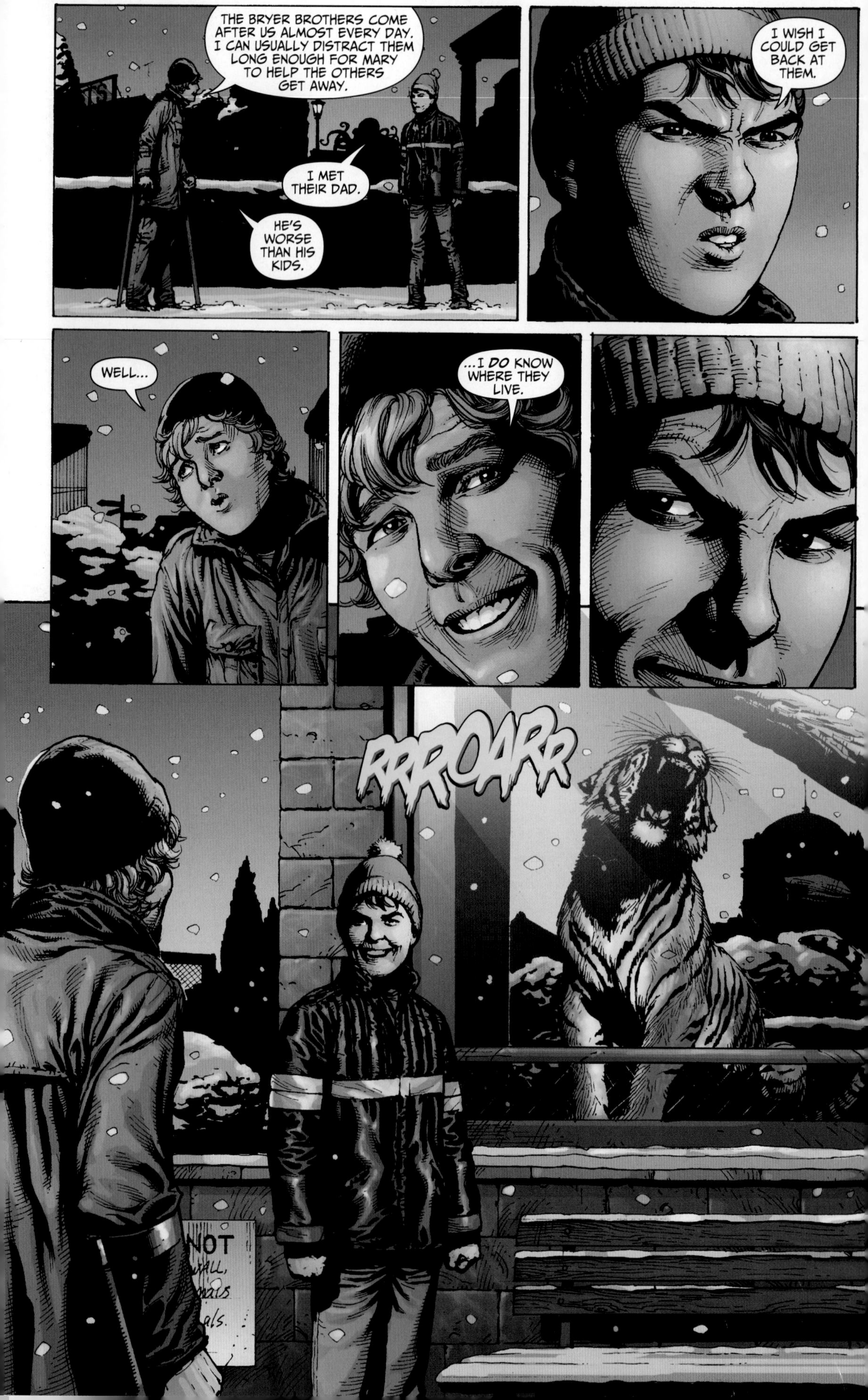
THE BRYER BROTHERS COME AFTER US ALMOST EVERY DAY. I CAN USUALLY DISTRACT THEM LONG ENOUGH FOR MARY TO HELP THE OTHERS GET AWAY.
I MET THEIR DAD.
HE'S WORSE THAN HIS KIDS.
I WISH I COULD GET BACK AT THEM.
WELL...
...I *DO* KNOW WHERE THEY LIVE.
RRRROARR
NOT

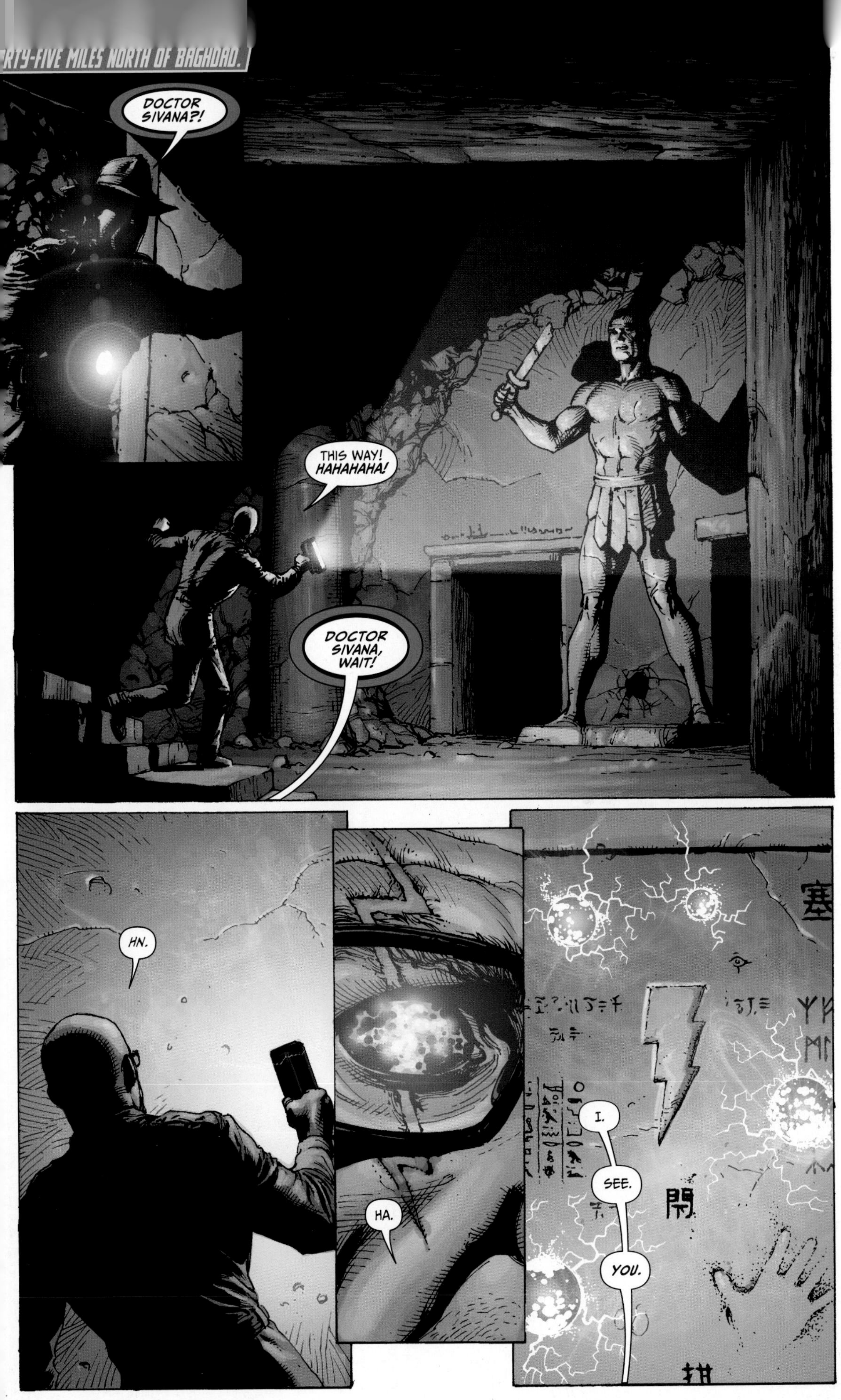
RTY-FIVE MILES NORTH OF BAGHDAD.
DOCTOR SIVANA?!
THIS WAY! HAHAHAHA!
DOCTOR SIVANA, WAIT!
HN.
HA.
I.
SEE.
YOU.

DOCTOR SIVANA? THERE'S NOTHING THERE. IT'S JUST A WALL.

BUT THE ROOM AHEAD, WE CAN SEE A GLITTER-ING.

< TREASURE! >

TREASURE, GABIR SAYS. WE'VE FOUND SOMETHING!

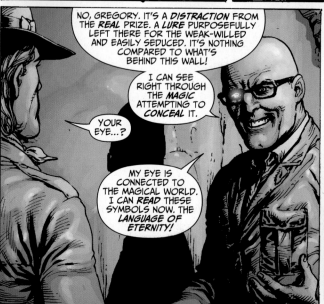

NO, GREGORY. IT'S A DISTRACTION FROM THE REAL PRIZE. A LURE PURPOSEFULLY LEFT THERE FOR THE WEAK-WILLED AND EASILY SEDUCED. IT'S NOTHING COMPARED TO WHAT'S BEHIND THIS WALL!

I CAN SEE RIGHT THROUGH THE MAGIC ATTEMPTING TO CONCEAL IT.

YOUR EYE...?

MY EYE IS CONNECTED TO THE MAGICAL WORLD. I CAN READ THESE SYMBOLS NOW. THE LANGUAGE OF ETERNITY!

IT SAYS HERE THAT BLACK ADAM WILL BE IMPRISONED UNTIL A BEING WHO CAN DESTROY HIM IS FOUND!

HIS ENEMIES PUT HIM HERE, BUT WE CAN RELEASE HIM--

--AND BRING MAGIC BACK TO THE WORLD!

IT SAYS THIS TOMB CANNOT BE OPENED BUT WITH ONE WORD...

SHA

KZZATTT   KZZATTT

...SHAZAM!

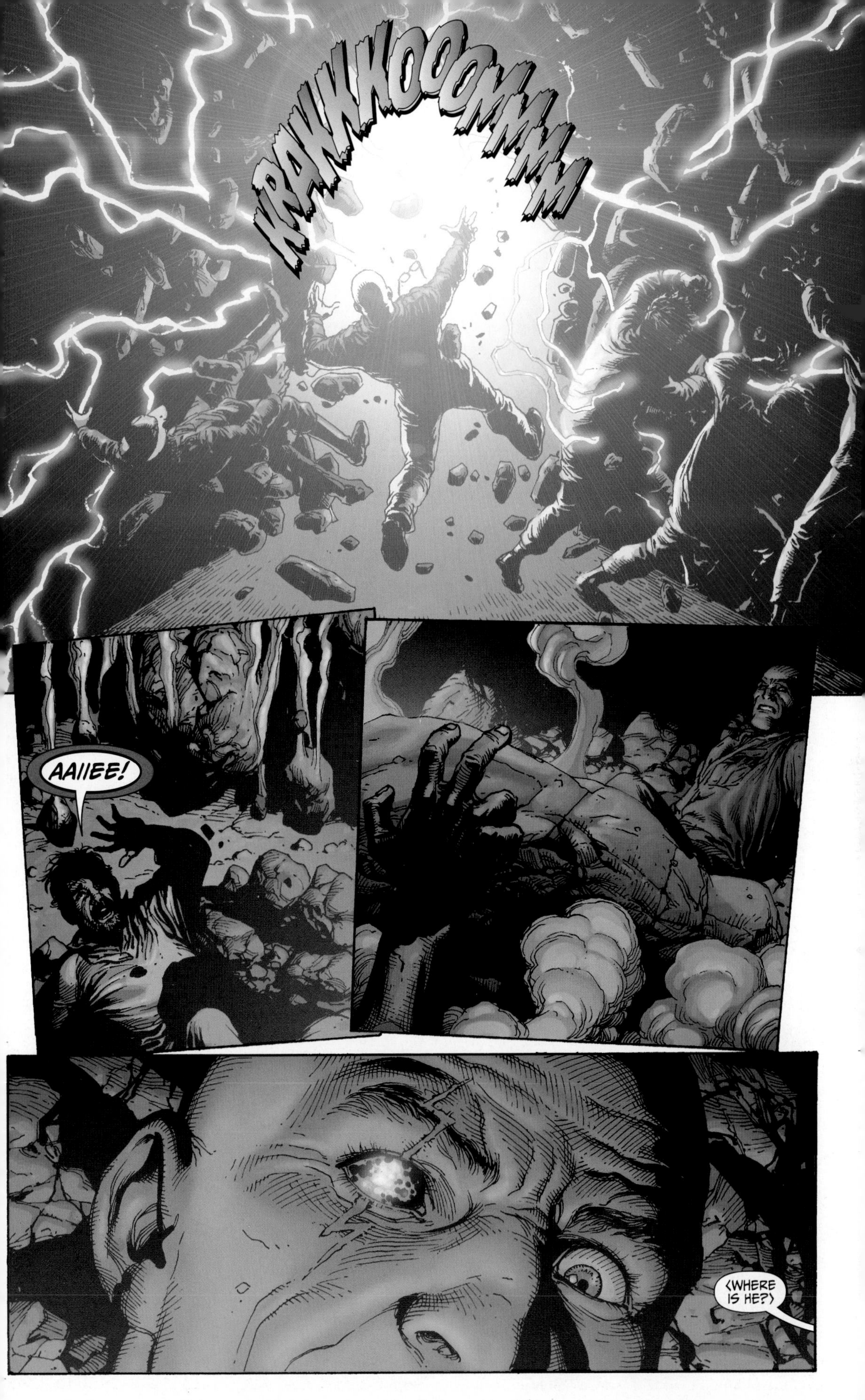
KRAKKOOOMMMM
AAIIEE!
<WHERE IS HE?>

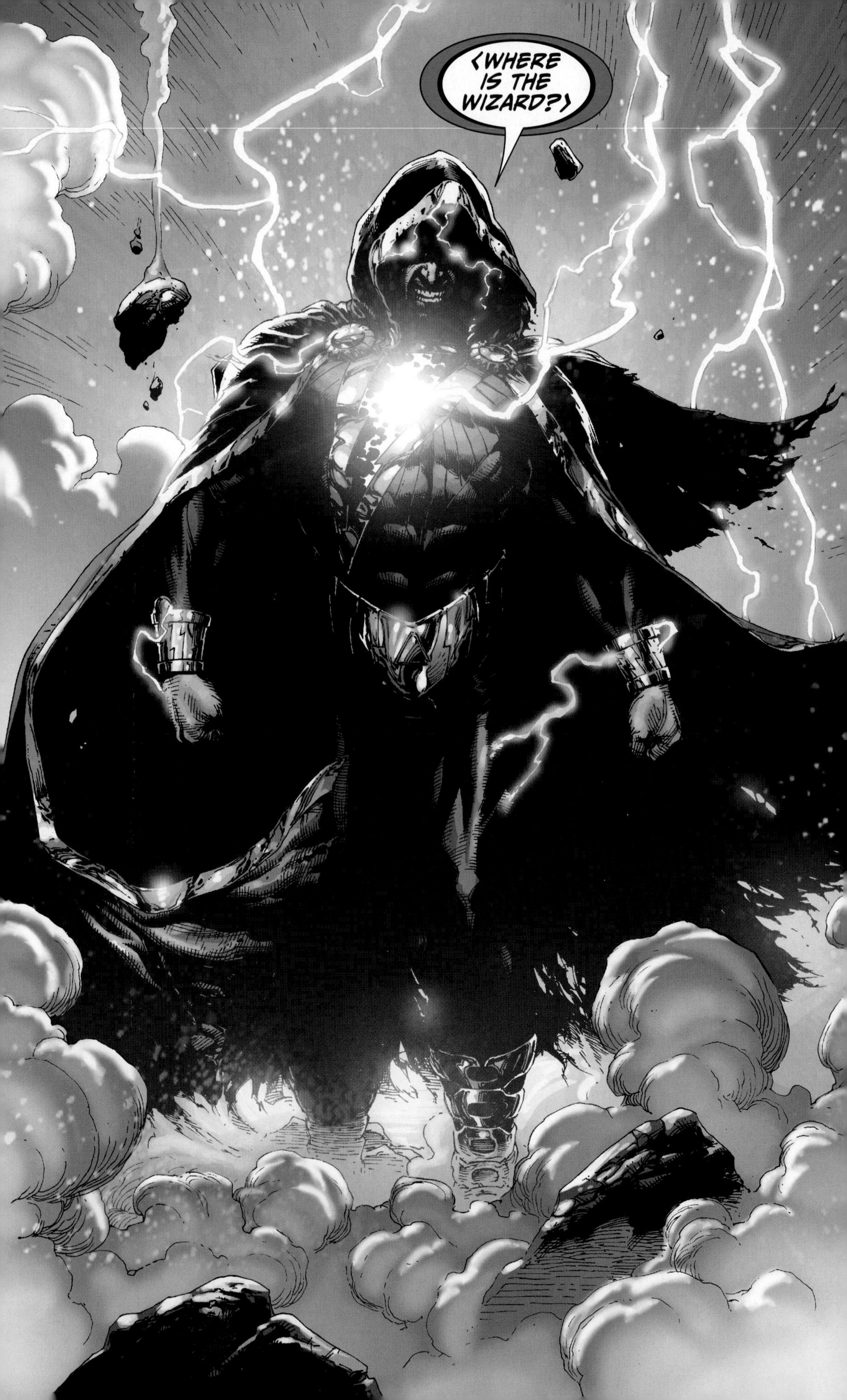
<WHERE IS THE WIZARD?>

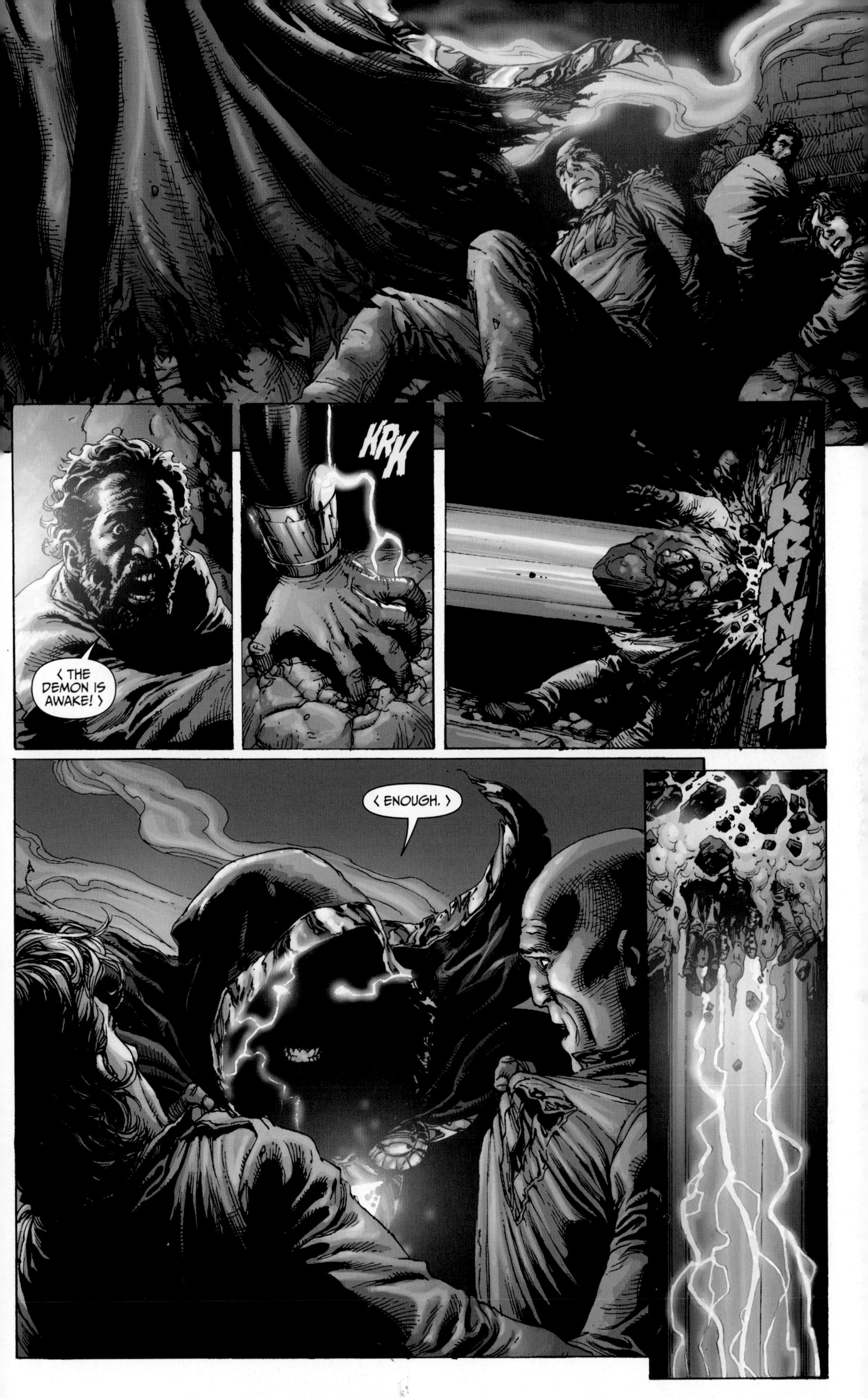

‹ THE DEMON IS AWAKE! ›
KRK
KRNNCH
‹ ENOUGH. ›

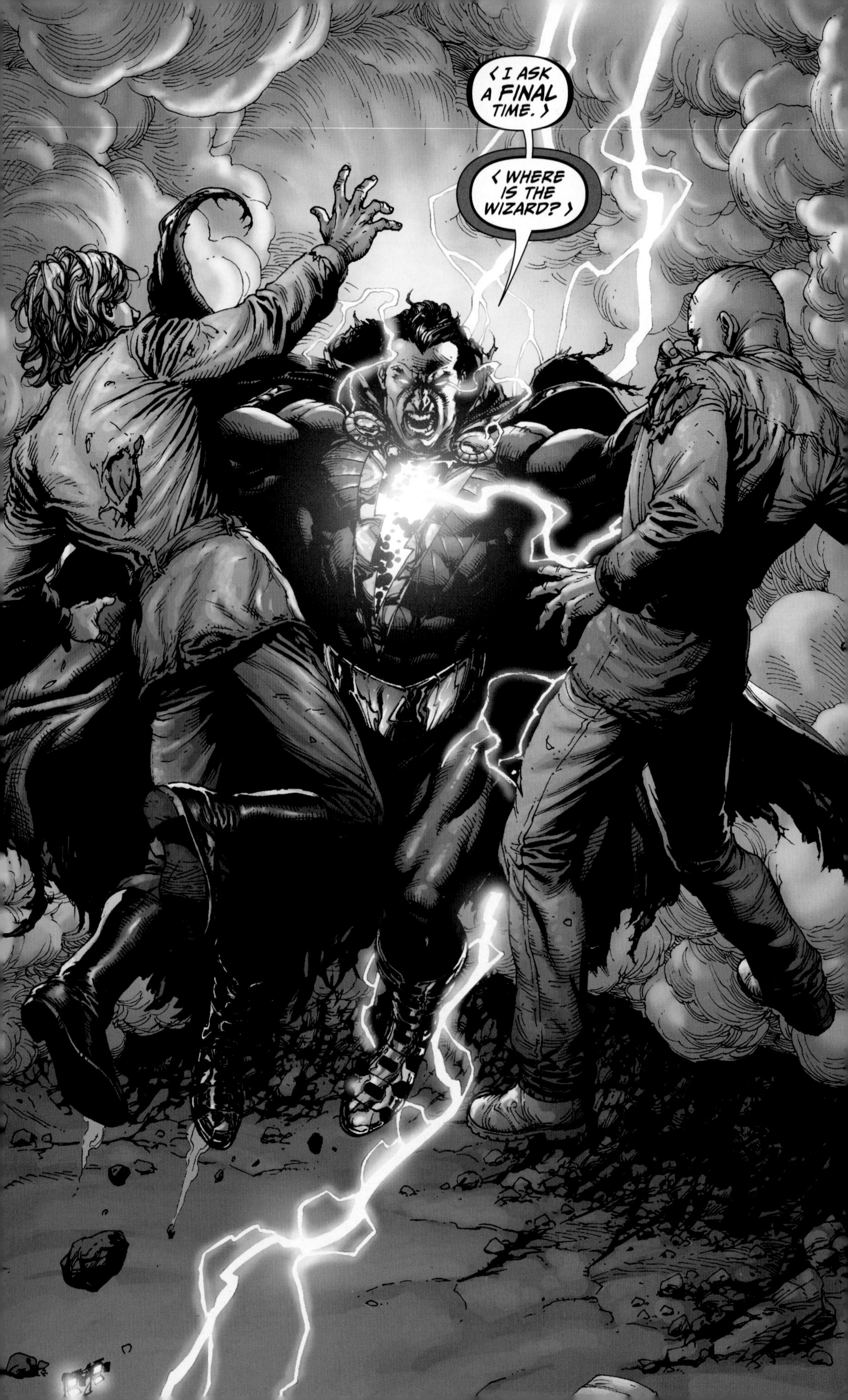
‹ I ASK A FINAL TIME. ›
‹ WHERE IS THE WIZARD? ›

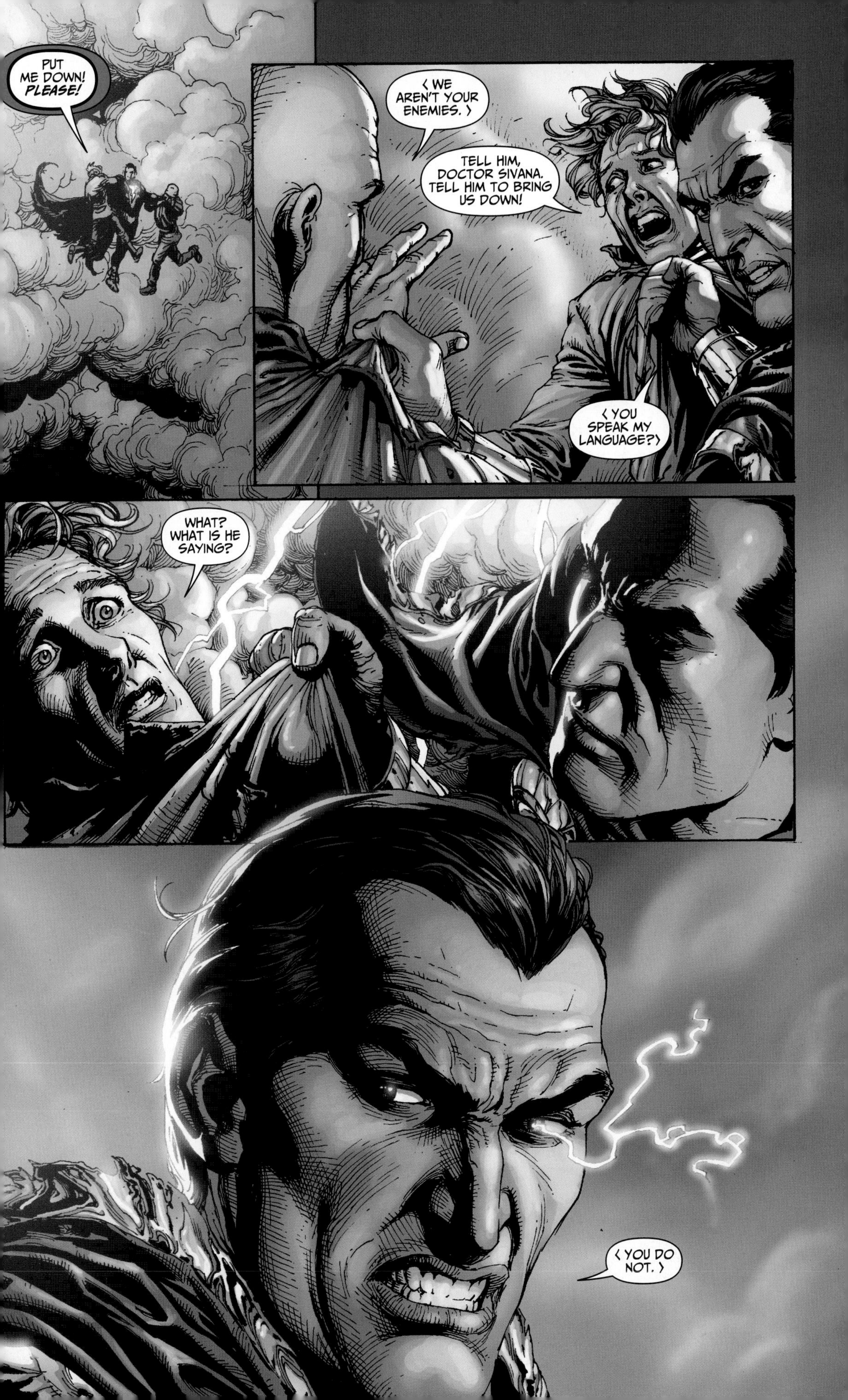
PUT ME DOWN! *PLEASE!*
‹ WE AREN'T YOUR ENEMIES. ›
TELL HIM, DOCTOR SIVANA. TELL HIM TO BRING US DOWN!
‹ YOU SPEAK MY LANGUAGE?›
WHAT? WHAT IS HE SAYING?
‹ YOU DO NOT. ›

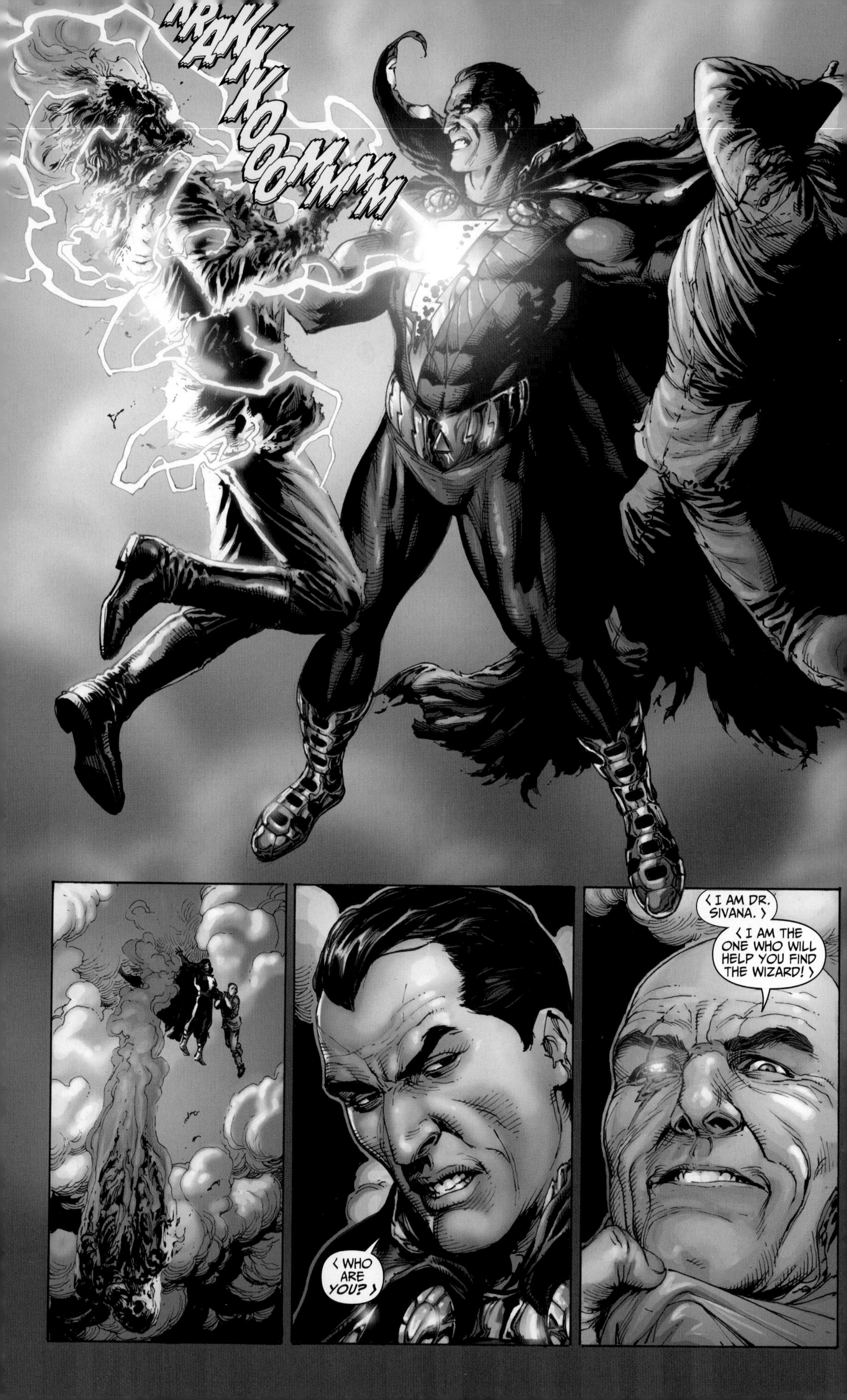
DRAKKKOOOMMMM
‹ WHO ARE YOU? ›
‹ I AM DR. SIVANA. ›
‹ I AM THE ONE WHO WILL HELP YOU FIND THE WIZARD! ›

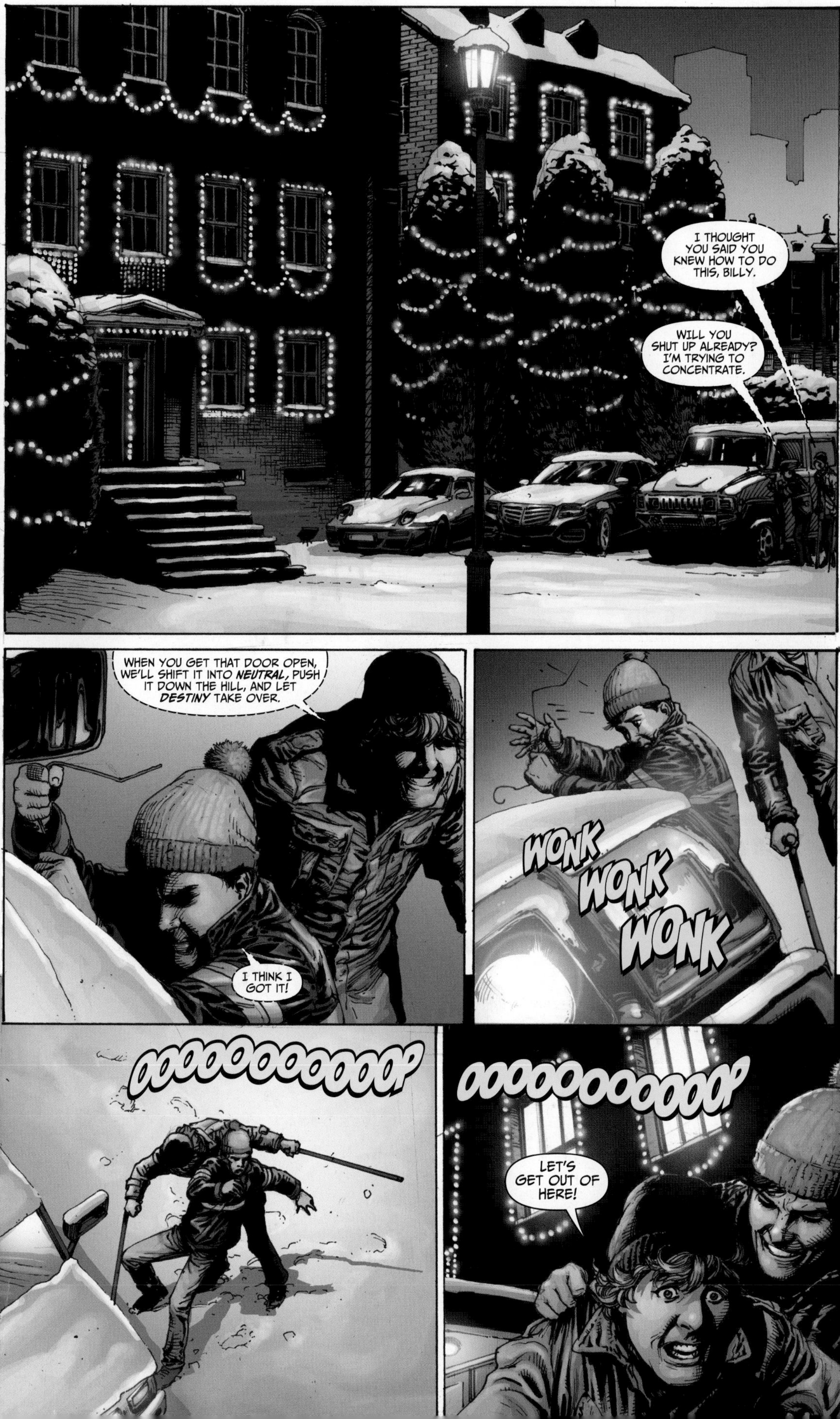
I THOUGHT YOU SAID YOU KNEW HOW TO DO THIS, BILLY.
WILL YOU SHUT UP ALREADY? I'M TRYING TO CONCENTRATE.
WHEN YOU GET THAT DOOR OPEN, WE'LL SHIFT IT INTO NEUTRAL, PUSH IT DOWN THE HILL, AND LET DESTINY TAKE OVER.
I THINK I GOT IT!
WONK
WONK
WONK
OOOOOOOOOOOP
OOOOOOOOOOOP
LET'S GET OUT OF HERE!

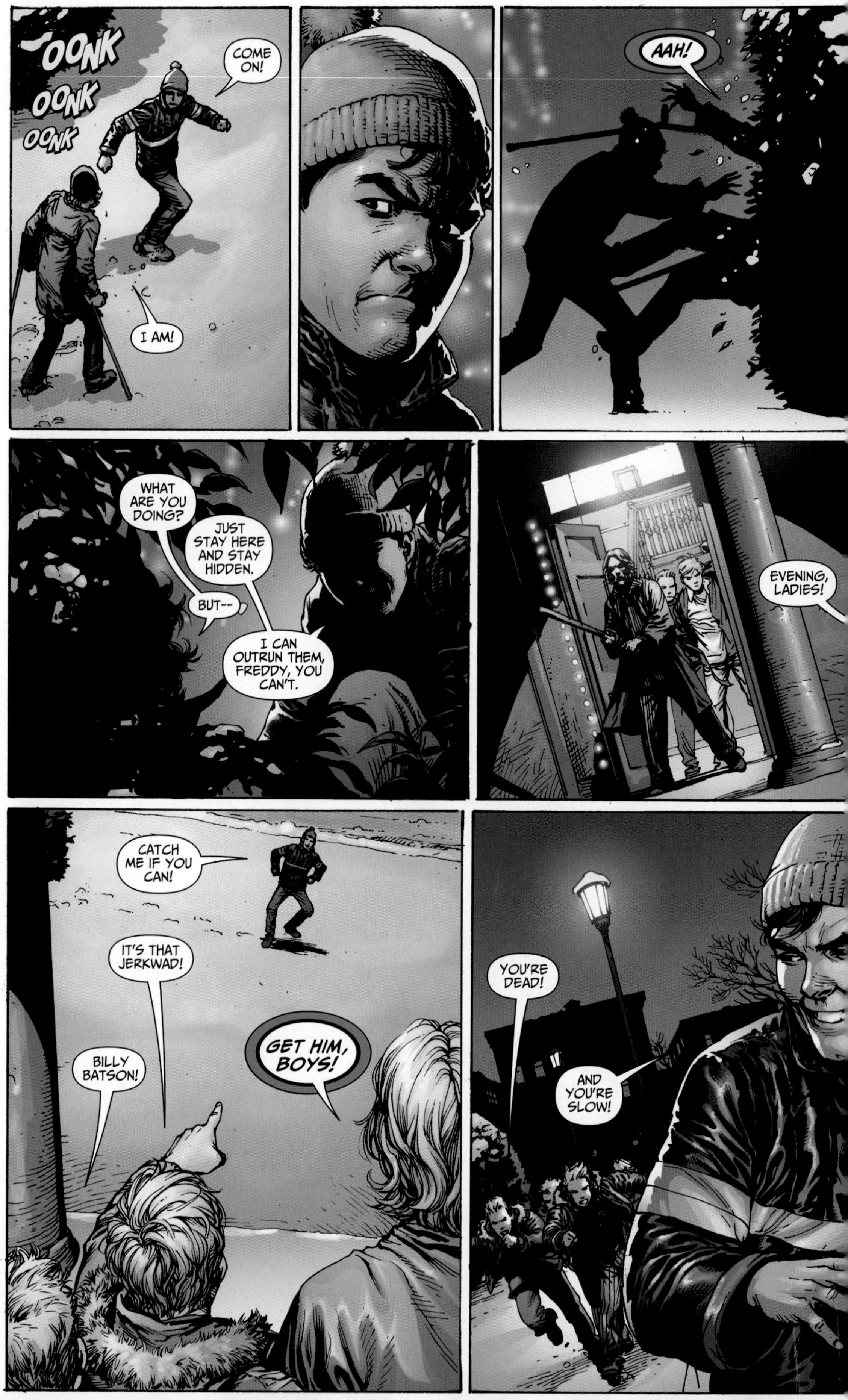
OONK
OONK
OONK
COME ON!
I AM!
AAH!
WHAT ARE YOU DOING?
JUST STAY HERE AND STAY HIDDEN.
BUT--
I CAN OUTRUN THEM, FREDDY, YOU CAN'T.
EVENING, LADIES!
CATCH ME IF YOU CAN!
IT'S THAT JERKWAD!
BILLY BATSON!
GET HIM, BOYS!
YOU'RE DEAD!
AND YOU'RE SLOW!

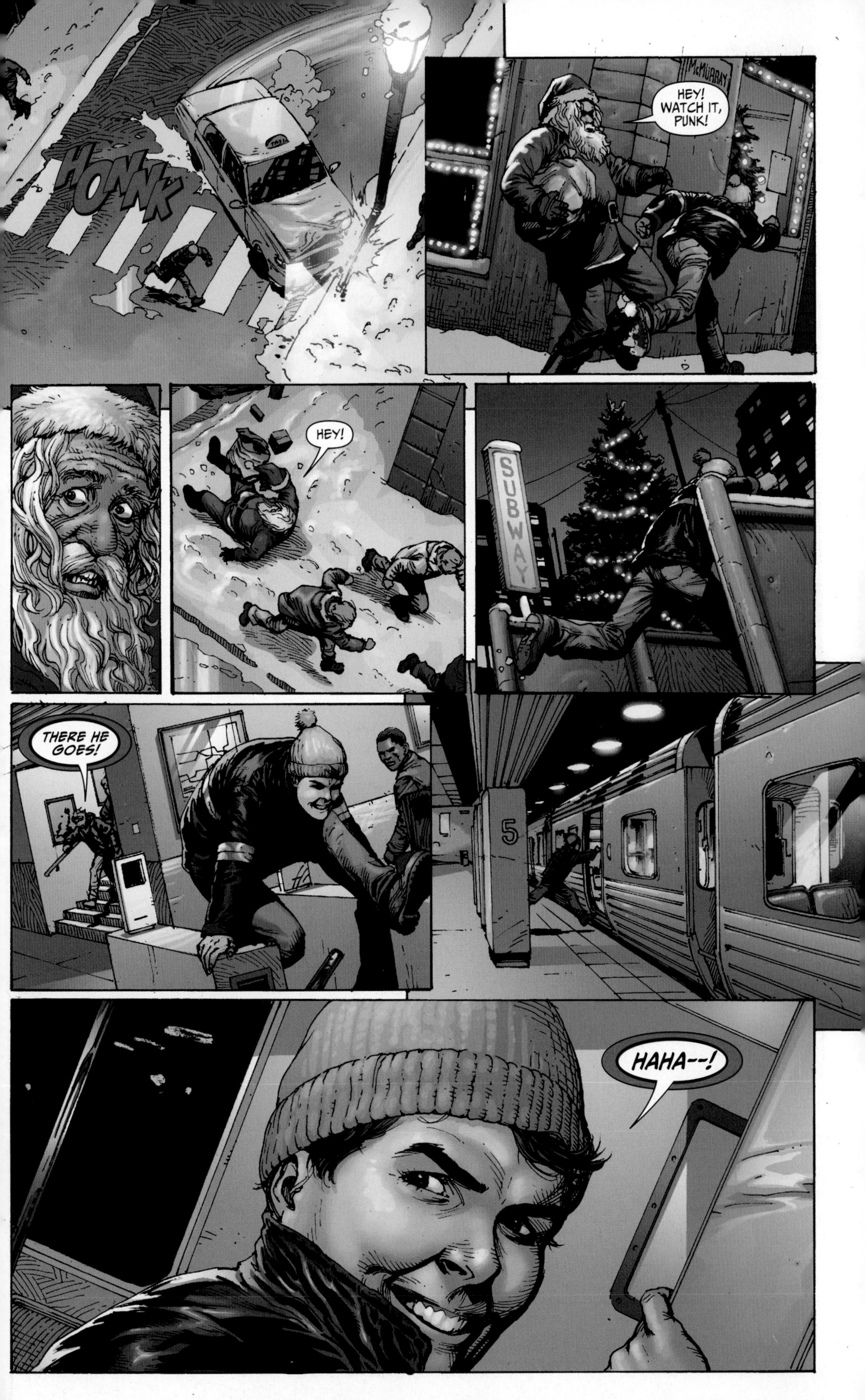
HONNK
HEY! WATCH IT, PUNK!
HEY!
SUBWAY
THERE HE GOES!
5
HAHA--!

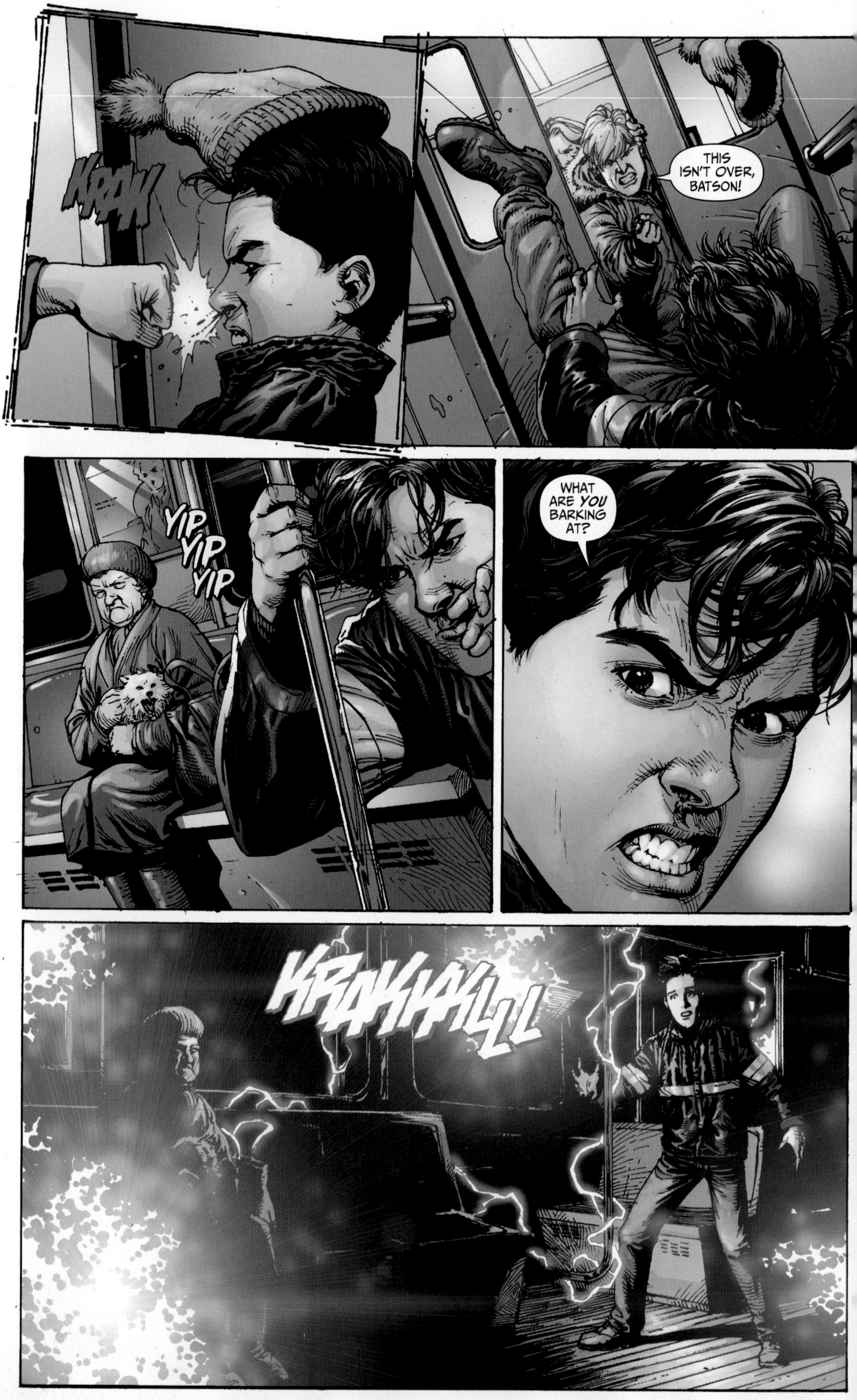
KRAK
THIS ISN'T OVER, BATSON!
YIP YIP YIP
WHAT ARE *YOU* BARKING AT?
KRAKKALLL

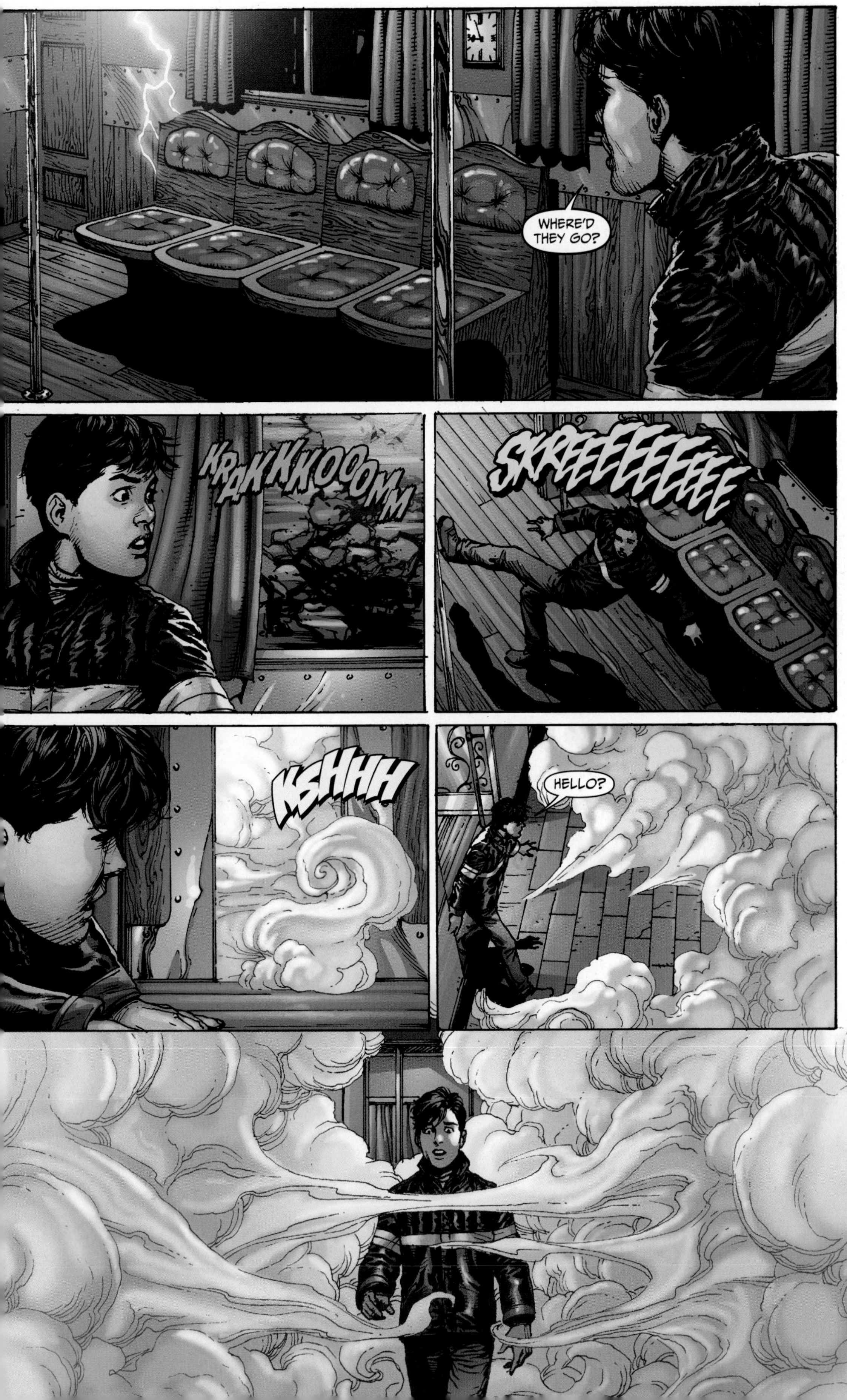
WHERE'D THEY GO?
KRAKKKOOOMM
SKREEEEEEEEE
KSHHH
HELLO?

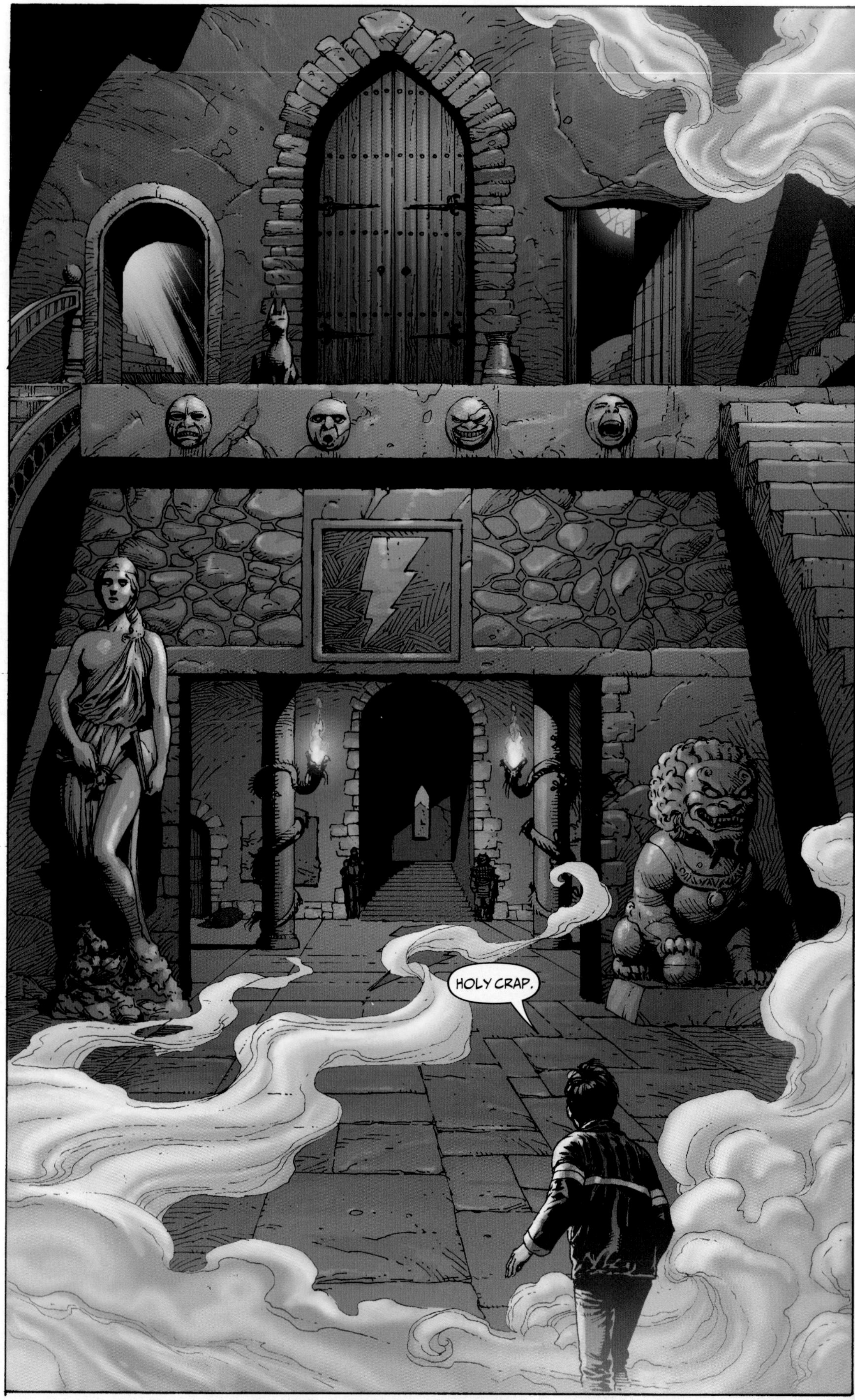
HOLY CRAP.

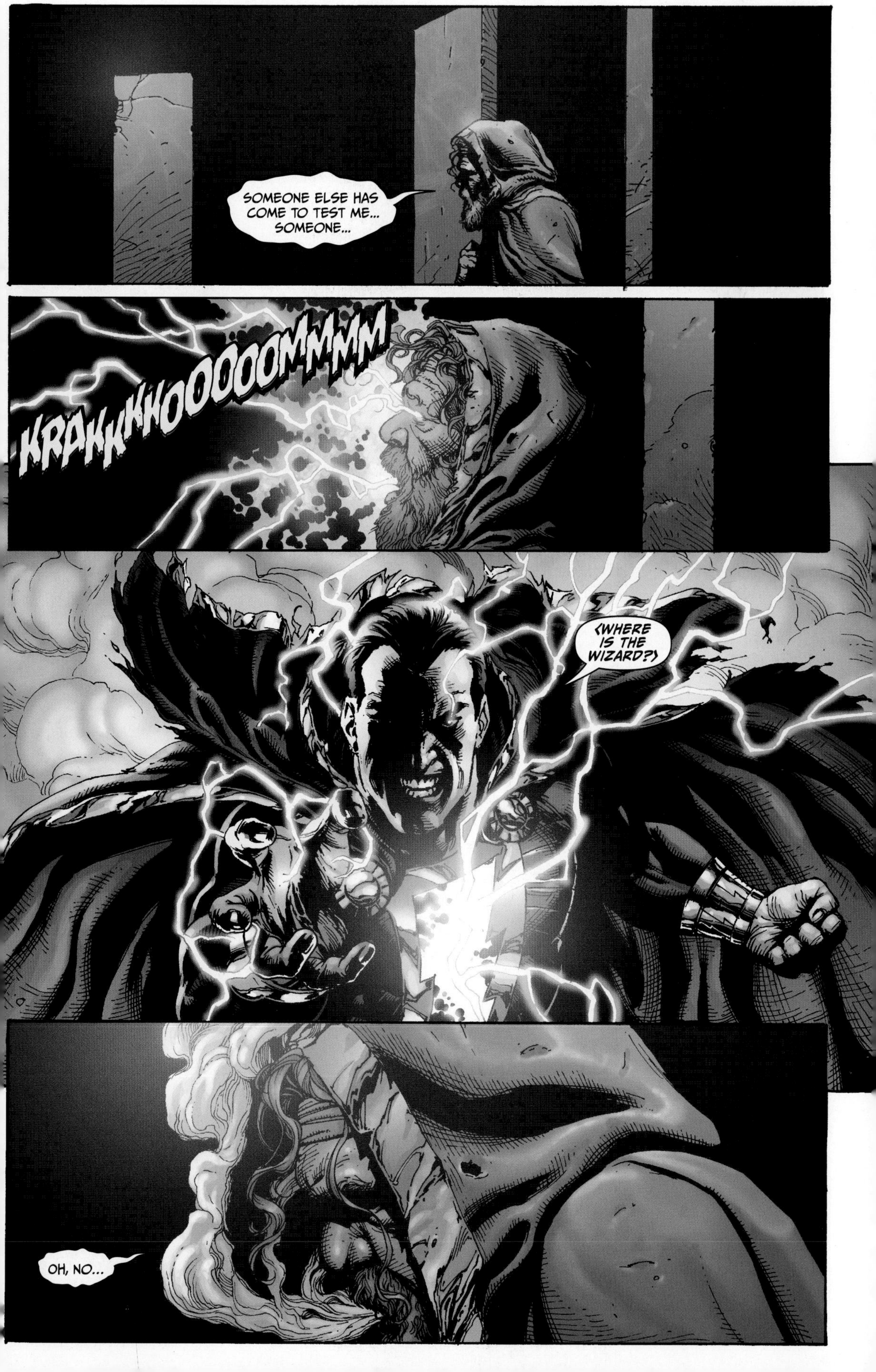
SOMEONE ELSE HAS COME TO TEST ME... SOMEONE...
KRAKKKOOOOOOMMMM
‹WHERE IS THE WIZARD?›
OH, NO...

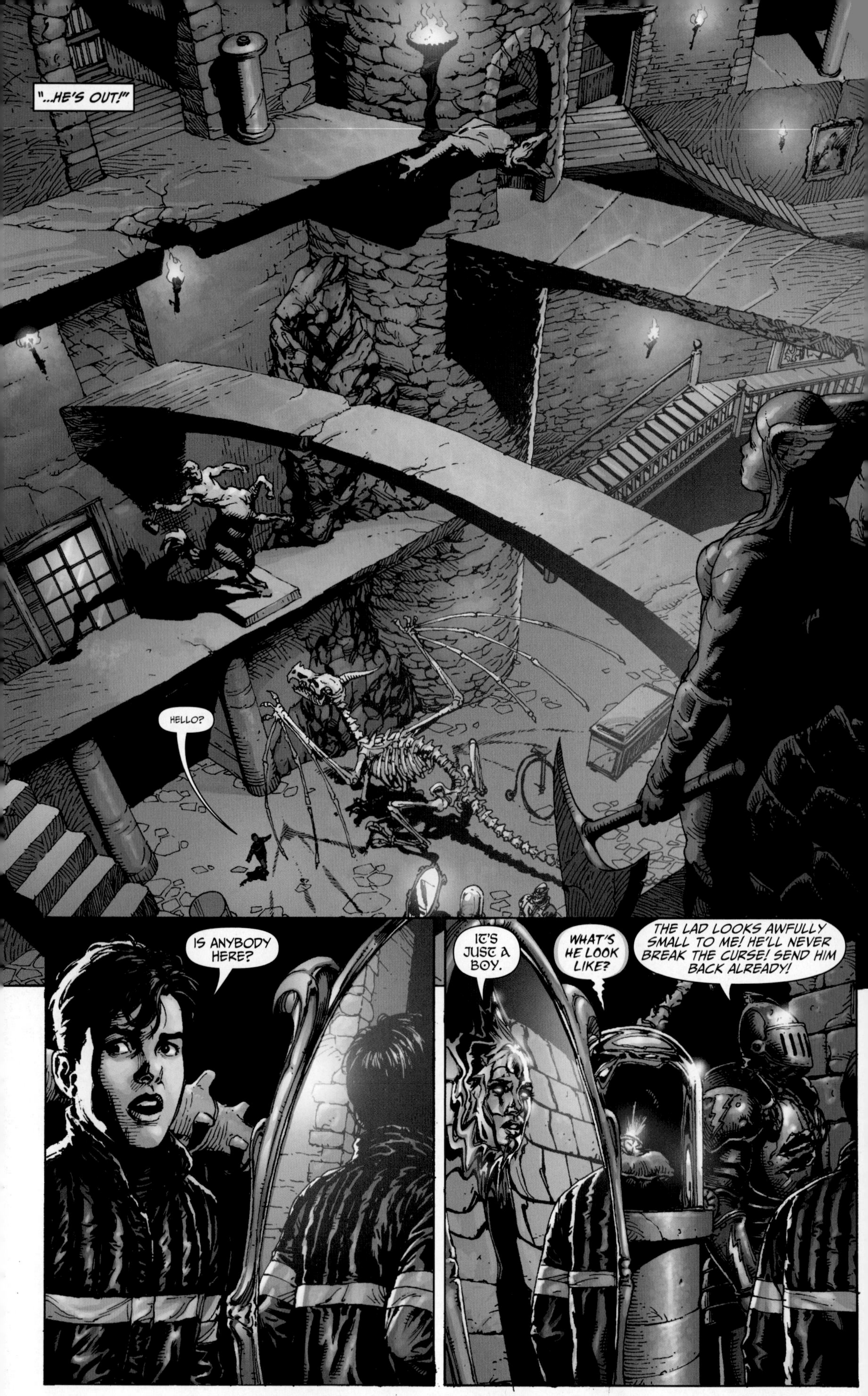
"...HE'S OUT!"
HELLO?
IS ANYBODY HERE?
IT'S JUST A BOY.
WHAT'S HE LOOK LIKE?
THE LAD LOOKS AWFULLY SMALL TO ME! HE'LL NEVER BREAK THE CURSE! SEND HIM BACK ALREADY!

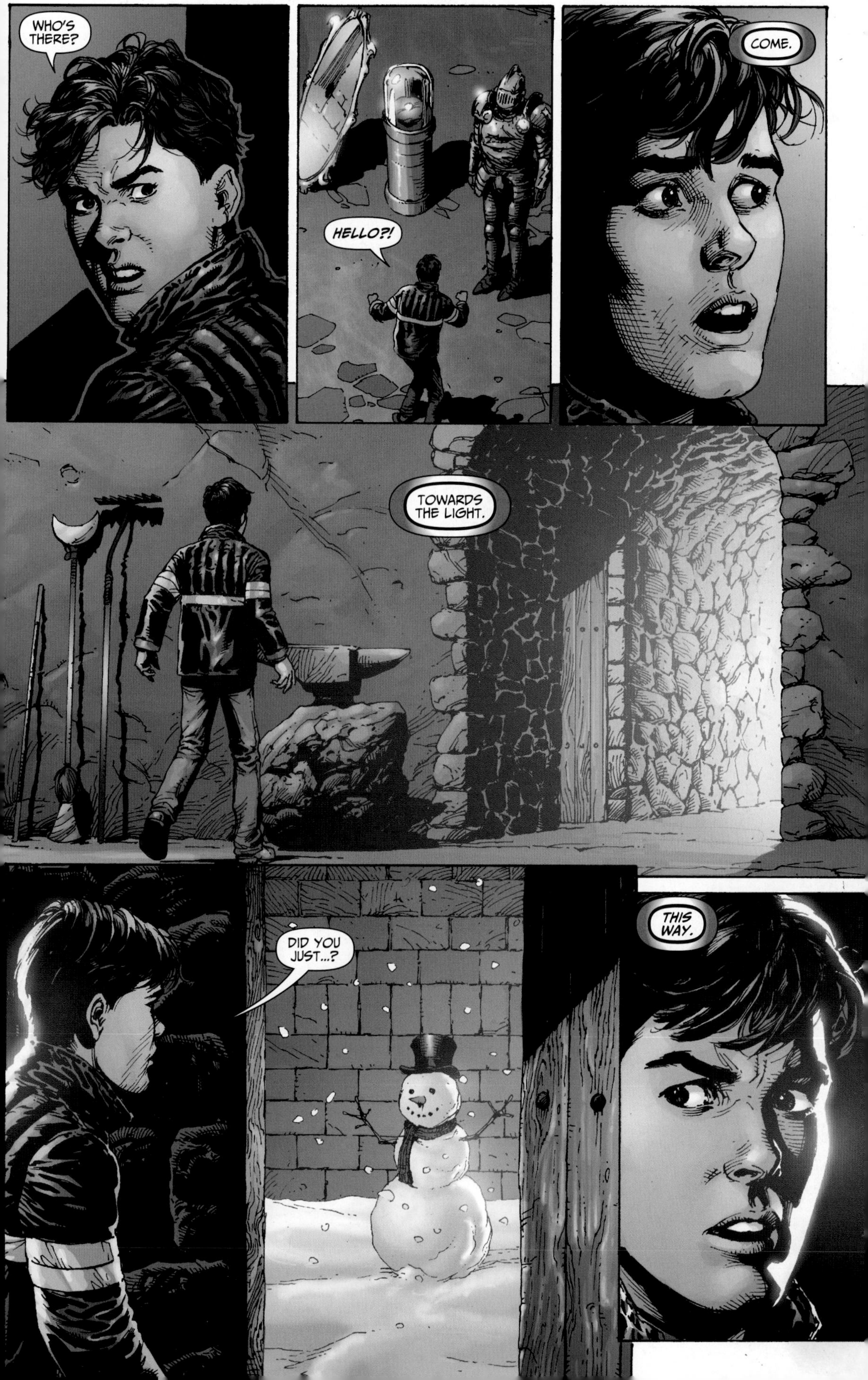
WHO'S THERE?
HELLO?!
COME.
TOWARDS THE LIGHT.
DID YOU JUST...?
THIS WAY.

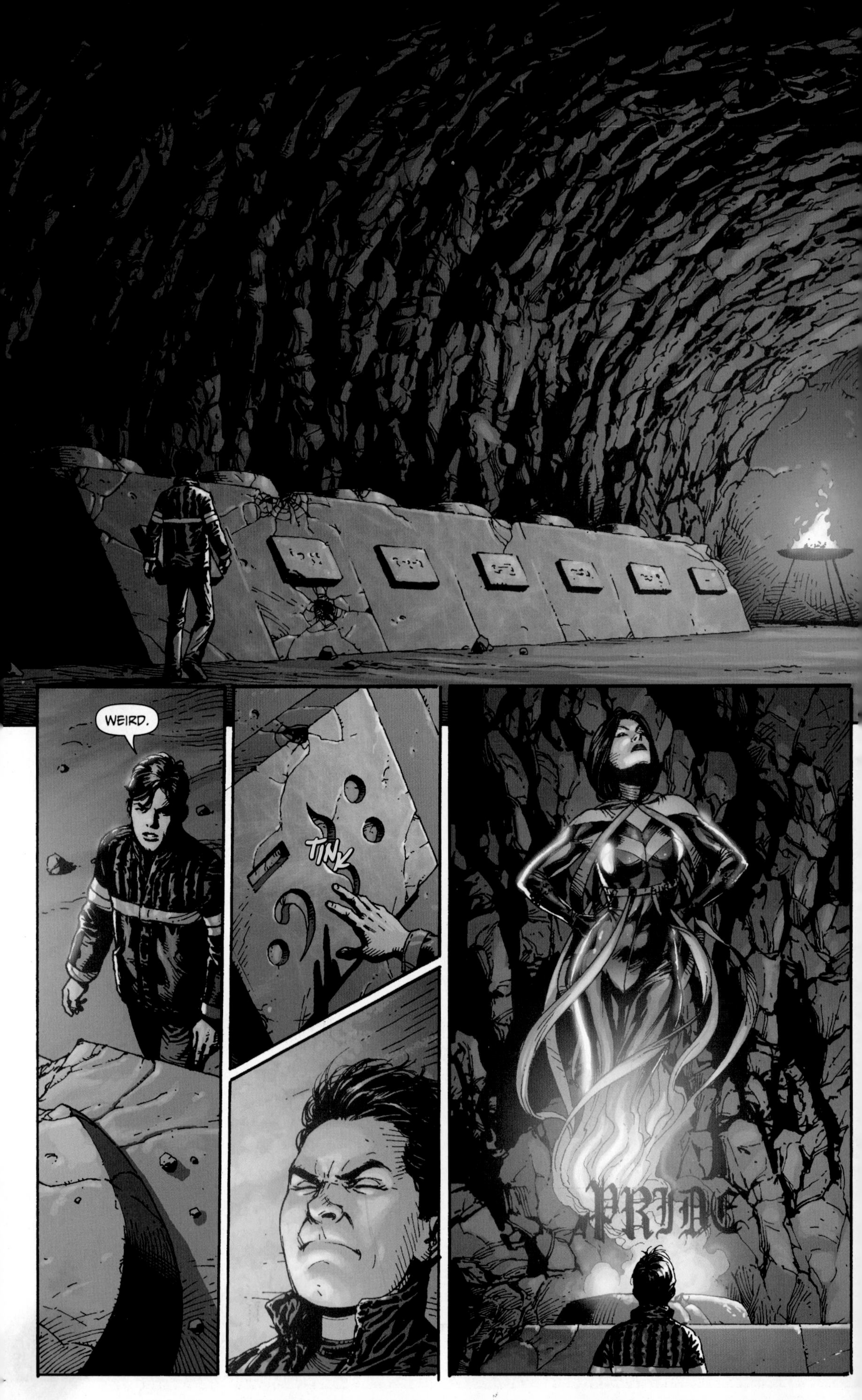
WEIRD.
TINK
PRIDE

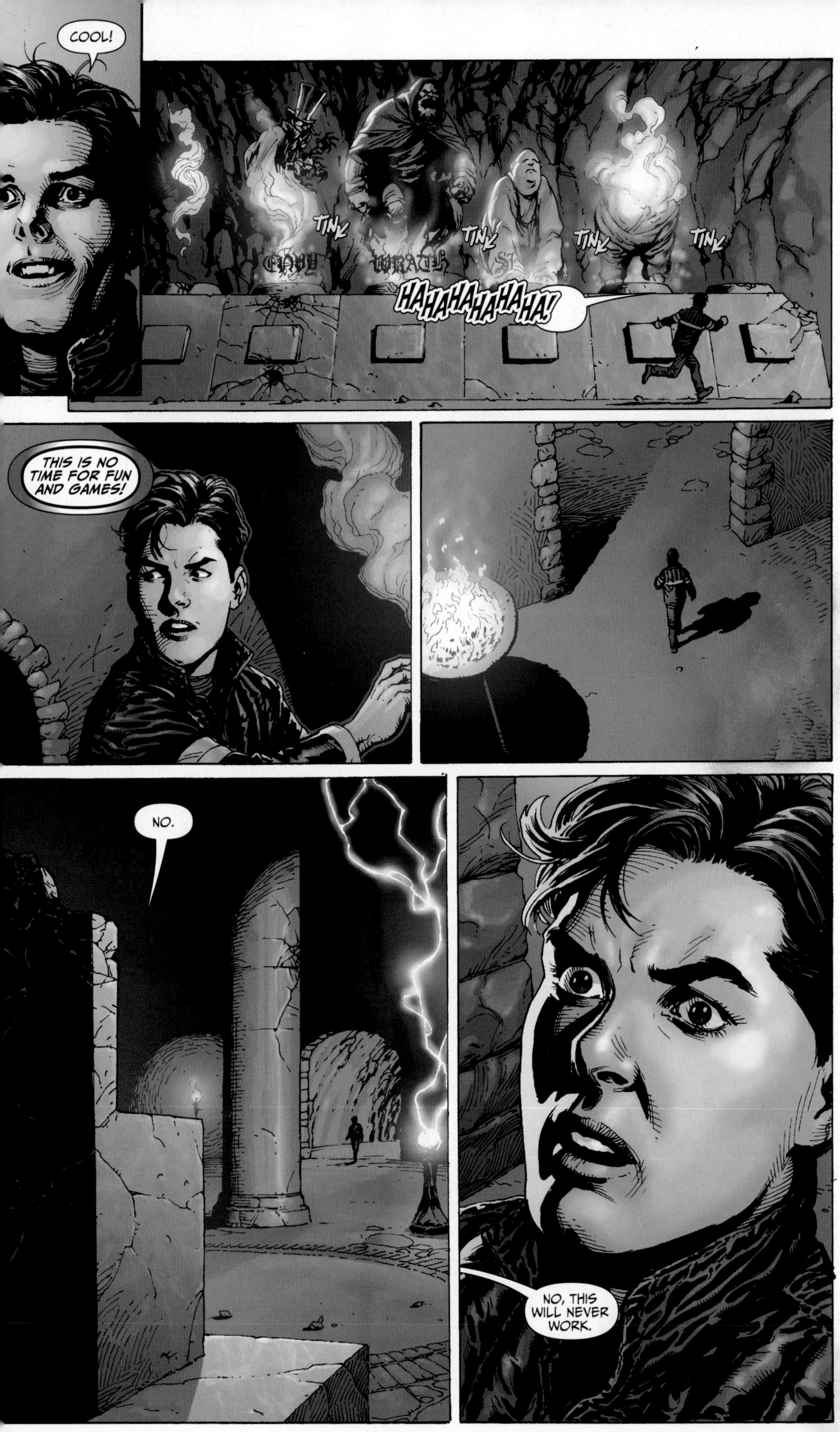
COOL!
TINK
TINK
TINK
TINK
HAHAHAHAHAHAHA!
THIS IS NO TIME FOR FUN AND GAMES!
NO.
NO, THIS WILL NEVER WORK.

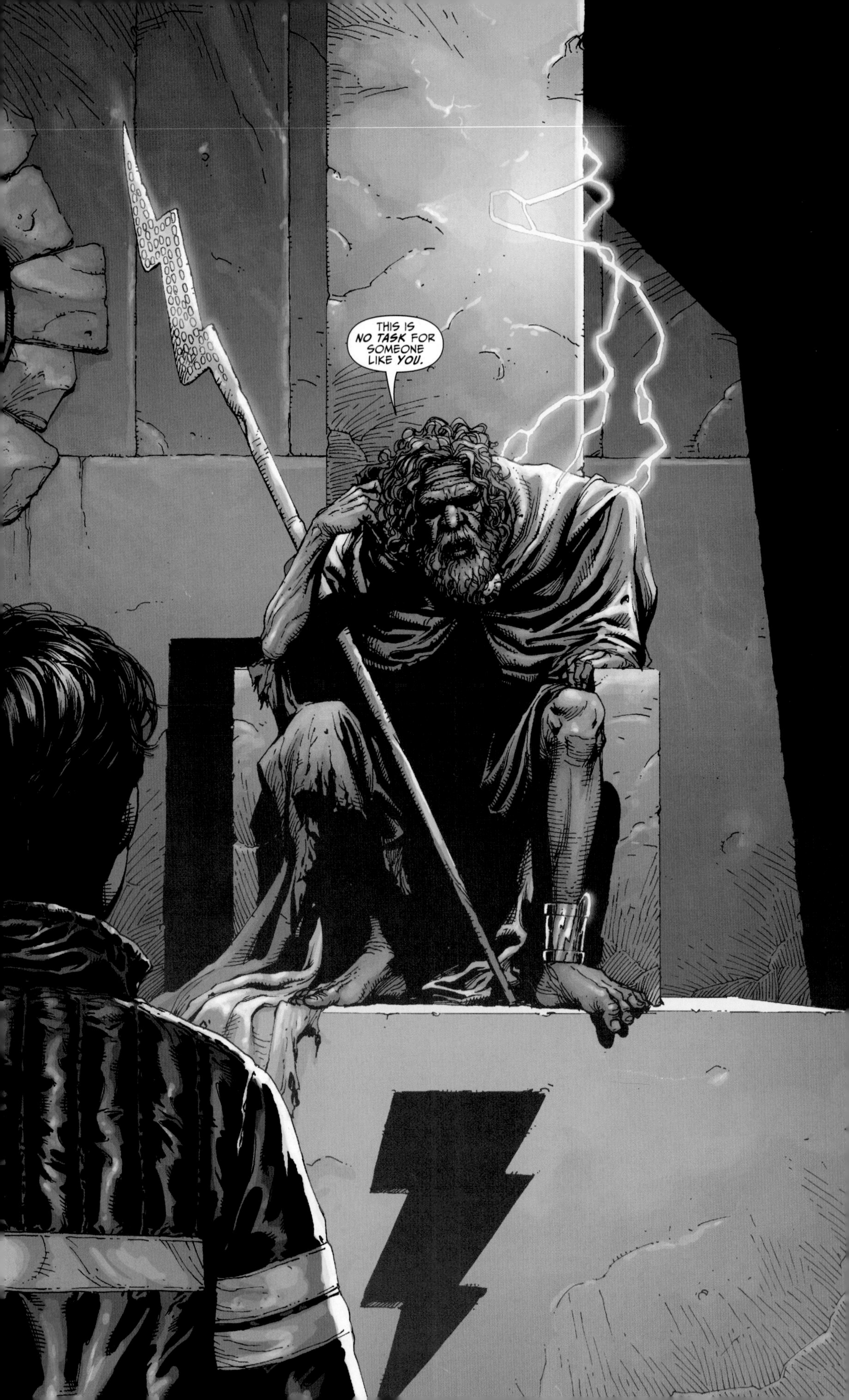
THIS IS NO TASK FOR SOMEONE LIKE YOU.

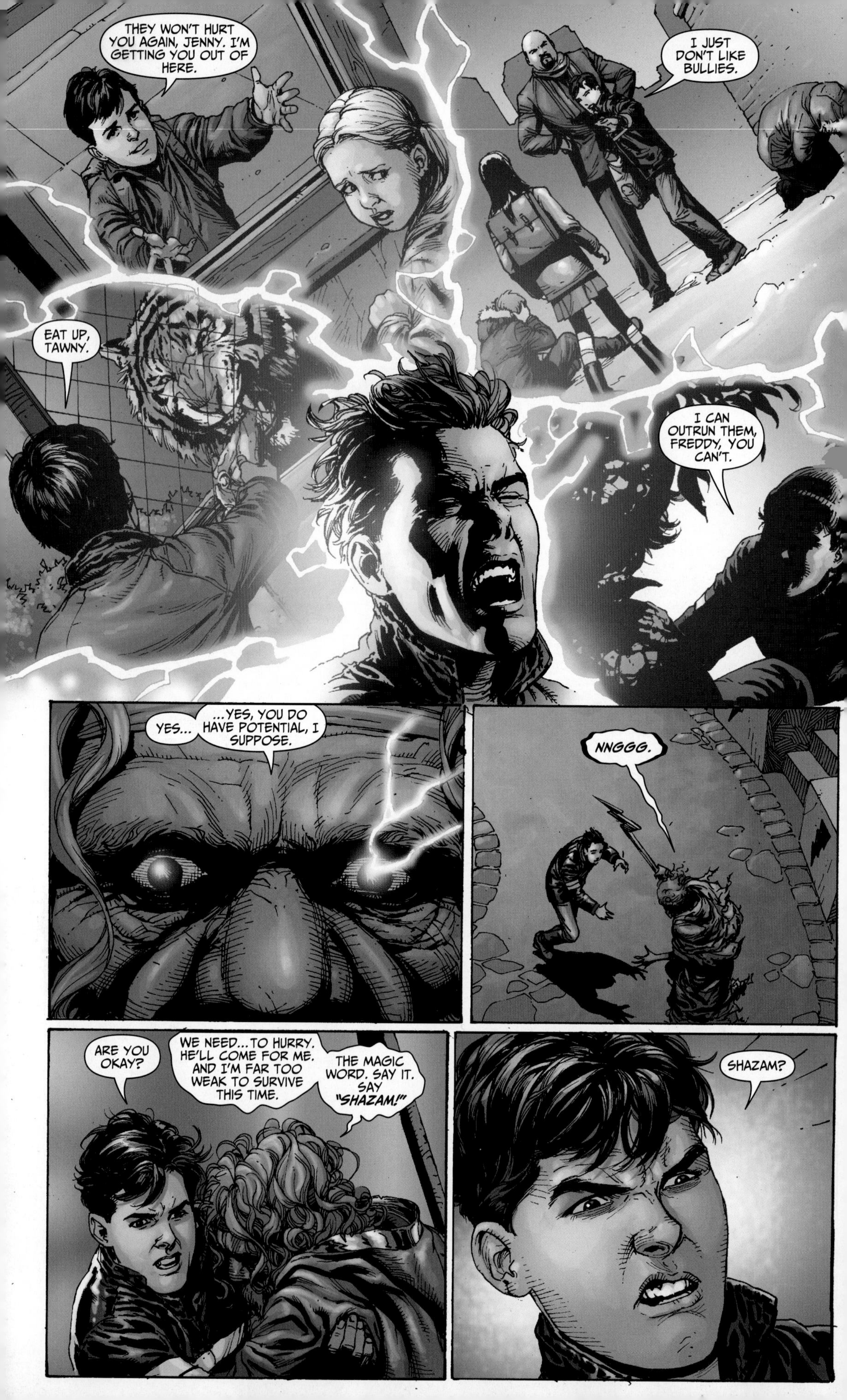
THEY WON'T HURT YOU AGAIN, JENNY. I'M GETTING YOU OUT OF HERE.
I JUST DON'T LIKE BULLIES.
EAT UP, TAWNY.
I CAN OUTRUN THEM, FREDDY, YOU CAN'T.
YES...
...YES, YOU DO HAVE POTENTIAL, I SUPPOSE.
NNGGG.
ARE YOU OKAY?
WE NEED... TO HURRY. HE'LL COME FOR ME. AND I'M FAR TOO WEAK TO SURVIVE THIS TIME.
THE MAGIC WORD. SAY IT. SAY "SHAZAM!"
SHAZAM?

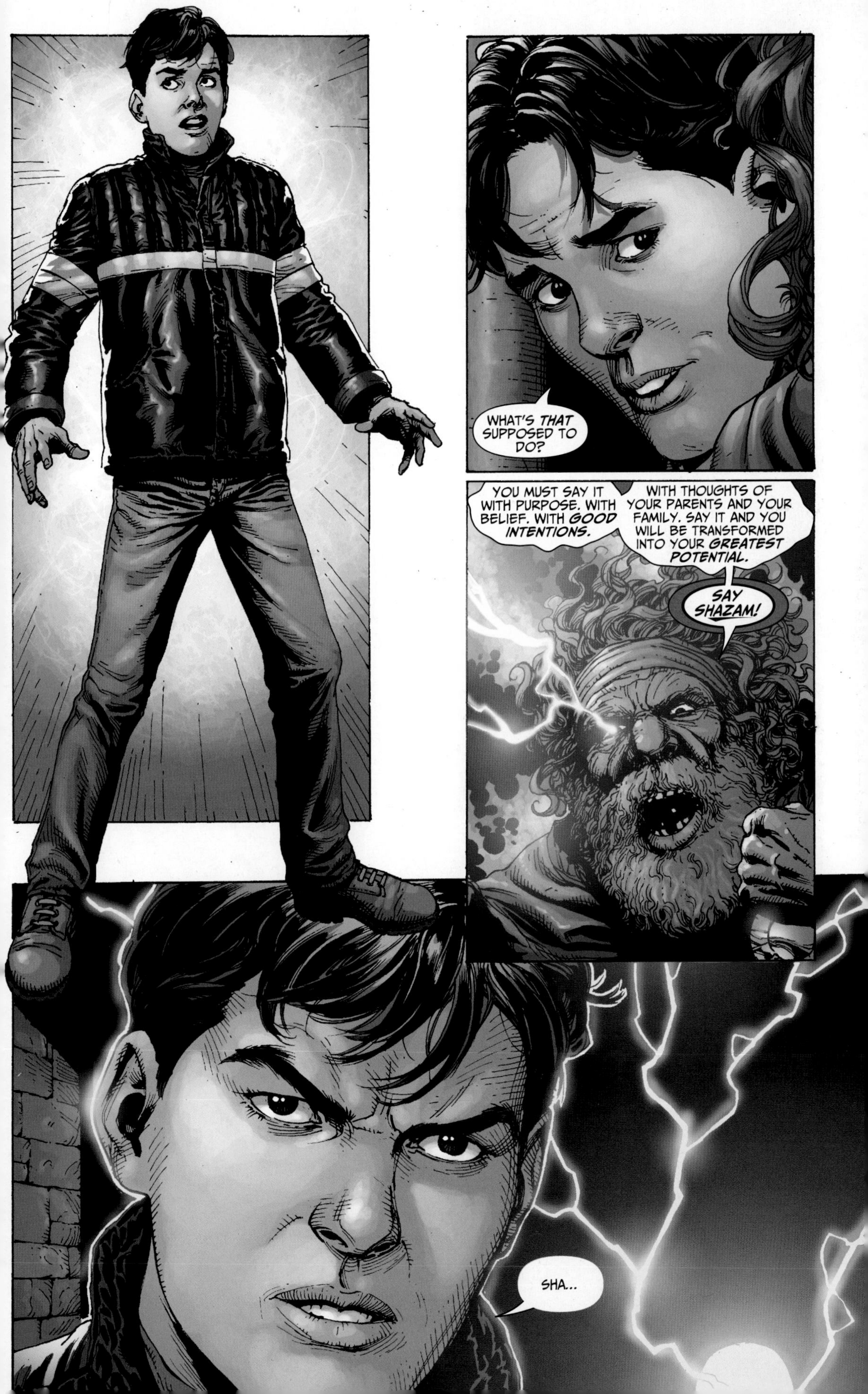
WHAT'S *THAT* SUPPOSED TO DO?
YOU MUST SAY IT WITH PURPOSE. WITH BELIEF. WITH *GOOD INTENTIONS.*
WITH THOUGHTS OF YOUR PARENTS AND YOUR FAMILY. SAY IT AND YOU WILL BE TRANSFORMED INTO YOUR *GREATEST POTENTIAL.*
SAY SHAZAM!
SHA...

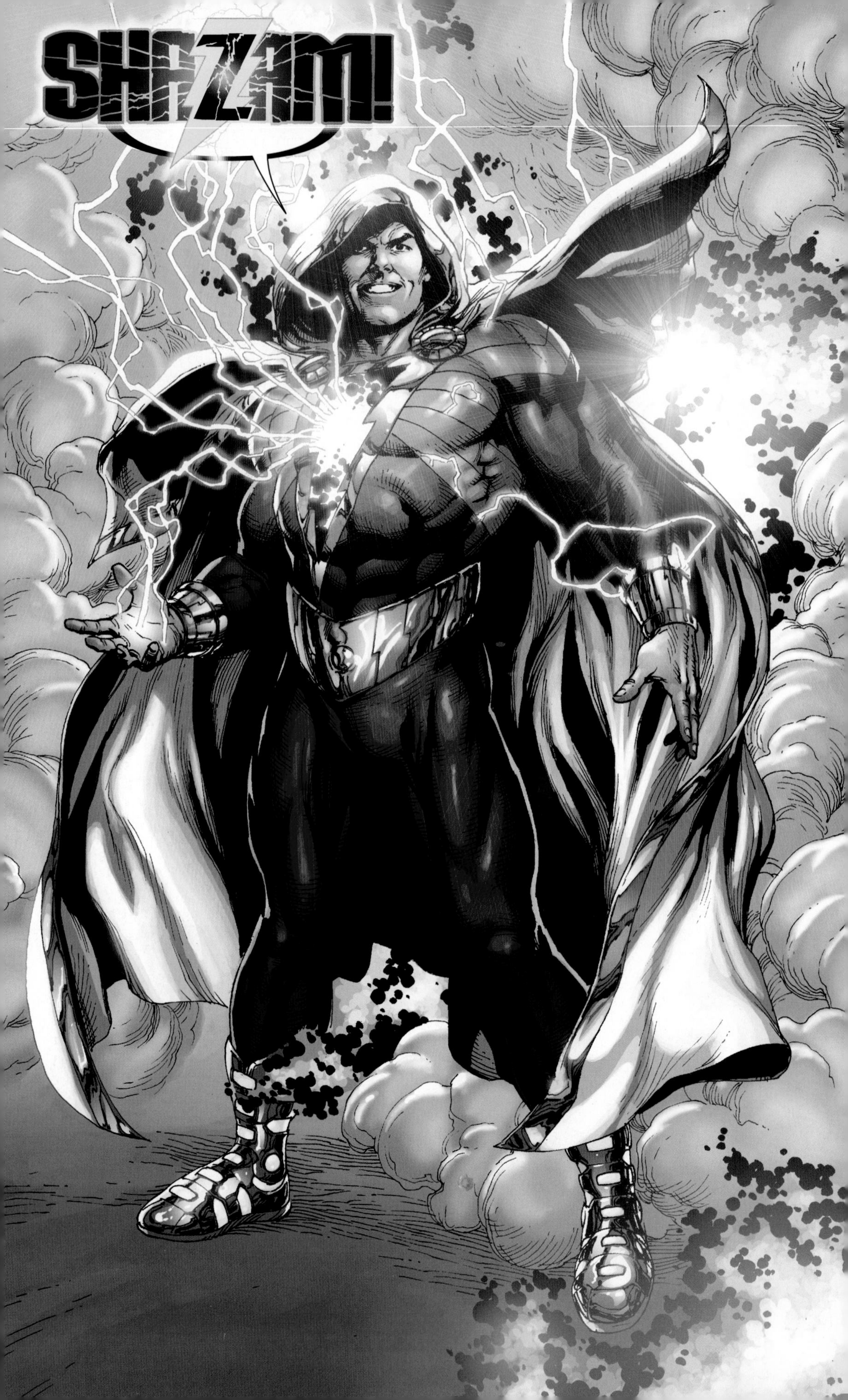
SHAZAM!

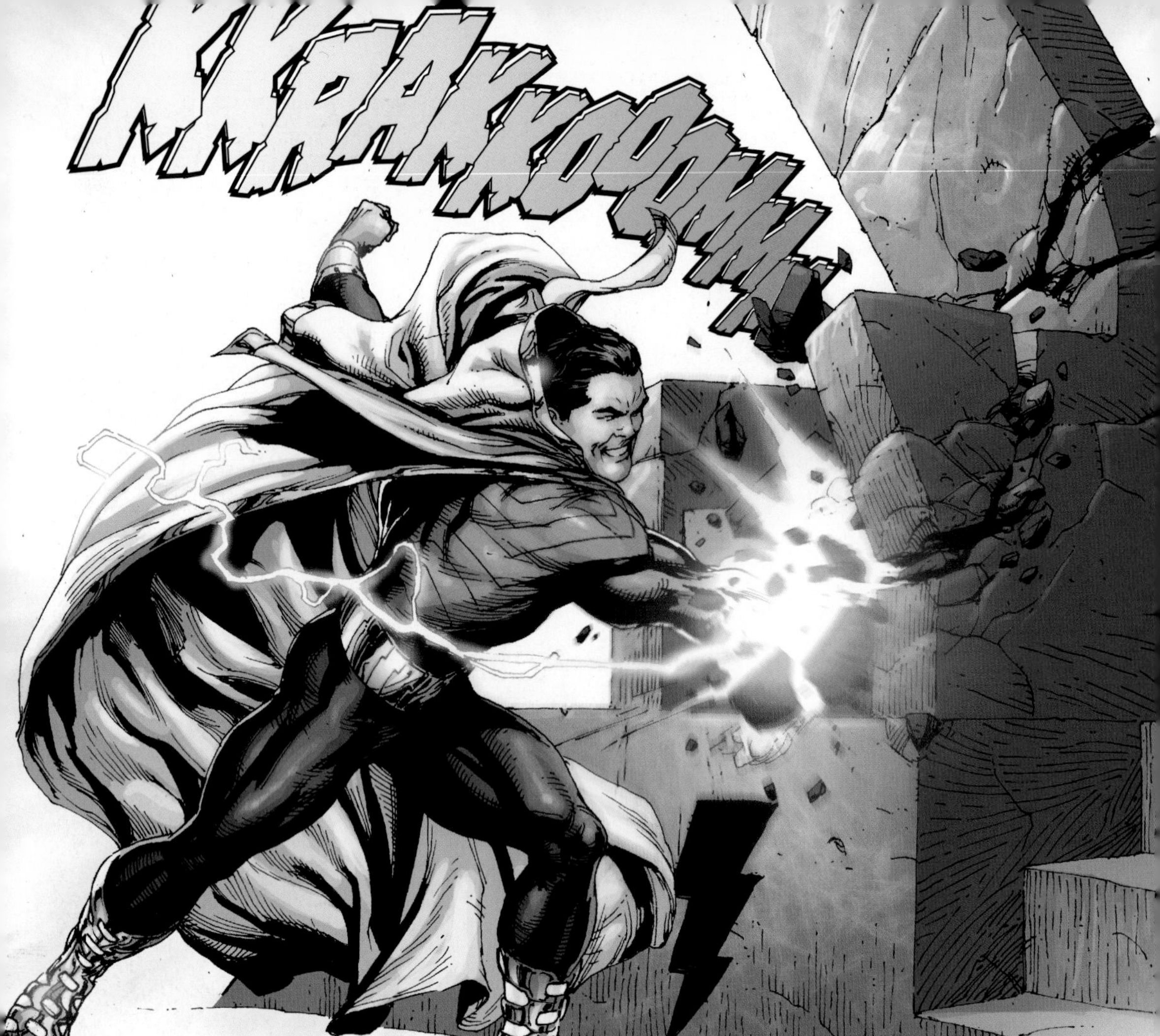
KKRAKKOOOMM

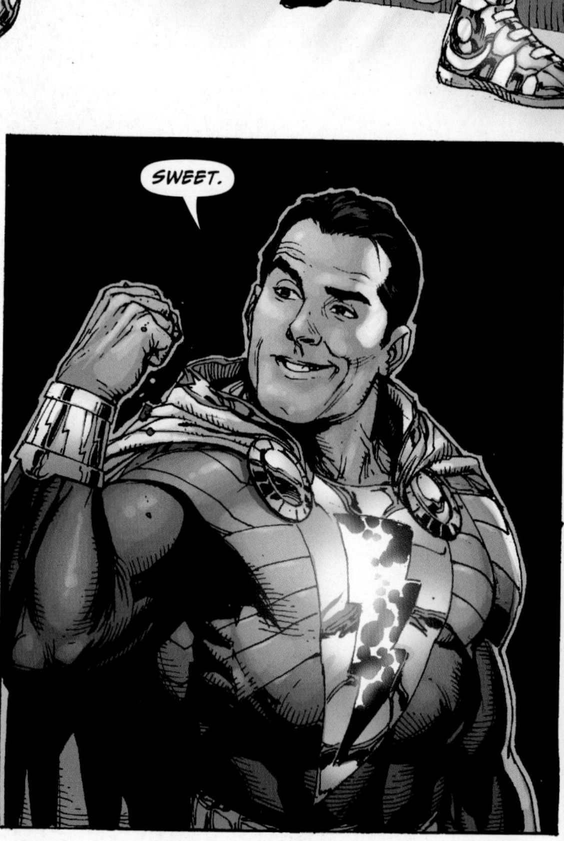
SWEET.

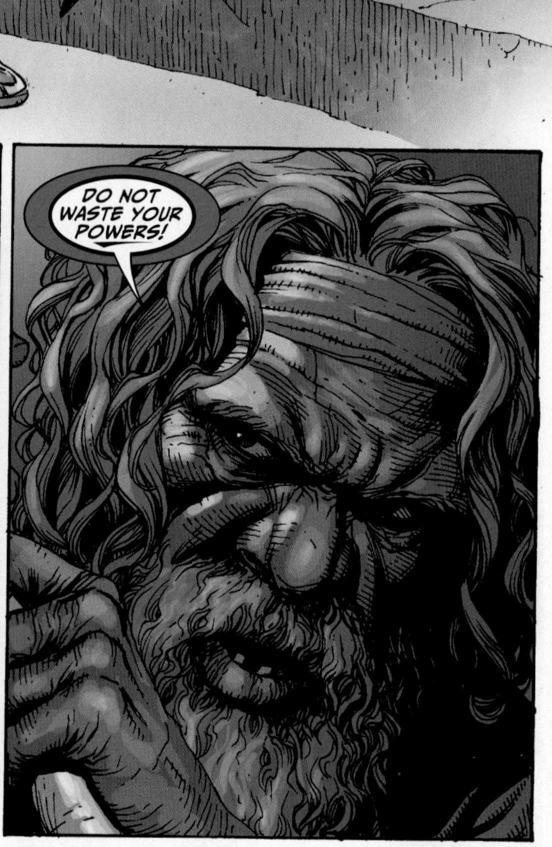
DO NOT WASTE YOUR POWERS!

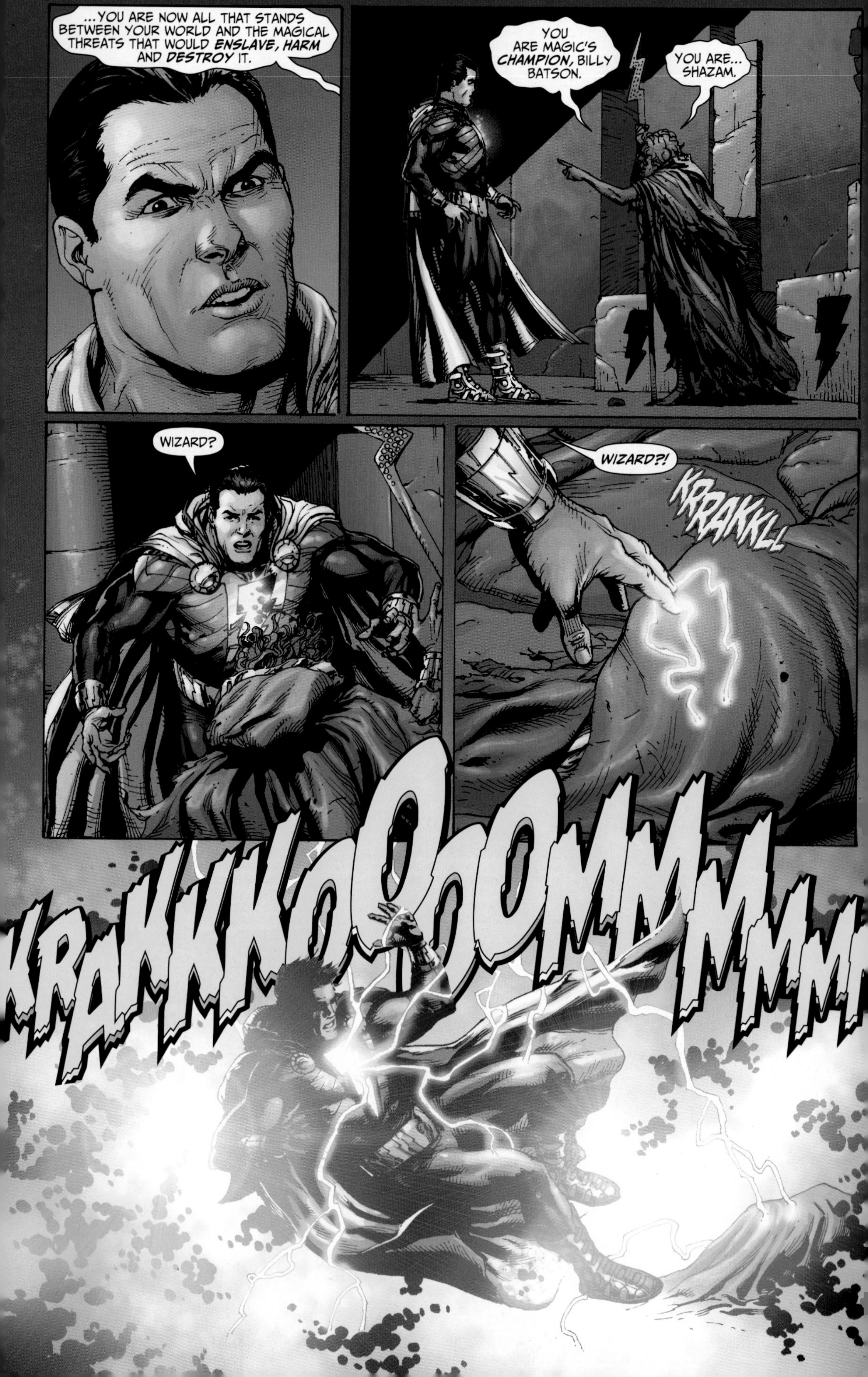
...YOU ARE NOW ALL THAT STANDS BETWEEN YOUR WORLD AND THE MAGICAL THREATS THAT WOULD ENSLAVE, HARM AND DESTROY IT.
YOU ARE MAGIC'S CHAMPION, BILLY BATSON.
YOU ARE... SHAZAM.
WIZARD?
WIZARD?!
KRRAKKLL
KRAKKKOOOOOMMMMMMMM

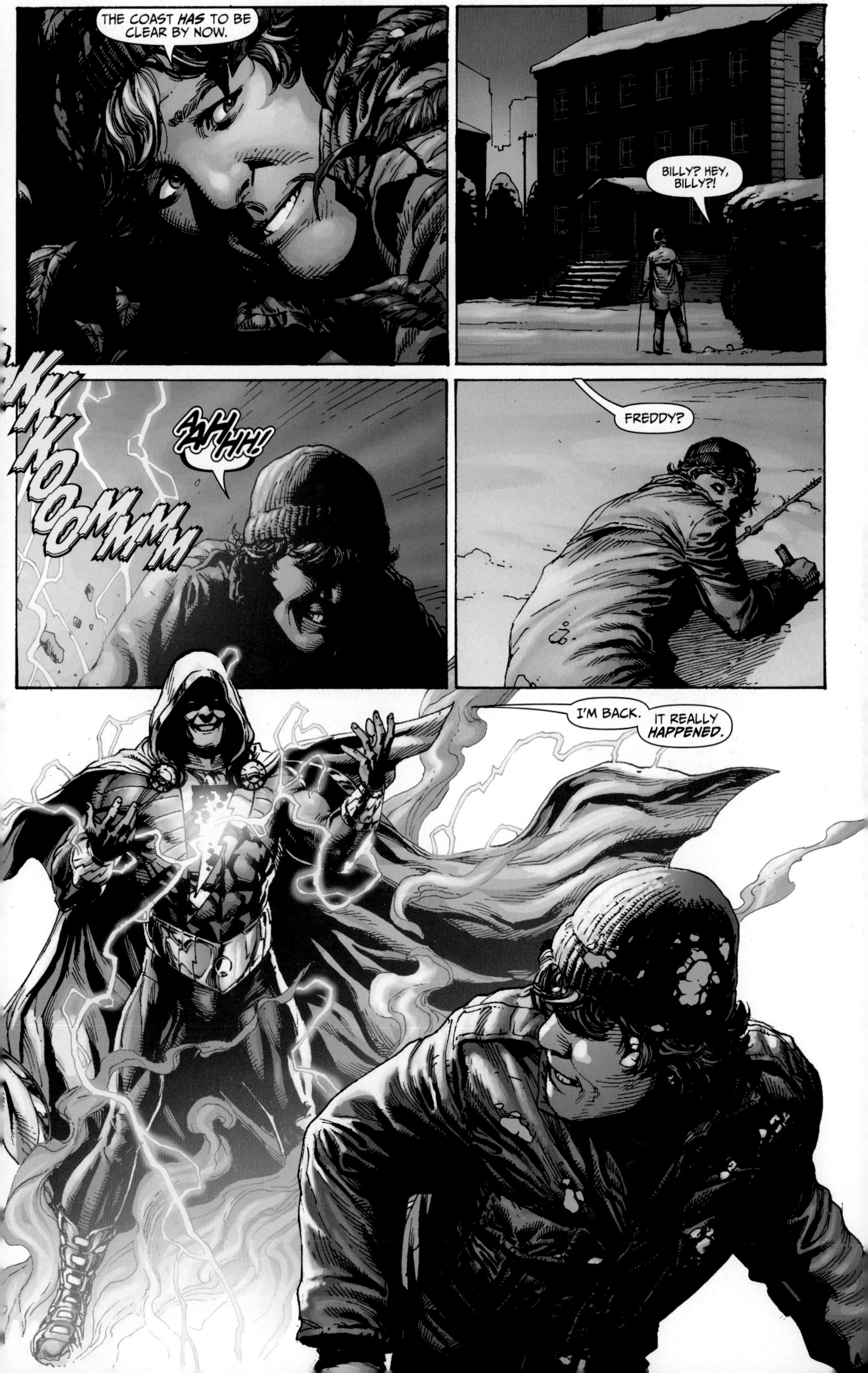

THE COAST HAS TO BE CLEAR BY NOW.
BILLY? HEY, BILLY?!
KKKHOOOMMMM
AAHHH!
FREDDY?
I'M BACK.
IT REALLY HAPPENED.

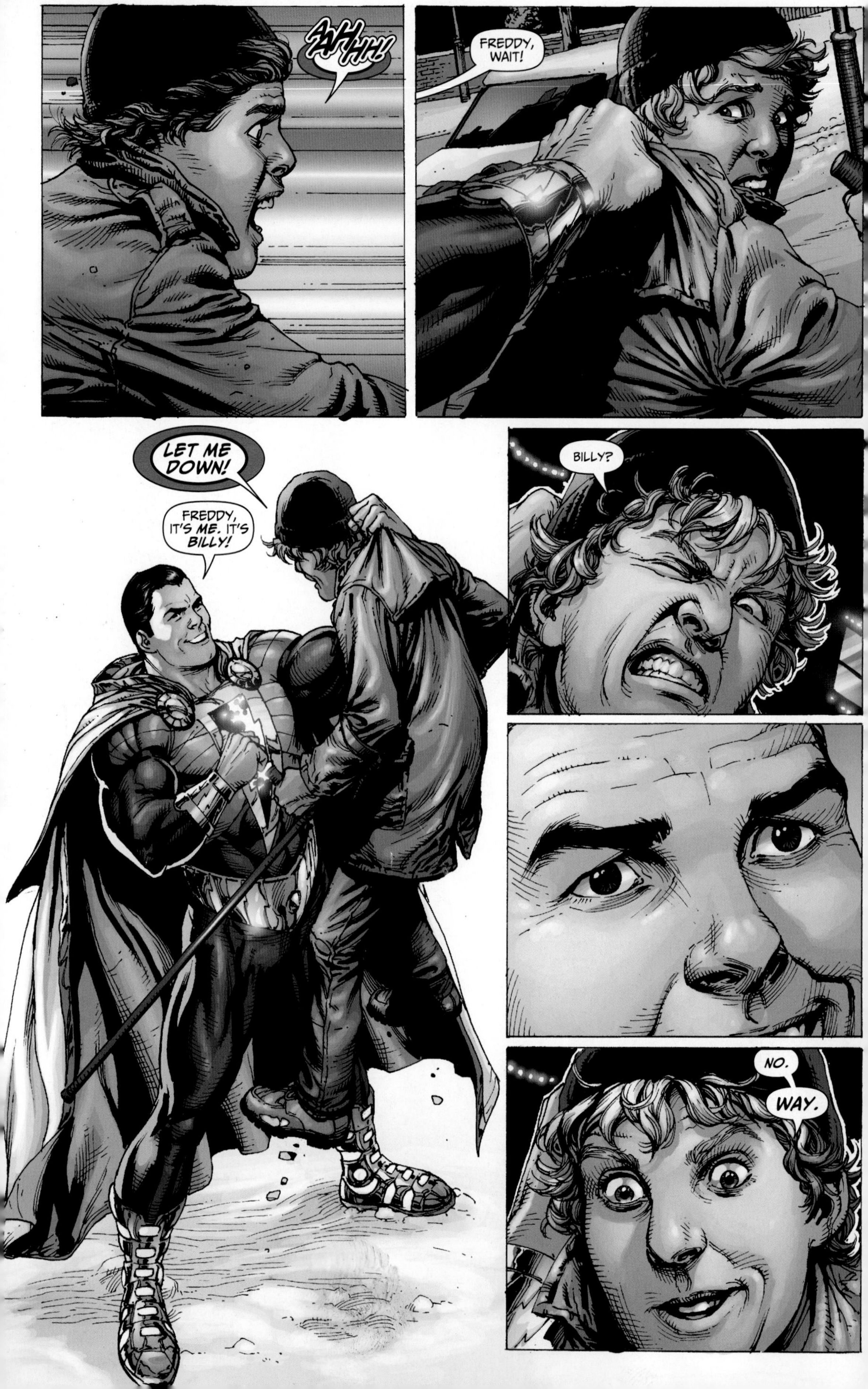
AAHHH!
FREDDY, WAIT!
LET ME DOWN!
FREDDY, IT'S ME. IT'S BILLY!
BILLY?
NO.
WAY.

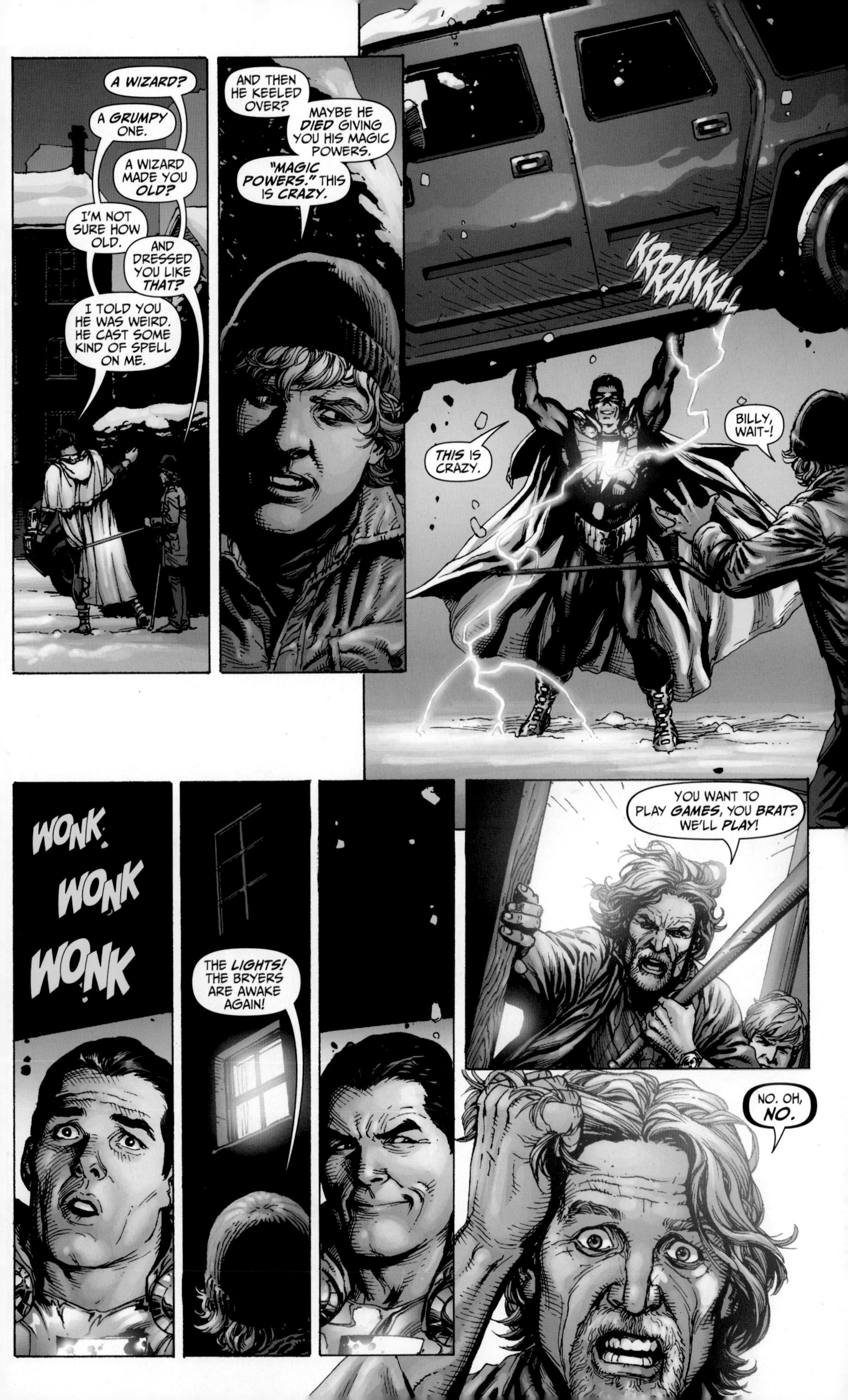
A WIZARD?
A GRUMPY ONE.
A WIZARD MADE YOU OLD?
I'M NOT SURE HOW OLD.
AND DRESSED YOU LIKE THAT?
I TOLD YOU HE WAS WEIRD. HE CAST SOME KIND OF SPELL ON ME.
AND THEN HE KEELED OVER?
MAYBE HE DIED GIVING YOU HIS MAGIC POWERS.
"MAGIC POWERS." THIS IS CRAZY.
KRRAKKL!
THIS IS CRAZY.
BILLY, WAIT-!
WONK
WONK
WONK
THE LIGHTS! THE BRYERS ARE AWAKE AGAIN!
YOU WANT TO PLAY GAMES, YOU BRAT? WE'LL PLAY!
NO. OH, NO.

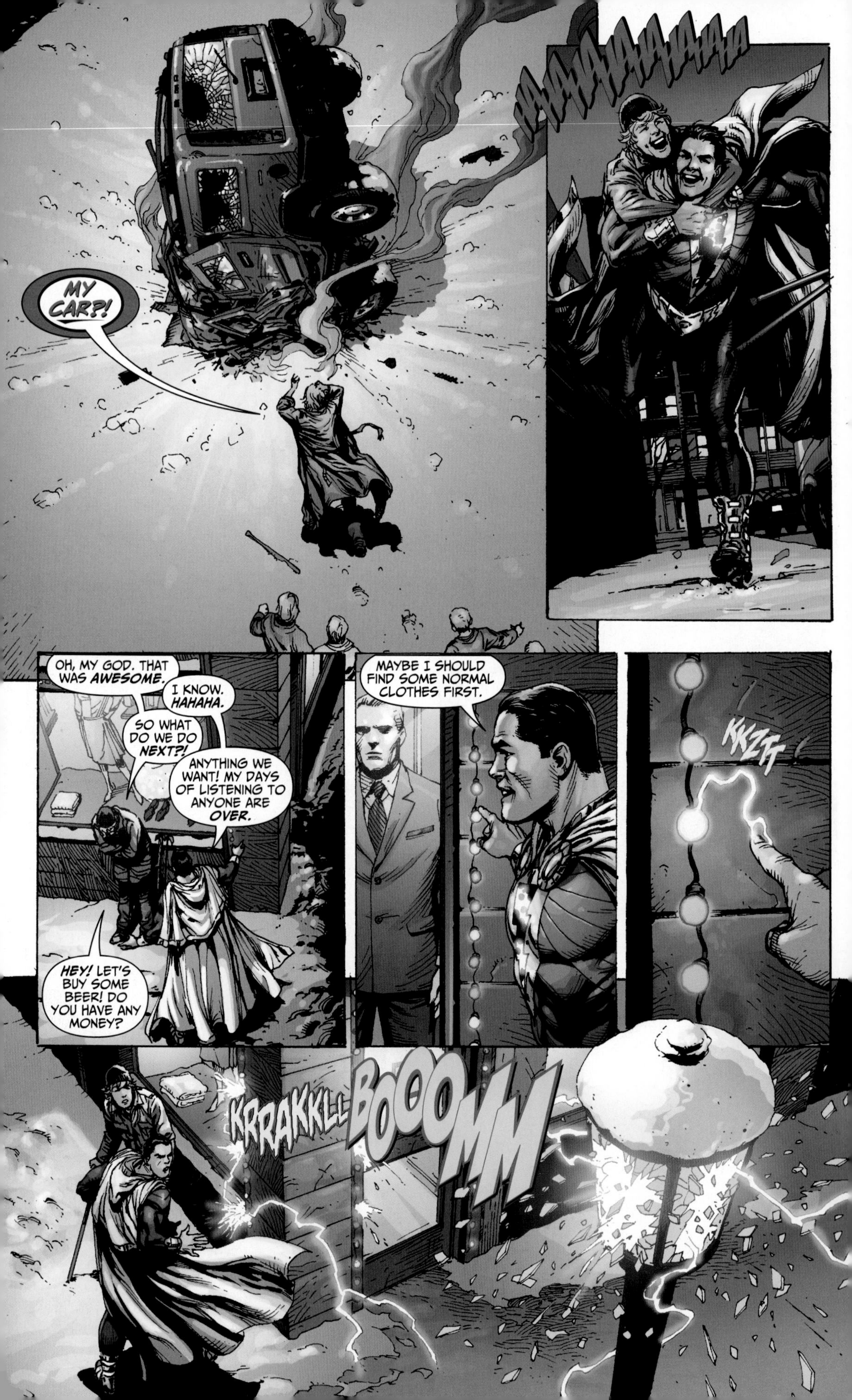
MY CAR?!
AAAAAAAAAAAAAA
OH, MY GOD. THAT WAS AWESOME.
I KNOW. HAHAHA.
SO WHAT DO WE DO NEXT?!
ANYTHING WE WANT! MY DAYS OF LISTENING TO ANYONE ARE OVER.
HEY! LET'S BUY SOME BEER! DO YOU HAVE ANY MONEY?
MAYBE I SHOULD FIND SOME NORMAL CLOTHES FIRST.
KKZTT
KRRAKKLL BOOOMM

WHAT'D YOU DO?

I DON'T KNOW.

THE LIGHTS ON THE CAR EXPLODED WHEN YOU LIFTED IT UP. MAYBE YOU CAN'T TOUCH ANYTHING TOO ELECTRICAL.

WELL, *THAT* WOULD SUCK.

JUST TAKE IT.

PLEASE. THESE ARE PRESENTS FOR THE CHILDREN'S HOSPITAL. THEY'RE JUST *TOYS*.

SHUT UP.

YOU SEE THAT?

PLEASE, DON'T HURT ME.

DO WHAT I SAY AND I WON'T.

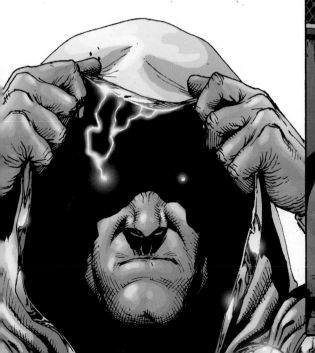

HEY!

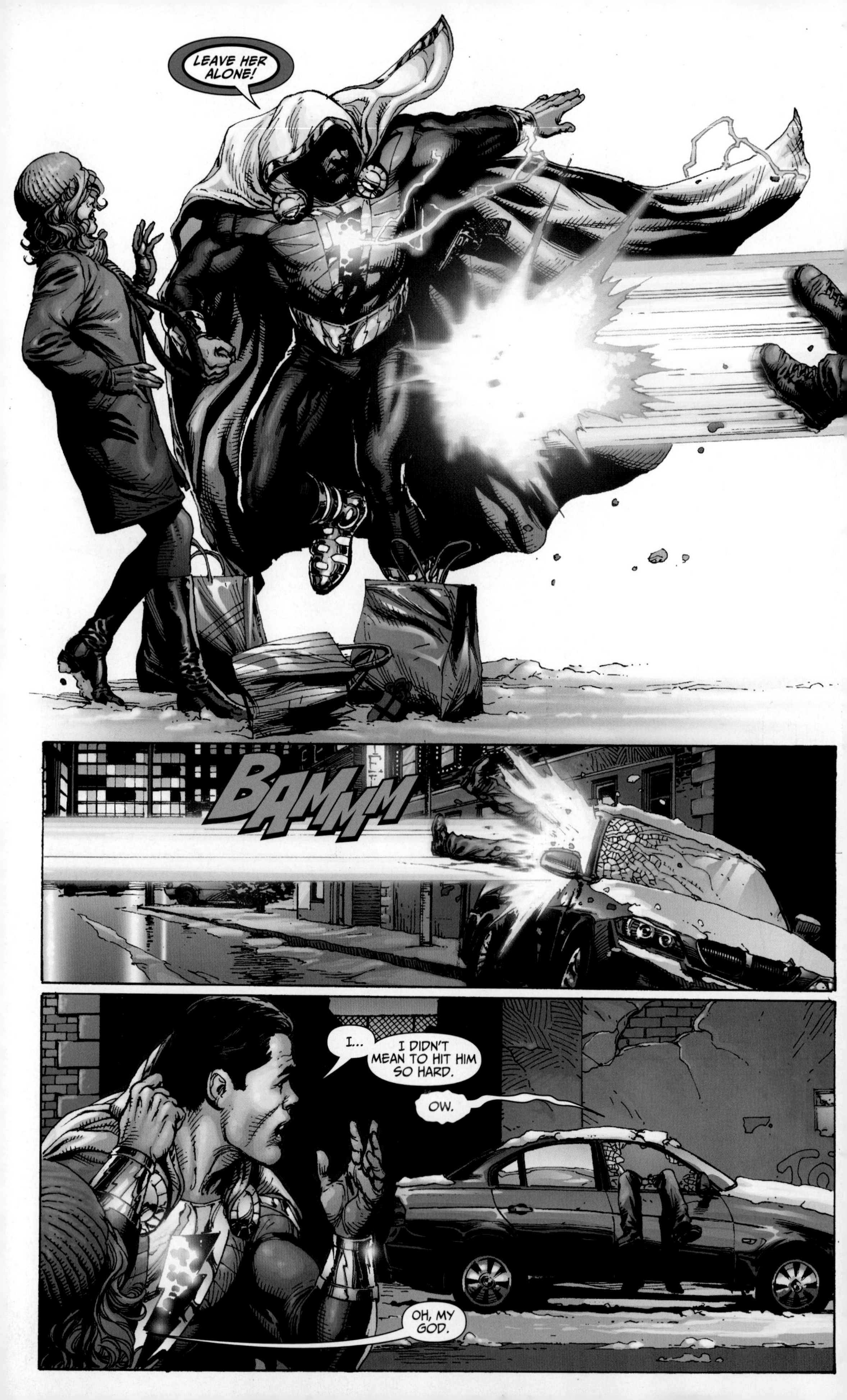
LEAVE HER ALONE!
BAMMM
I...
I DIDN'T MEAN TO HIT HIM SO HARD.
OW.
OH, MY GOD.

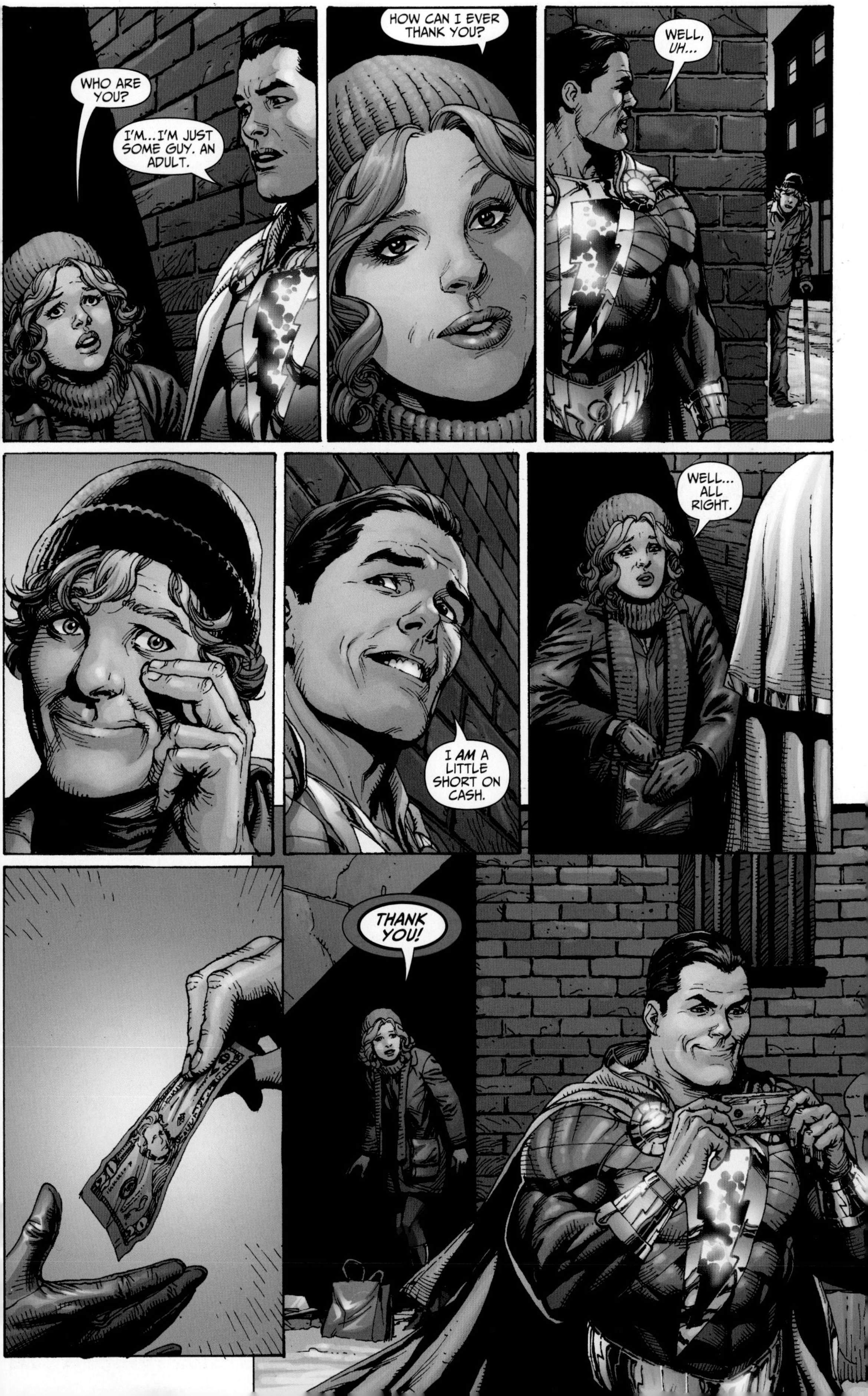
WHO ARE YOU?
I'M...I'M JUST SOME GUY. AN ADULT.
HOW CAN I EVER THANK YOU?
WELL, UH...
I AM A LITTLE SHORT ON CASH.
WELL... ALL RIGHT.
THANK YOU!

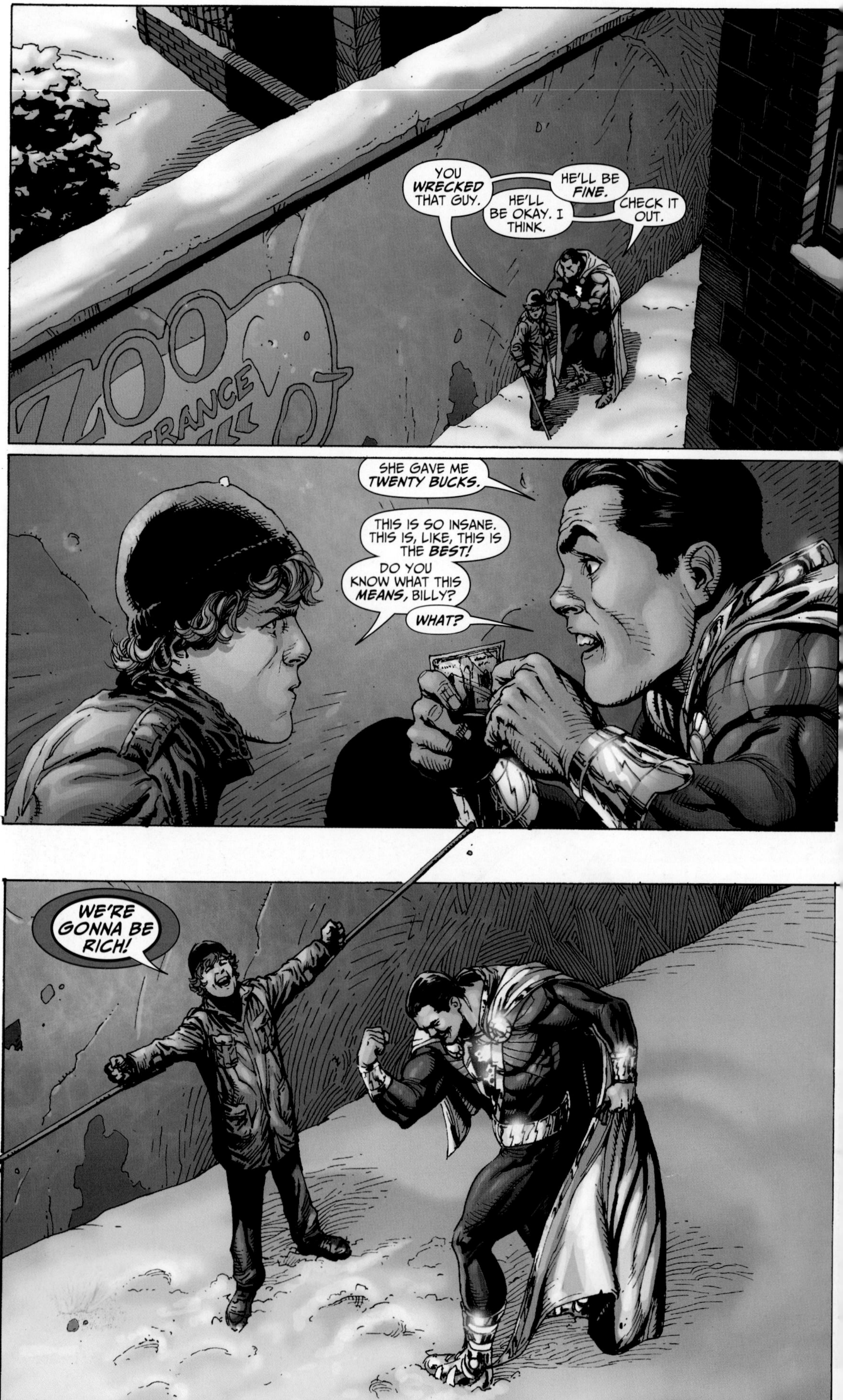
YOU WRECKED THAT GUY.
HE'LL BE OKAY. I THINK.
HE'LL BE FINE.
CHECK IT OUT.
SHE GAVE ME TWENTY BUCKS.
THIS IS SO INSANE. THIS IS, LIKE, THIS IS THE BEST!
DO YOU KNOW WHAT THIS MEANS, BILLY?
WHAT?
WE'RE GONNA BE RICH!

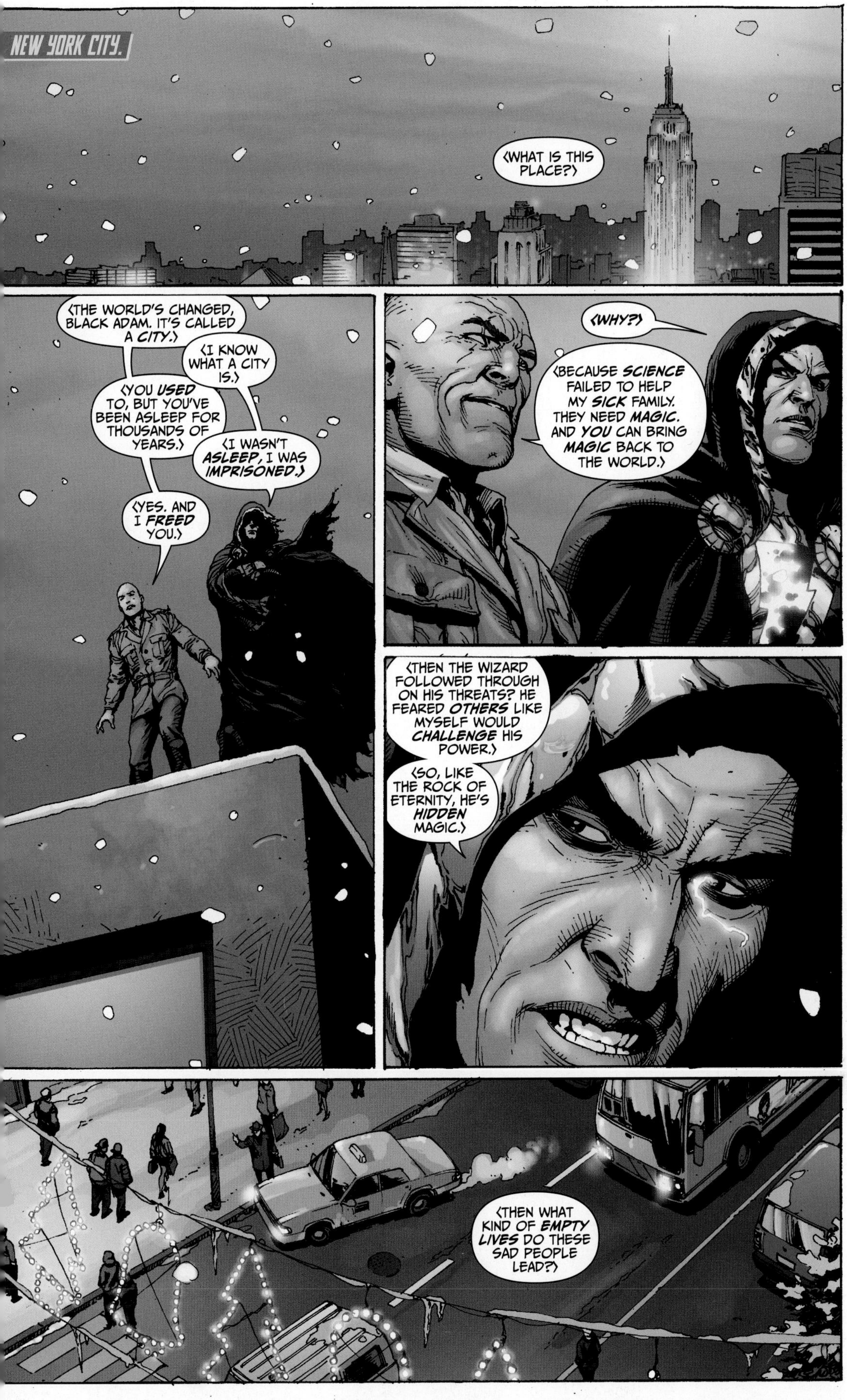
NEW YORK CITY.
‹WHAT IS THIS PLACE?›
‹THE WORLD'S CHANGED, BLACK ADAM. IT'S CALLED A CITY.›
‹I KNOW WHAT A CITY IS.›
‹YOU USED TO, BUT YOU'VE BEEN ASLEEP FOR THOUSANDS OF YEARS.›
‹I WASN'T ASLEEP, I WAS IMPRISONED.›
‹YES. AND I FREED YOU.›
‹WHY?›
‹BECAUSE SCIENCE FAILED TO HELP MY SICK FAMILY. THEY NEED MAGIC. AND YOU CAN BRING MAGIC BACK TO THE WORLD.›
‹THEN THE WIZARD FOLLOWED THROUGH ON HIS THREATS? HE FEARED OTHERS LIKE MYSELF WOULD CHALLENGE HIS POWER.›
‹SO, LIKE THE ROCK OF ETERNITY, HE'S HIDDEN MAGIC.›
‹THEN WHAT KIND OF EMPTY LIVES DO THESE SAD PEOPLE LEAD?›

THOOOOMMM

OONNK

BAAAAASHHH

⟨THIS CITY IS STRANGE.⟩

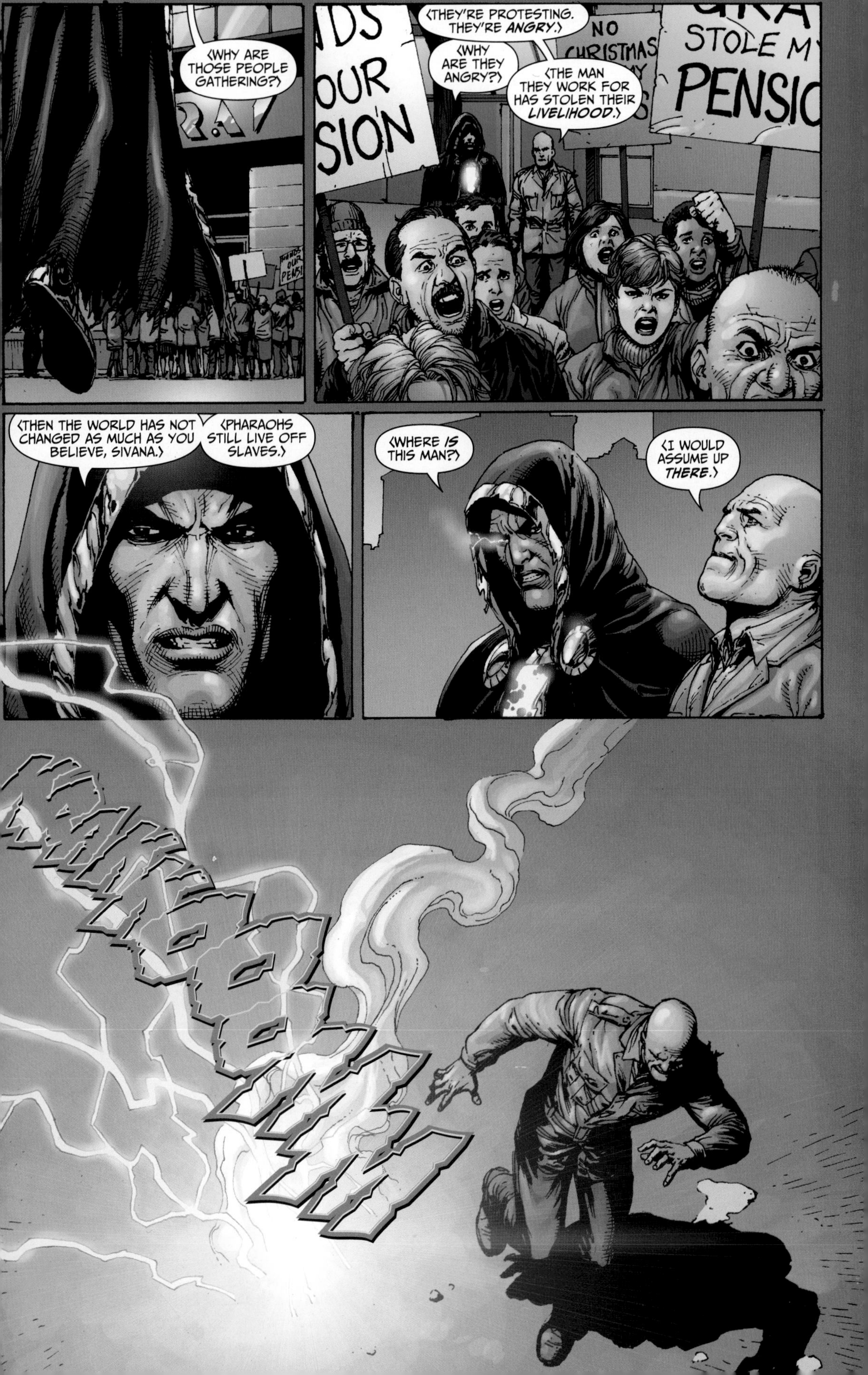

‹WHY ARE THOSE PEOPLE GATHERING?›
‹THEY'RE PROTESTING. THEY'RE *ANGRY*.›
‹WHY ARE THEY ANGRY?›
‹THE MAN THEY WORK FOR HAS STOLEN THEIR *LIVELIHOOD*.›
‹THEN THE WORLD HAS NOT CHANGED AS MUCH AS YOU BELIEVE, SIVANA.›
‹PHARAOHS STILL LIVE OFF SLAVES.›
‹WHERE *IS* THIS MAN?›
‹I WOULD ASSUME UP *THERE*.›

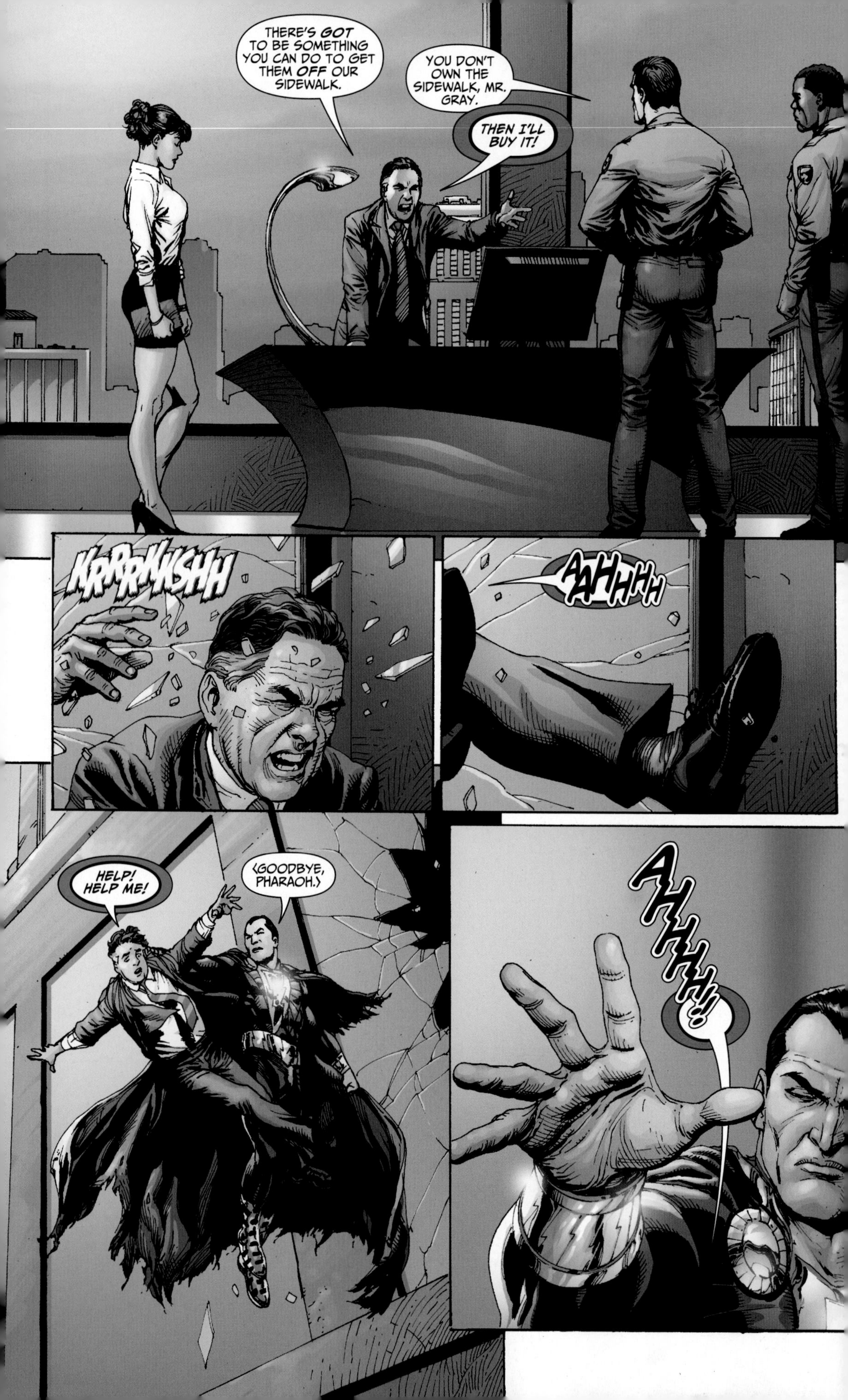
THERE'S GOT TO BE SOMETHING YOU CAN DO TO GET THEM OFF OUR SIDEWALK.
YOU DON'T OWN THE SIDEWALK, MR. GRAY.
THEN I'LL BUY IT!
KRRRKKSHH
AAHHHH
HELP! HELP ME!
‹GOODBYE, PHARAOH.›
AHHHH!!

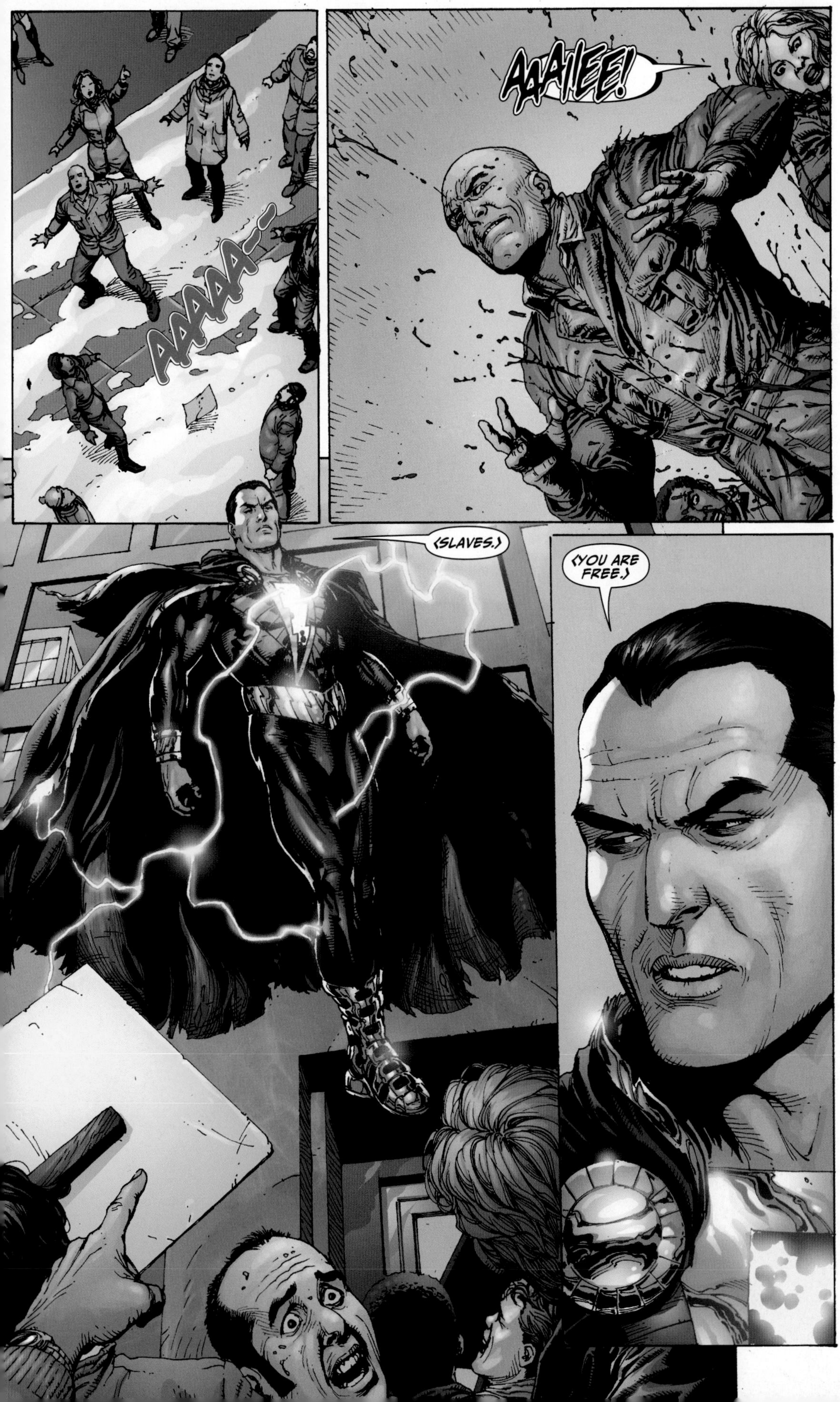

AAAAA--!
AAAIEE!
‹SLAVES.›
‹YOU ARE FREE.›

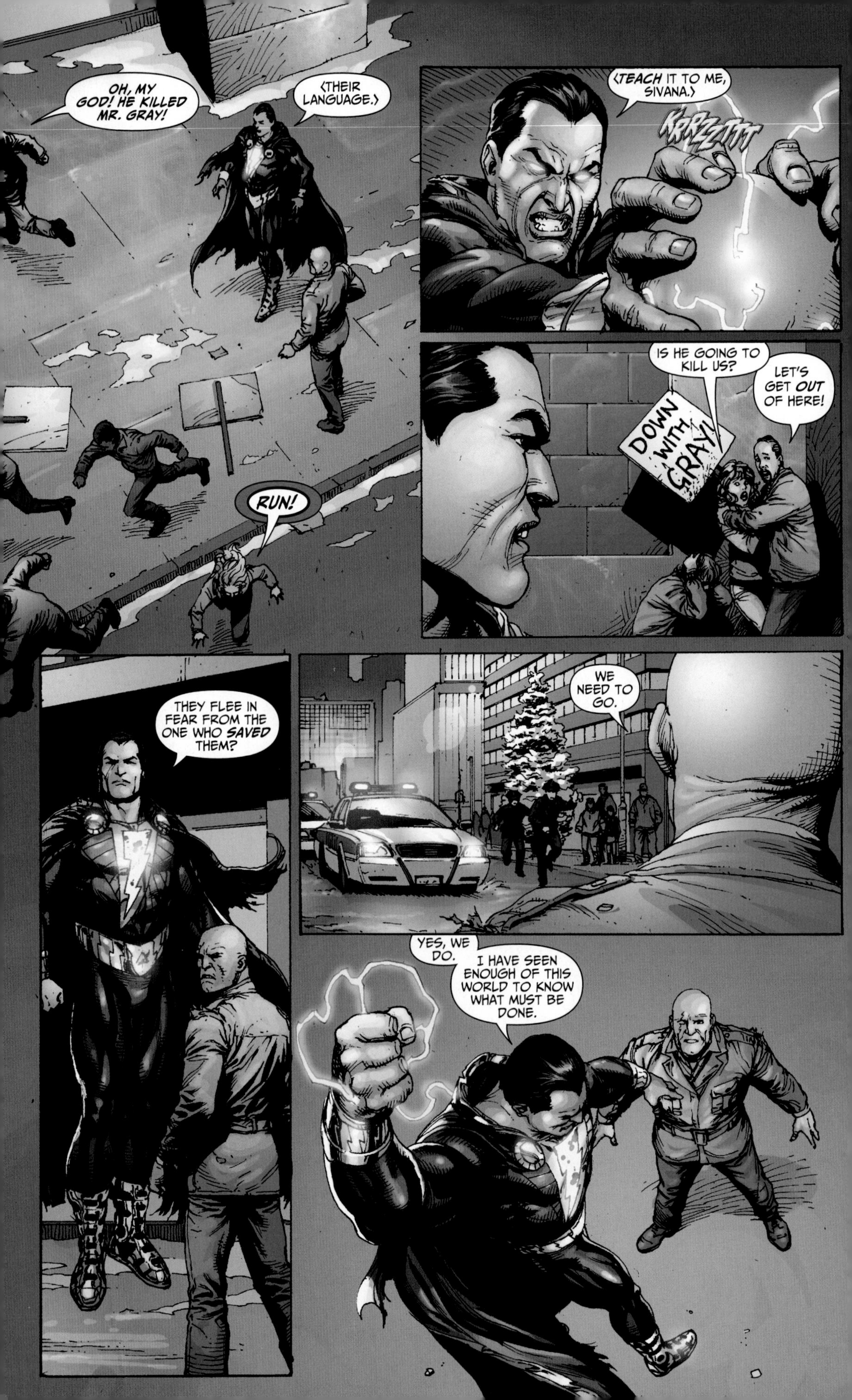
OH, MY GOD! HE KILLED MR. GRAY!
‹THEIR LANGUAGE.›
RUN!
‹TEACH IT TO ME, SIVANA.›
KRRZZTTT
DOWN WITH GRAY!
IS HE GOING TO KILL US?
LET'S GET OUT OF HERE!
THEY FLEE IN FEAR FROM THE ONE WHO SAVED THEM?
WE NEED TO GO.
YES, WE DO.
I HAVE SEEN ENOUGH OF THIS WORLD TO KNOW WHAT MUST BE DONE.

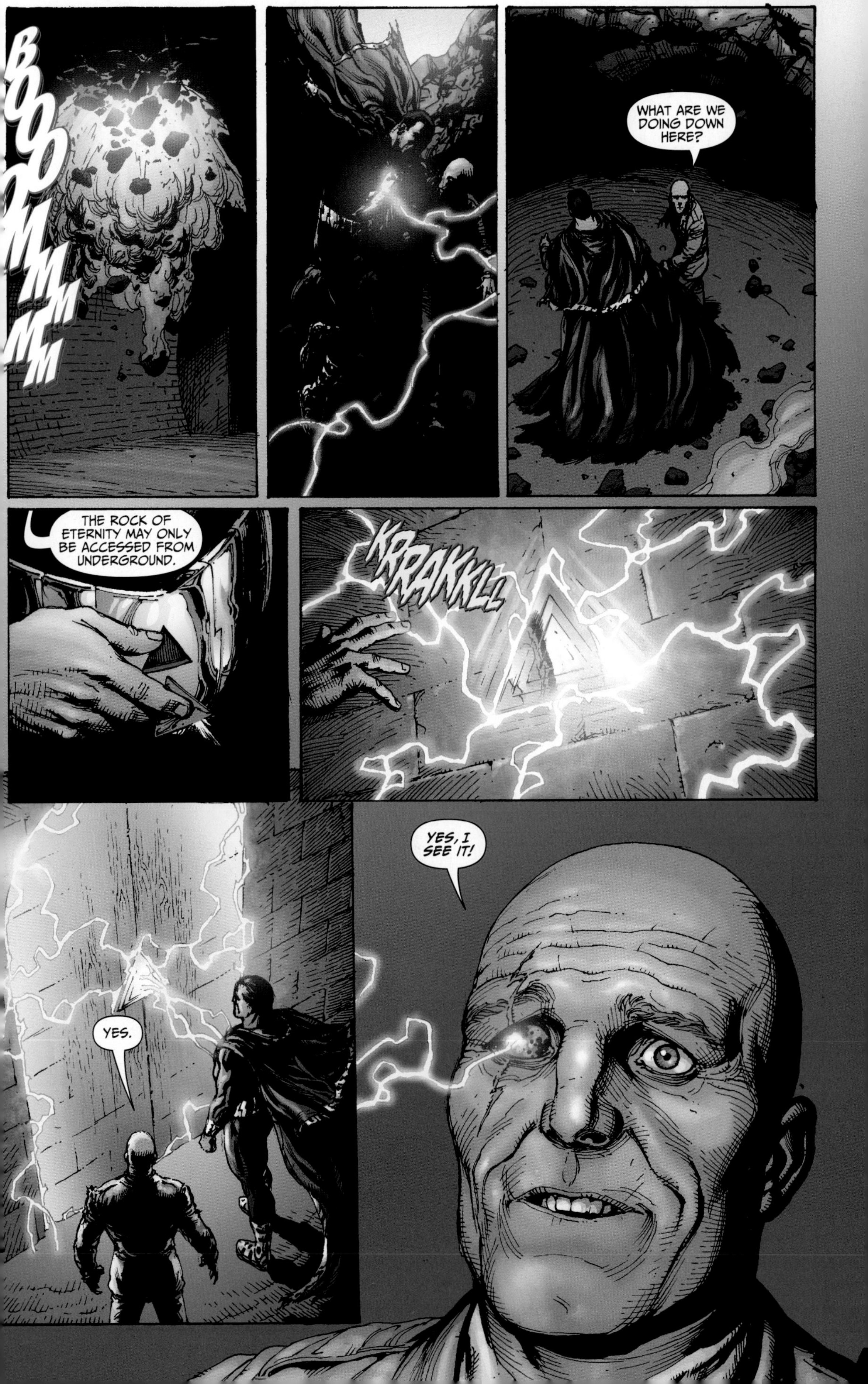
BOOOMMMMMMM
WHAT ARE WE DOING DOWN HERE?
THE ROCK OF ETERNITY MAY ONLY BE ACCESSED FROM UNDERGROUND.
KRRAKKLL
YES, I SEE IT!
YES.

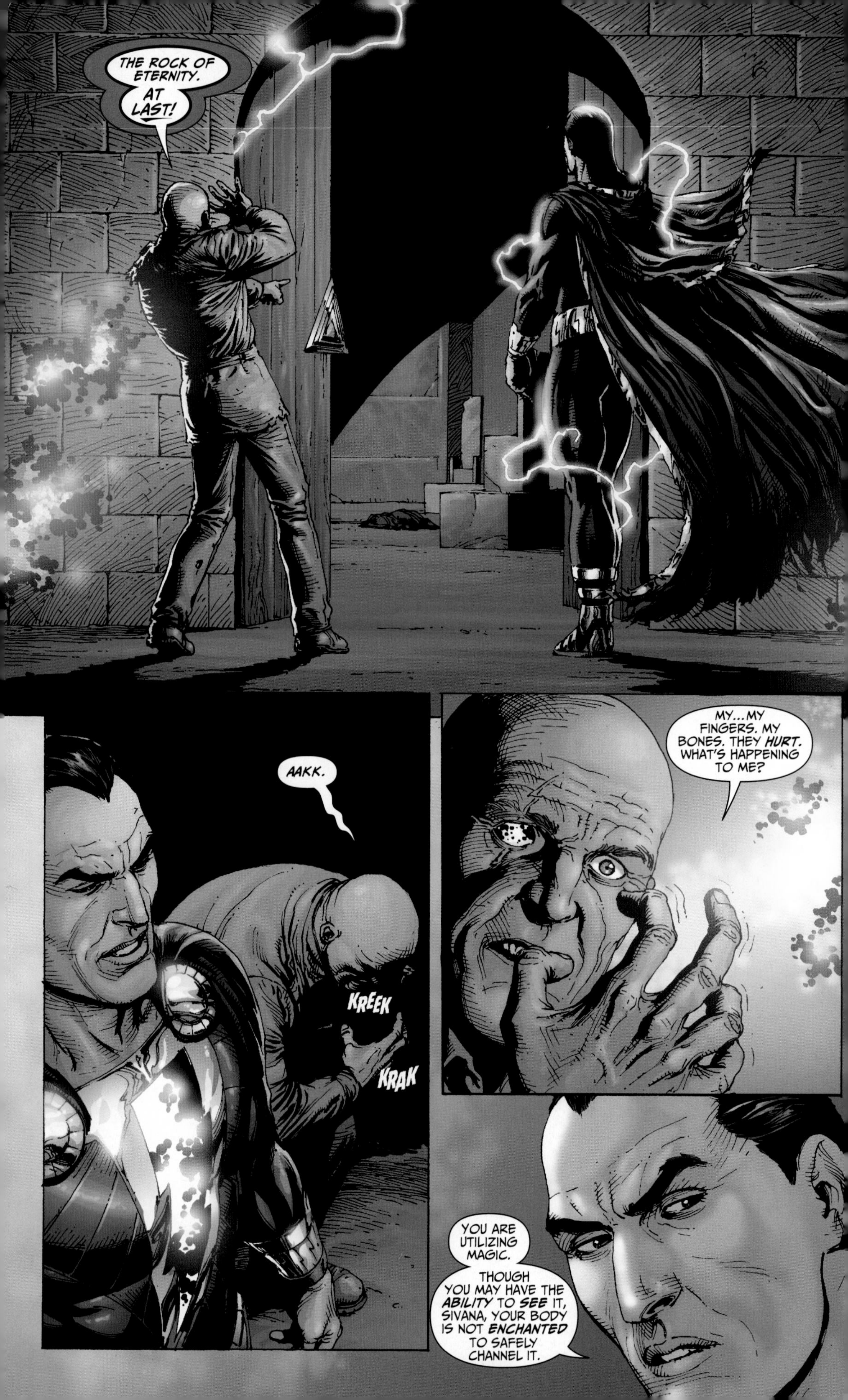
THE ROCK OF ETERNITY. AT LAST!
AAKK.
KREEK
KRAK
MY...MY FINGERS. MY BONES. THEY HURT. WHAT'S HAPPENING TO ME?
YOU ARE UTILIZING MAGIC.
THOUGH YOU MAY HAVE THE ABILITY TO SEE IT, SIVANA, YOUR BODY IS NOT ENCHANTED TO SAFELY CHANNEL IT.

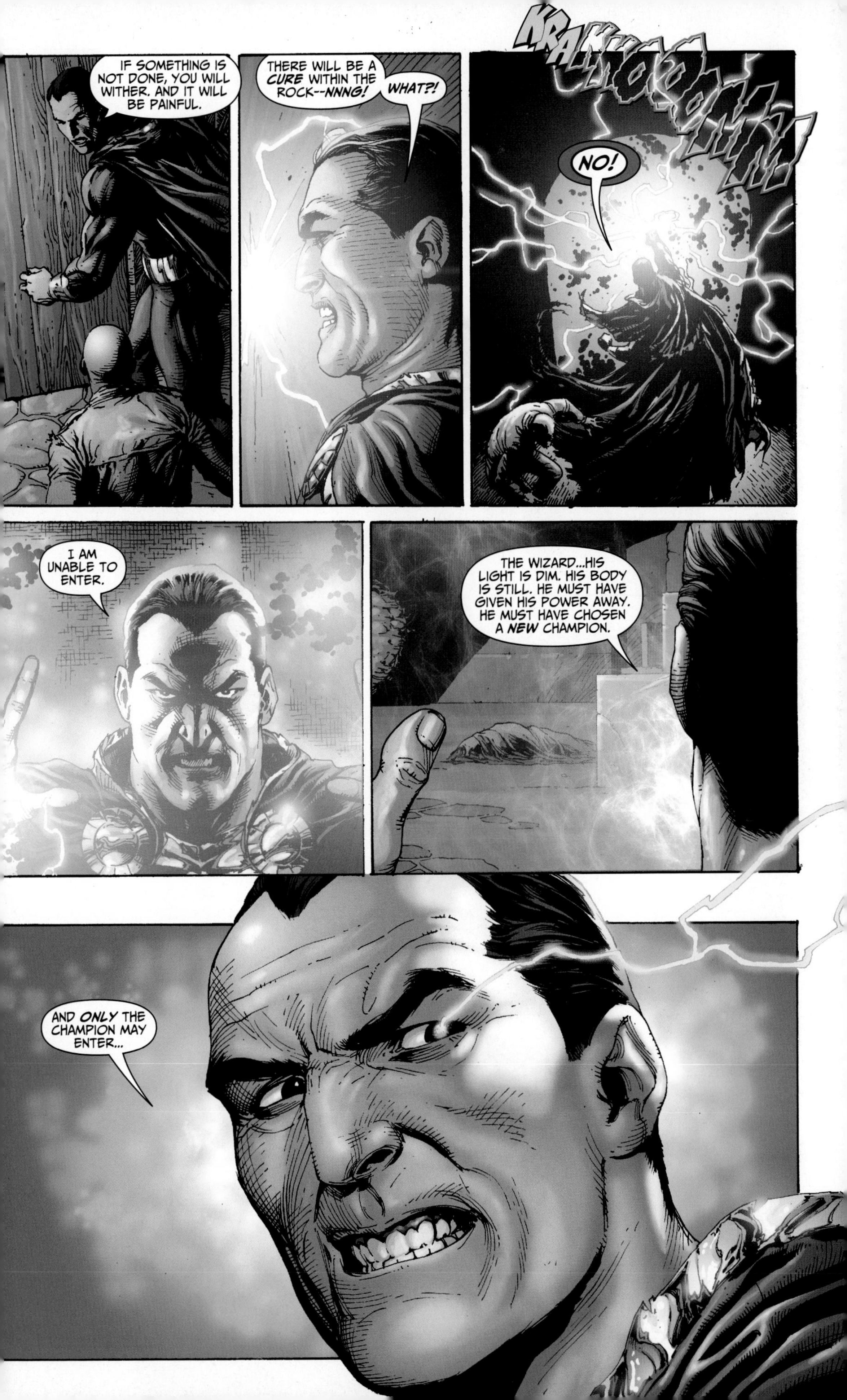
IF SOMETHING IS NOT DONE, YOU WILL WITHER. AND IT WILL BE PAINFUL.
THERE WILL BE A CURE WITHIN THE ROCK--NNNG!
WHAT?!
NO!
I AM UNABLE TO ENTER.
THE WIZARD...HIS LIGHT IS DIM. HIS BODY IS STILL. HE MUST HAVE GIVEN HIS POWER AWAY. HE MUST HAVE CHOSEN A NEW CHAMPION.
AND ONLY THE CHAMPION MAY ENTER...

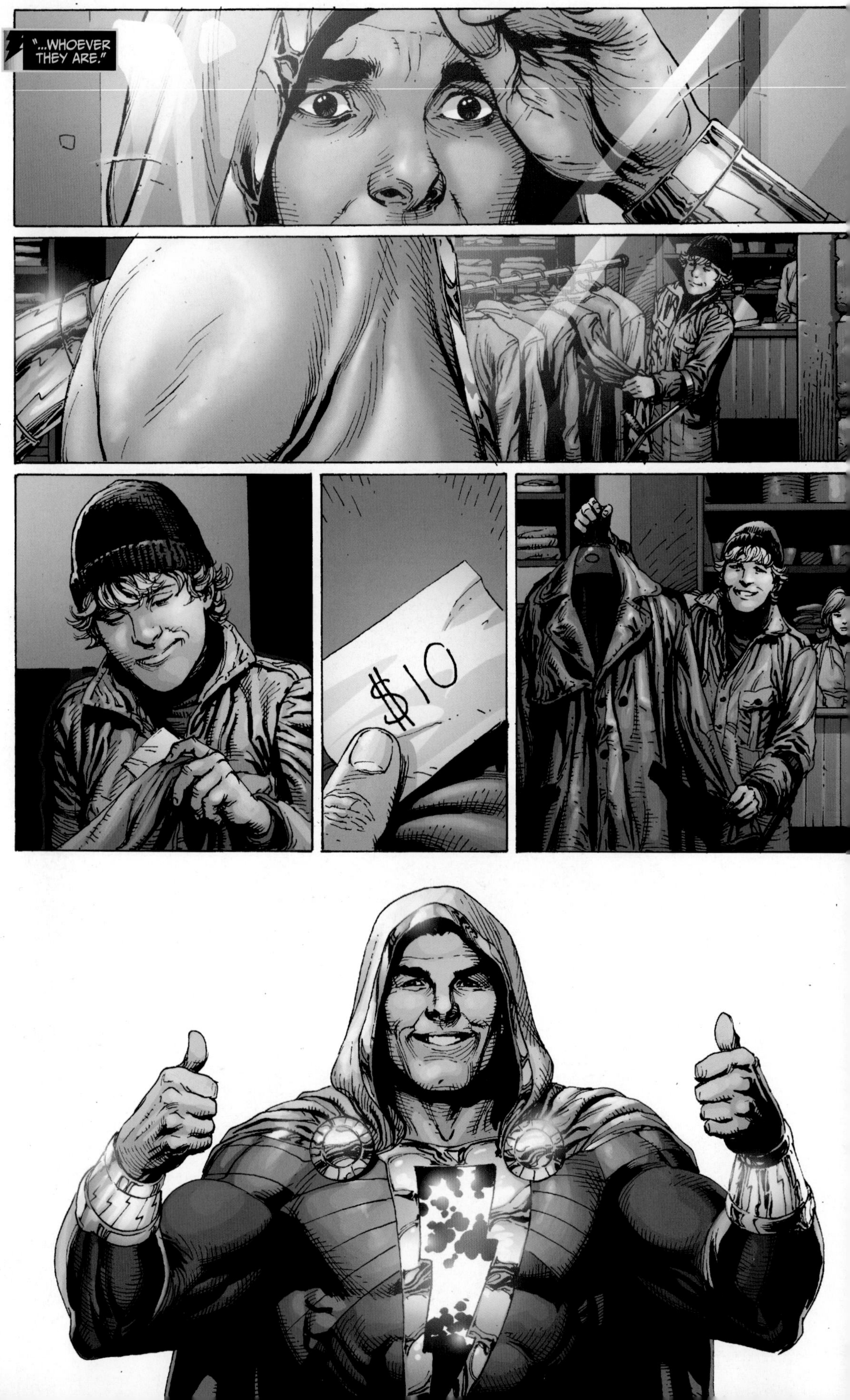
"...WHOEVER THEY ARE."
$10

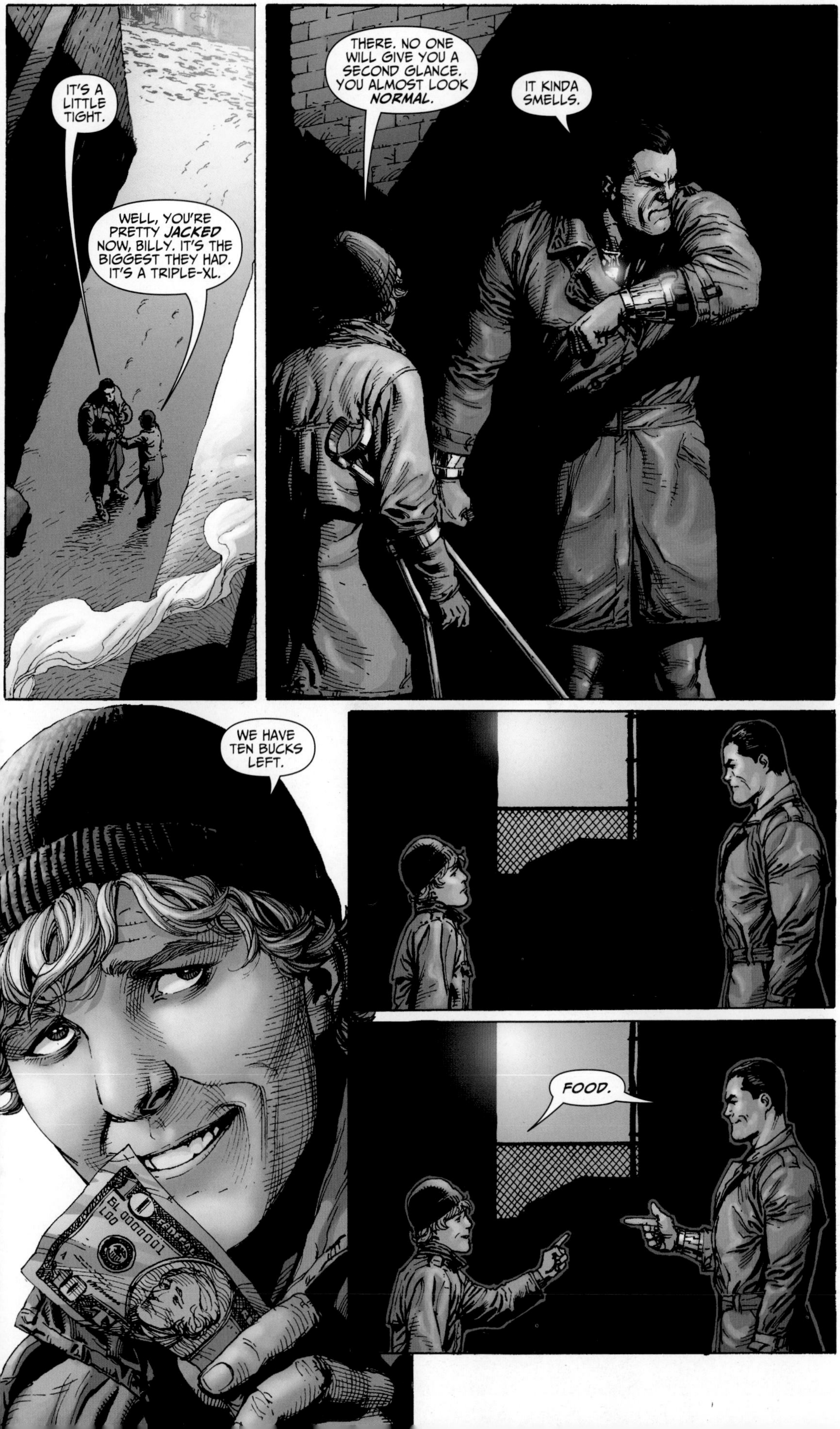
IT'S A LITTLE TIGHT.
WELL, YOU'RE PRETTY **JACKED** NOW, BILLY. IT'S THE BIGGEST THEY HAD. IT'S A TRIPLE-XL.
THERE. NO ONE WILL GIVE YOU A SECOND GLANCE. YOU ALMOST LOOK **NORMAL**.
IT KINDA SMELLS.
WE HAVE TEN BUCKS LEFT.
FOOD.

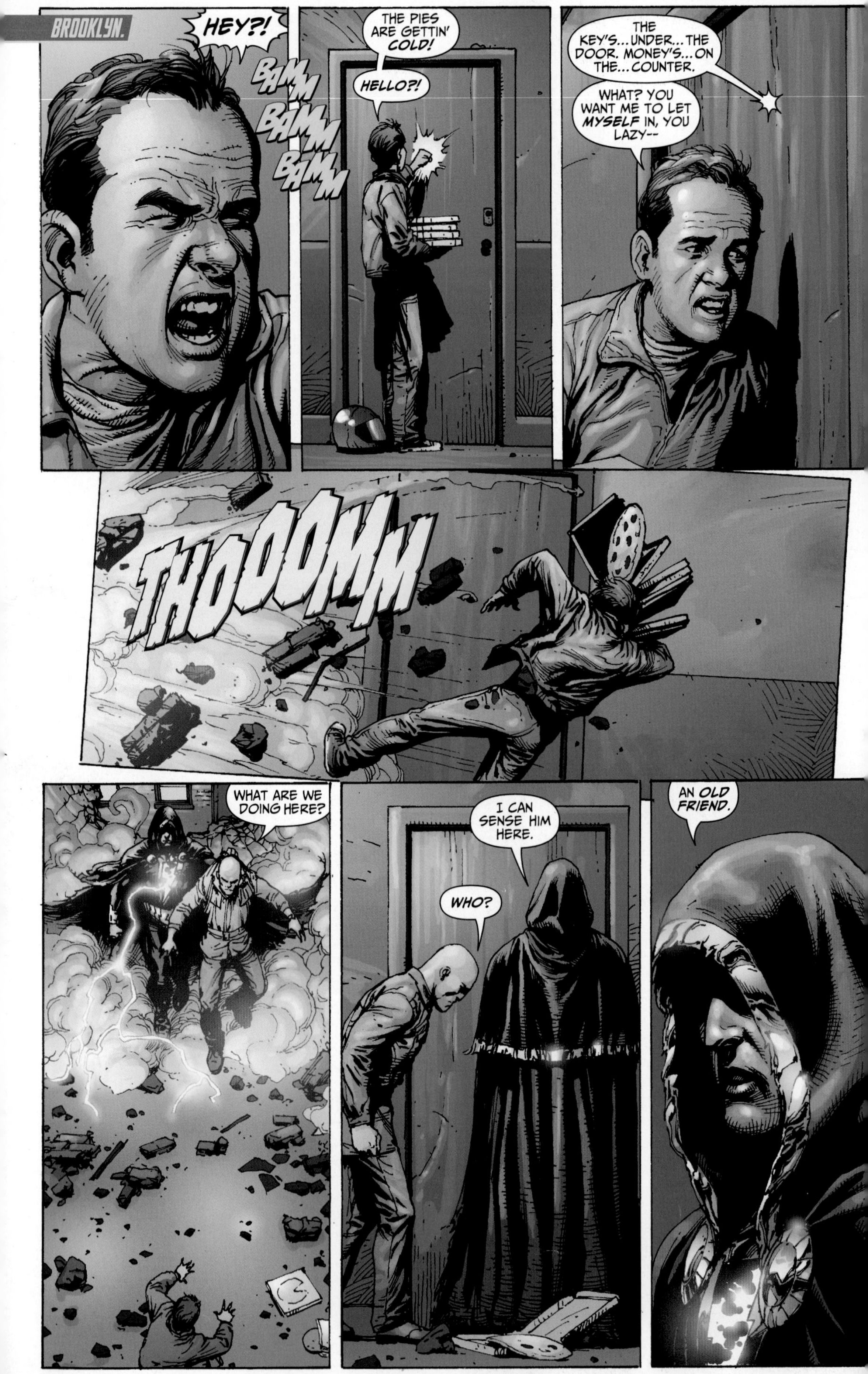
BROOKLYN.
HEY?!
BAMM
BAMM
BAMM
THE PIES ARE GETTIN' COLD!
HELLO?!
THE KEY'S...UNDER...THE DOOR. MONEY'S...ON THE...COUNTER.
WHAT? YOU WANT ME TO LET MYSELF IN, YOU LAZY--
THOOOMM
WHAT ARE WE DOING HERE?
I CAN SENSE HIM HERE.
WHO?
AN OLD FRIEND.

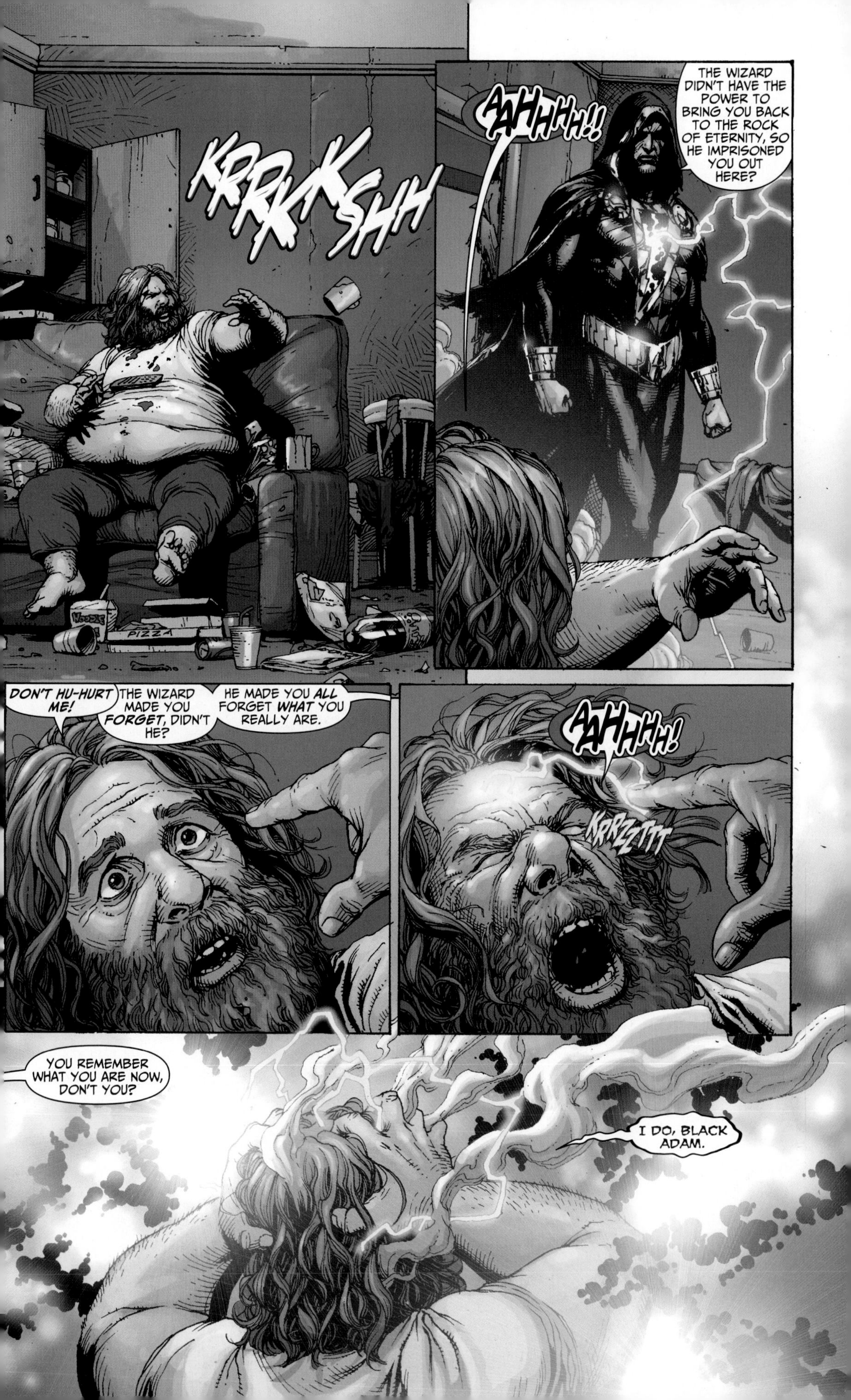
KRRKKKSHH
AAHHHH!!
THE WIZARD DIDN'T HAVE THE POWER TO BRING YOU BACK TO THE ROCK OF ETERNITY, SO HE IMPRISONED YOU OUT HERE?
PIZZA
DON'T HU-HURT ME!
THE WIZARD MADE YOU FORGET, DIDN'T HE?
HE MADE YOU ALL FORGET WHAT YOU REALLY ARE.
AAHHHH!
KRRZZTTT
YOU REMEMBER WHAT YOU ARE NOW, DON'T YOU?
I DO, BLACK ADAM.

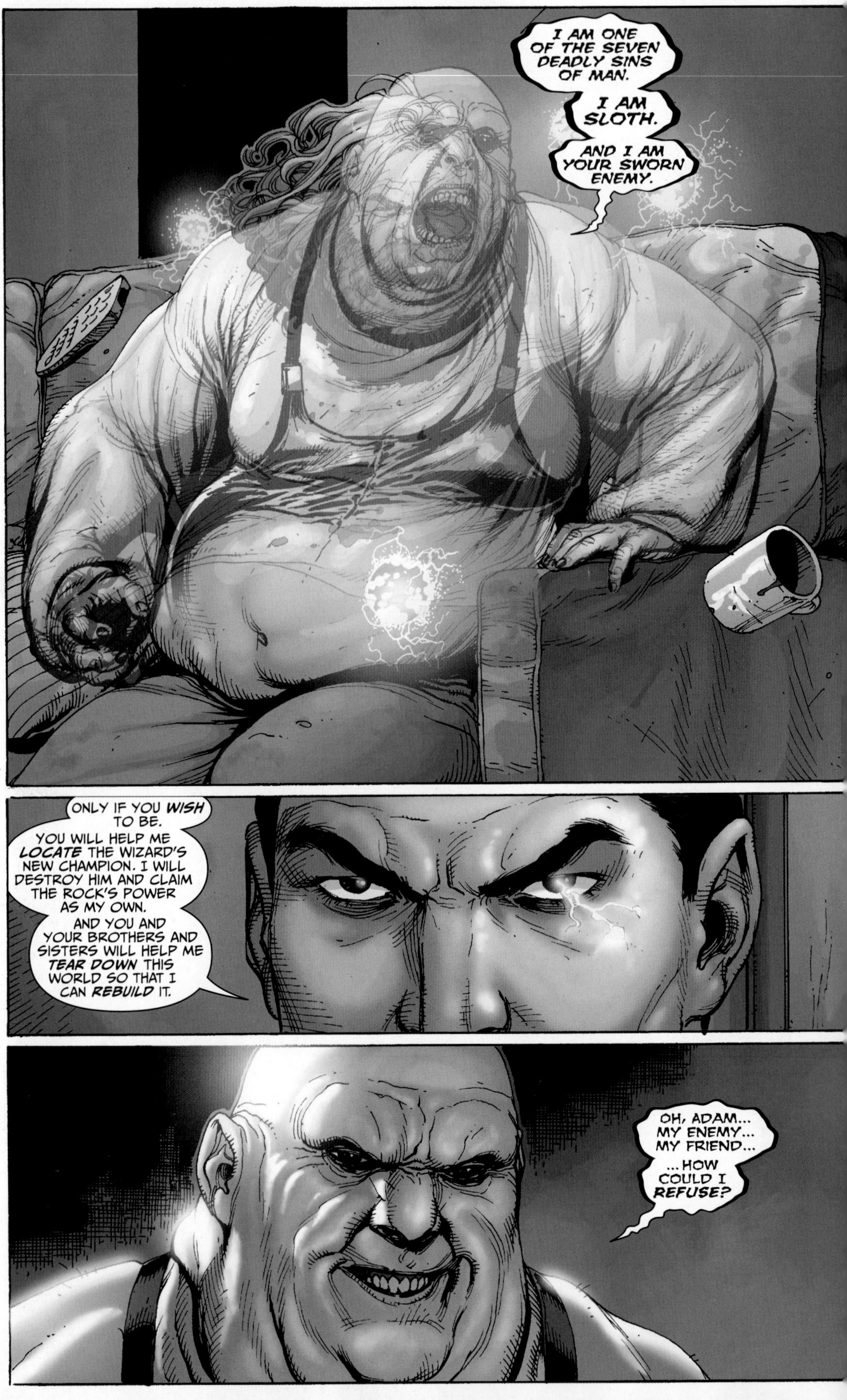
I AM ONE OF THE SEVEN DEADLY SINS OF MAN.
I AM SLOTH.
AND I AM YOUR SWORN ENEMY.
ONLY IF YOU WISH TO BE.
YOU WILL HELP ME LOCATE THE WIZARD'S NEW CHAMPION. I WILL DESTROY HIM AND CLAIM THE ROCK'S POWER AS MY OWN.
AND YOU AND YOUR BROTHERS AND SISTERS WILL HELP ME TEAR DOWN THIS WORLD SO THAT I CAN REBUILD IT.
OH, ADAM... MY ENEMY... MY FRIEND...
...HOW COULD I REFUSE?

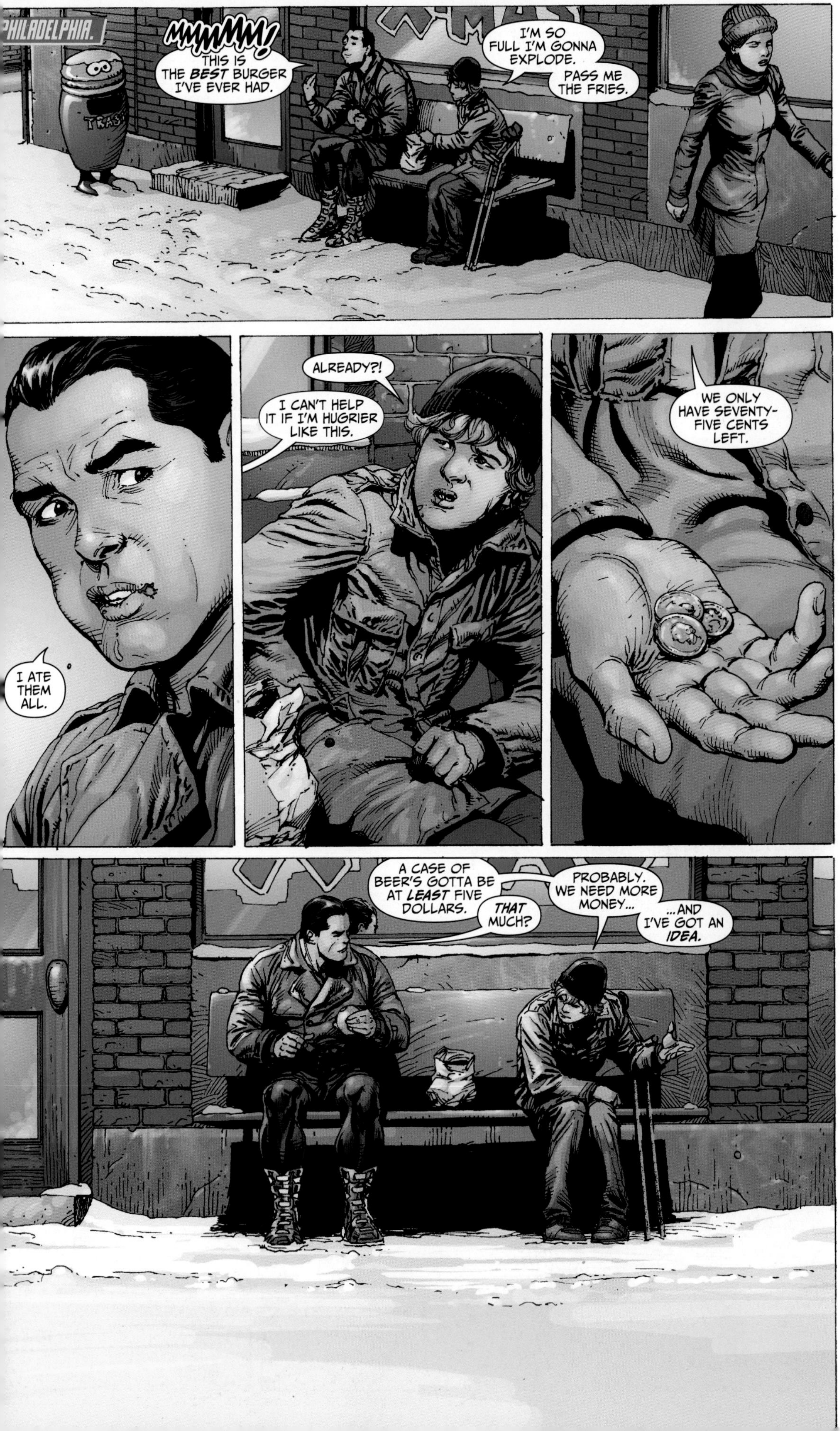
PHILADELPHIA.
MMMMM! THIS IS THE BEST BURGER I'VE EVER HAD.
I'M SO FULL I'M GONNA EXPLODE.
PASS ME THE FRIES.
TRASH
I ATE THEM ALL.
ALREADY?!
I CAN'T HELP IT IF I'M HUGRIER LIKE THIS.
WE ONLY HAVE SEVENTY-FIVE CENTS LEFT.
A CASE OF BEER'S GOTTA BE AT LEAST FIVE DOLLARS.
THAT MUCH?
PROBABLY. WE NEED MORE MONEY...
...AND I'VE GOT AN IDEA.

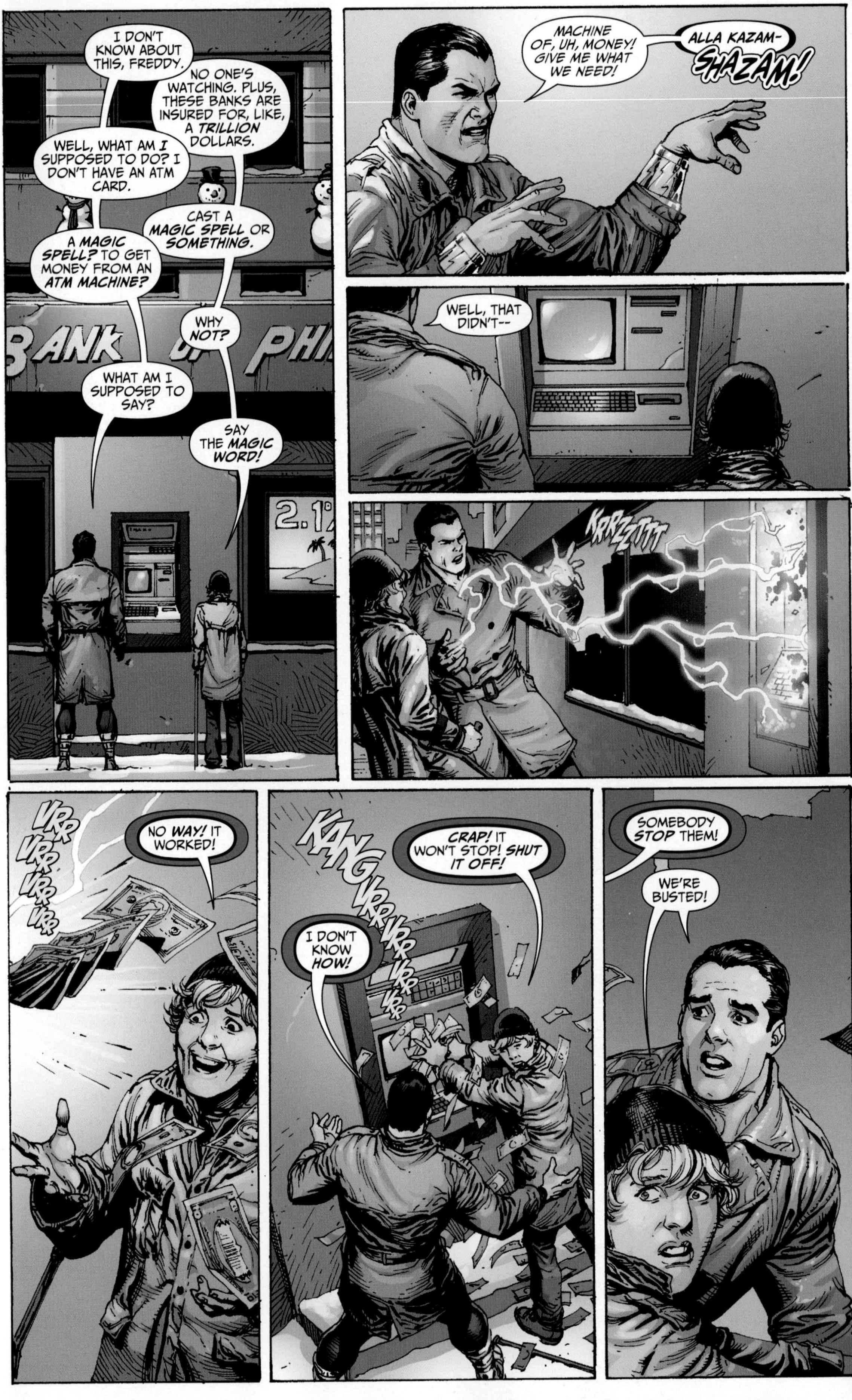
I DON'T KNOW ABOUT THIS, FREDDY.
NO ONE'S WATCHING. PLUS, THESE BANKS ARE INSURED FOR, LIKE, A TRILLION DOLLARS.
WELL, WHAT AM I SUPPOSED TO DO? I DON'T HAVE AN ATM CARD.
CAST A MAGIC SPELL OR SOMETHING.
A MAGIC SPELL? TO GET MONEY FROM AN ATM MACHINE?
WHY NOT?
BANK OF PHI
WHAT AM I SUPPOSED TO SAY?
SAY THE MAGIC WORD!
MACHINE OF, UH, MONEY! GIVE ME WHAT WE NEED!
ALLA KAZAM-SHAZAM!
WELL, THAT DIDN'T--
KRRZZTTT
VRR VRR VRR VRR
NO WAY! IT WORKED!
KANG VRR VRR VRR VRR
CRAP! IT WON'T STOP! SHUT IT OFF!
I DON'T KNOW HOW!
SOMEBODY STOP THEM!
WE'RE BUSTED!

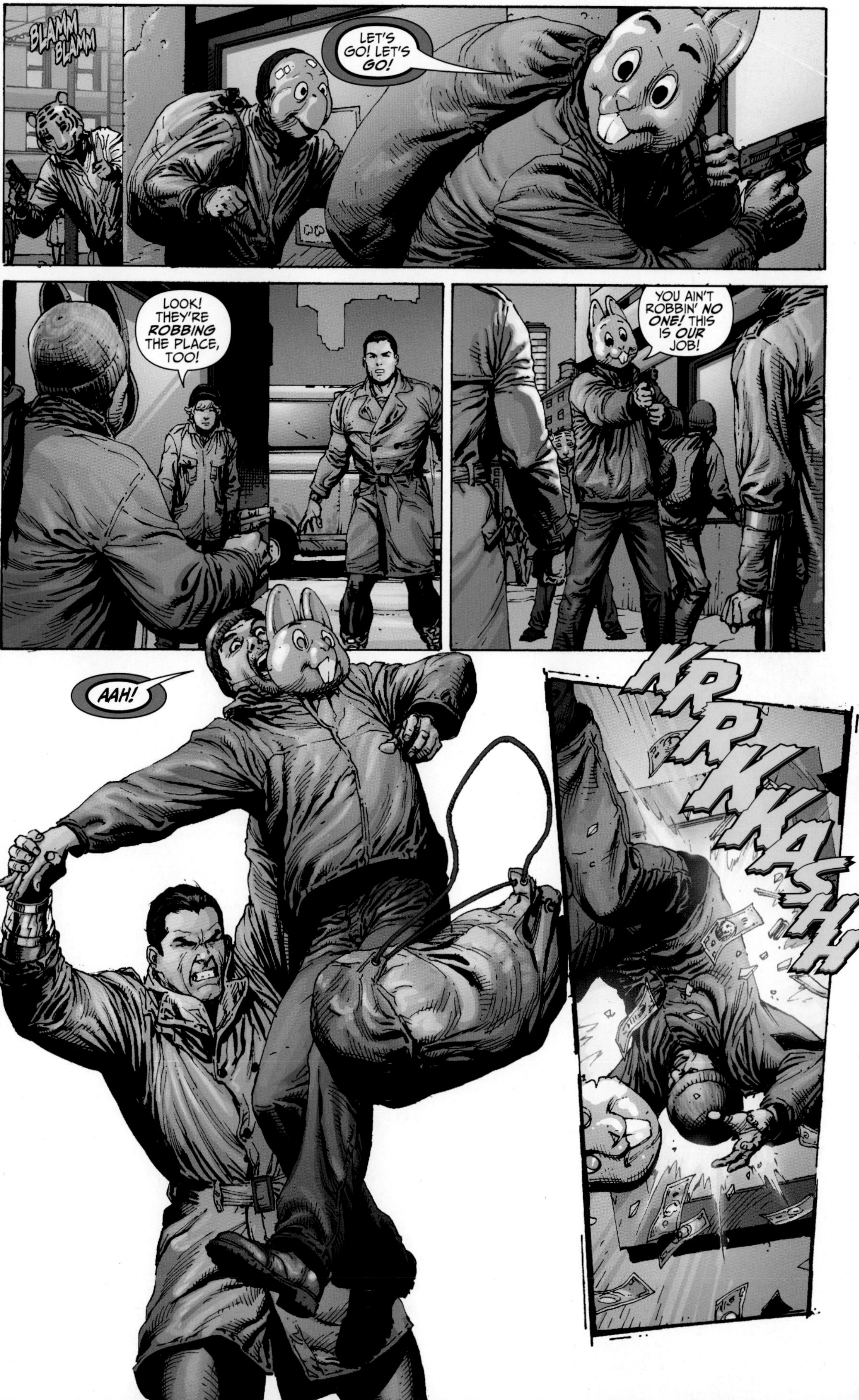
BLAMM BLAMM
LET'S GO! LET'S GO!
LOOK! THEY'RE ROBBING THE PLACE, TOO!
YOU AIN'T ROBBIN' NO ONE! THIS IS OUR JOB!
AAH!
KRKKASH

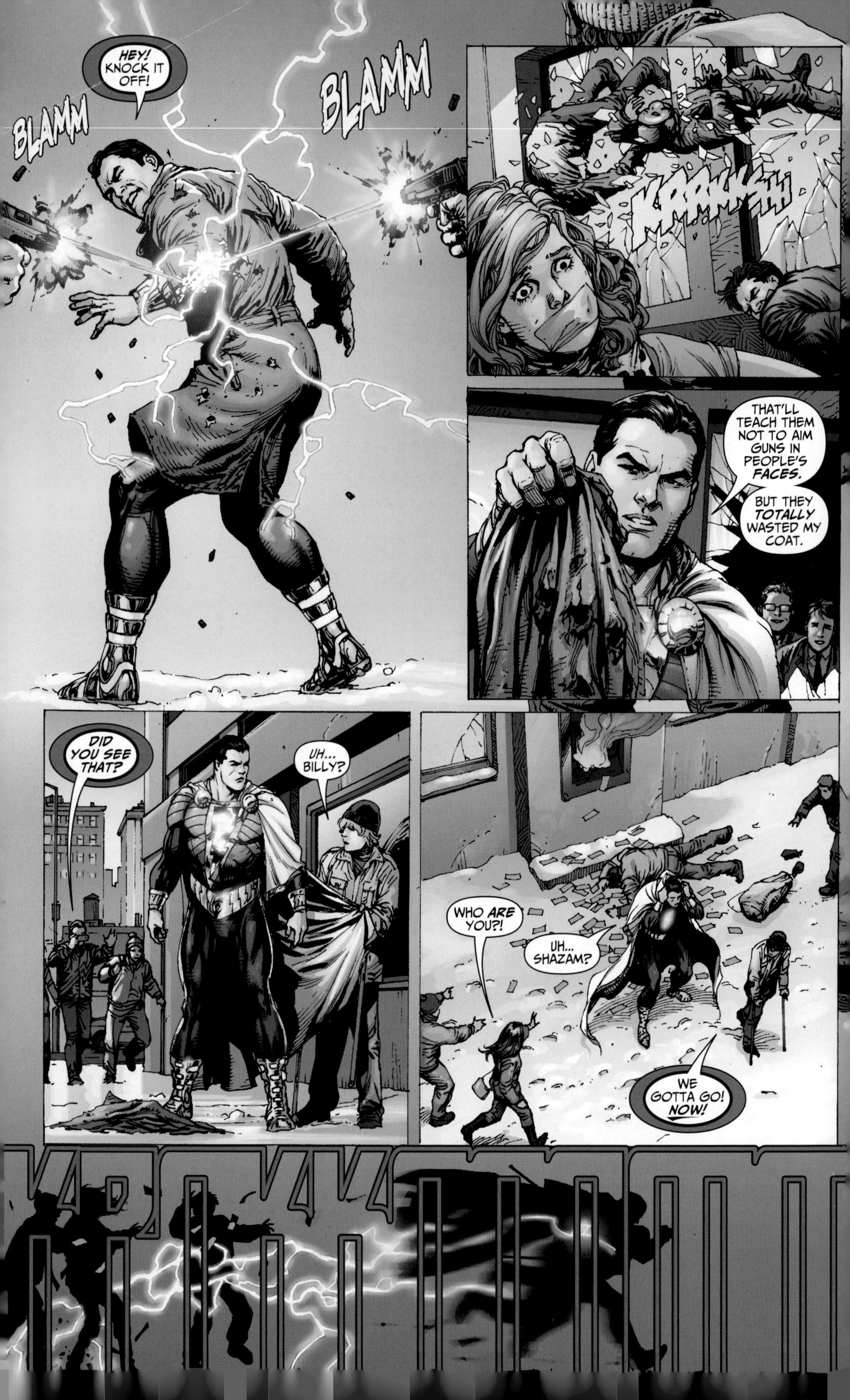
HEY! KNOCK IT OFF!
BLAMM
BLAMM
KRRKKSH
THAT'LL TEACH THEM NOT TO AIM GUNS IN PEOPLE'S FACES.
BUT THEY TOTALLY WASTED MY COAT.
DID YOU SEE THAT?
UH... BILLY?
WHO ARE YOU?!
UH... SHAZAM?
WE GOTTA GO! NOW!

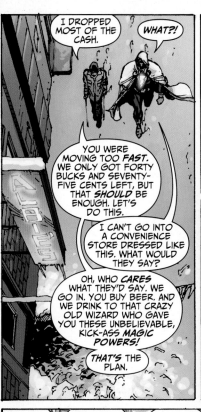

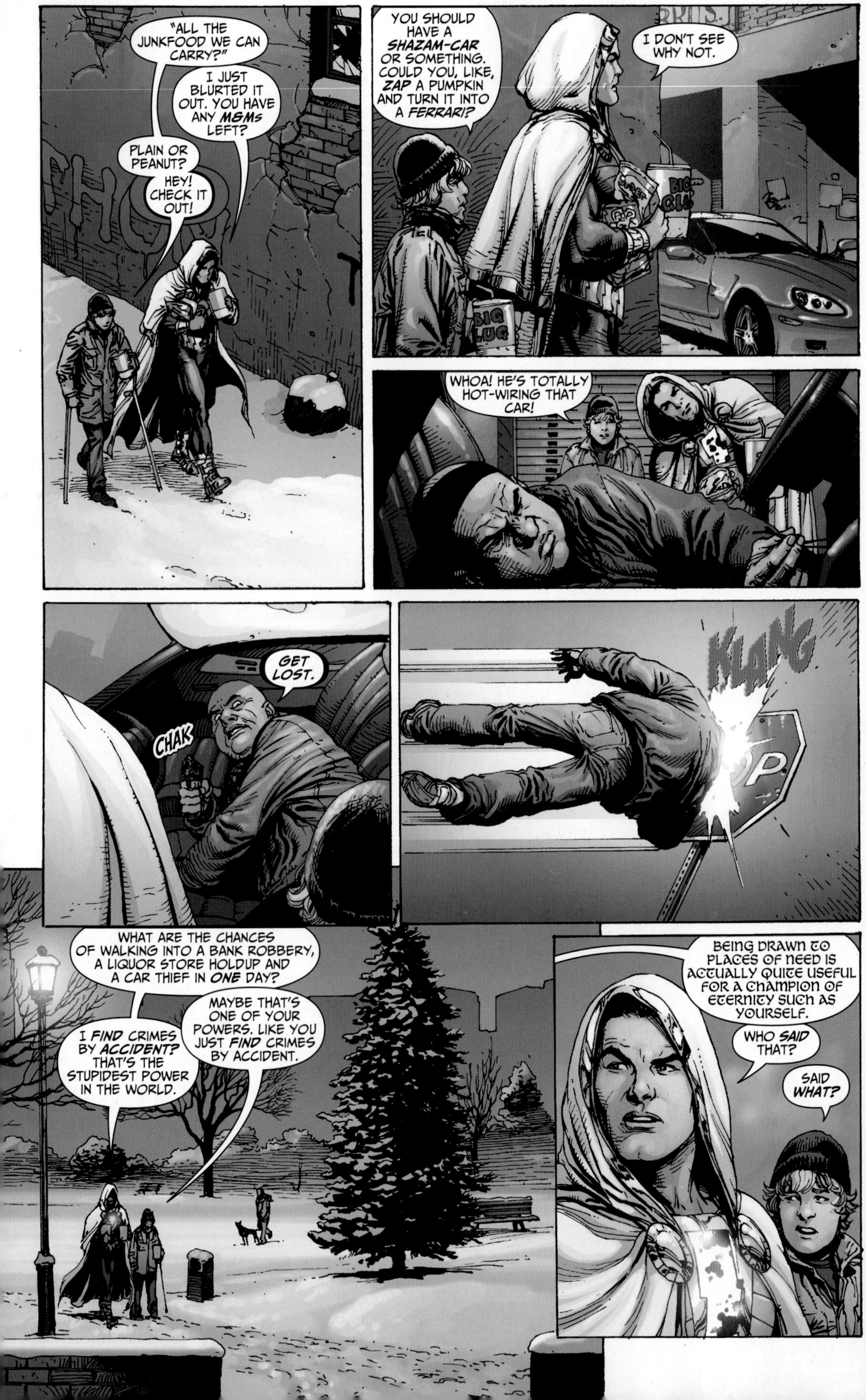

"ALL THE JUNKFOOD WE CAN CARRY?"
I JUST BLURTED IT OUT. YOU HAVE ANY M&Ms LEFT?
PLAIN OR PEANUT?
HEY! CHECK IT OUT!
YOU SHOULD HAVE A SHAZAM-CAR OR SOMETHING. COULD YOU, LIKE, ZAP A PUMPKIN AND TURN IT INTO A FERRARI!?
I DON'T SEE WHY NOT.
WHOA! HE'S TOTALLY HOT-WIRING THAT CAR!
GET LOST.
CHAK
KLANG
WHAT ARE THE CHANCES OF WALKING INTO A BANK ROBBERY, A LIQUOR STORE HOLDUP AND A CAR THIEF IN ONE DAY?
MAYBE THAT'S ONE OF YOUR POWERS. LIKE YOU JUST FIND CRIMES BY ACCIDENT.
I FIND CRIMES BY ACCIDENT? THAT'S THE STUPIDEST POWER IN THE WORLD.
BEING DRAWN TO PLACES OF NEED IS ACTUALLY QUITE USEFUL FOR A CHAMPION OF ETERNITY SUCH AS YOURSELF.
WHO SAID THAT?
SAID WHAT?

DO YOU **SEE** THAT?

SEE WHAT?

A **FACE.** IN THE MIRROR. YOU DON'T SEE THAT?

MY NAME IS FRANCESCA. I SAW YOU IN THE ROCK OF ETERNITY.

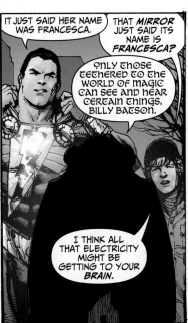

IT JUST SAID HER NAME WAS FRANCESCA.

THAT **MIRROR** JUST SAID ITS NAME IS **FRANCESCA?**

ONLY THOSE TETHERED TO THE WORLD OF MAGIC CAN SEE AND HEAR CERTAIN THINGS, BILLY BATSON.

I THINK ALL THAT ELECTRICITY MIGHT BE GETTING TO YOUR **BRAIN.**

YOU MUST PREPARE YOURSELF.

BE THE CHAMPION YOU'RE EMPOWERED TO BE, BILLY BATSON.

AND BEWARE **BLACK ADAM!** HE KNOWS!

KKRSH

IT JUST SHATTERED! WHAT'D YOU DO?

I SWEAR, I DIDN'T DO ANYTHING! BUT THERE WAS A LADY'S FACE IN IT.

WHAT?

UH... BILLY?

I DON'T THINK YOU NEED A **SHAZAM-CAR** ANYMORE.

WHY?

BECAUSE YOU'RE FREAKING **FLYING!**

I CAN **FLY?!**

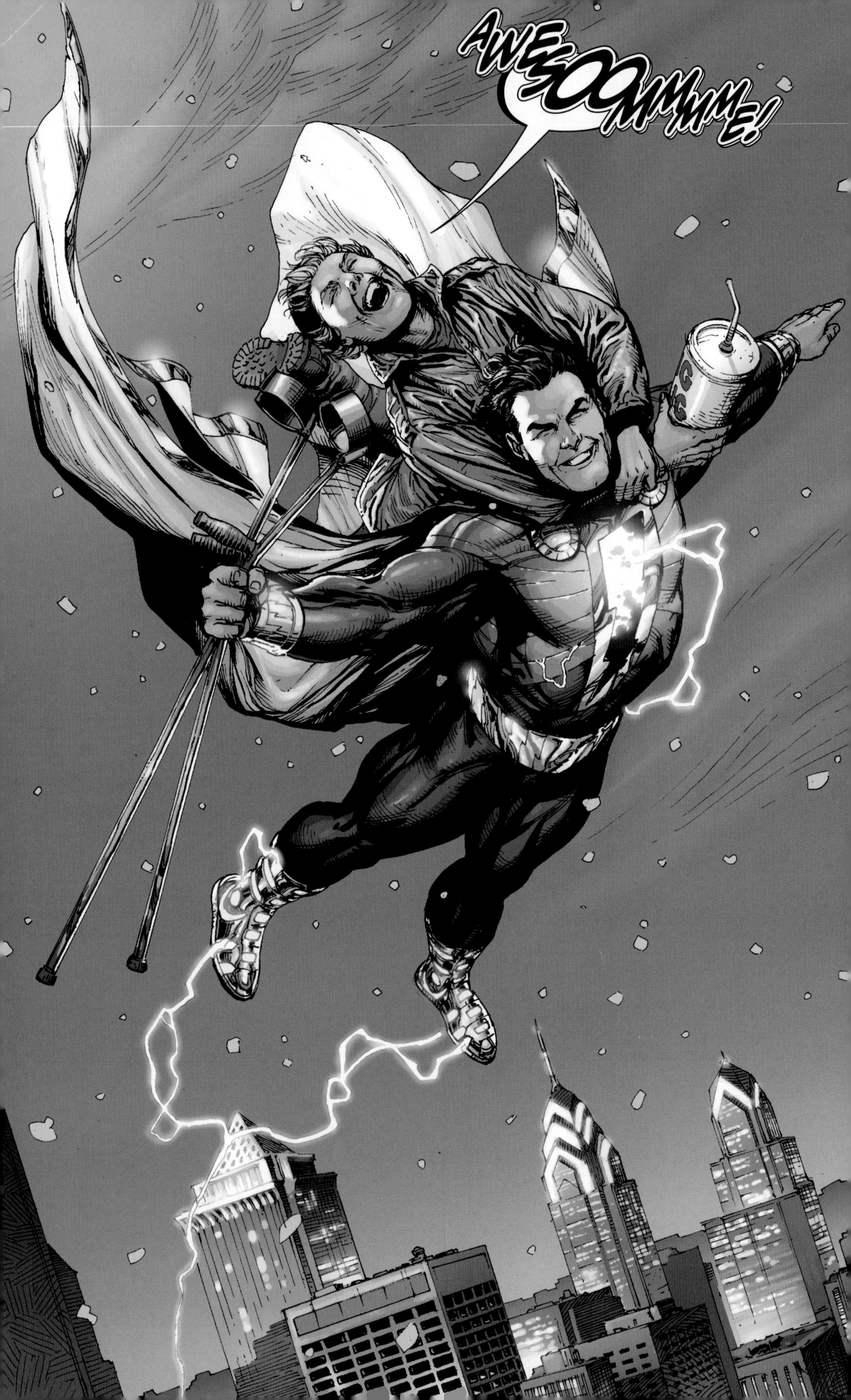
AWESOOMMMMME!

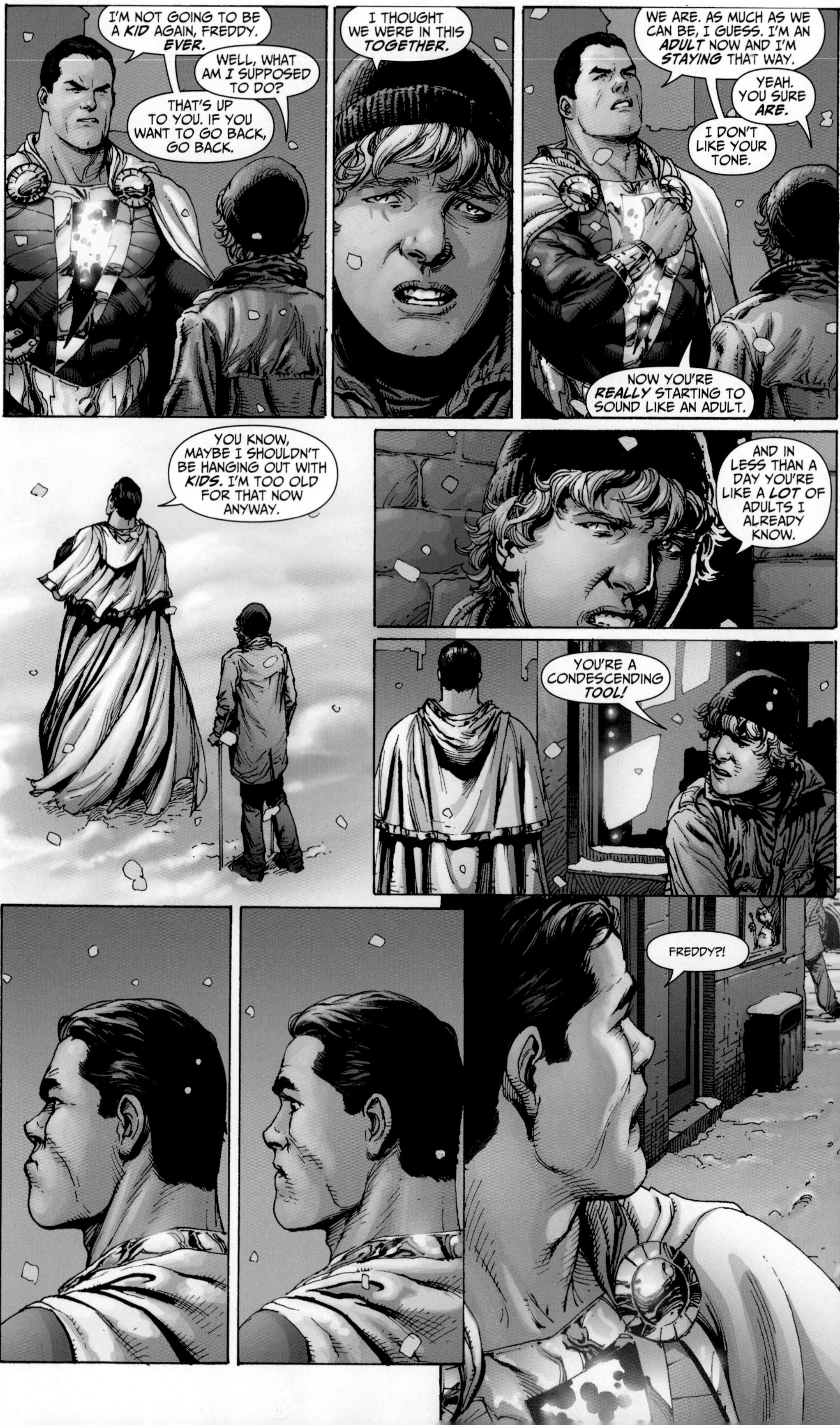
I'M NOT GOING TO BE A KID AGAIN, FREDDY. EVER.
WELL, WHAT AM I SUPPOSED TO DO?
THAT'S UP TO YOU. IF YOU WANT TO GO BACK, GO BACK.
I THOUGHT WE WERE IN THIS TOGETHER.
WE ARE. AS MUCH AS WE CAN BE, I GUESS. I'M AN ADULT NOW AND I'M STAYING THAT WAY.
YEAH. YOU SURE ARE.
I DON'T LIKE YOUR TONE.
NOW YOU'RE REALLY STARTING TO SOUND LIKE AN ADULT.
YOU KNOW, MAYBE I SHOULDN'T BE HANGING OUT WITH KIDS. I'M TOO OLD FOR THAT NOW ANYWAY.
AND IN LESS THAN A DAY YOU'RE LIKE A LOT OF ADULTS I ALREADY KNOW.
YOU'RE A CONDESCENDING TOOL!
FREDDY?!

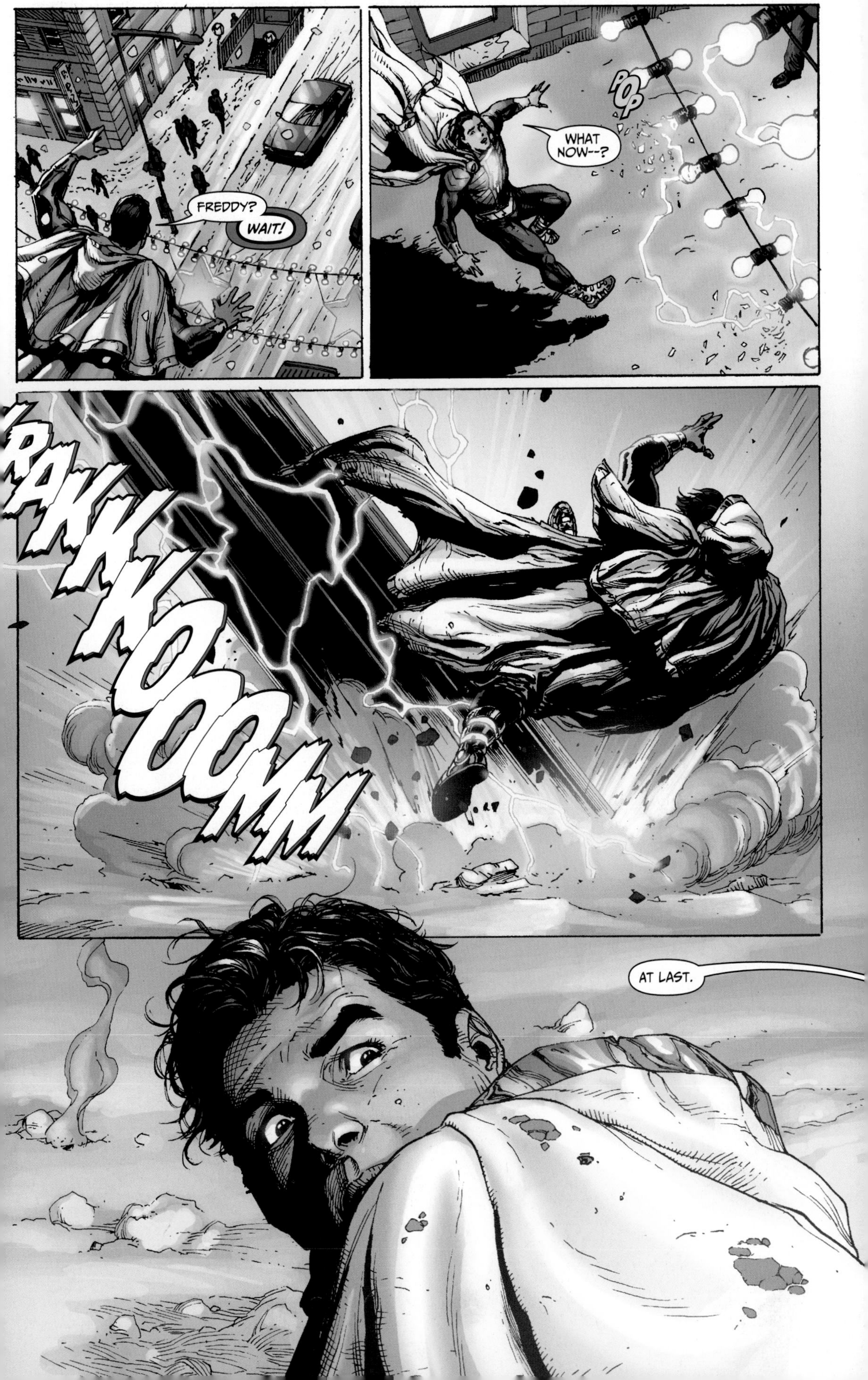
FREDDY?
WAIT!
POP
WHAT NOW--?
KRAKKOOOMM
AT LAST.

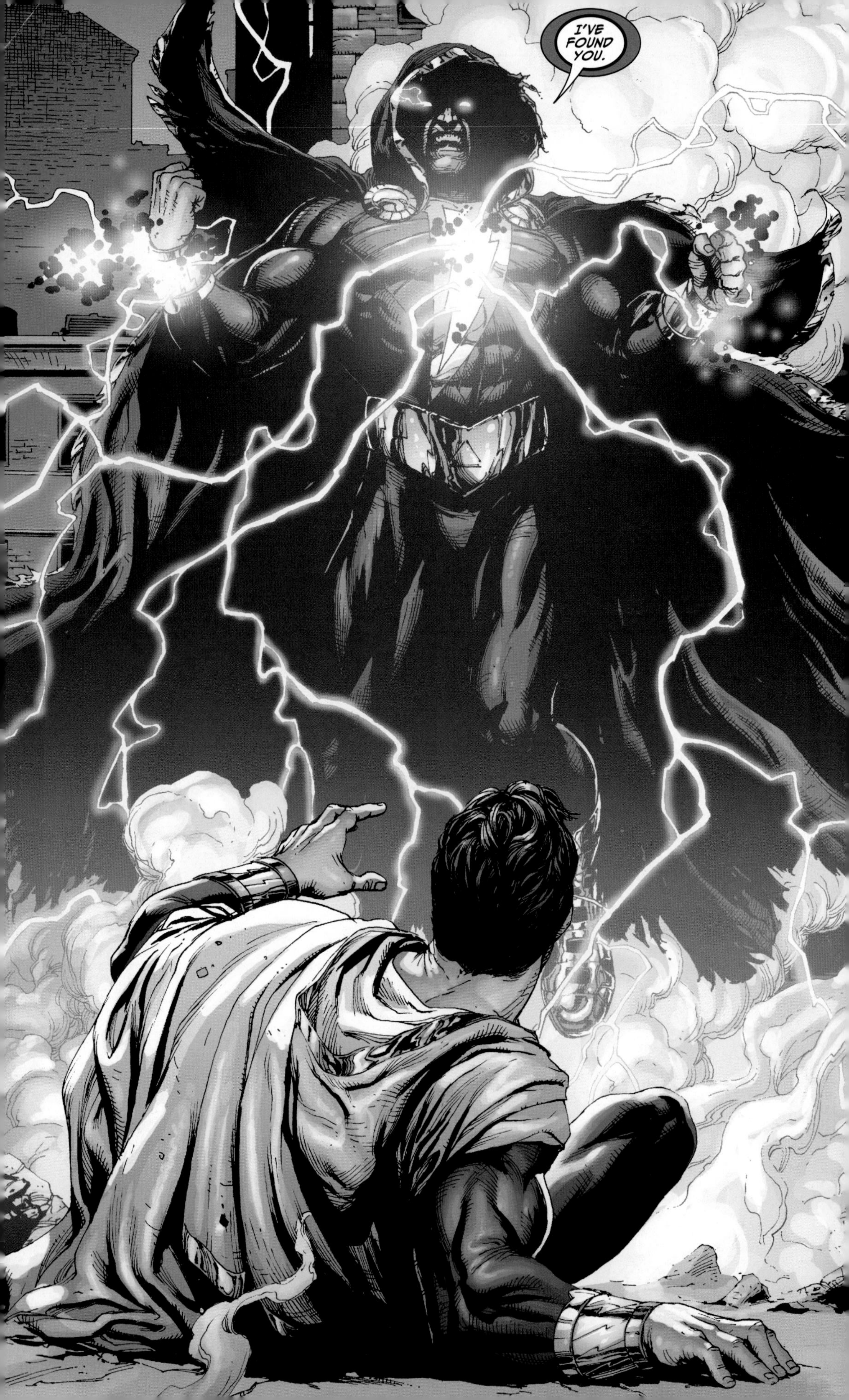
I'VE FOUND YOU.

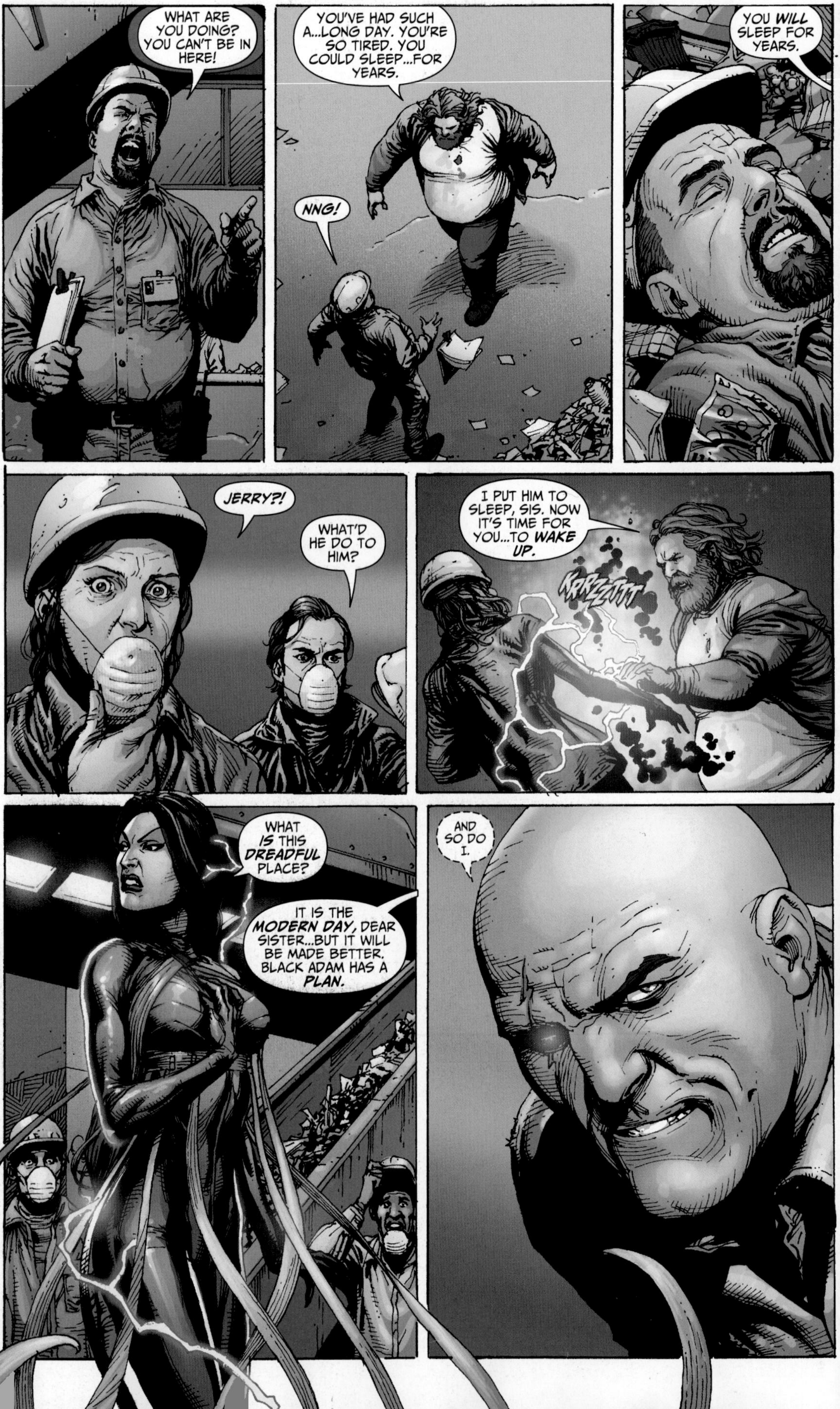
WHAT ARE YOU DOING? YOU CAN'T BE IN HERE!
YOU'VE HAD SUCH A...LONG DAY. YOU'RE SO TIRED. YOU COULD SLEEP...FOR YEARS.
NNG!
YOU WILL SLEEP FOR YEARS.
JERRY?!
WHAT'D HE DO TO HIM?
I PUT HIM TO SLEEP, SIS. NOW IT'S TIME FOR YOU...TO WAKE UP.
KRRZZTTT
WHAT IS THIS DREADFUL PLACE?
IT IS THE MODERN DAY, DEAR SISTER...BUT IT WILL BE MADE BETTER. BLACK ADAM HAS A PLAN.
AND SO DO I.

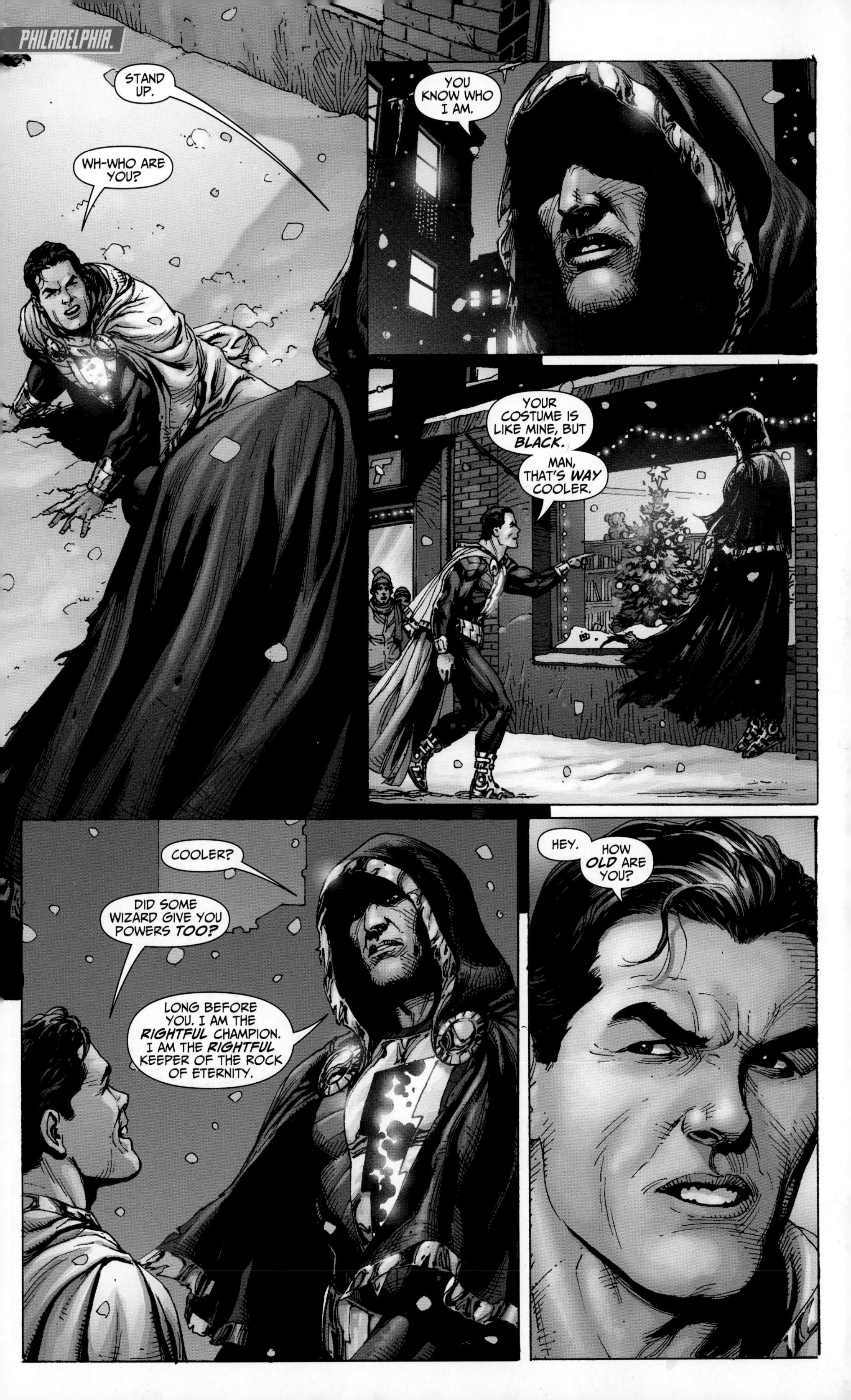
PHILADELPHIA.
STAND UP.
WH-WHO ARE YOU?
YOU KNOW WHO I AM.
YOUR COSTUME IS LIKE MINE, BUT BLACK.
MAN, THAT'S WAY COOLER.
COOLER?
DID SOME WIZARD GIVE YOU POWERS TOO?
LONG BEFORE YOU. I AM THE RIGHTFUL CHAMPION. I AM THE RIGHTFUL KEEPER OF THE ROCK OF ETERNITY.
HEY.
HOW OLD ARE YOU?

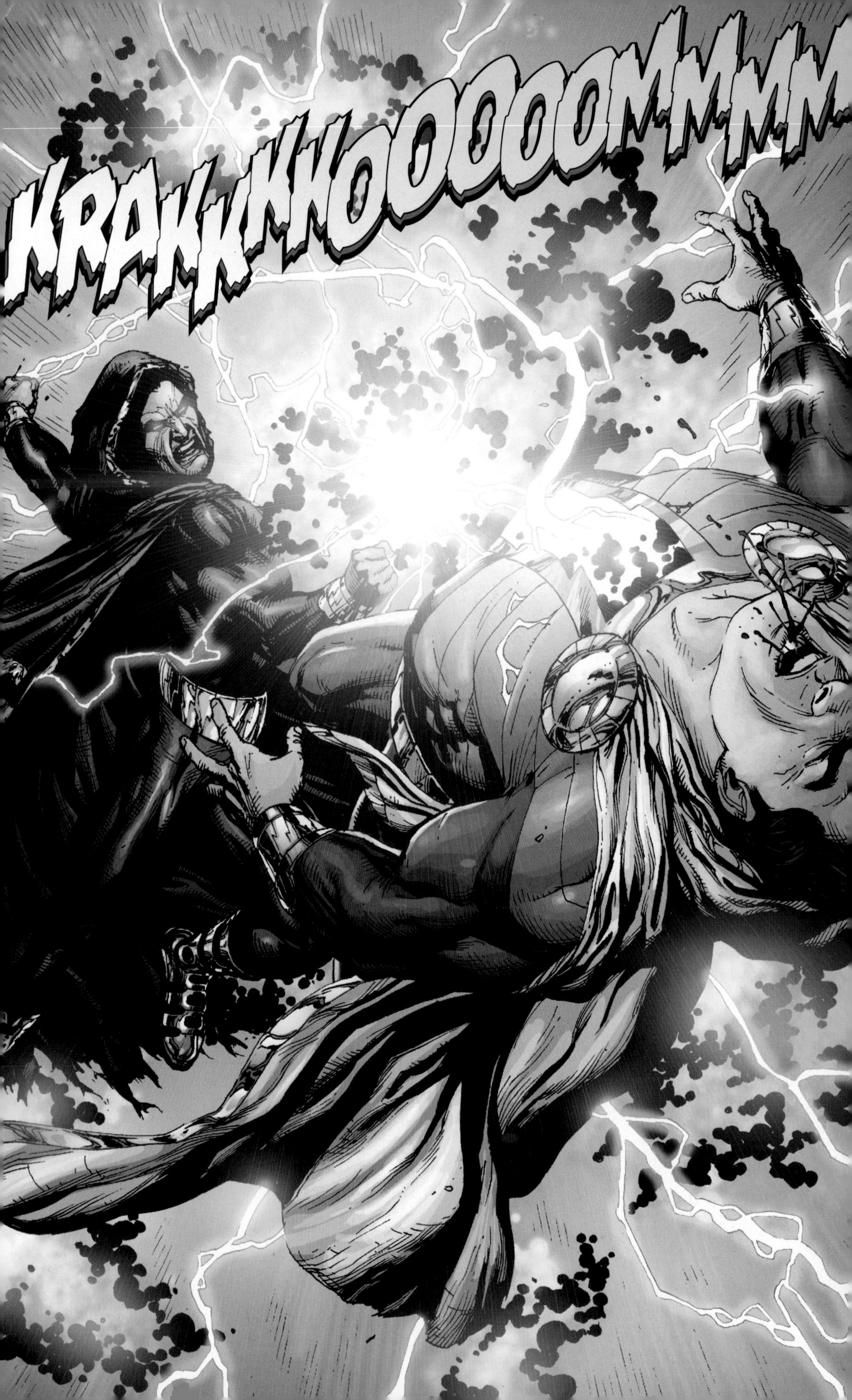
KRAKKKOOOOOOMMMM

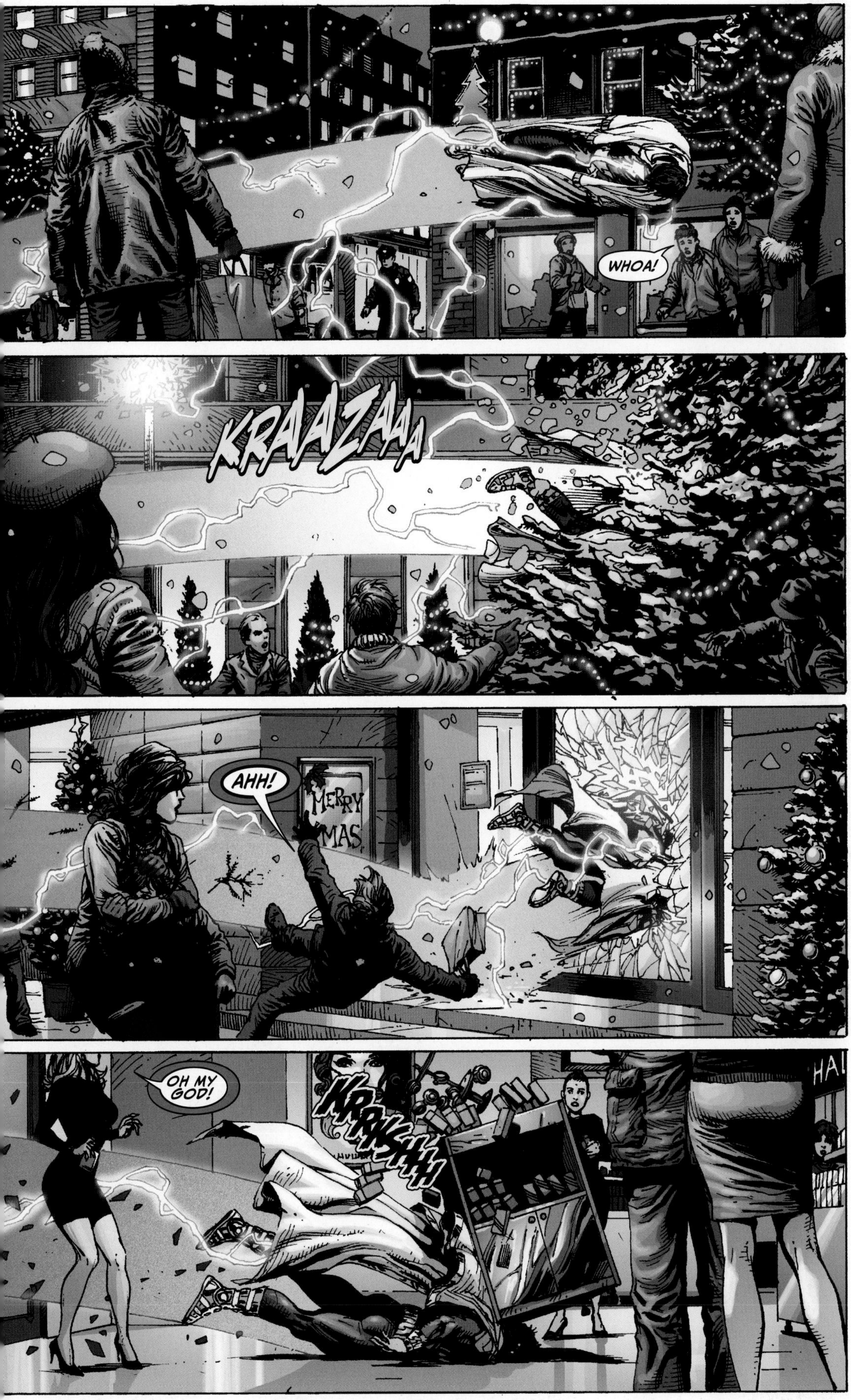
WHOA!
KRAAZAAA
AHH!
MERRY
MAS
OH MY GOD!
KRRNSHHH

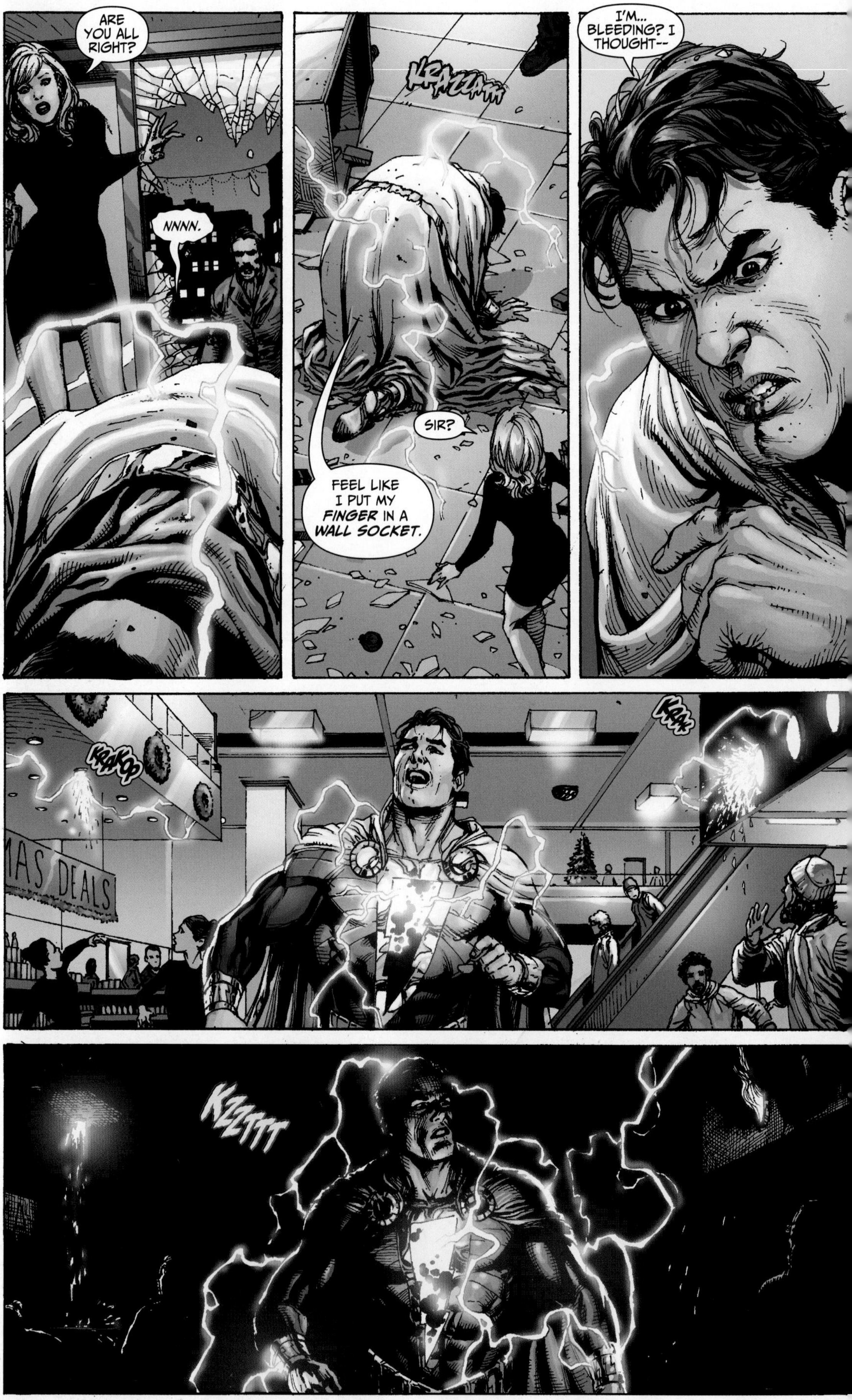

ARE YOU ALL RIGHT?
NNNN.
KRAZZAM
SIR?
FEEL LIKE I PUT MY FINGER IN A WALL SOCKET.
I'M... BLEEDING? I THOUGHT--
KRAKOOP
KRAK
MAS DEALS
KZZTTT

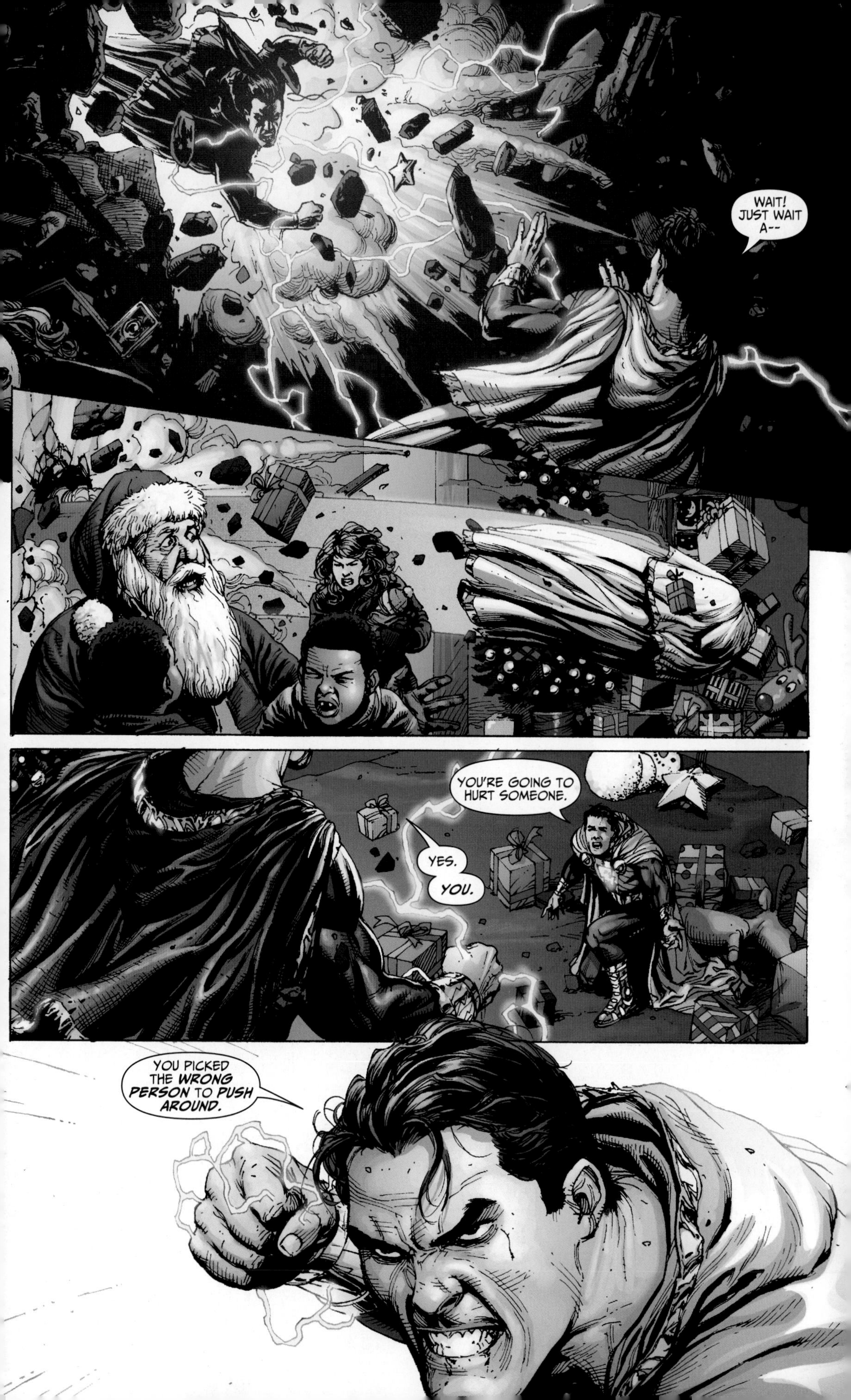
WAIT! JUST WAIT A--
YOU'RE GOING TO HURT SOMEONE.
YES. YOU.
YOU PICKED THE WRONG PERSON TO PUSH AROUND.

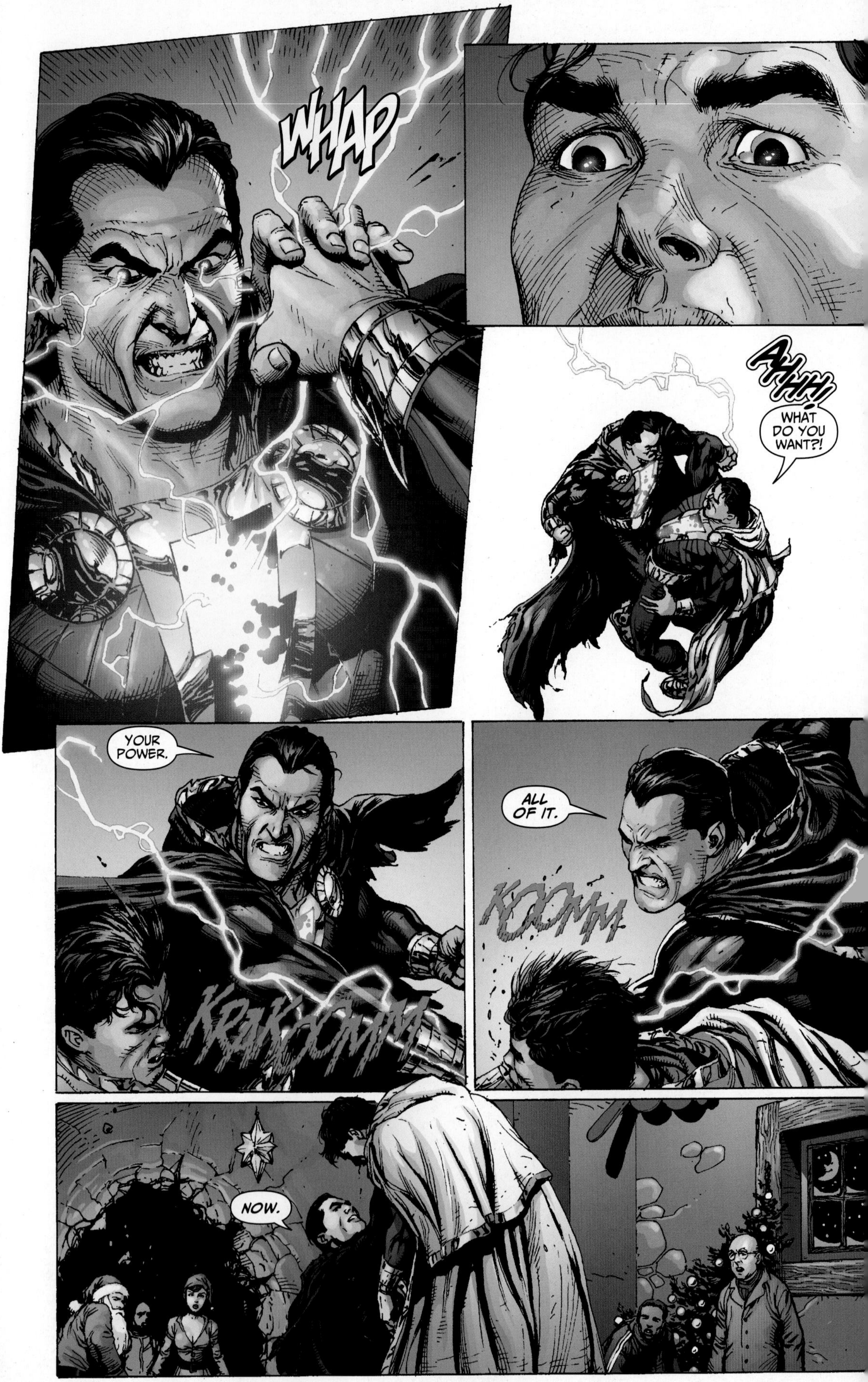
WHAP
AHHH!
WHAT DO YOU WANT?!
YOUR POWER.
KRAKOOM
ALL OF IT.
KOOM
NOW.

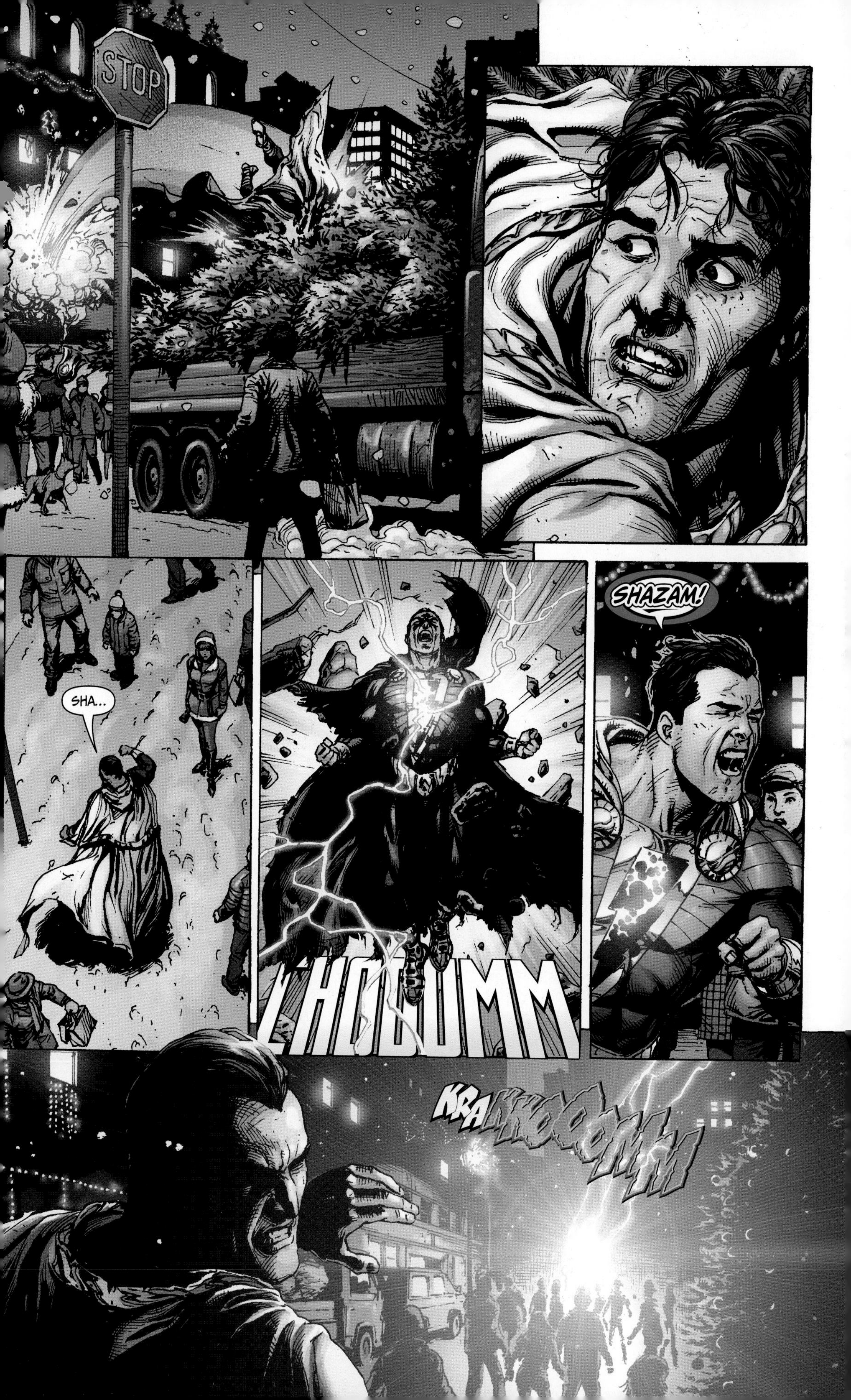
STOP
SHA...
CHOOOMM
SHAZAM!
KRAKOOOMM

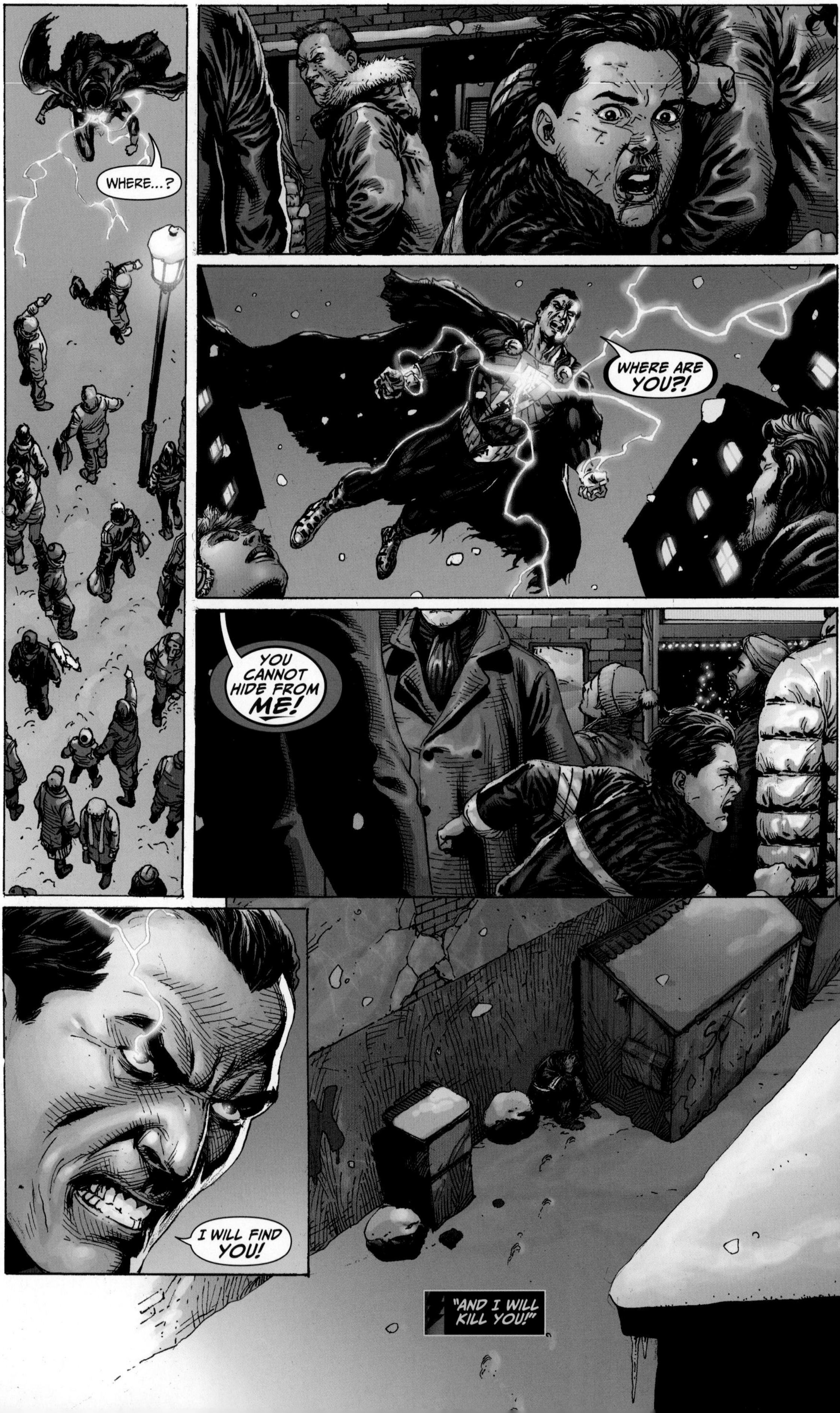
WHERE...?
WHERE ARE YOU?!
YOU CANNOT HIDE FROM ME!
I WILL FIND YOU!
"AND I WILL KILL YOU!"

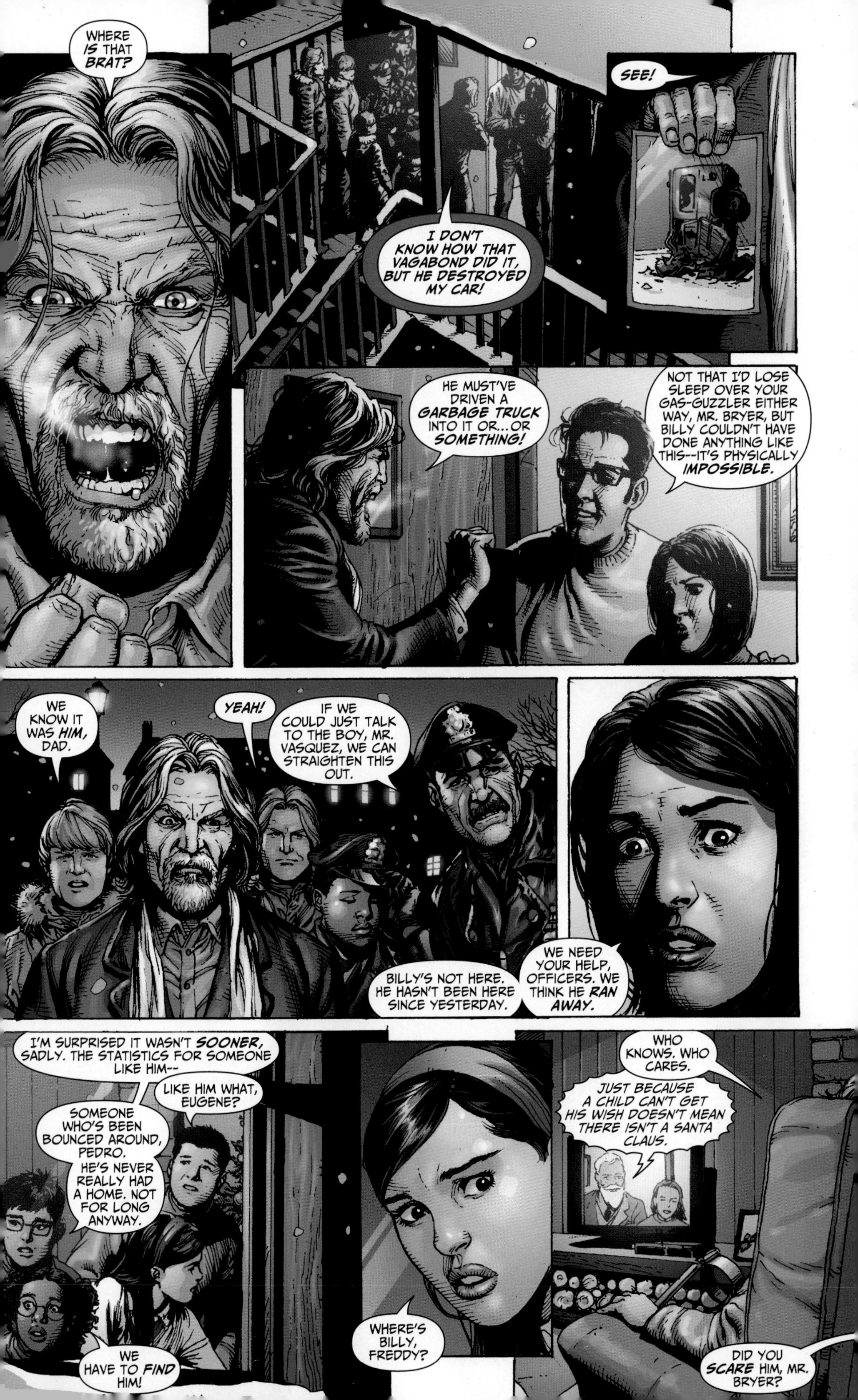
WHERE IS THAT BRAT?
I DON'T KNOW HOW THAT VAGABOND DID IT, BUT HE DESTROYED MY CAR!
SEE!
HE MUST'VE DRIVEN A GARBAGE TRUCK INTO IT OR...OR SOMETHING!
NOT THAT I'D LOSE SLEEP OVER YOUR GAS-GUZZLER EITHER WAY, MR. BRYER, BUT BILLY COULDN'T HAVE DONE ANYTHING LIKE THIS--IT'S PHYSICALLY IMPOSSIBLE.
WE KNOW IT WAS HIM, DAD.
YEAH!
IF WE COULD JUST TALK TO THE BOY, MR. VASQUEZ, WE CAN STRAIGHTEN THIS OUT.
BILLY'S NOT HERE. HE HASN'T BEEN HERE SINCE YESTERDAY.
WE NEED YOUR HELP, OFFICERS. WE THINK HE RAN AWAY.
I'M SURPRISED IT WASN'T SOONER, SADLY. THE STATISTICS FOR SOMEONE LIKE HIM--
LIKE HIM WHAT, EUGENE?
SOMEONE WHO'S BEEN BOUNCED AROUND, PEDRO.
HE'S NEVER REALLY HAD A HOME. NOT FOR LONG ANYWAY.
WE HAVE TO FIND HIM!
WHERE'S BILLY, FREDDY?
WHO KNOWS. WHO CARES.
JUST BECAUSE A CHILD CAN'T GET HIS WISH DOESN'T MEAN THERE ISN'T A SANTA CLAUS.
DID YOU SCARE HIM, MR. BRYER?

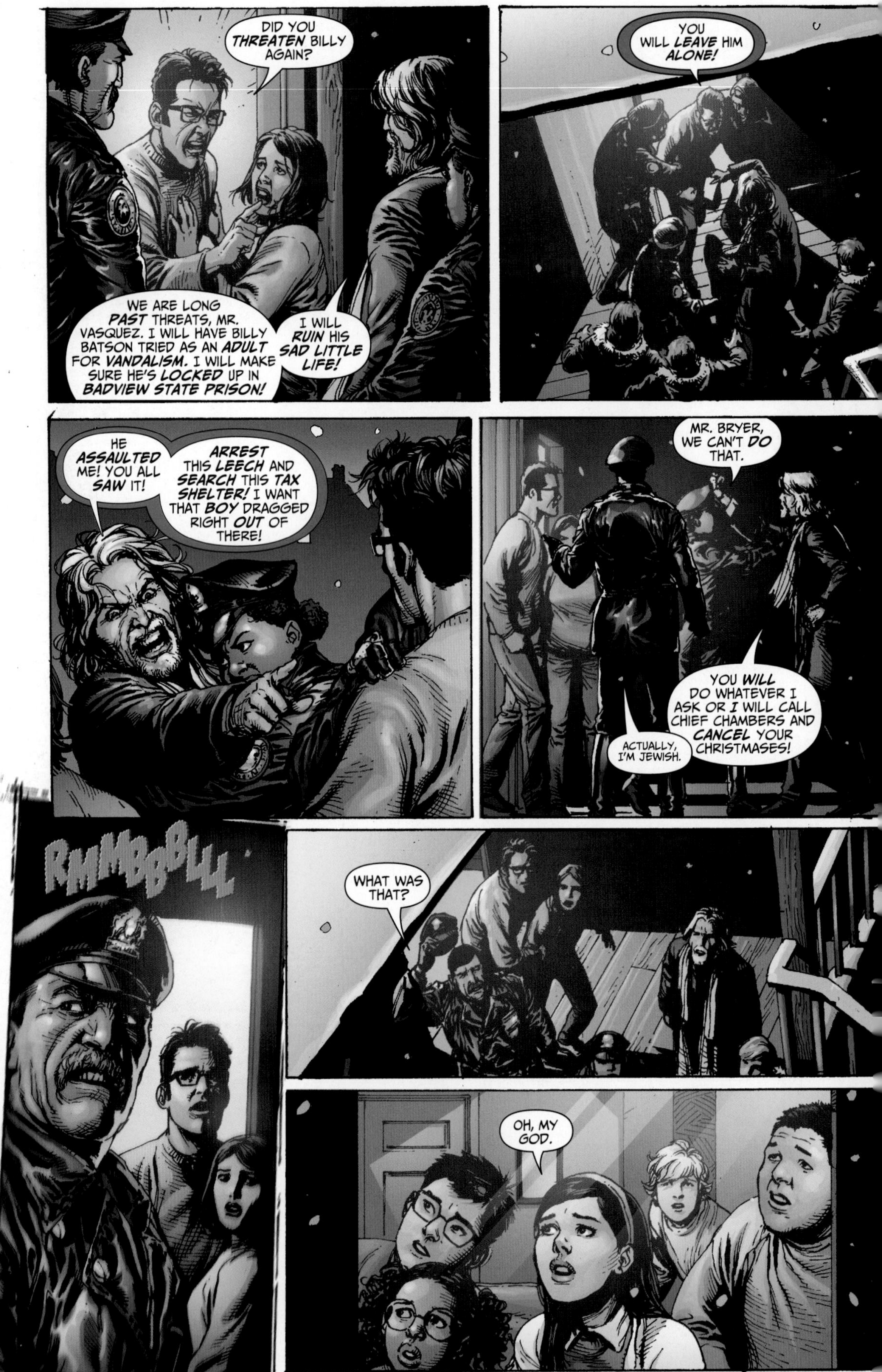
DID YOU THREATEN BILLY AGAIN?
WE ARE LONG PAST THREATS, MR. VASQUEZ. I WILL HAVE BILLY BATSON TRIED AS AN ADULT FOR VANDALISM. I WILL MAKE SURE HE'S LOCKED UP IN BADVIEW STATE PRISON!
I WILL RUIN HIS SAD LITTLE LIFE!
YOU WILL LEAVE HIM ALONE!
HE ASSAULTED ME! YOU ALL SAW IT!
ARREST THIS LEECH AND SEARCH THIS TAX SHELTER! I WANT THAT BOY DRAGGED RIGHT OUT OF THERE!
MR. BRYER, WE CAN'T DO THAT.
YOU WILL DO WHATEVER I ASK OR I WILL CALL CHIEF CHAMBERS AND CANCEL YOUR CHRISTMASES!
ACTUALLY, I'M JEWISH.
RMMBBLL
WHAT WAS THAT?
OH, MY GOD.

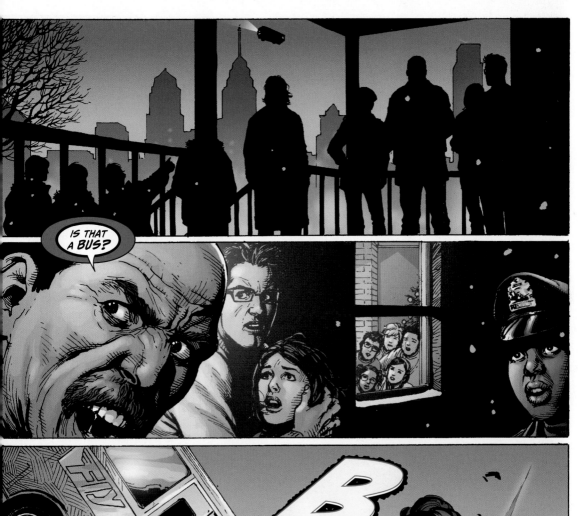

IS THAT A BUS?

BOOOOOOOMM

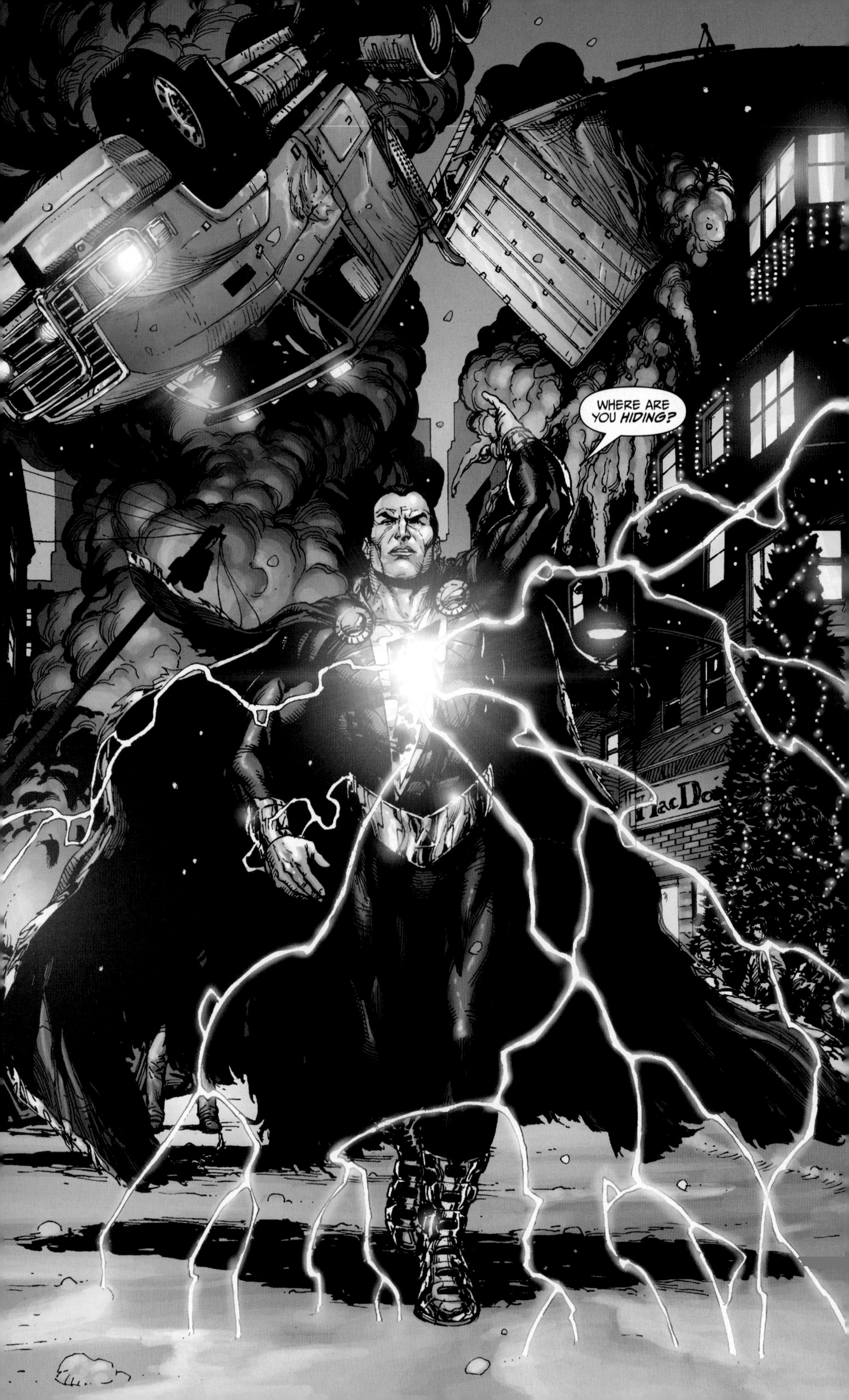
WHERE ARE YOU HIDING?

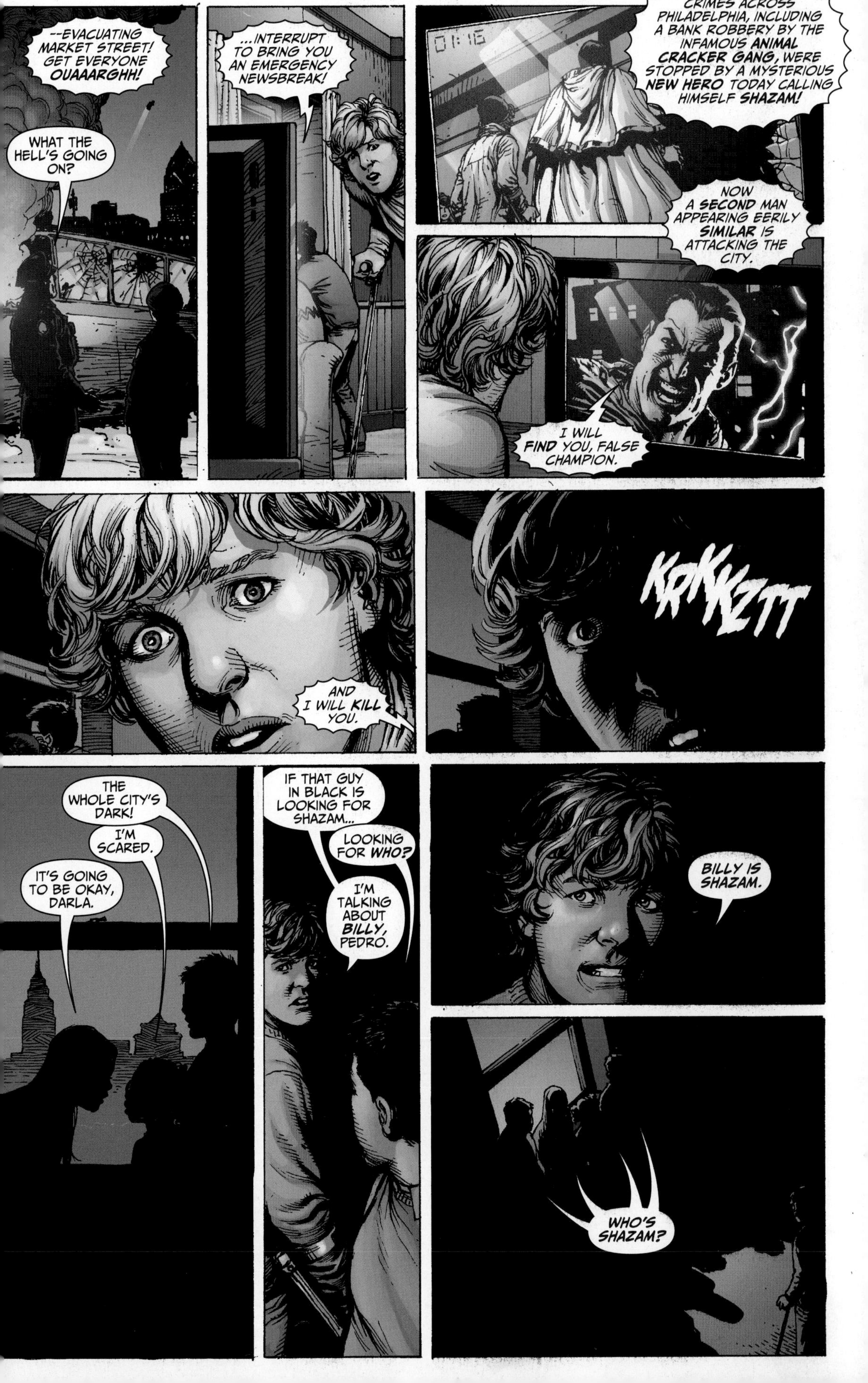
--EVACUATING MARKET STREET! GET EVERYONE OUAAARGHH!
WHAT THE HELL'S GOING ON?
...INTERRUPT TO BRING YOU AN EMERGENCY NEWSBREAK!
SEVERAL CRIMES ACROSS PHILADELPHIA, INCLUDING A BANK ROBBERY BY THE INFAMOUS ANIMAL CRACKER GANG, WERE STOPPED BY A MYSTERIOUS NEW HERO TODAY CALLING HIMSELF SHAZAM!
01:16
NOW A SECOND MAN APPEARING EERILY SIMILAR IS ATTACKING THE CITY.
I WILL FIND YOU, FALSE CHAMPION.
AND I WILL KILL YOU.
KRKKZTT
THE WHOLE CITY'S DARK!
I'M SCARED.
IT'S GOING TO BE OKAY, DARLA.
IF THAT GUY IN BLACK IS LOOKING FOR SHAZAM...
LOOKING FOR WHO?
I'M TALKING ABOUT BILLY, PEDRO.
BILLY IS SHAZAM.
WHO'S SHAZAM?

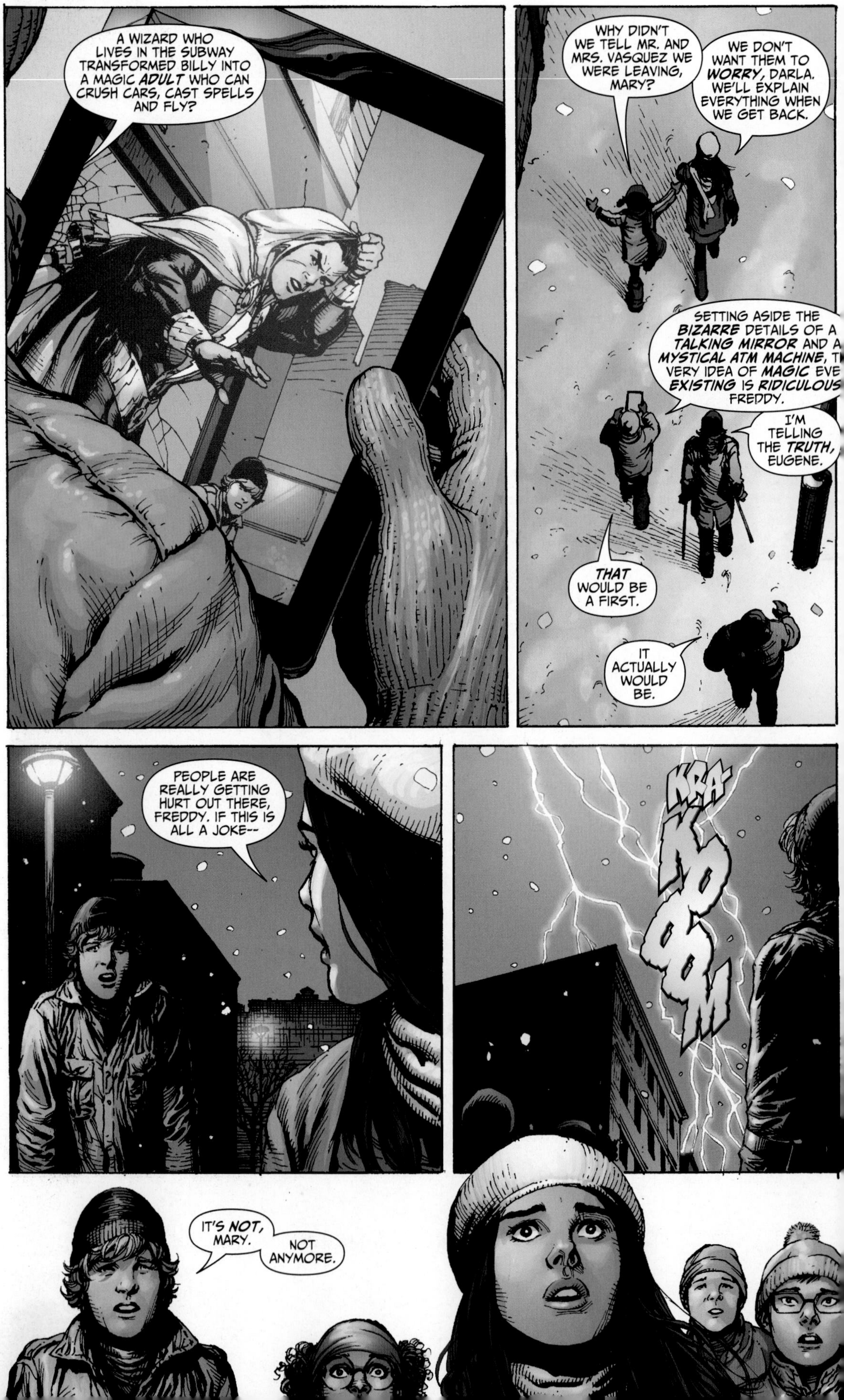
A WIZARD WHO LIVES IN THE SUBWAY TRANSFORMED BILLY INTO A MAGIC ADULT WHO CAN CRUSH CARS, CAST SPELLS AND FLY?
WHY DIDN'T WE TELL MR. AND MRS. VASQUEZ WE WERE LEAVING, MARY?
WE DON'T WANT THEM TO WORRY, DARLA. WE'LL EXPLAIN EVERYTHING WHEN WE GET BACK.
SETTING ASIDE THE BIZARRE DETAILS OF A TALKING MIRROR AND A MYSTICAL ATM MACHINE, THE VERY IDEA OF MAGIC EVER EXISTING IS RIDICULOUS, FREDDY.
I'M TELLING THE TRUTH, EUGENE.
THAT WOULD BE A FIRST.
IT ACTUALLY WOULD BE.
PEOPLE ARE REALLY GETTING HURT OUT THERE, FREDDY. IF THIS IS ALL A JOKE--
KRA-KOOOM
IT'S NOT, MARY.
NOT ANYMORE.

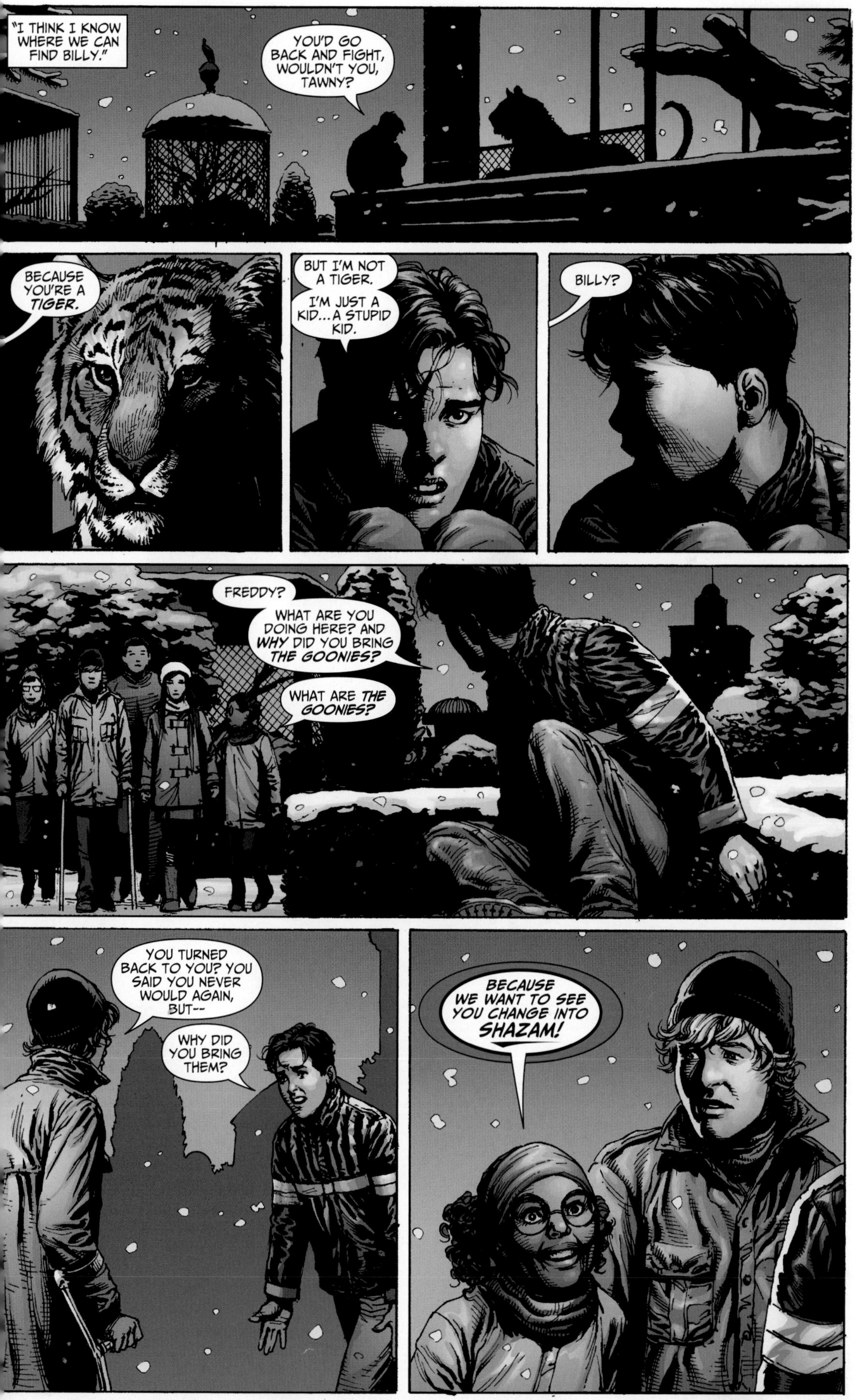
"I THINK I KNOW WHERE WE CAN FIND BILLY."
YOU'D GO BACK AND FIGHT, WOULDN'T YOU, TAWNY?
BECAUSE YOU'RE A *TIGER.*
BUT I'M NOT A TIGER.
I'M JUST A KID... A STUPID KID.
BILLY?
FREDDY?
WHAT ARE YOU DOING HERE? AND *WHY* DID YOU BRING *THE GOONIES?*
WHAT ARE *THE GOONIES?*
YOU TURNED BACK TO YOU? YOU SAID YOU NEVER WOULD AGAIN, BUT--
WHY DID YOU BRING THEM?
BECAUSE WE WANT TO SEE YOU CHANGE INTO ***SHAZAM!***

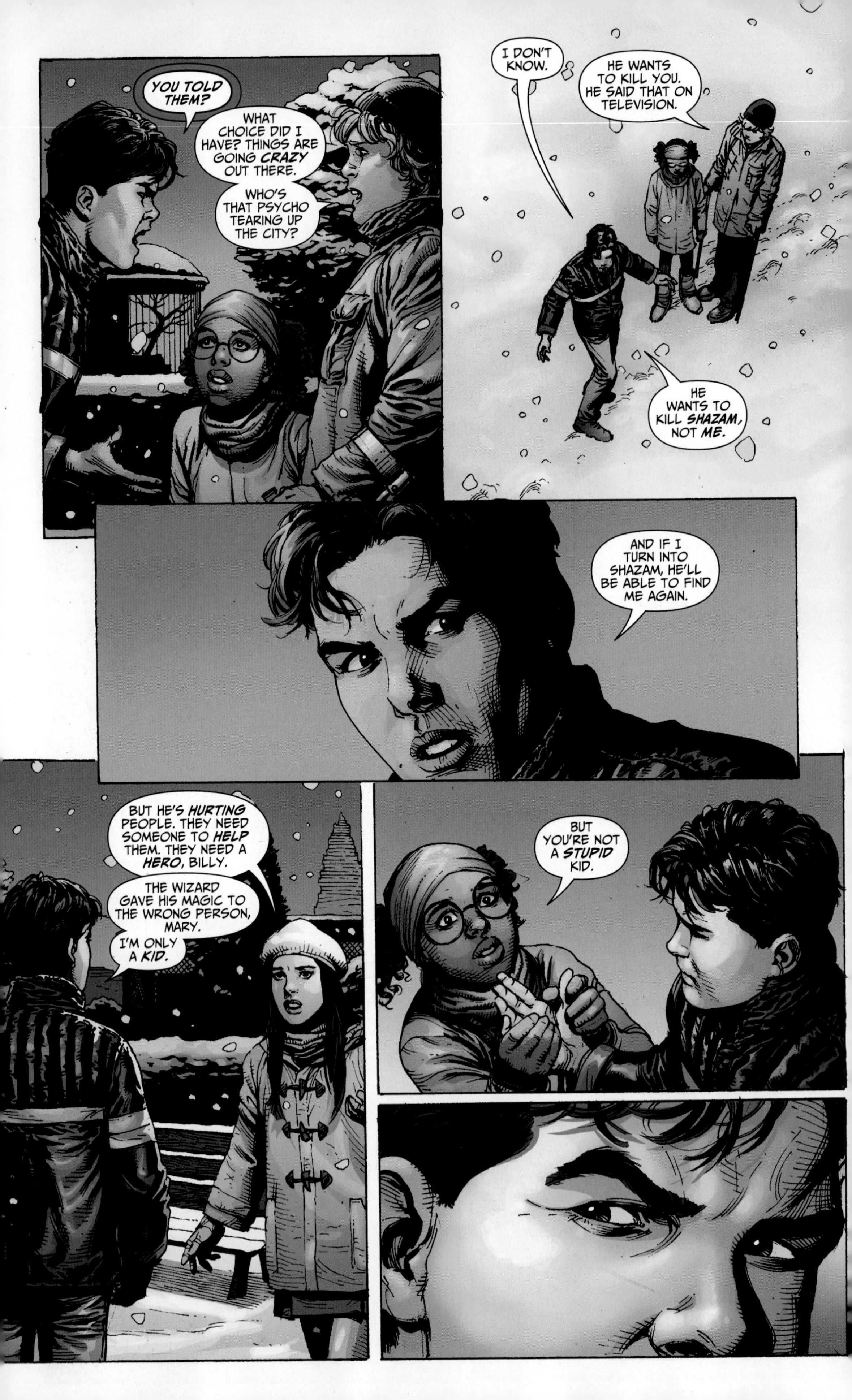
YOU TOLD THEM?
WHAT CHOICE DID I HAVE? THINGS ARE GOING CRAZY OUT THERE.
WHO'S THAT PSYCHO TEARING UP THE CITY?
I DON'T KNOW.
HE WANTS TO KILL YOU. HE SAID THAT ON TELEVISION.
HE WANTS TO KILL SHAZAM, NOT ME.
AND IF I TURN INTO SHAZAM, HE'LL BE ABLE TO FIND ME AGAIN.
BUT HE'S HURTING PEOPLE. THEY NEED SOMEONE TO HELP THEM. THEY NEED A HERO, BILLY.
THE WIZARD GAVE HIS MAGIC TO THE WRONG PERSON, MARY.
I'M ONLY A KID.
BUT YOU'RE NOT A STUPID KID.

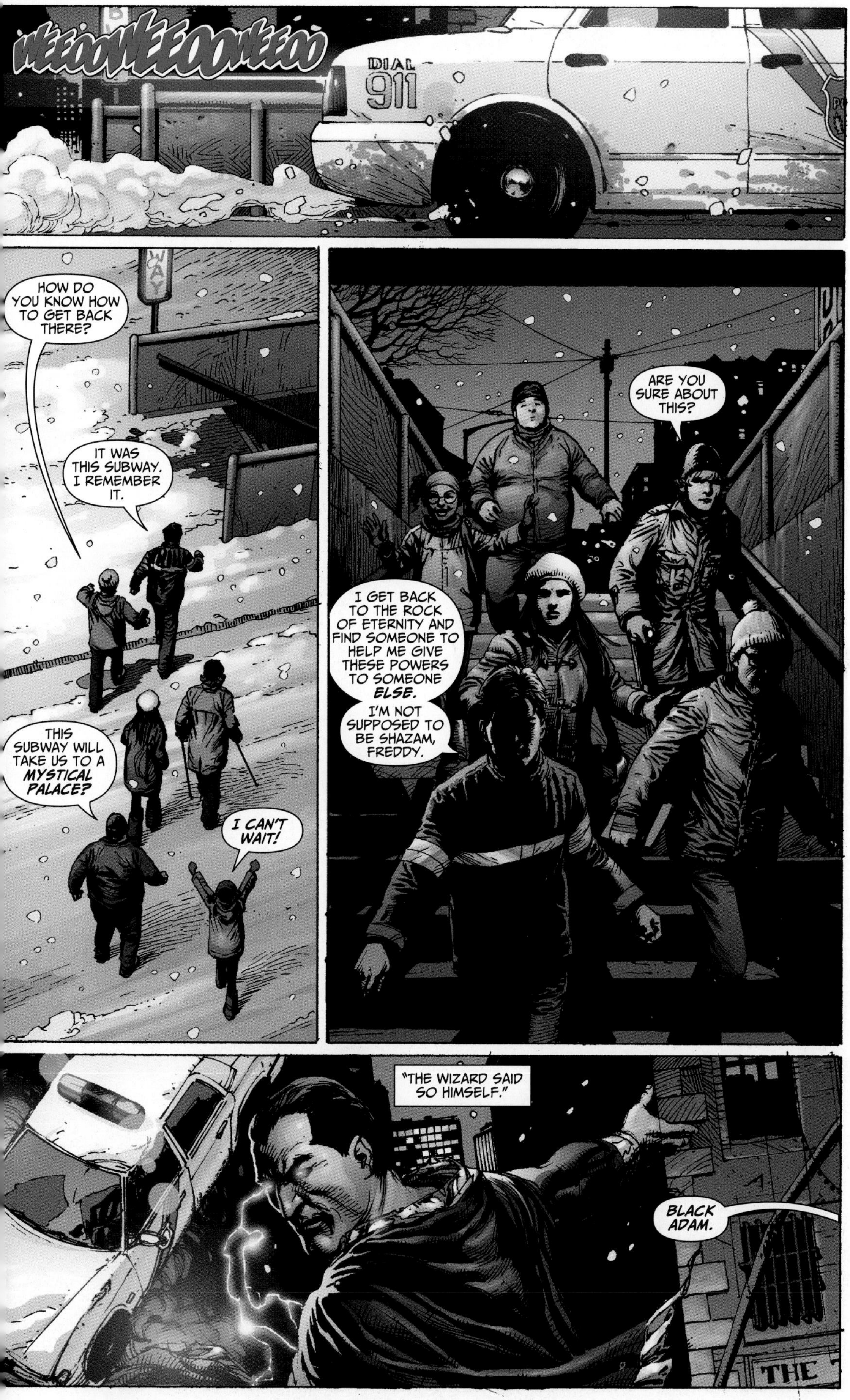
WEEOOWEEOOWEEOO
DIAL 911
HOW DO YOU KNOW HOW TO GET BACK THERE?
IT WAS THIS SUBWAY. I REMEMBER IT.
THIS SUBWAY WILL TAKE US TO A *MYSTICAL PALACE?*
I CAN'T WAIT!
ARE YOU SURE ABOUT THIS?
I GET BACK TO THE ROCK OF ETERNITY AND FIND SOMEONE TO HELP ME GIVE THESE POWERS TO SOMEONE *ELSE.*
I'M NOT SUPPOSED TO BE SHAZAM, FREDDY.
"THE WIZARD SAID SO HIMSELF."
BLACK ADAM.
THE

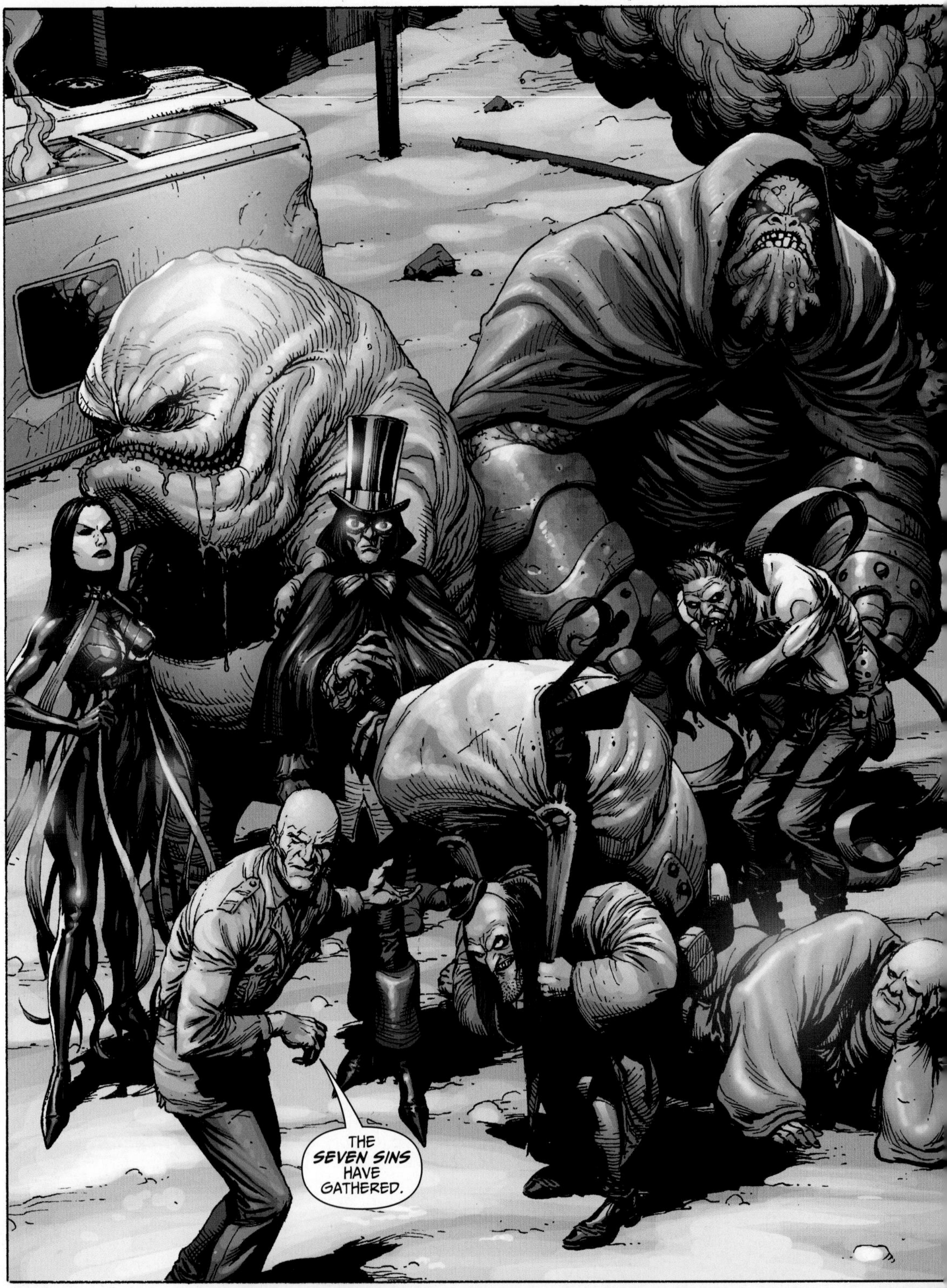
THE SEVEN SINS HAVE GATHERED.

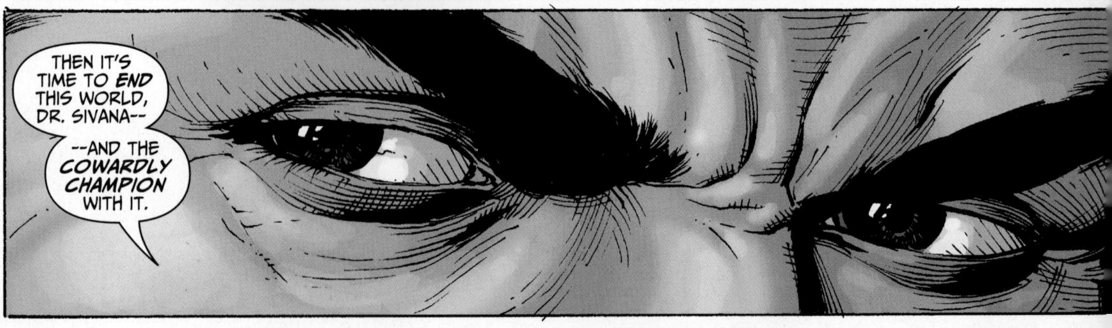
THEN IT'S TIME TO END THIS WORLD, DR. SIVANA--
--AND THE COWARDLY CHAMPION WITH IT.

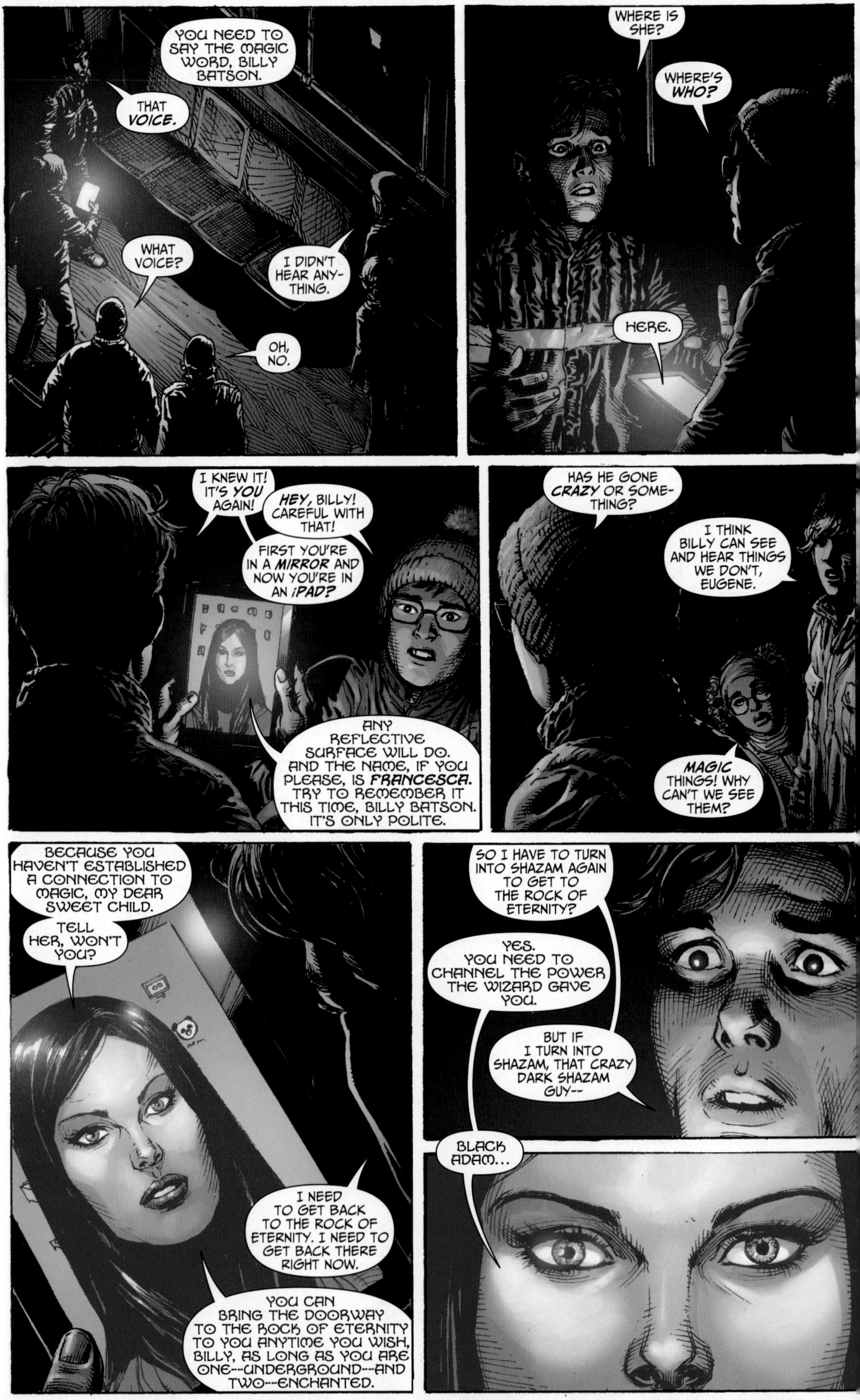

YOU NEED TO SAY THE MAGIC WORD, BILLY BATSON.
THAT VOICE.
WHAT VOICE?
I DIDN'T HEAR ANY-THING.
OH, NO.
WHERE IS SHE?
WHERE'S WHO?
HERE.
I KNEW IT! IT'S YOU AGAIN!
HEY, BILLY! CAREFUL WITH THAT!
FIRST YOU'RE IN A MIRROR AND NOW YOU'RE IN AN iPAD?
ANY REFLECTIVE SURFACE WILL DO. AND THE NAME, IF YOU PLEASE, IS FRANCESCA. TRY TO REMEMBER IT THIS TIME, BILLY BATSON. IT'S ONLY POLITE.
HAS HE GONE CRAZY OR SOME-THING?
I THINK BILLY CAN SEE AND HEAR THINGS WE DON'T, EUGENE.
MAGIC THINGS! WHY CAN'T WE SEE THEM?
BECAUSE YOU HAVEN'T ESTABLISHED A CONNECTION TO MAGIC, MY DEAR SWEET CHILD.
TELL HER, WON'T YOU?
I NEED TO GET BACK TO THE ROCK OF ETERNITY. I NEED TO GET BACK THERE RIGHT NOW.
YOU CAN BRING THE DOORWAY TO THE ROCK OF ETERNITY TO YOU ANYTIME YOU WISH, BILLY, AS LONG AS YOU ARE ONE--UNDERGROUND--AND TWO--ENCHANTED.
SO I HAVE TO TURN INTO SHAZAM AGAIN TO GET TO THE ROCK OF ETERNITY?
YES. YOU NEED TO CHANNEL THE POWER THE WIZARD GAVE YOU.
BUT IF I TURN INTO SHAZAM, THAT CRAZY DARK SHAZAM GUY--
BLACK ADAM...

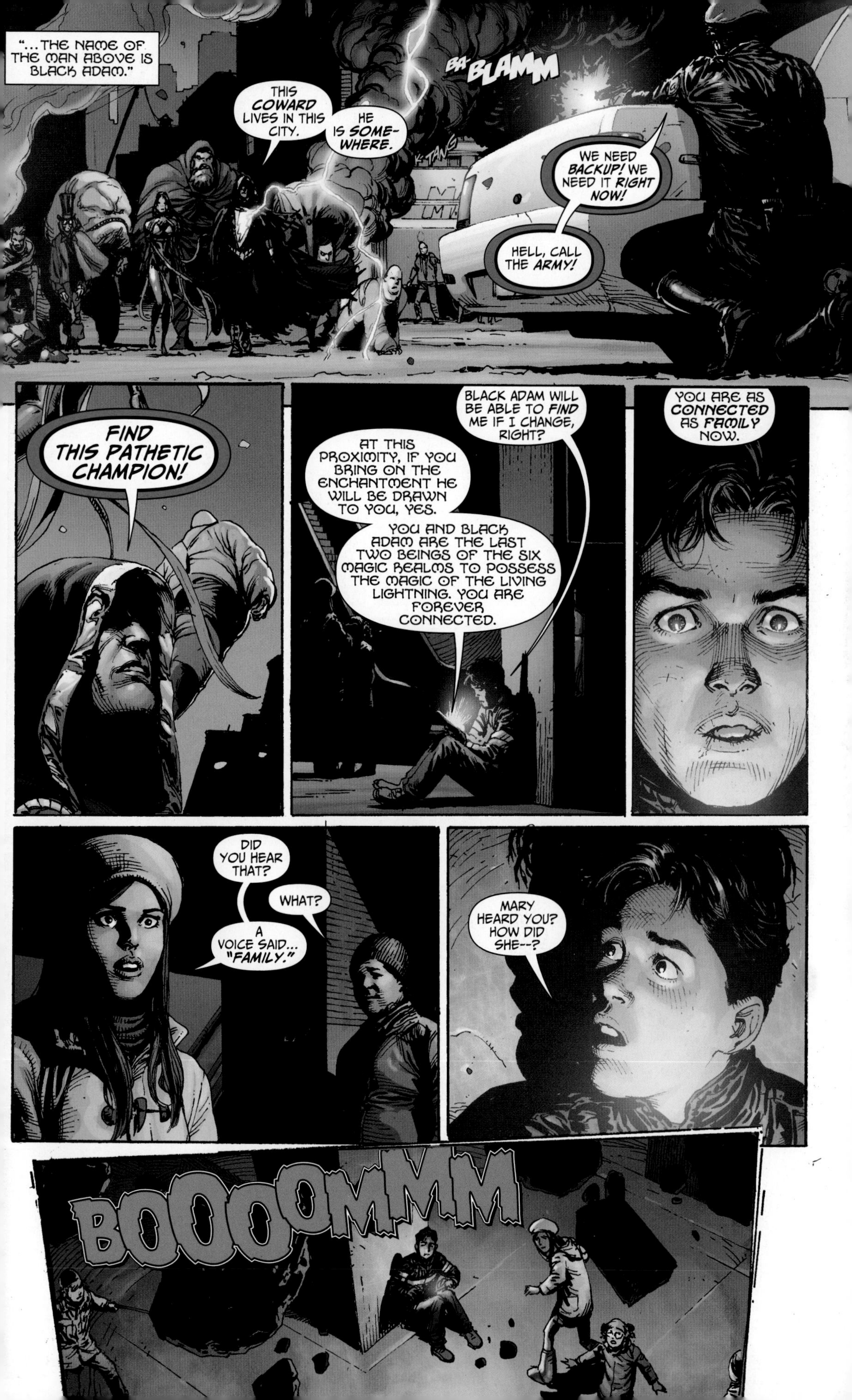
"...THE NAME OF THE MAN ABOVE IS BLACK ADAM."
THIS COWARD LIVES IN THIS CITY.
HE IS SOME-WHERE.
BA-BLAMM
K-TANG
WE NEED BACKUP! WE NEED IT RIGHT NOW!
HELL, CALL THE ARMY!
FIND THIS PATHETIC CHAMPION!
BLACK ADAM WILL BE ABLE TO FIND ME IF I CHANGE, RIGHT?
AT THIS PROXIMITY, IF YOU BRING ON THE ENCHANTMENT HE WILL BE DRAWN TO YOU, YES.
YOU AND BLACK ADAM ARE THE LAST TWO BEINGS OF THE SIX MAGIC REALMS TO POSSESS THE MAGIC OF THE LIVING LIGHTNING. YOU ARE FOREVER CONNECTED.
YOU ARE AS CONNECTED AS FAMILY NOW.
DID YOU HEAR THAT?
WHAT?
A VOICE SAID... "FAMILY."
MARY HEARD YOU? HOW DID SHE--?
BOOOOMMM

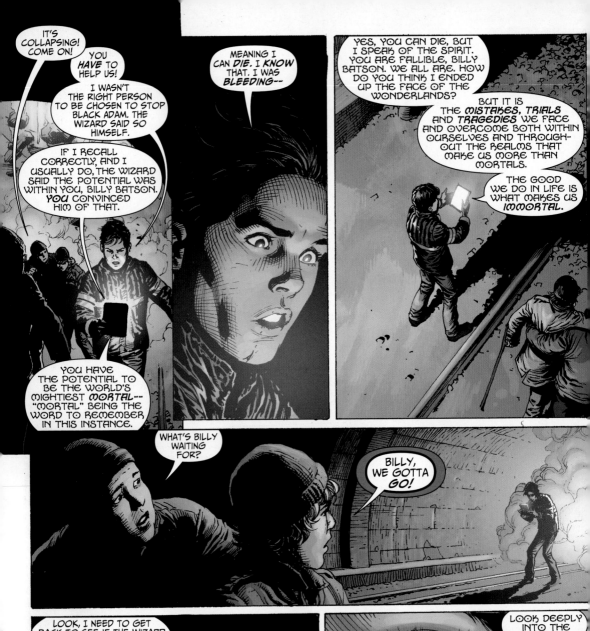

IT'S COLLAPSING! COME ON!

YOU *HAVE* TO HELP US!

I WASN'T THE RIGHT PERSON TO BE CHOSEN TO STOP BLACK ADAM. THE WIZARD SAID SO HIMSELF.

IF I RECALL CORRECTLY, AND I USUALLY DO, THE WIZARD SAID THE POTENTIAL WAS WITHIN YOU, BILLY BATSON. *YOU* CONVINCED HIM OF THAT.

YOU HAVE THE POTENTIAL TO BE THE WORLD'S MIGHTIEST *MORTAL*-- "MORTAL" BEING THE WORD TO REMEMBER IN THIS INSTANCE.

MEANING I CAN *DIE*. I *KNOW* THAT. I WAS *BLEEDING*--

YES, YOU CAN DIE, BUT I SPEAK OF THE SPIRIT. YOU ARE FALLIBLE, BILLY BATSON. WE ALL ARE. HOW DO YOU THINK I ENDED UP THE FACE OF THE WONDERLANDS?

BUT IT IS THE *MISTAKES, TRIALS* AND *TRAGEDIES* WE FACE AND OVERCOME BOTH WITHIN OURSELVES AND THROUGH-OUT THE REALMS THAT MAKE US MORE THAN MORTALS.

THE GOOD WE DO IN LIFE IS WHAT MAKES US *IMMORTAL*.

WHAT'S BILLY WAITING FOR?

BILLY, WE GOTTA *GO!*

LOOK, I NEED TO GET BACK TO SEE IF THE WIZARD IS STILL ALIVE. IF HE IS, HE CAN TAKE THESE POWERS BACK AND GIVE THEM TO SOME-ONE WHO KNOWS WHAT THEY'RE DOING.

EVEN IF HE WERE STILL ALIVE, ONCE THE WIZARD BESTOWS THE CONNECTION TO THE LIVING LIGHTNING IT CANNOT BE *SEVERED*.

THAT'S WHY BLACK ADAM STILL HOLDS THE POWER. THAT'S WHY YOU ARE THE ONLY ONE LEFT TO STOP HIM.

WELL, WHO THE HELL *IS* HE ANYWAY? WHAT DOES HE WANT?

LOOK DEEPLY INTO THE MIRROR...

...AND I'LL SHOW YOU.

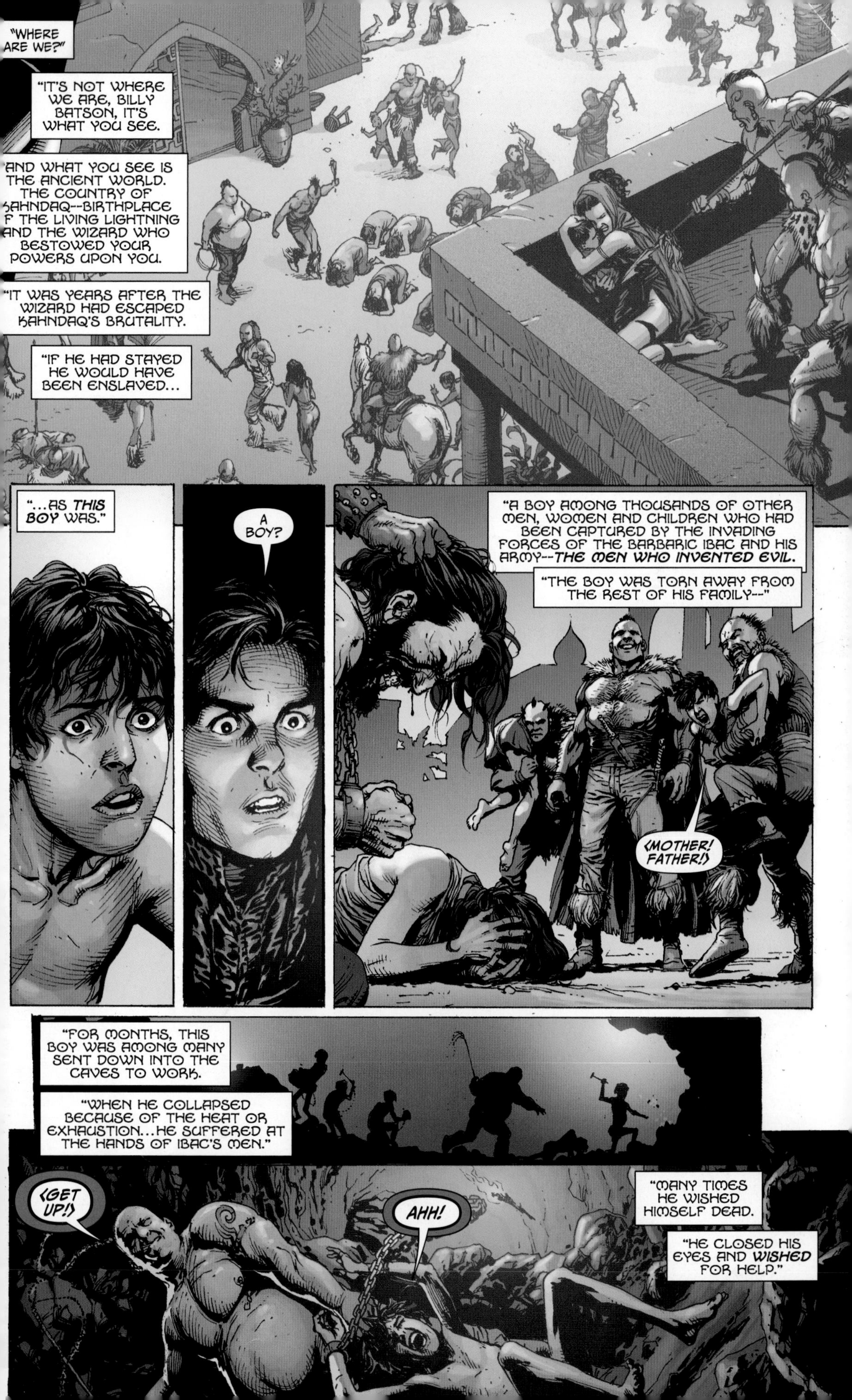
"WHERE ARE WE?"
"IT'S NOT WHERE WE ARE, BILLY BATSON, IT'S WHAT YOU SEE.
"AND WHAT YOU SEE IS THE ANCIENT WORLD. THE COUNTRY OF KAHNDAQ--BIRTHPLACE OF THE LIVING LIGHTNING AND THE WIZARD WHO BESTOWED YOUR POWERS UPON YOU.
"IT WAS YEARS AFTER THE WIZARD HAD ESCAPED KAHNDAQ'S BRUTALITY.
"IF HE HAD STAYED HE WOULD HAVE BEEN ENSLAVED...
"...AS THIS BOY WAS."
A BOY?
"A BOY AMONG THOUSANDS OF OTHER MEN, WOMEN AND CHILDREN WHO HAD BEEN CAPTURED BY THE INVADING FORCES OF THE BARBARIC IBAC AND HIS ARMY--THE MEN WHO INVENTED EVIL.
"THE BOY WAS TORN AWAY FROM THE REST OF HIS FAMILY--"
<MOTHER! FATHER!>
"FOR MONTHS, THIS BOY WAS AMONG MANY SENT DOWN INTO THE CAVES TO WORK.
"WHEN HE COLLAPSED BECAUSE OF THE HEAT OR EXHAUSTION...HE SUFFERED AT THE HANDS OF IBAC'S MEN."
<GET UP!>
AHH!
"MANY TIMES HE WISHED HIMSELF DEAD.
"HE CLOSED HIS EYES AND WISHED FOR HELP."

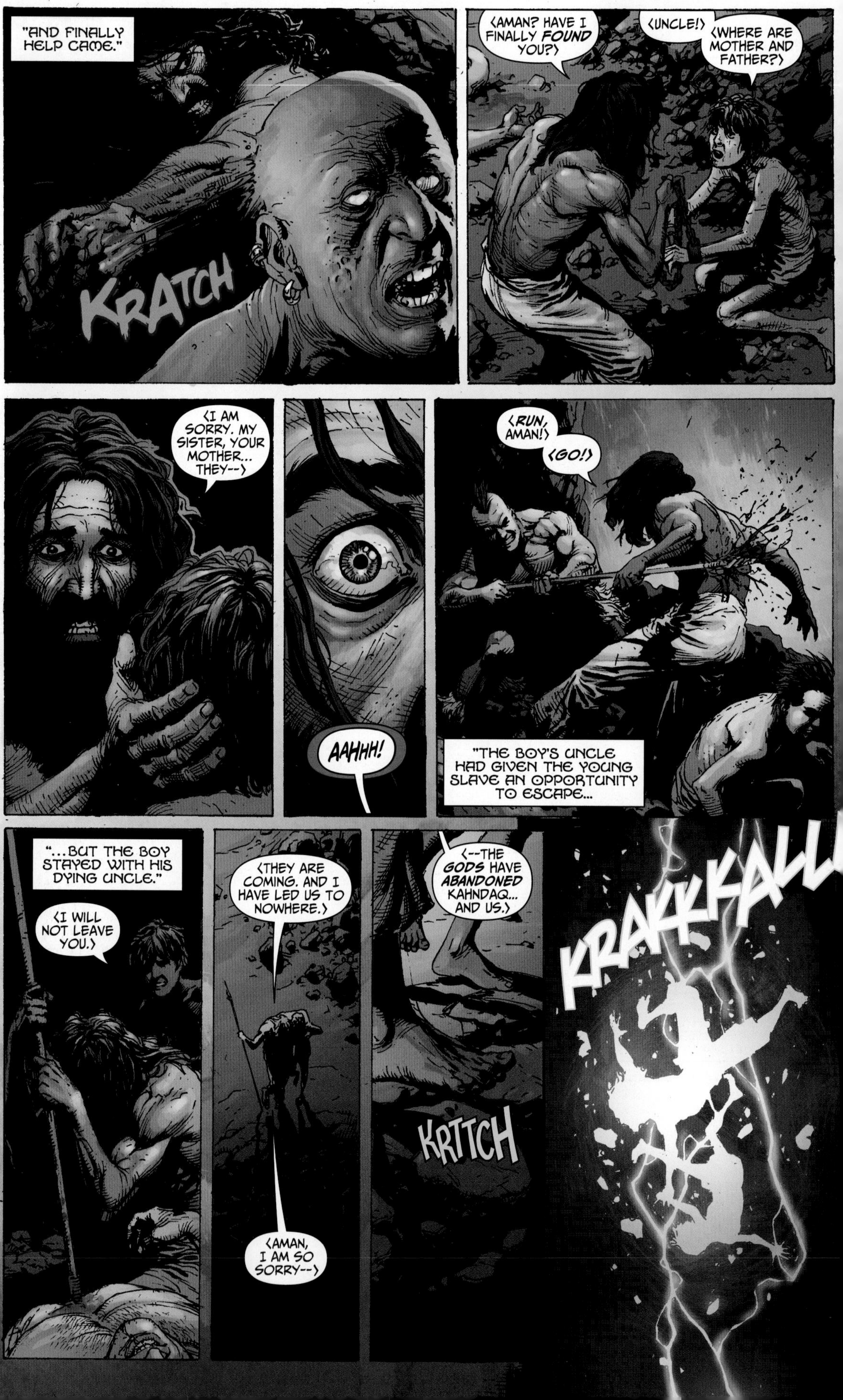
"AND FINALLY HELP CAME."
KRATCH
‹AMAN? HAVE I FINALLY FOUND YOU?›
‹UNCLE!›
‹WHERE ARE MOTHER AND FATHER?›
‹I AM SORRY. MY SISTER, YOUR MOTHER... THEY--›
AAHHH!
‹RUN, AMAN!›
‹GO!›
"THE BOY'S UNCLE HAD GIVEN THE YOUNG SLAVE AN OPPORTUNITY TO ESCAPE...
"...BUT THE BOY STAYED WITH HIS DYING UNCLE."
‹I WILL NOT LEAVE YOU.›
‹THEY ARE COMING. AND I HAVE LED US TO NOWHERE.›
‹AMAN, I AM SO SORRY--›
‹--THE GODS HAVE ABANDONED KAHNDAQ... AND US.›
KRITCH
KRAKKALL

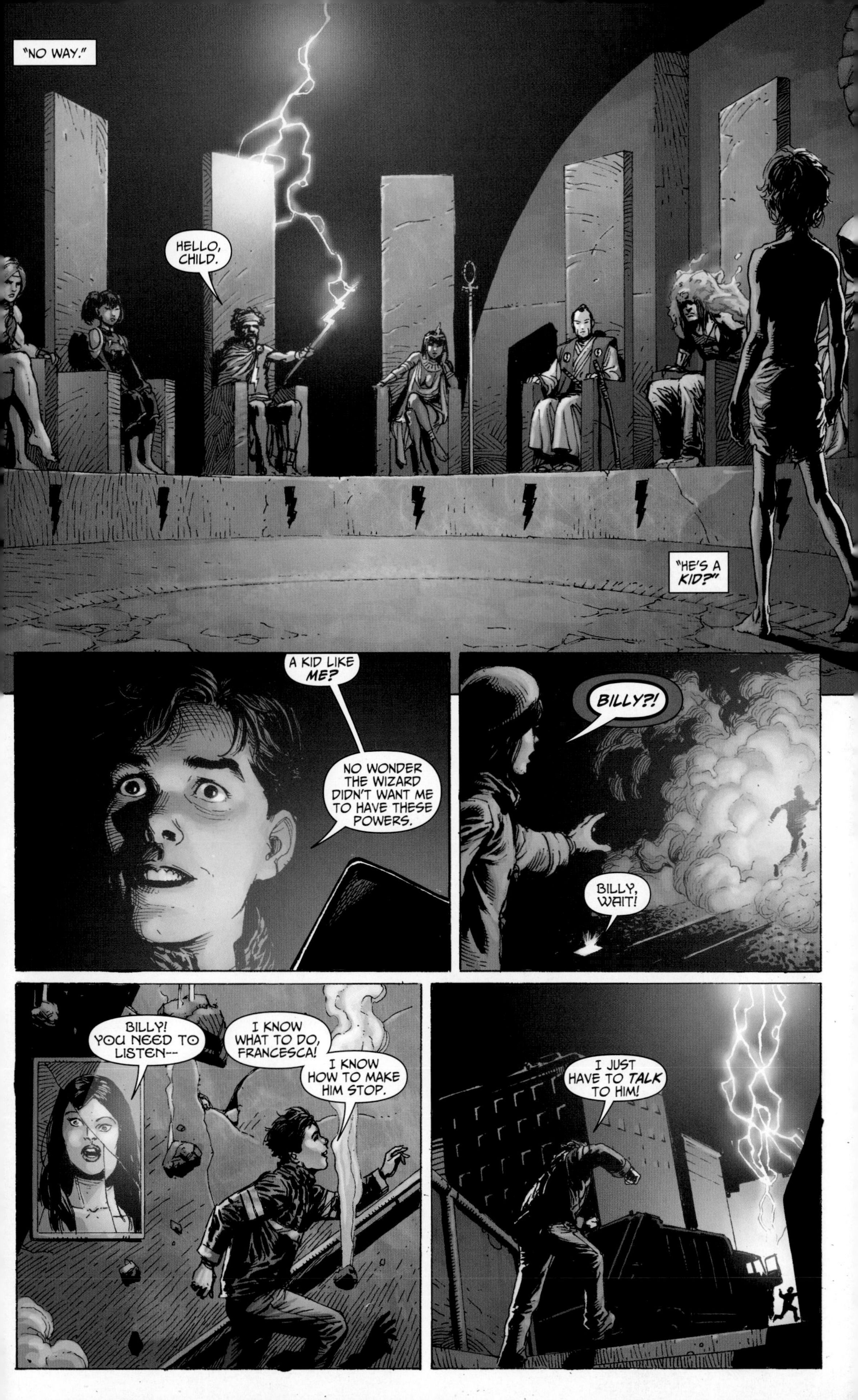
"NO WAY."
HELLO, CHILD.
"HE'S A KID?"
A KID LIKE ME?
NO WONDER THE WIZARD DIDN'T WANT ME TO HAVE THESE POWERS.
BILLY?!
BILLY, WAIT!
BILLY! YOU NEED TO LISTEN--
I KNOW WHAT TO DO, FRANCESCA!
I KNOW HOW TO MAKE HIM STOP.
I JUST HAVE TO TALK TO HIM!

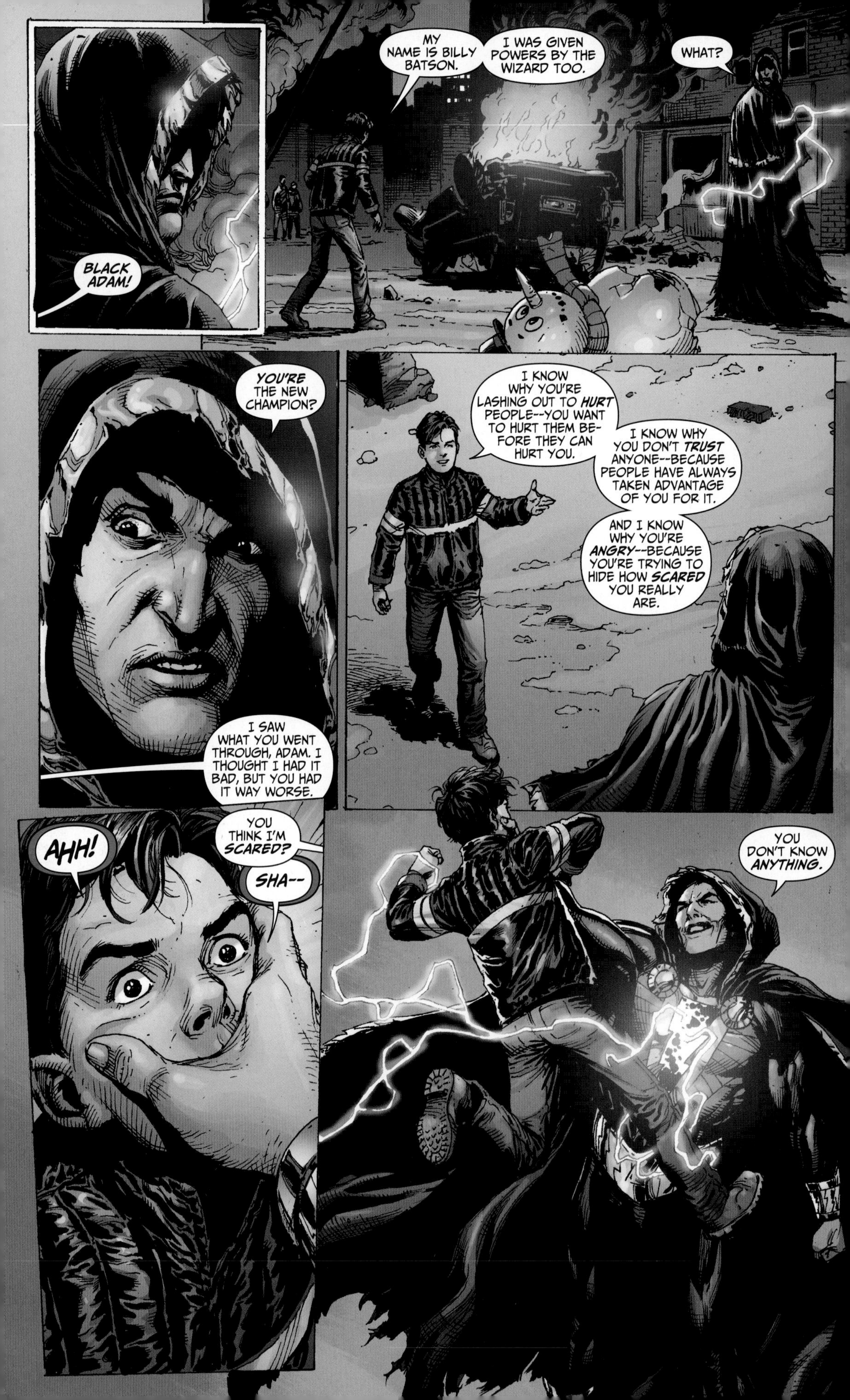

BLACK ADAM!
MY NAME IS BILLY BATSON.
I WAS GIVEN POWERS BY THE WIZARD TOO.
WHAT?
YOU'RE THE NEW CHAMPION?
I SAW WHAT YOU WENT THROUGH, ADAM. I THOUGHT I HAD IT BAD, BUT YOU HAD IT WAY WORSE.
I KNOW WHY YOU'RE LASHING OUT TO HURT PEOPLE--YOU WANT TO HURT THEM BEFORE THEY CAN HURT YOU.
I KNOW WHY YOU DON'T TRUST ANYONE--BECAUSE PEOPLE HAVE ALWAYS TAKEN ADVANTAGE OF YOU FOR IT.
AND I KNOW WHY YOU'RE ANGRY--BECAUSE YOU'RE TRYING TO HIDE HOW SCARED YOU REALLY ARE.
AHH!
YOU THINK I'M SCARED?
SHA--
YOU DON'T KNOW ANYTHING.

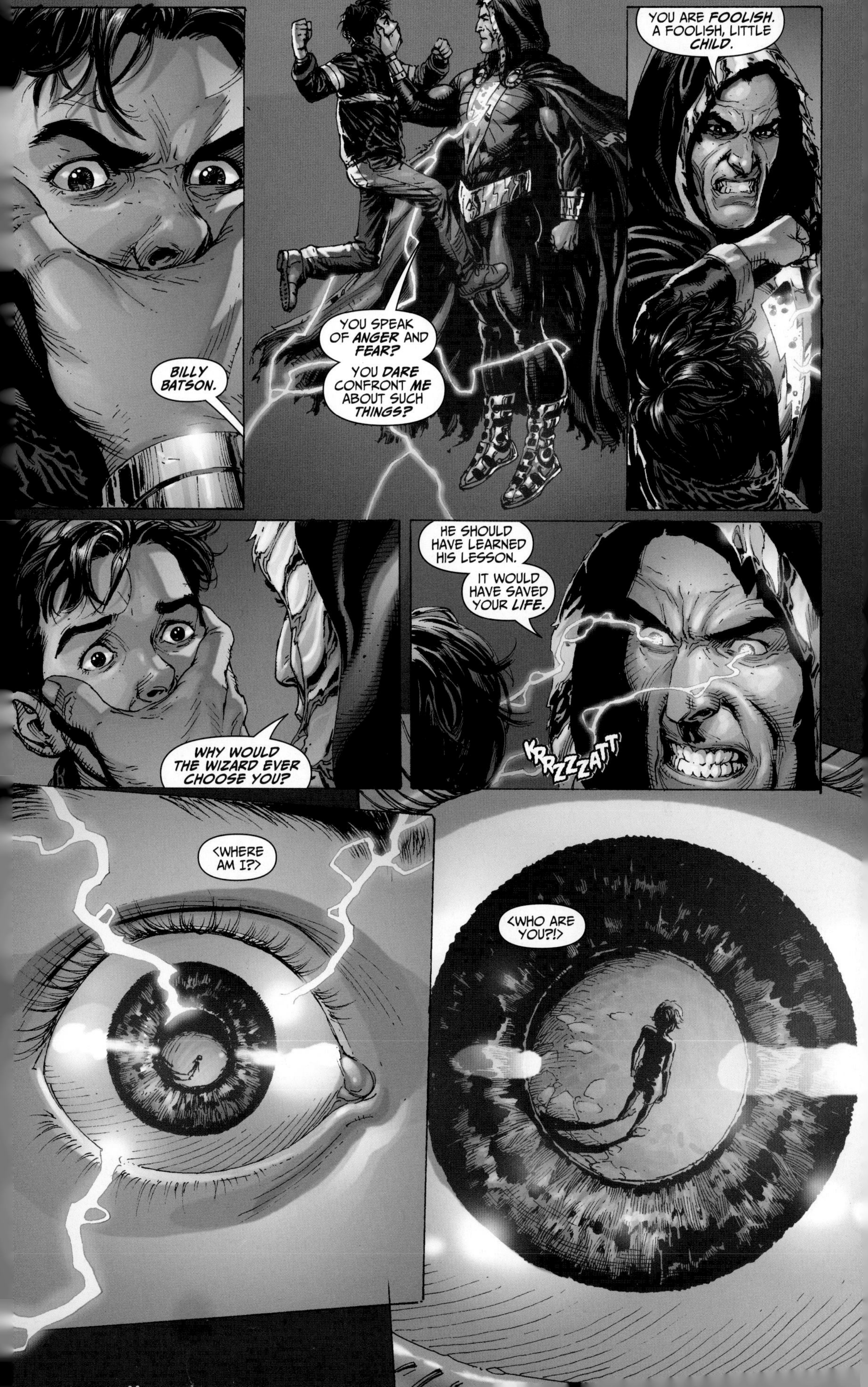
BILLY BATSON.
YOU SPEAK OF ANGER AND FEAR?
YOU DARE CONFRONT ME ABOUT SUCH THINGS?
YOU ARE FOOLISH. A FOOLISH, LITTLE CHILD.
WHY WOULD THE WIZARD EVER CHOOSE YOU?
HE SHOULD HAVE LEARNED HIS LESSON.
IT WOULD HAVE SAVED YOUR LIFE.
KRRZZZZATT
<WHERE AM I?>
<WHO ARE YOU?!>

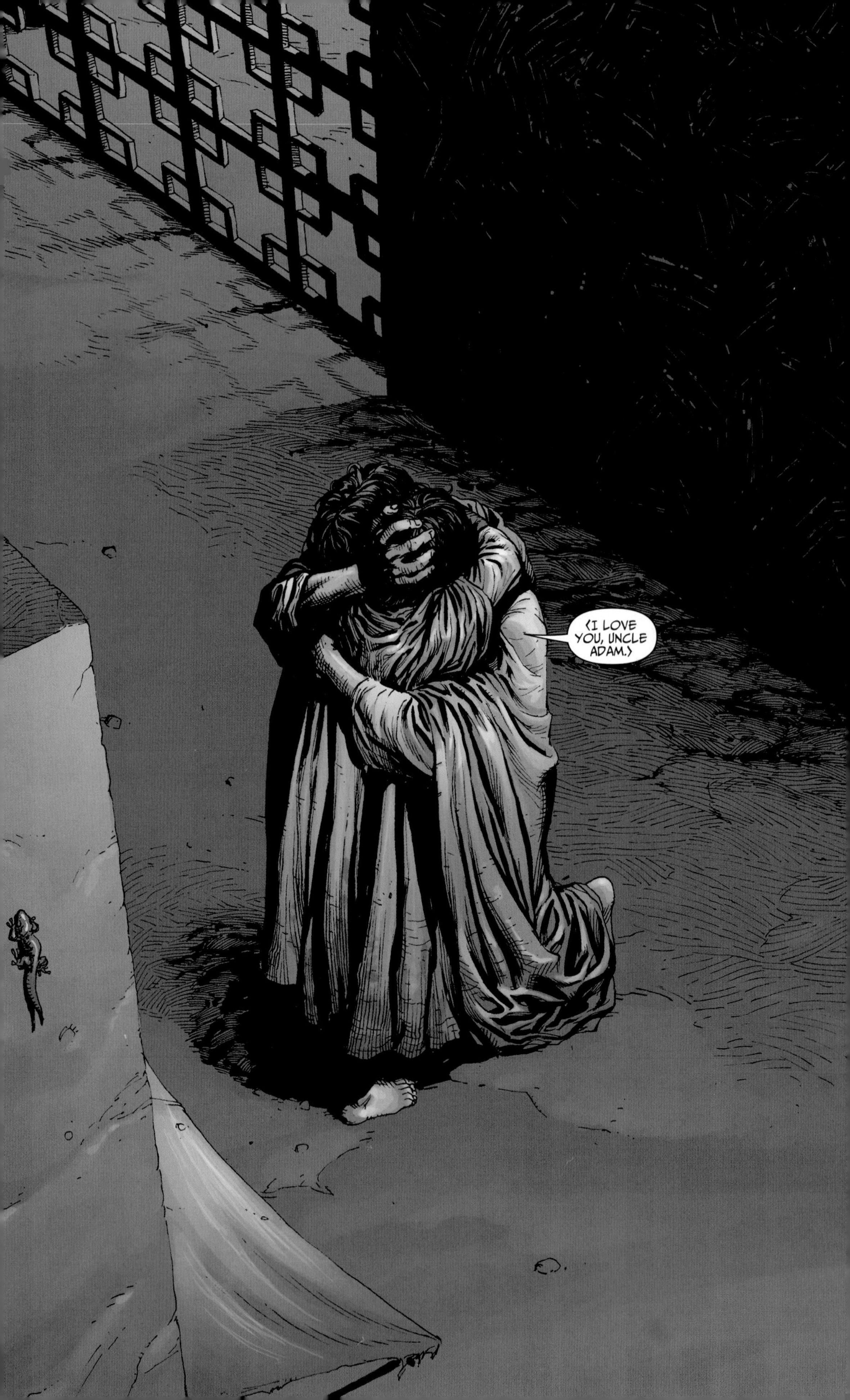
‹I LOVE YOU, UNCLE ADAM.›

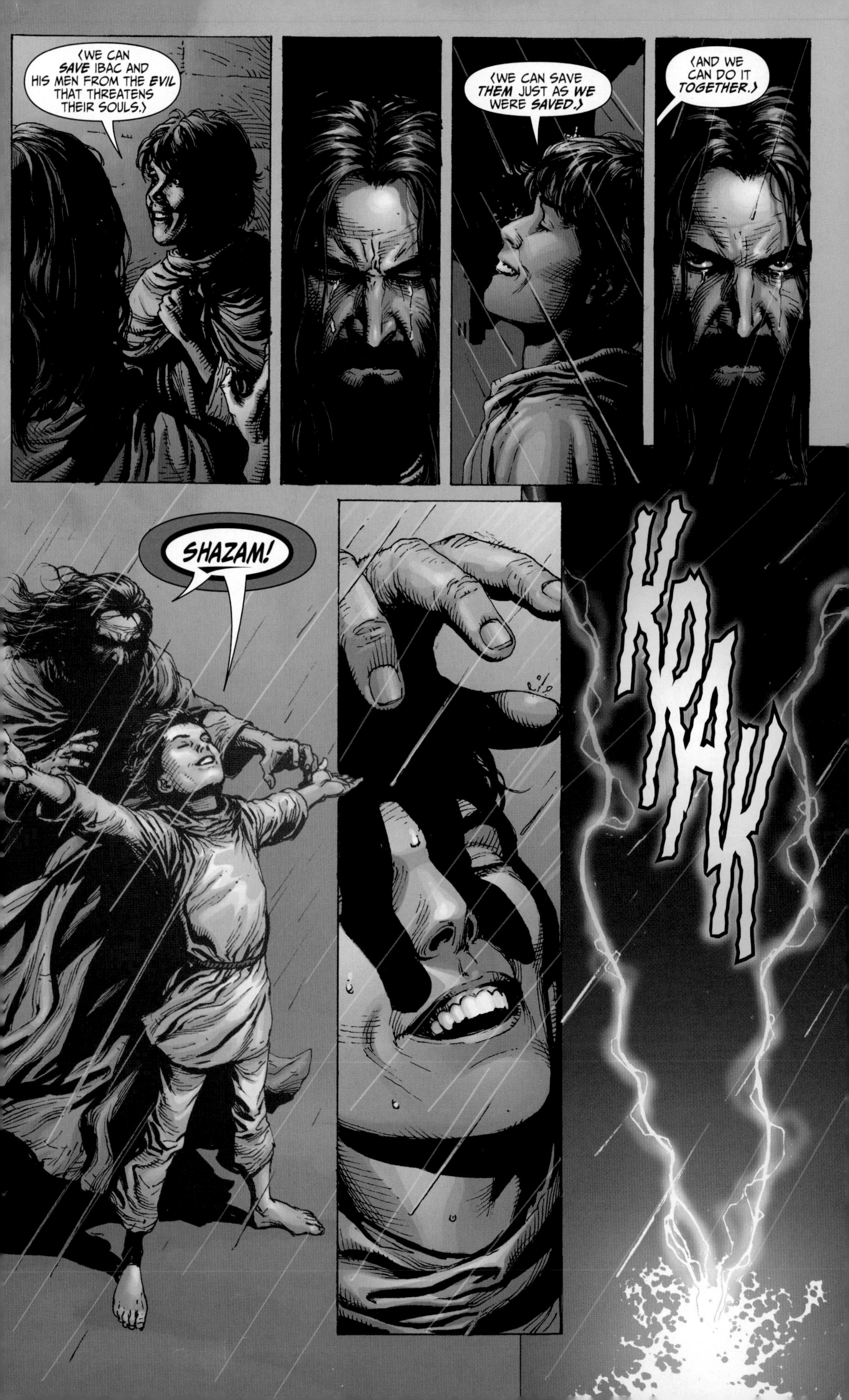

‹WE CAN SAVE IBAC AND HIS MEN FROM THE EVIL THAT THREATENS THEIR SOULS.›
‹WE CAN SAVE THEM JUST AS WE WERE SAVED.›
‹AND WE CAN DO IT TOGETHER.›
SHAZAM!
KRAKK

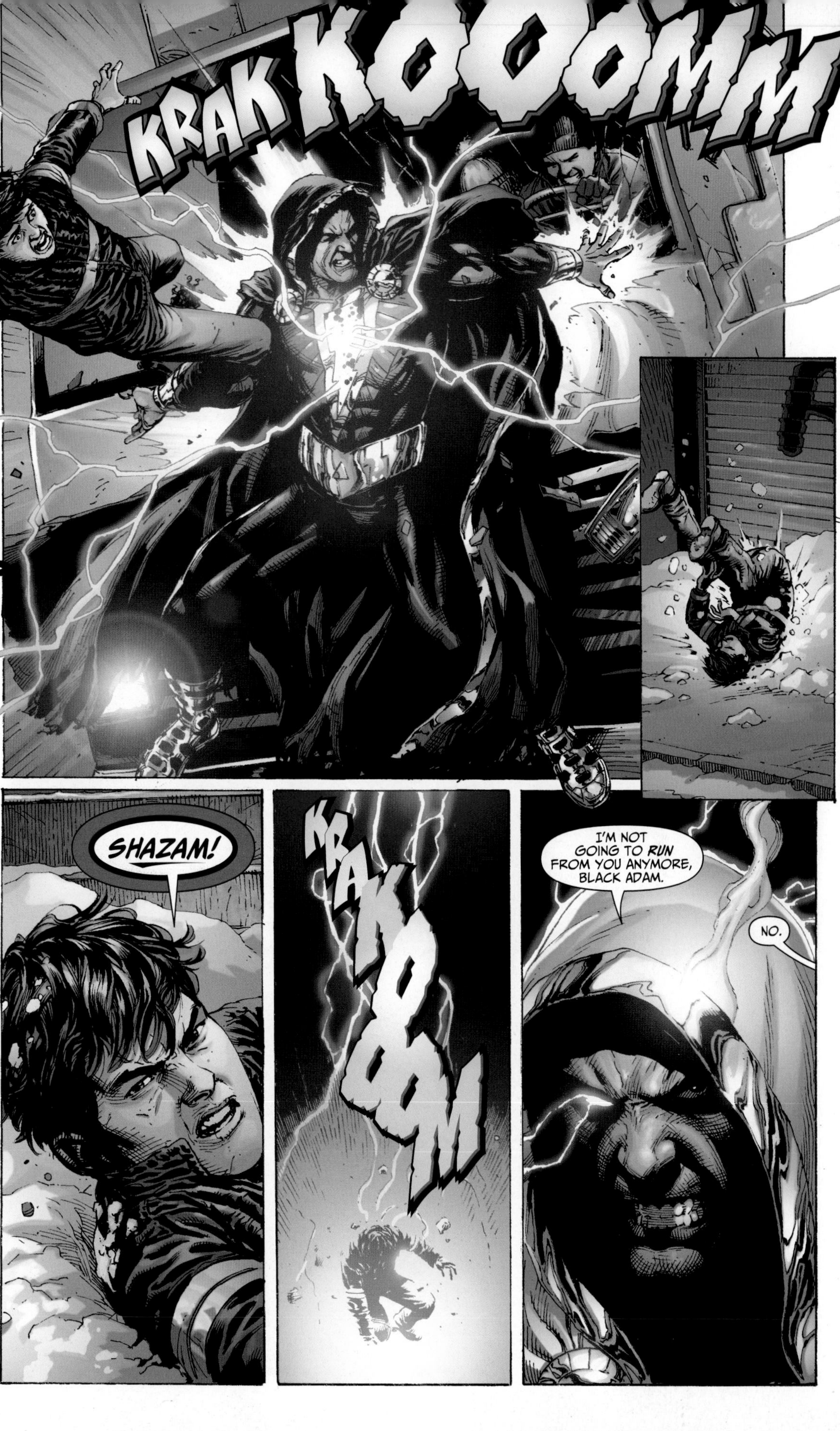
KRAK KOOOMM
SHAZAM!
KRAKOOOM
I'M NOT GOING TO *RUN* FROM YOU ANYMORE, BLACK ADAM.
NO.

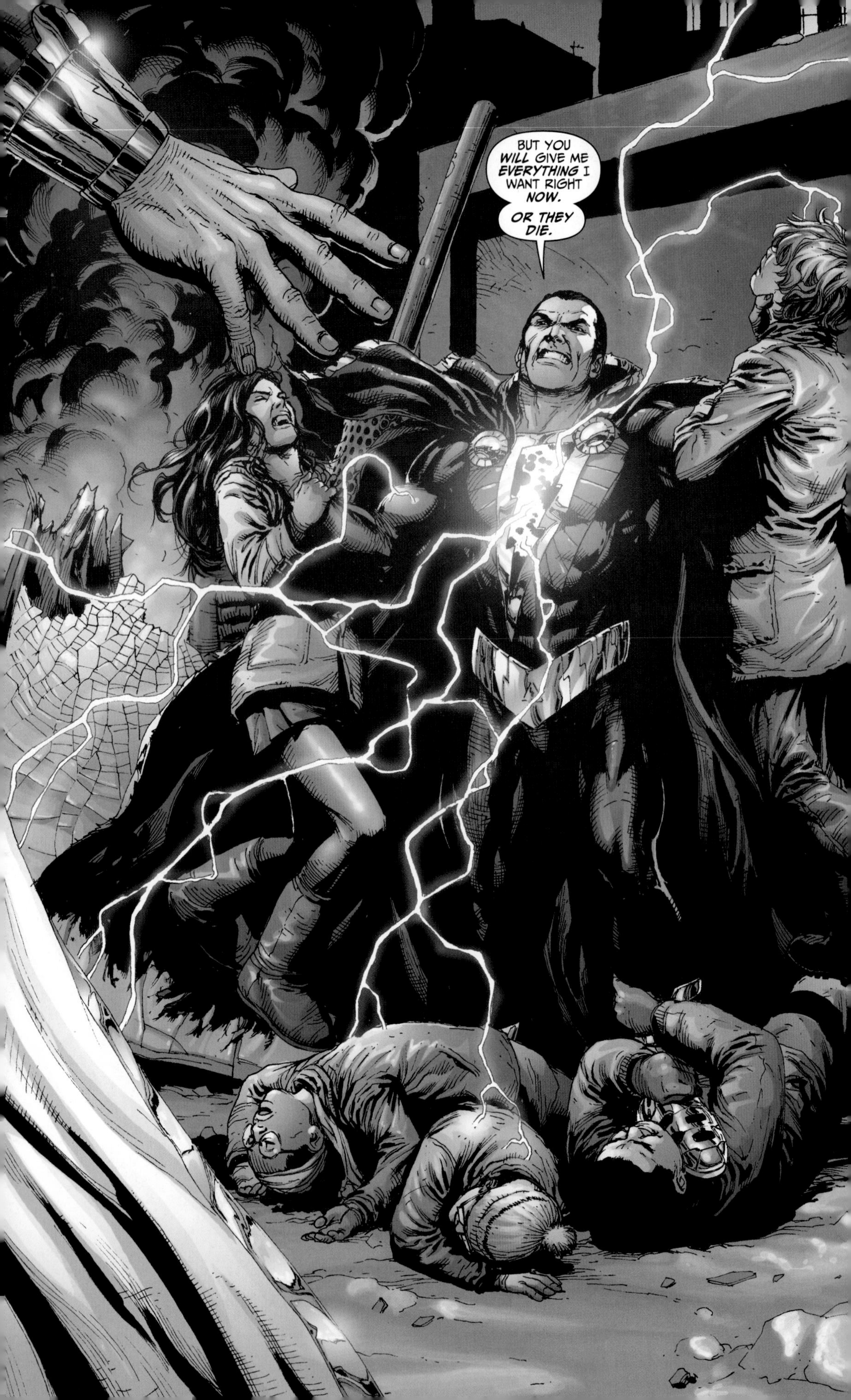
BUT YOU WILL GIVE ME EVERYTHING I WANT RIGHT NOW. OR THEY DIE.

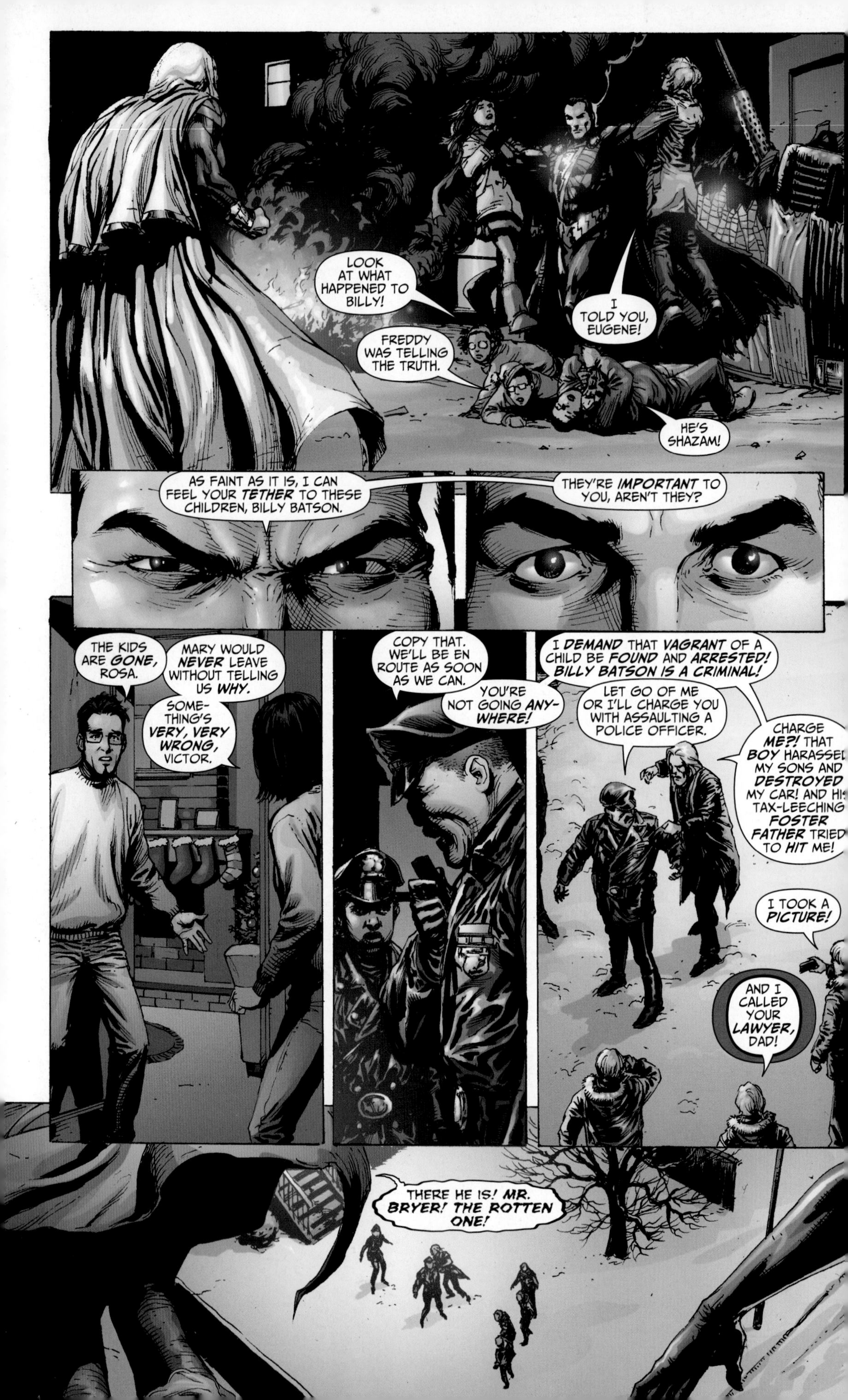
LOOK AT WHAT HAPPENED TO BILLY!
FREDDY WAS TELLING THE TRUTH.
I TOLD YOU, EUGENE!
HE'S SHAZAM!
AS FAINT AS IT IS, I CAN FEEL YOUR TETHER TO THESE CHILDREN, BILLY BATSON.
THEY'RE IMPORTANT TO YOU, AREN'T THEY?
THE KIDS ARE GONE, ROSA.
MARY WOULD NEVER LEAVE WITHOUT TELLING US WHY.
SOME-THING'S VERY, VERY WRONG, VICTOR.
COPY THAT. WE'LL BE EN ROUTE AS SOON AS WE CAN.
YOU'RE NOT GOING ANY-WHERE!
I DEMAND THAT VAGRANT OF A CHILD BE FOUND AND ARRESTED! BILLY BATSON IS A CRIMINAL!
LET GO OF ME OR I'LL CHARGE YOU WITH ASSAULTING A POLICE OFFICER.
CHARGE ME?! THAT BOY HARASSED MY SONS AND DESTROYED MY CAR! AND HIS TAX-LEECHING FOSTER FATHER TRIED TO HIT ME!
I TOOK A PICTURE!
AND I CALLED YOUR LAWYER, DAD!
THERE HE IS! MR. BRYER! THE ROTTEN ONE!

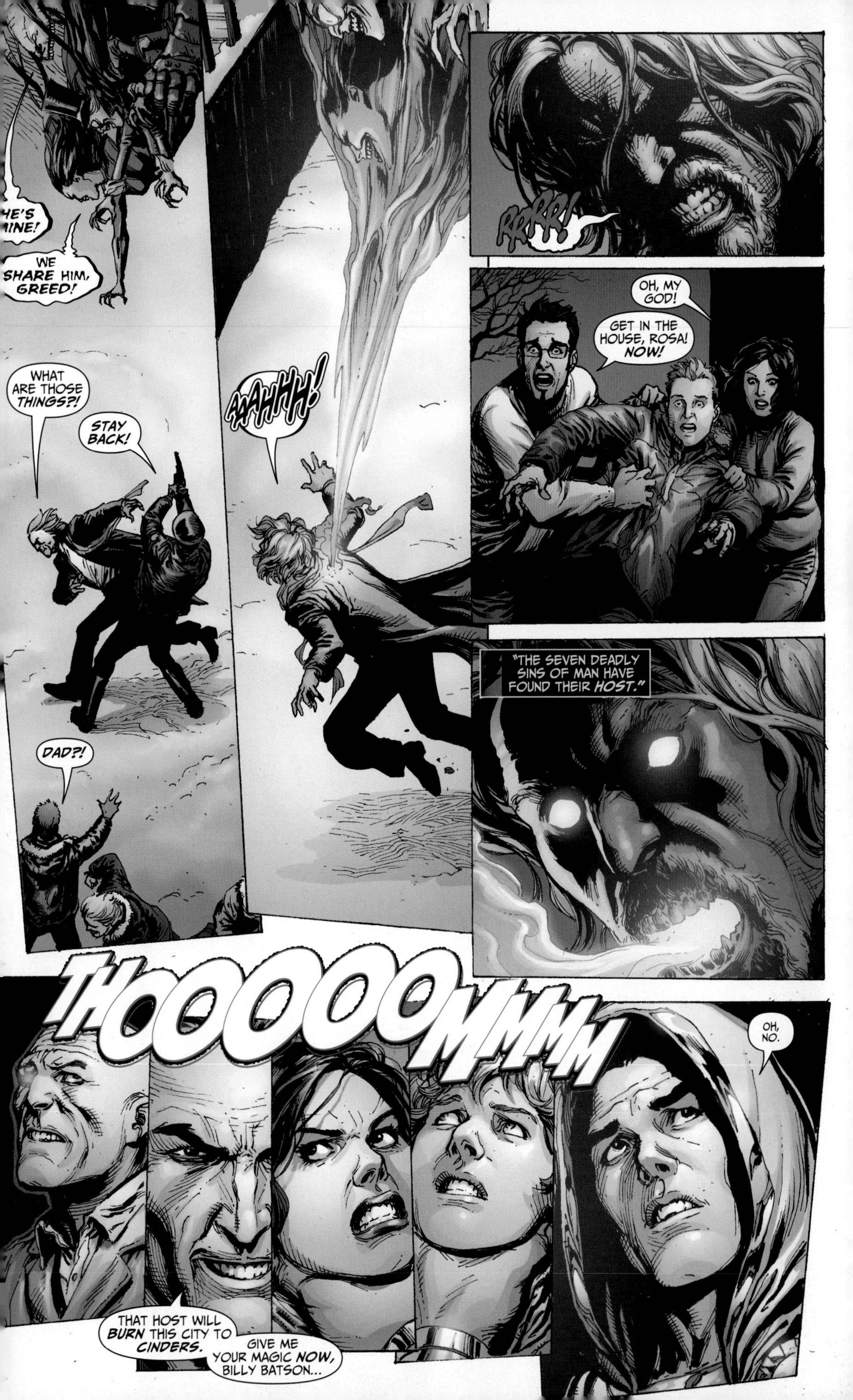

HE'S
MINE!
WE SHARE HIM, GREED!
RRRR!
OH, MY GOD!
GET IN THE HOUSE, ROSA! NOW!
WHAT ARE THOSE THINGS?!
STAY BACK!
AAAHHH!
DAD?!
"THE SEVEN DEADLY SINS OF MAN HAVE FOUND THEIR HOST."
THOOOOOMMMM
OH, NO.
THAT HOST WILL BURN THIS CITY TO CINDERS.
GIVE ME YOUR MAGIC NOW, BILLY BATSON...

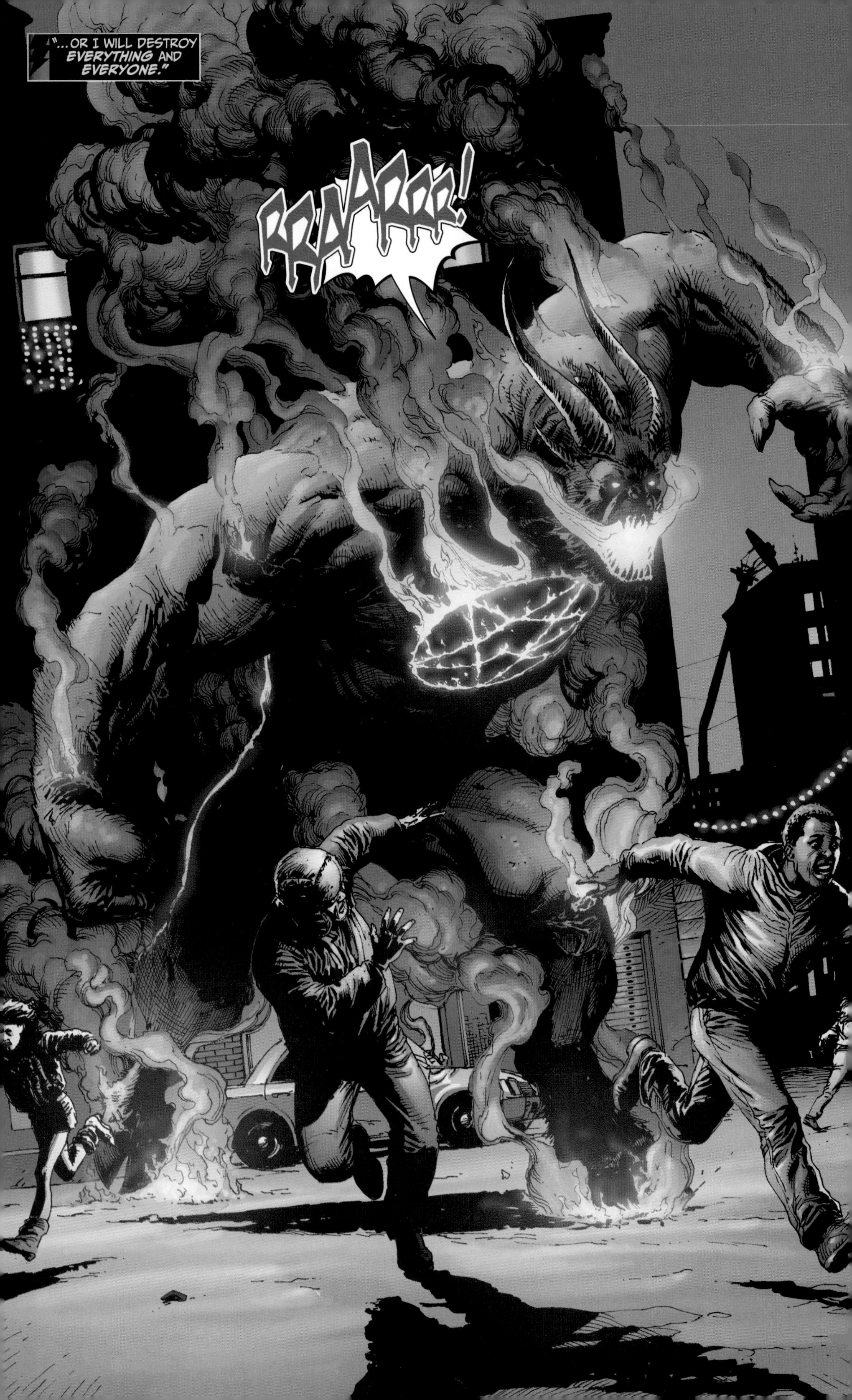
"...OR I WILL DESTROY *EVERYTHING* AND *EVERYONE*."
RRAAAAARR!

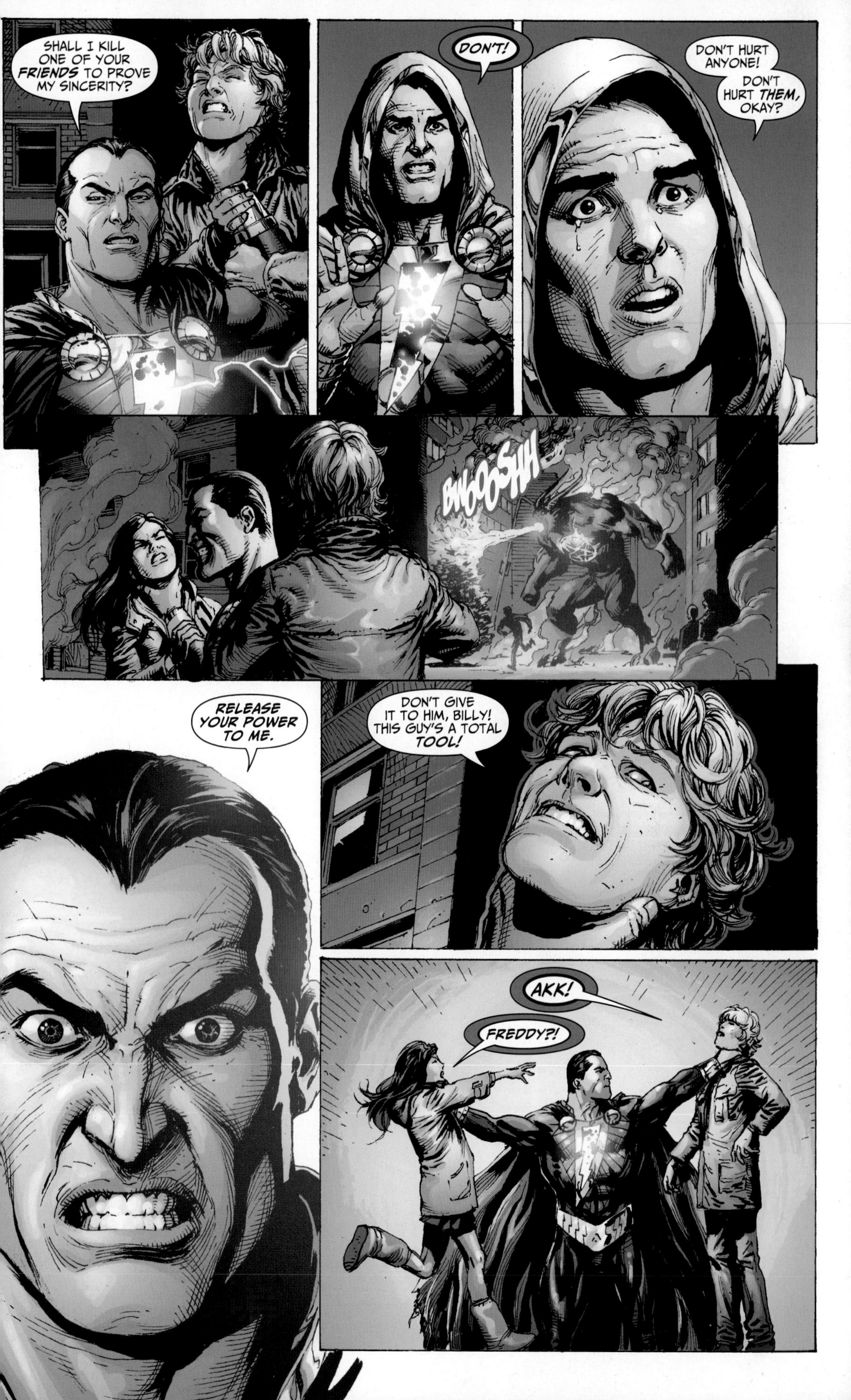
SHALL I KILL ONE OF YOUR FRIENDS TO PROVE MY SINCERITY?
DON'T!
DON'T HURT ANYONE!
DON'T HURT THEM, OKAY?
BWOOOSHH
RELEASE YOUR POWER TO ME.
DON'T GIVE IT TO HIM, BILLY! THIS GUY'S A TOTAL TOOL!
AKK!
FREDDY?!

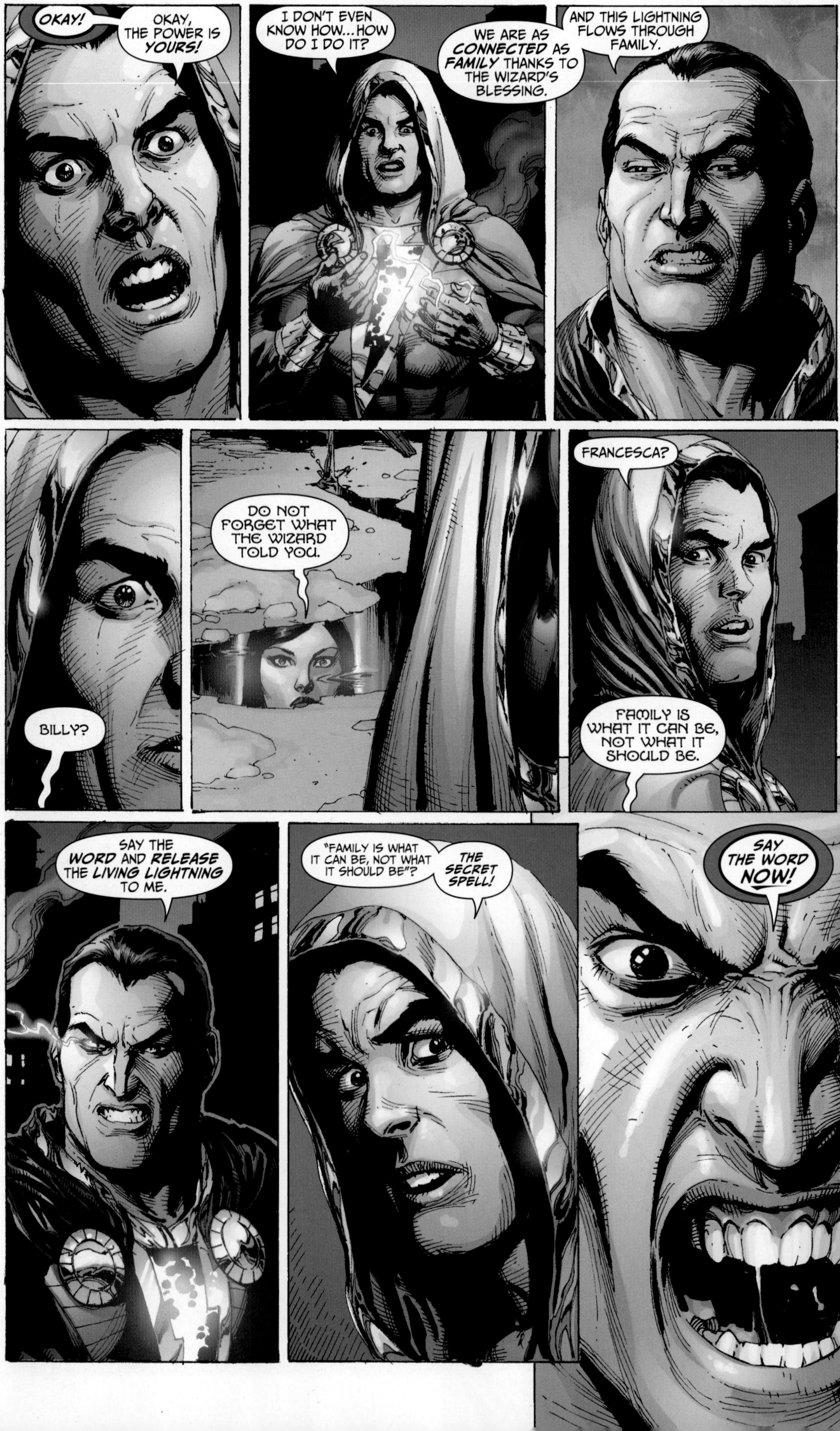
OKAY!
OKAY, THE POWER IS YOURS!
I DON'T EVEN KNOW HOW...HOW DO I DO IT?
WE ARE AS CONNECTED AS FAMILY THANKS TO THE WIZARD'S BLESSING.
AND THIS LIGHTNING FLOWS THROUGH FAMILY.
BILLY?
DO NOT FORGET WHAT THE WIZARD TOLD YOU.
FRANCESCA?
FAMILY IS WHAT IT CAN BE, NOT WHAT IT SHOULD BE.
SAY THE WORD AND RELEASE THE LIVING LIGHTNING TO ME.
"FAMILY IS WHAT IT CAN BE, NOT WHAT IT SHOULD BE"?
THE SECRET SPELL!
SAY THE WORD NOW!

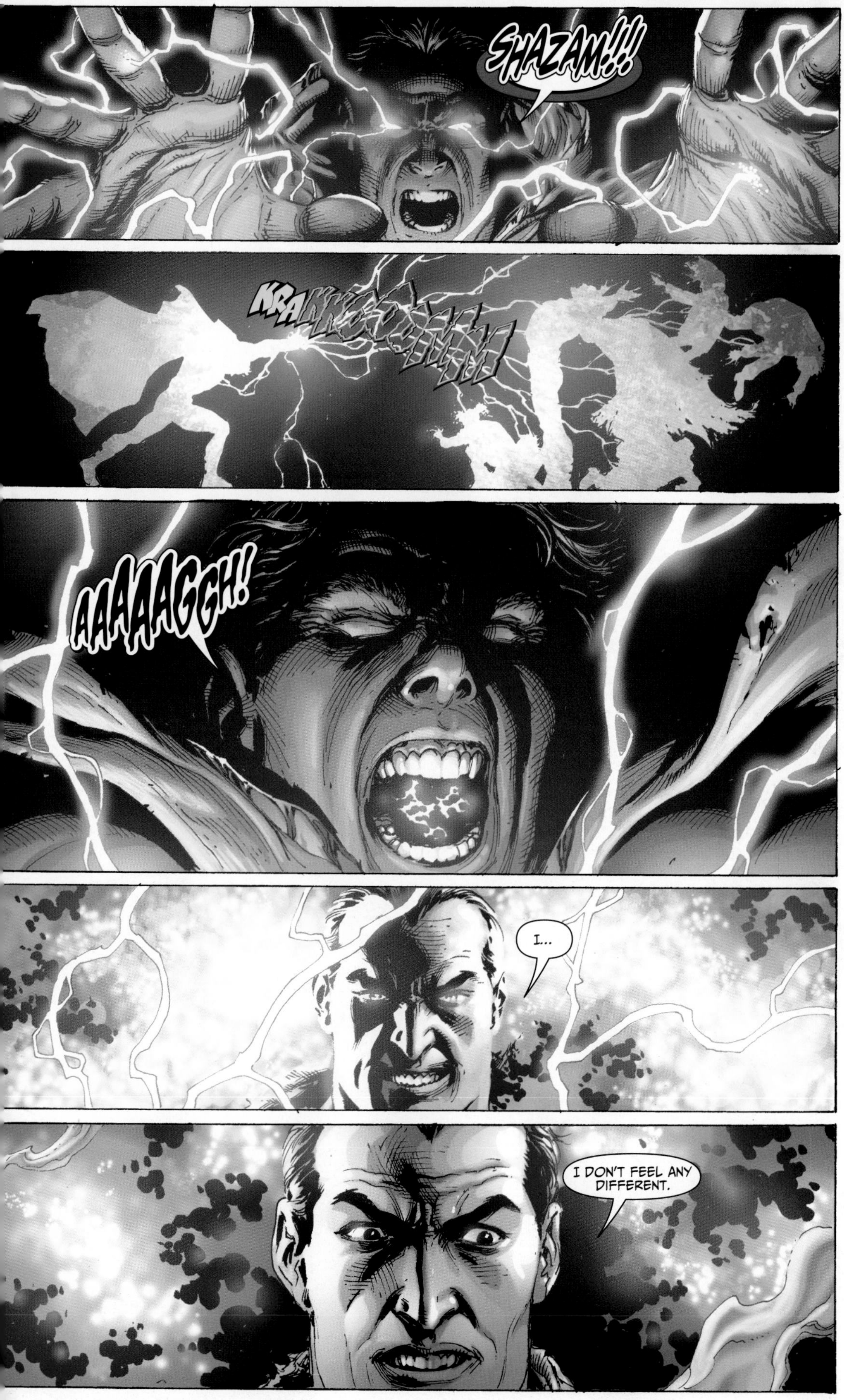

SHAZAM!!!
KRAKKOOOM
AAAAAGGH!
I...
I DON'T FEEL ANY DIFFERENT.

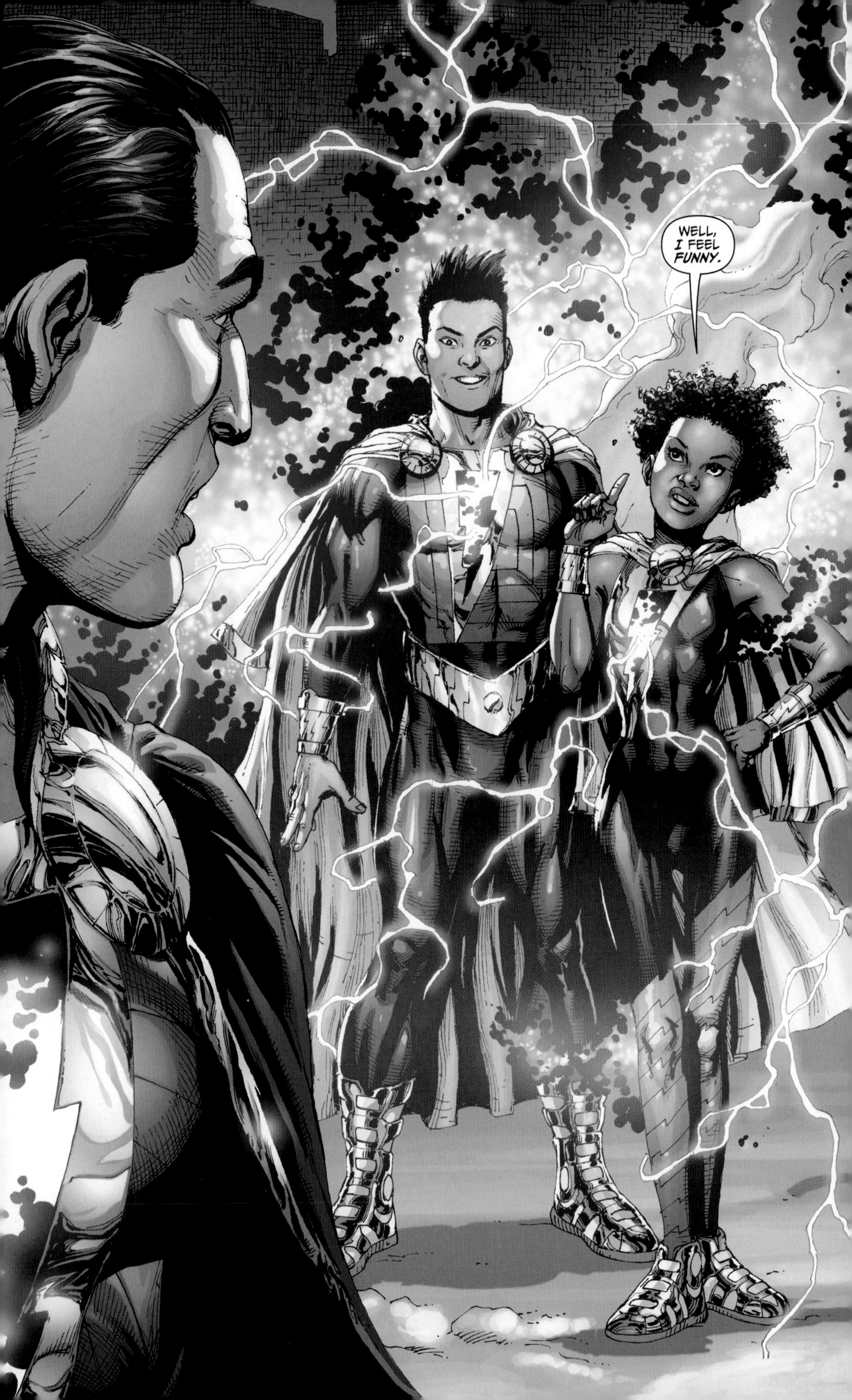
WELL, I FEEL *FUNNY*.

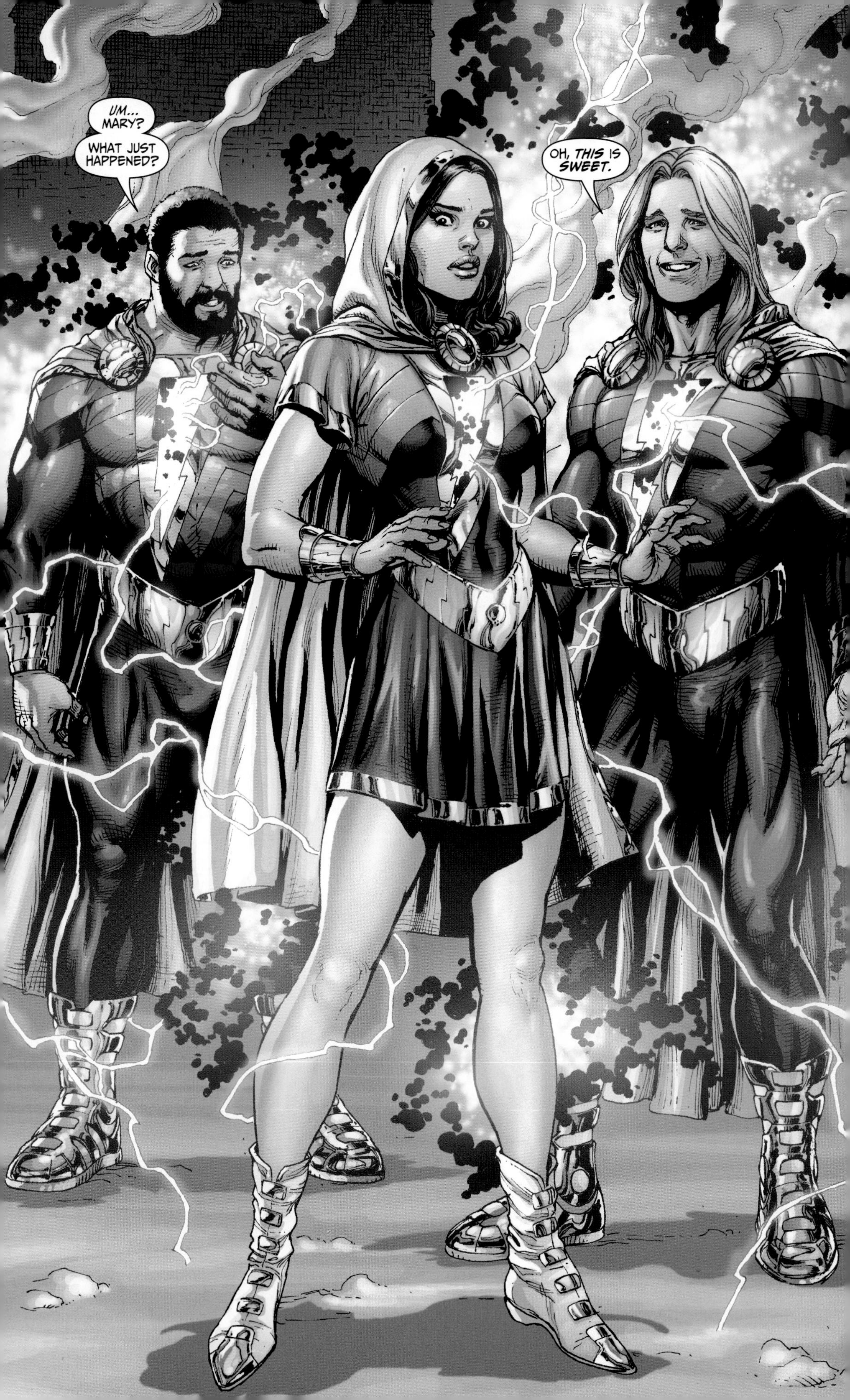
UM... MARY?
WHAT JUST HAPPENED?
OH, THIS IS SWEET.

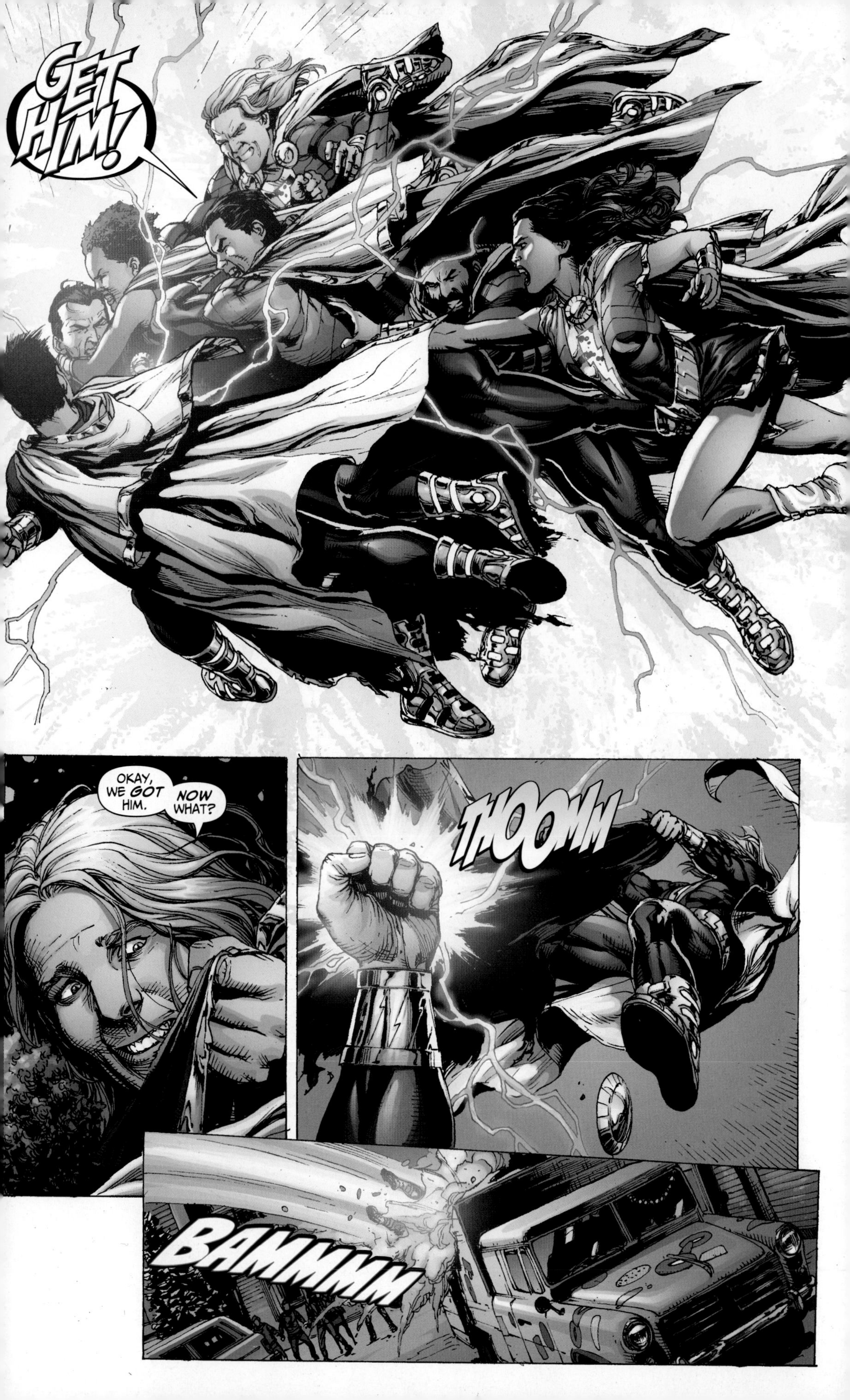
GET HIM!
OKAY, WE GOT HIM.
NOW WHAT?
THOOMM
BAMMMMM

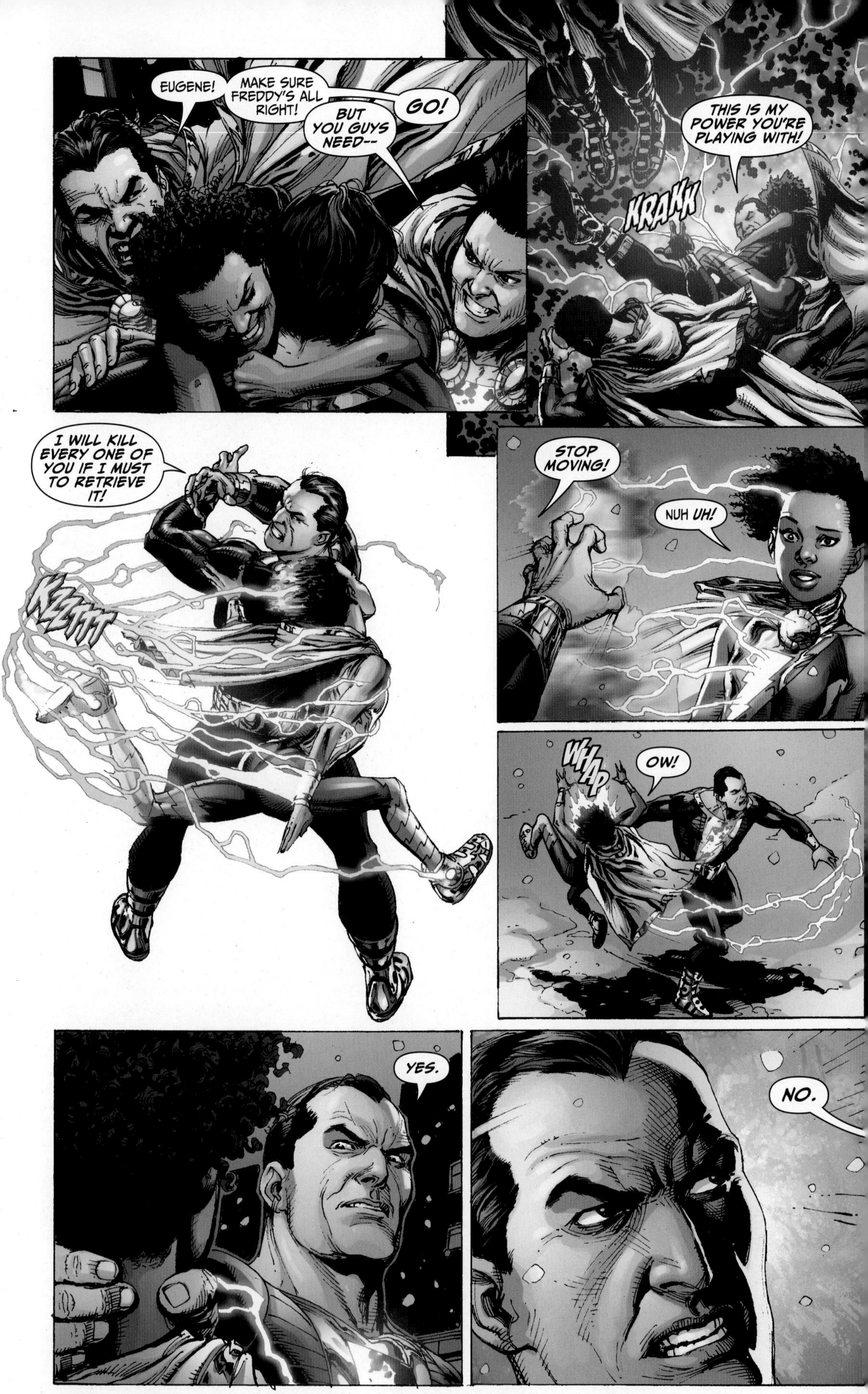
EUGENE!
MAKE SURE FREDDY'S ALL RIGHT!
GO!
BUT YOU GUYS NEED--
THIS IS MY POWER YOU'RE PLAYING WITH!
KRAKK
I WILL KILL EVERY ONE OF YOU IF I MUST TO RETRIEVE IT!
KZZTTT
STOP MOVING!
NUH UH!
WHAP
OW!
YES.
NO.

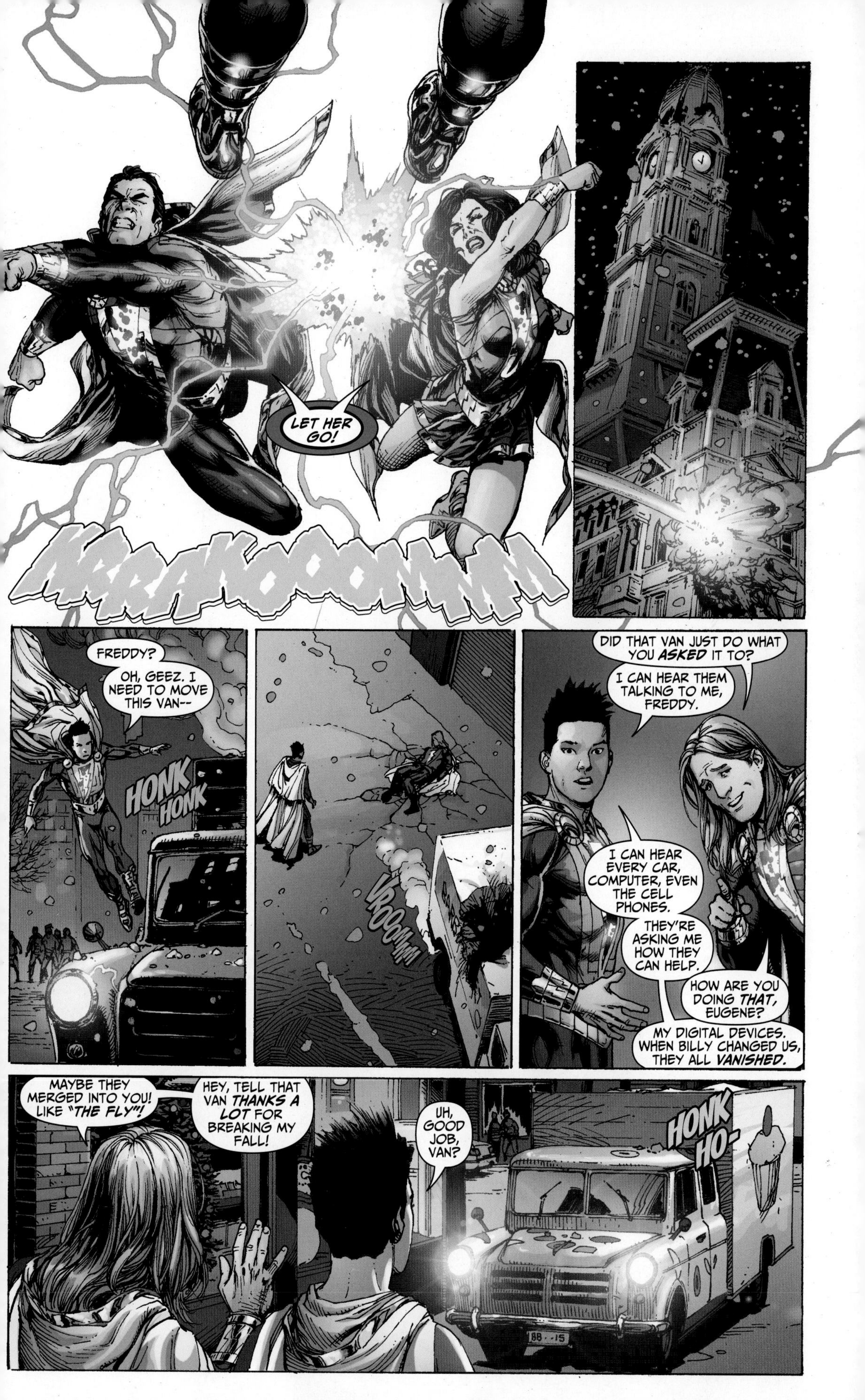
LET HER GO!
KRRAKOOOMMM
FREDDY?
OH, GEEZ. I NEED TO MOVE THIS VAN--
HONK HONK
VROOMMM
DID THAT VAN JUST DO WHAT YOU *ASKED* IT TO?
I CAN HEAR THEM TALKING TO ME, FREDDY.
I CAN HEAR EVERY CAR, COMPUTER, EVEN THE CELL PHONES.
THEY'RE ASKING ME HOW THEY CAN HELP.
HOW ARE YOU DOING *THAT*, EUGENE?
MY DIGITAL DEVICES. WHEN BILLY CHANGED US, THEY ALL *VANISHED*.
MAYBE THEY MERGED INTO YOU! LIKE *"THE FLY"*!
HEY, TELL THAT VAN *THANKS A LOT* FOR BREAKING MY FALL!
UH, GOOD JOB, VAN?
HONK HO-

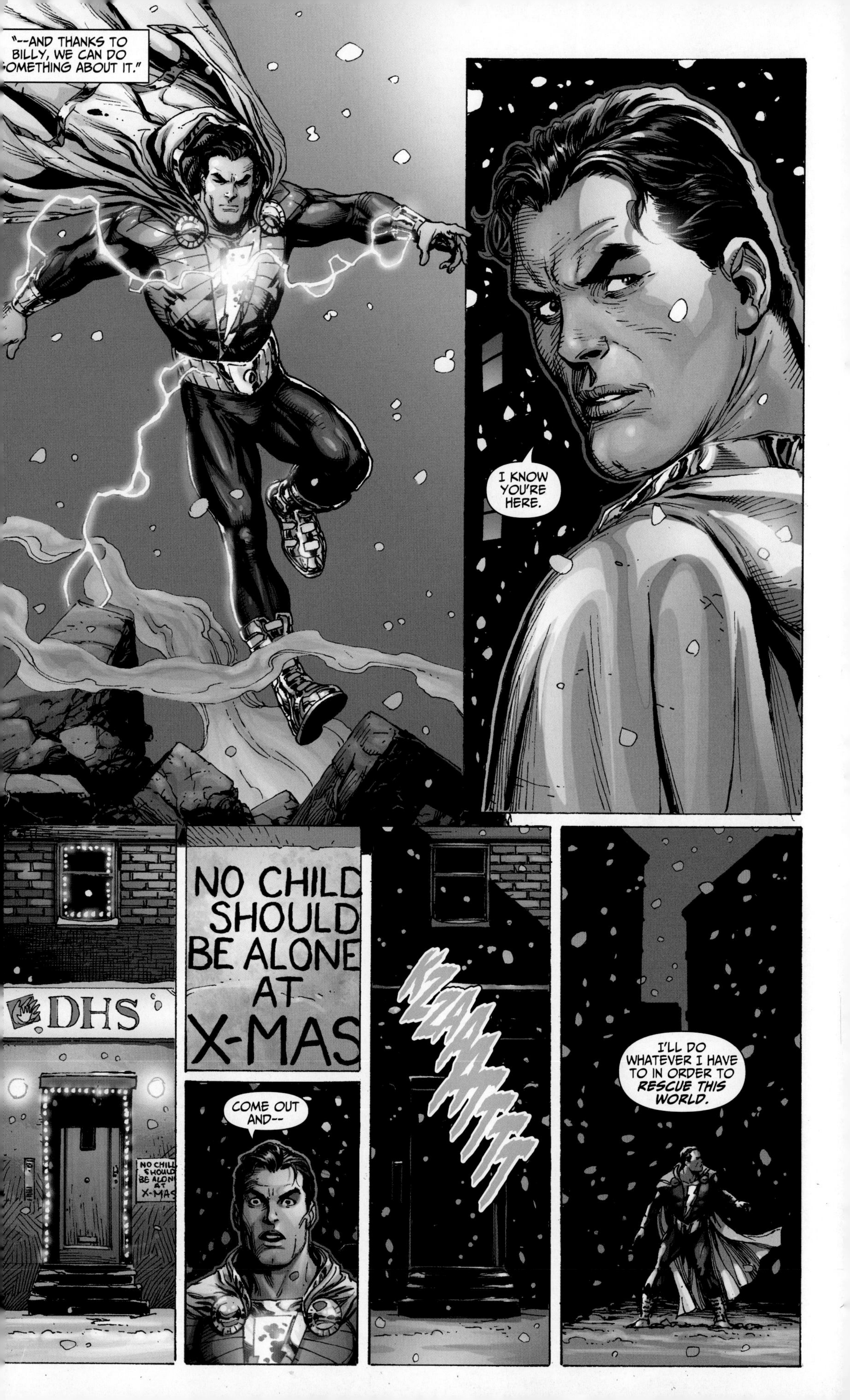
"--AND THANKS TO BILLY, WE CAN DO SOMETHING ABOUT IT."
I KNOW YOU'RE HERE.
DHS
NO CHILD SHOULD BE ALONE AT X-MAS
NO CHILD SHOULD BE ALONE AT X-MAS
COME OUT AND--
KZZAAAKTTTT
I'LL DO WHATEVER I HAVE TO IN ORDER TO RESCUE THIS WORLD.

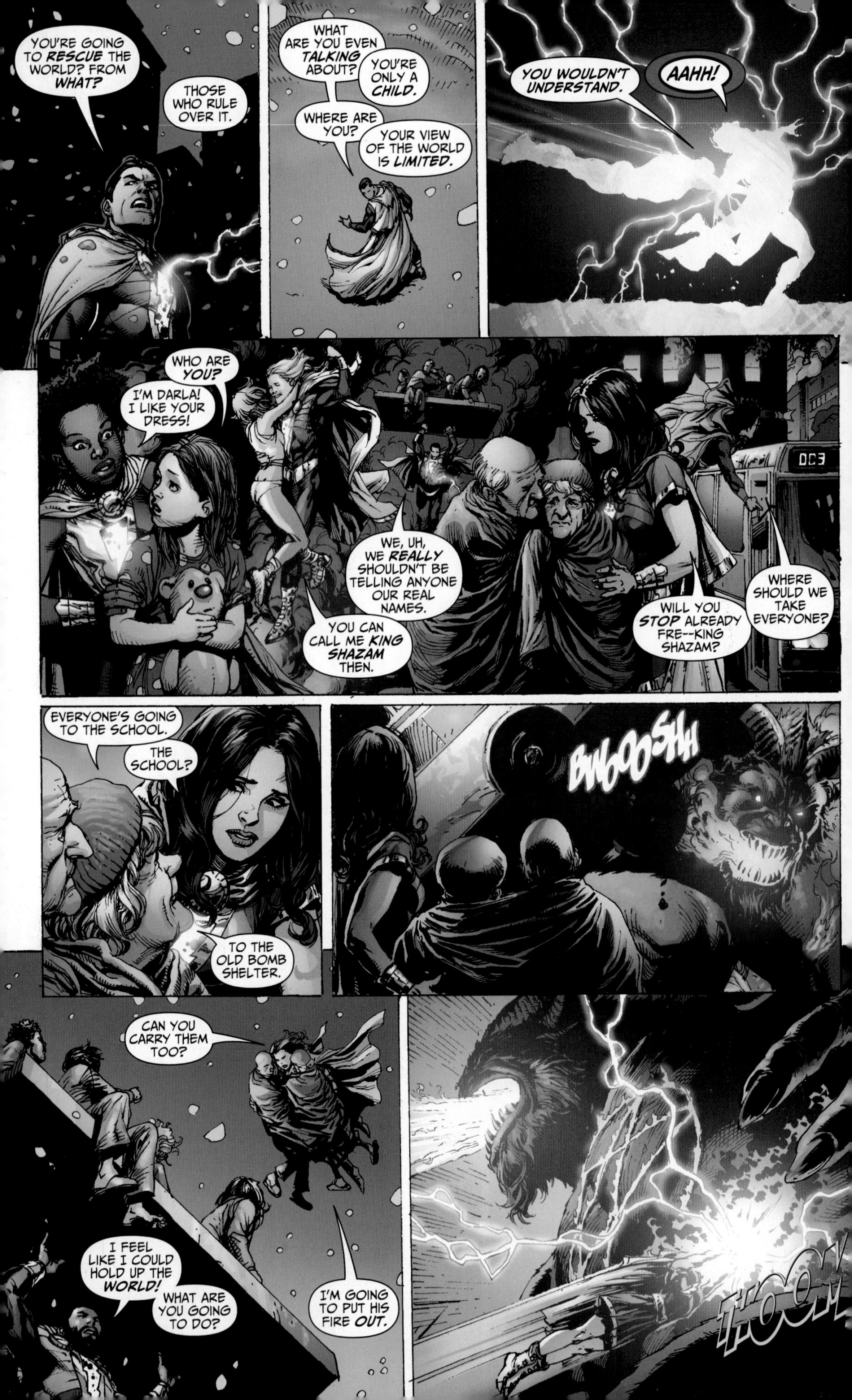
YOU'RE GOING TO RESCUE THE WORLD? FROM WHAT?
THOSE WHO RULE OVER IT.
WHAT ARE YOU EVEN TALKING ABOUT?
YOU'RE ONLY A CHILD.
WHERE ARE YOU?
YOUR VIEW OF THE WORLD IS LIMITED.
YOU WOULDN'T UNDERSTAND.
AAHH!
WHO ARE YOU?
I'M DARLA! I LIKE YOUR DRESS!
WE, UH, WE REALLY SHOULDN'T BE TELLING ANYONE OUR REAL NAMES.
YOU CAN CALL ME KING SHAZAM THEN.
WILL YOU STOP ALREADY FRE--KING SHAZAM?
WHERE SHOULD WE TAKE EVERYONE?
DC3
EVERYONE'S GOING TO THE SCHOOL.
THE SCHOOL?
TO THE OLD BOMB SHELTER.
BWOOOSHH
CAN YOU CARRY THEM TOO?
I FEEL LIKE I COULD HOLD UP THE WORLD!
WHAT ARE YOU GOING TO DO?
I'M GOING TO PUT HIS FIRE OUT.
THOOOM

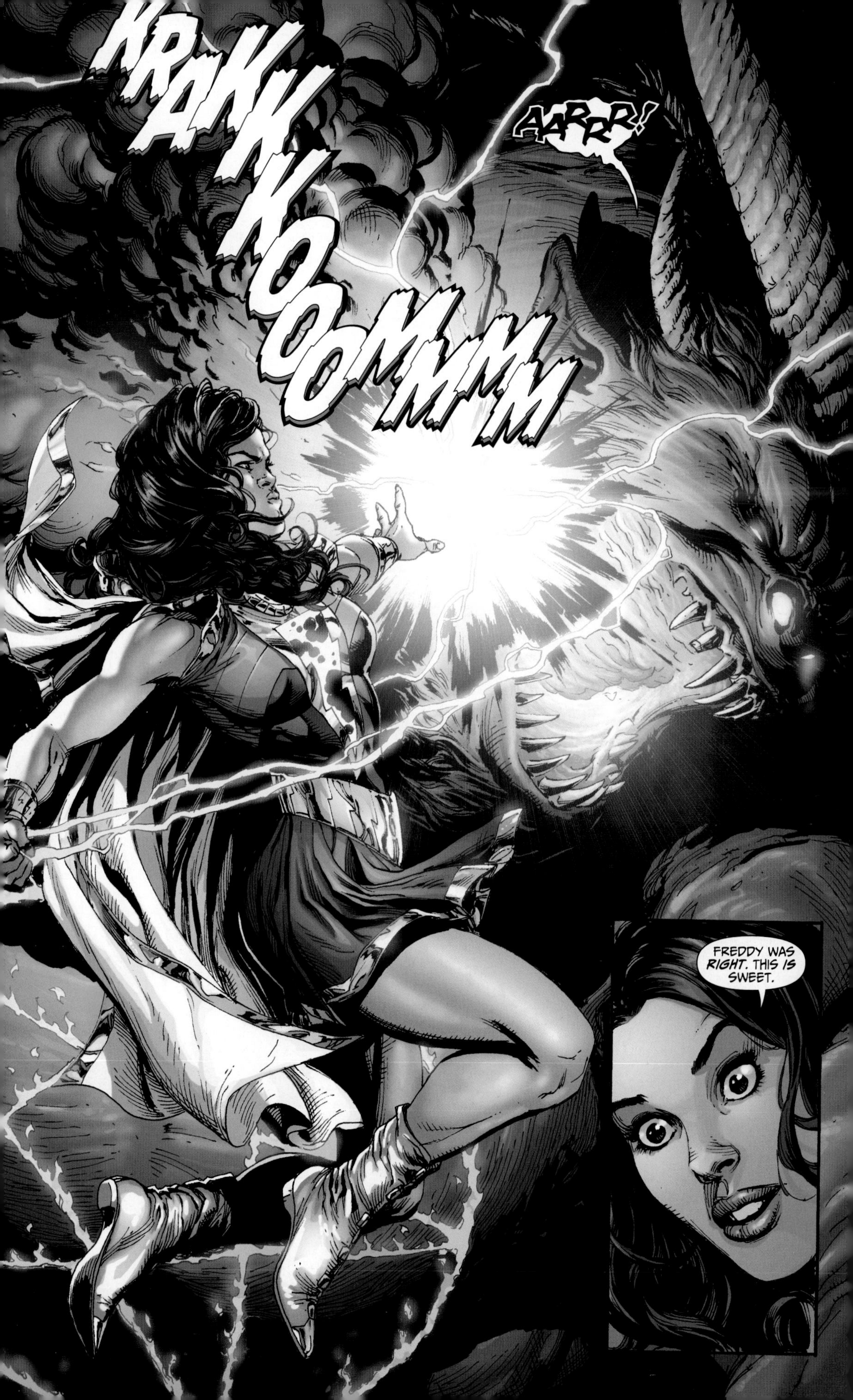
KRAKKOOMMM
AARRR!
FREDDY WAS RIGHT. THIS IS SWEET.

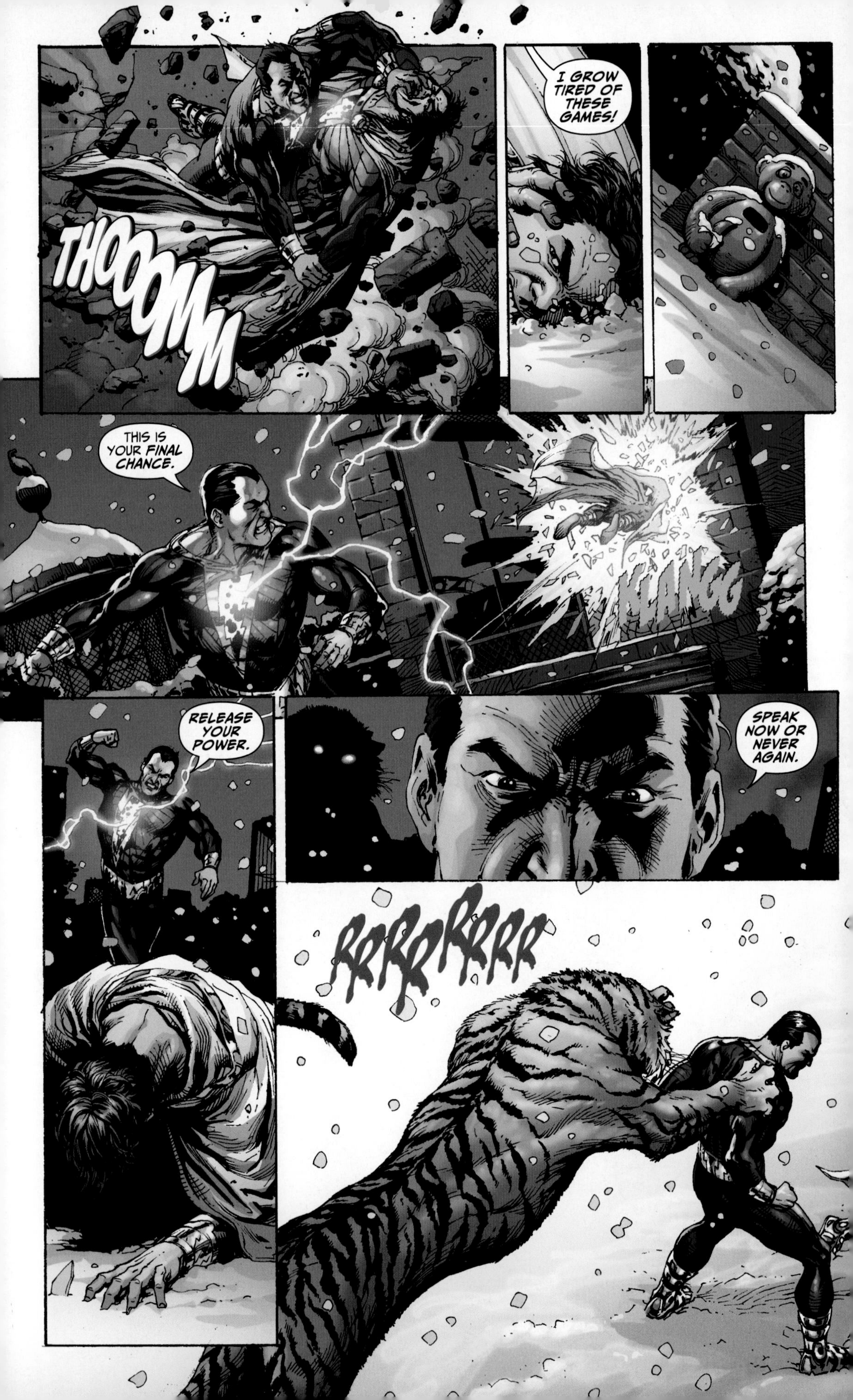
THOOOOMMM
I GROW TIRED OF THESE GAMES!
THIS IS YOUR FINAL CHANCE.
KLANGG
RELEASE YOUR POWER.
SPEAK NOW OR NEVER AGAIN.
RRRRRRRRRR

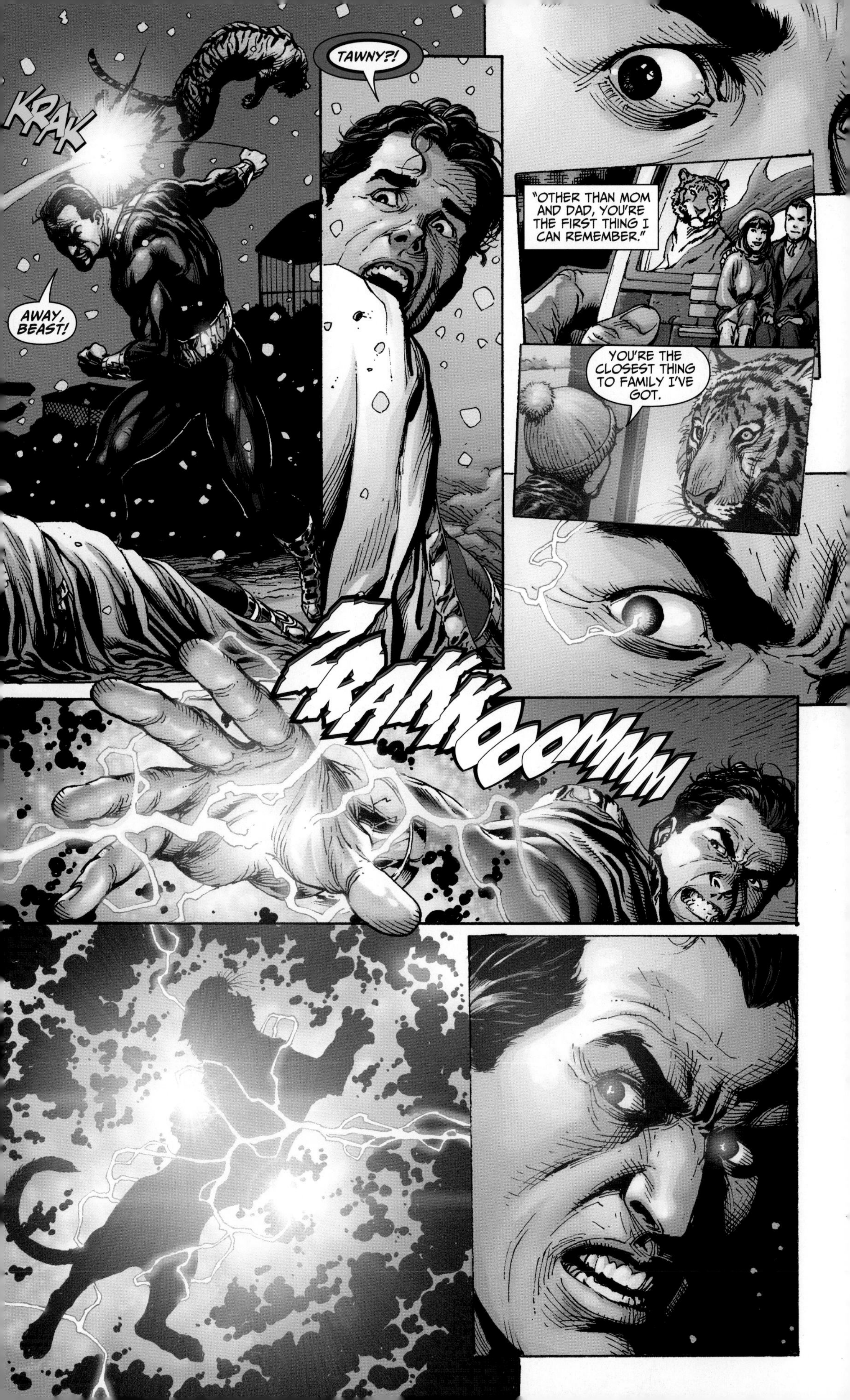
KRAK
AWAY, BEAST!
TAWNY?!
"OTHER THAN MOM AND DAD, YOU'RE THE FIRST THING I CAN REMEMBER."
YOU'RE THE CLOSEST THING TO FAMILY I'VE GOT.
KRAKOOOMMM

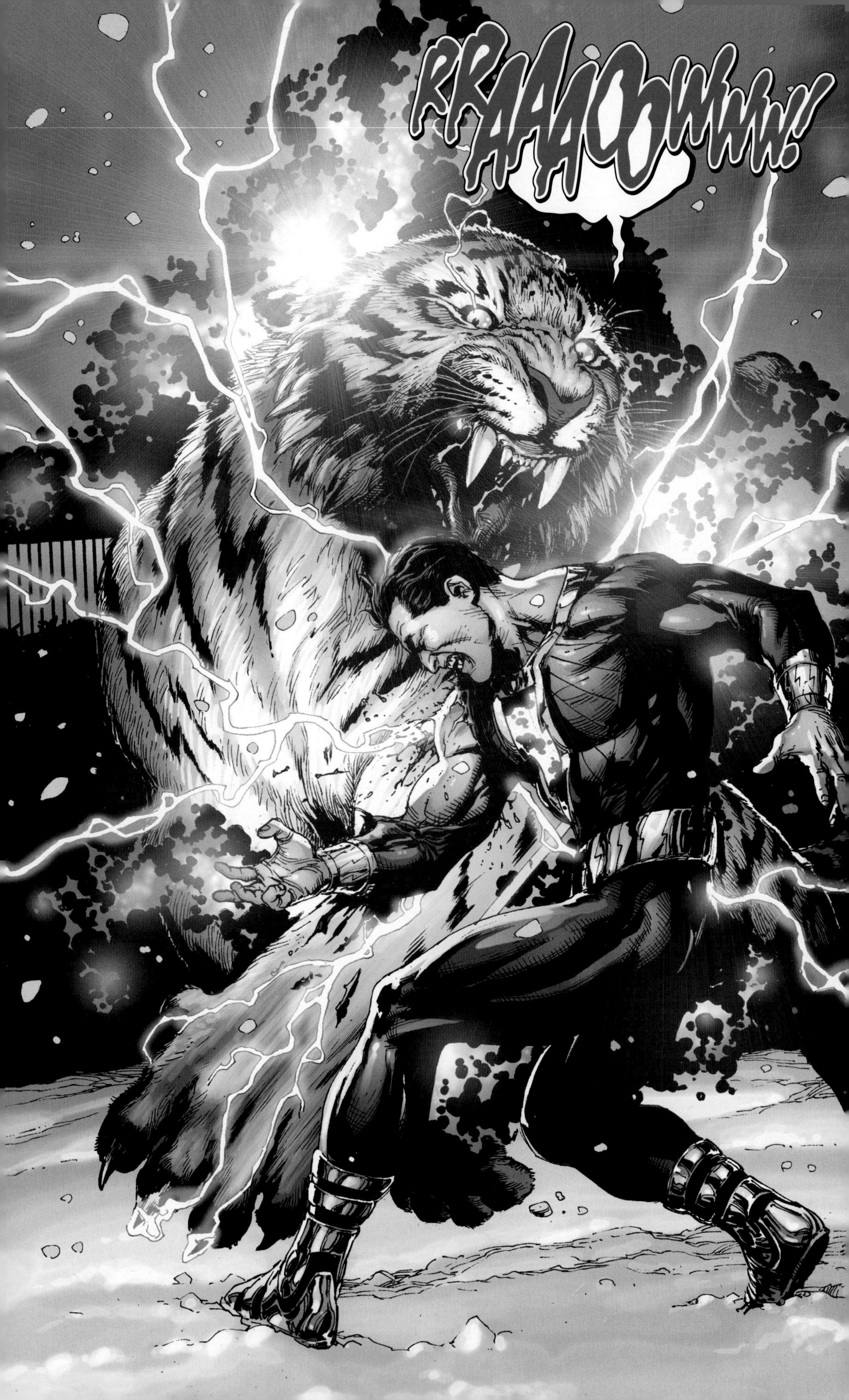
RRAAAOOWWW!

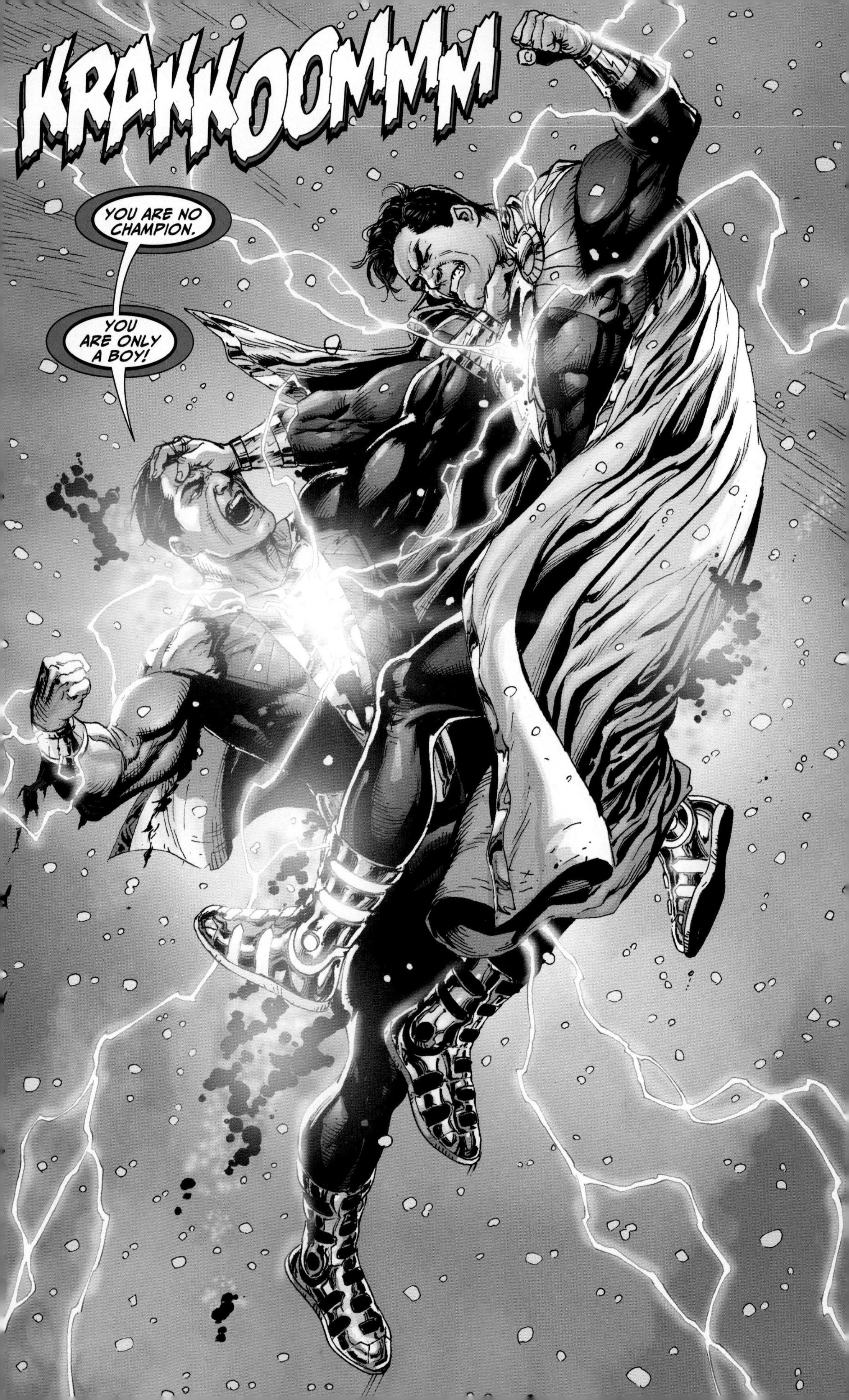
KRAKKOOMMM
YOU ARE NO CHAMPION.
YOU ARE ONLY A BOY!

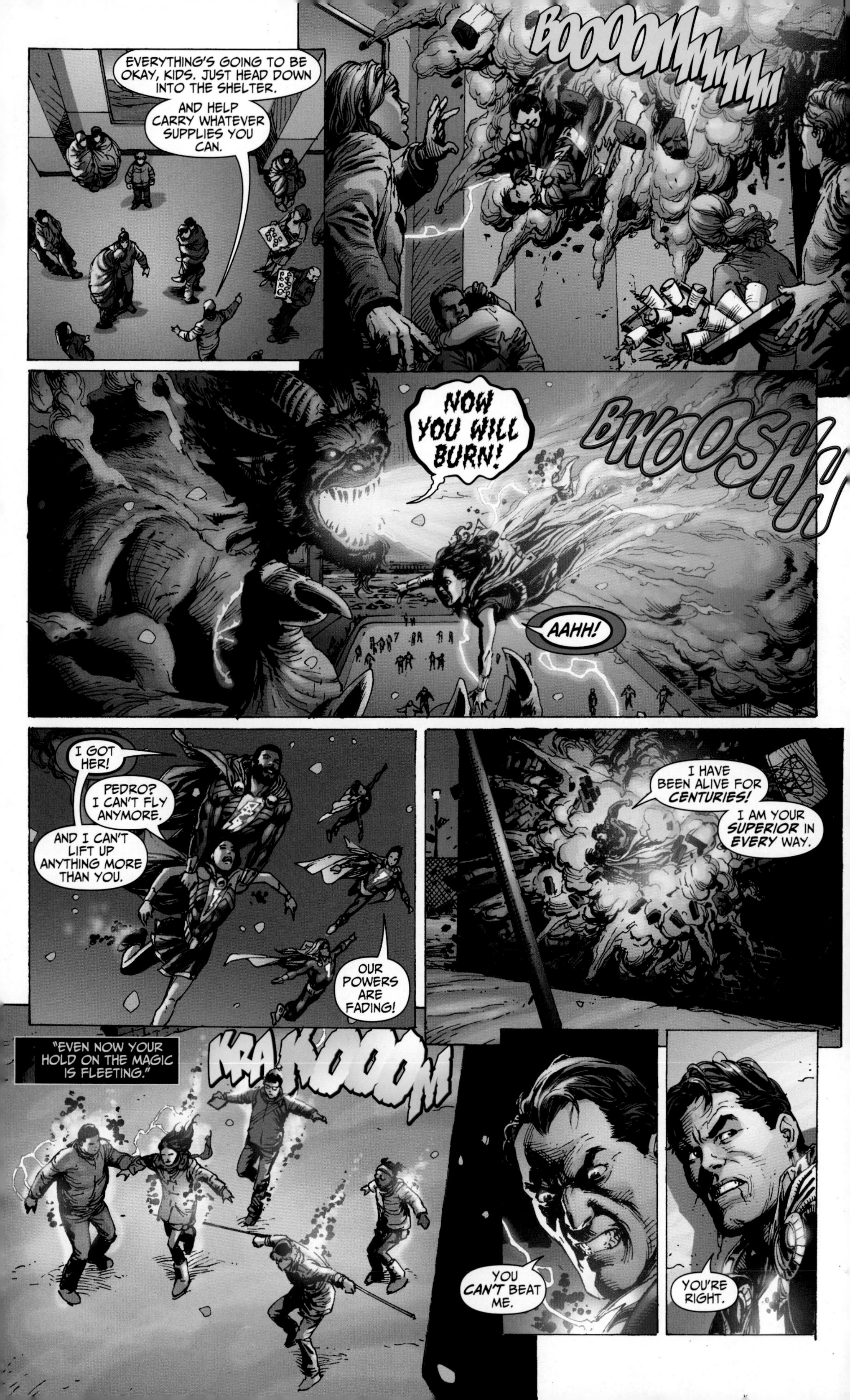
EVERYTHING'S GOING TO BE OKAY, KIDS. JUST HEAD DOWN INTO THE SHELTER.
AND HELP CARRY WHATEVER SUPPLIES YOU CAN.
BOOOOMMMMM
NOW YOU WILL BURN!
BWOOSH
AAHH!
I GOT HER!
PEDRO? I CAN'T FLY ANYMORE.
AND I CAN'T LIFT UP ANYTHING MORE THAN YOU.
OUR POWERS ARE FADING!
I HAVE BEEN ALIVE FOR CENTURIES!
I AM YOUR SUPERIOR IN EVERY WAY.
"EVEN NOW YOUR HOLD ON THE MAGIC IS FLEETING."
KRAKOOOM
YOU CAN'T BEAT ME.
YOU'RE RIGHT.

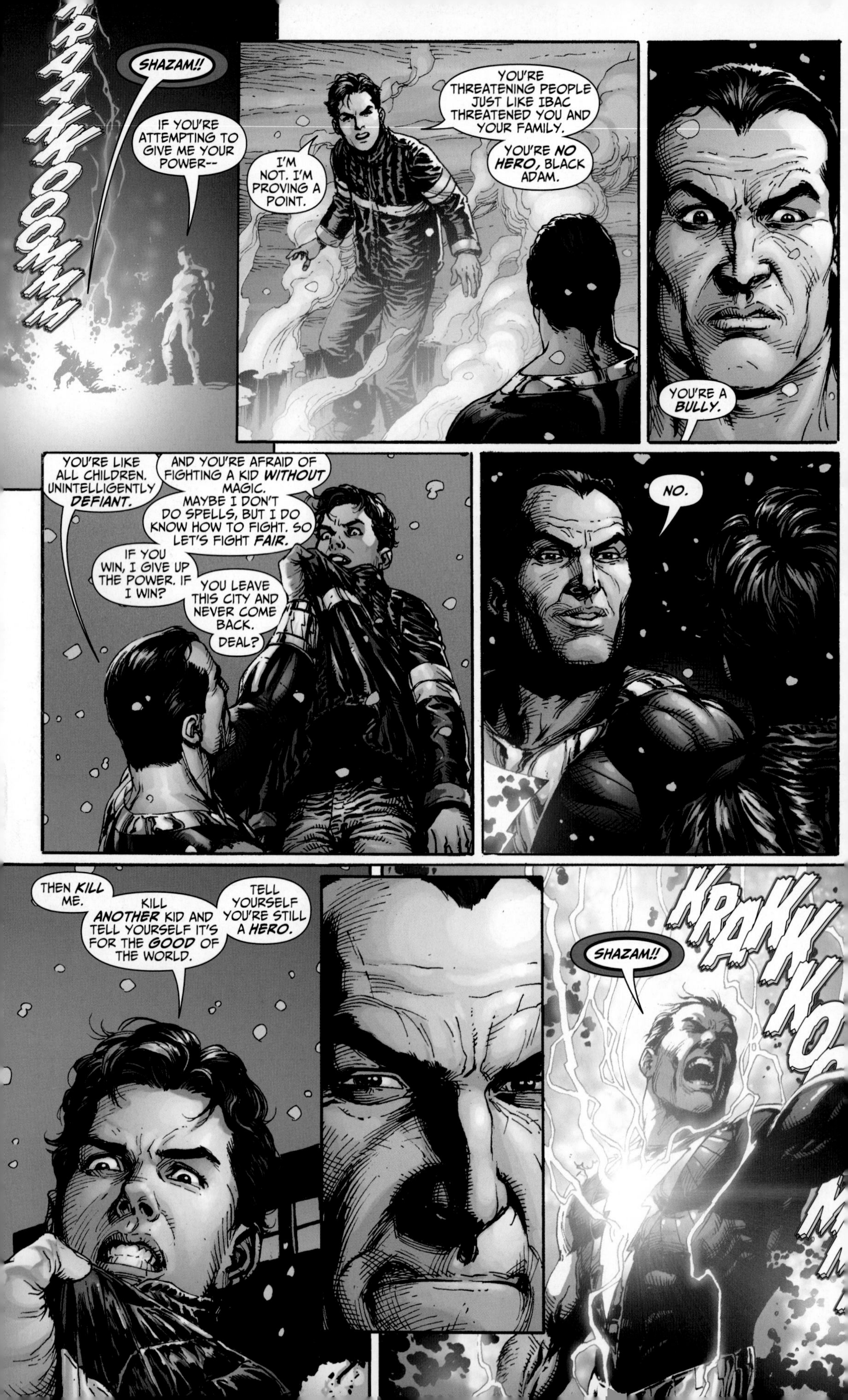
KRAAKOOOOMMM
SHAZAM!!
IF YOU'RE ATTEMPTING TO GIVE ME YOUR POWER--
I'M NOT. I'M PROVING A POINT.
YOU'RE THREATENING PEOPLE JUST LIKE IBAC THREATENED YOU AND YOUR FAMILY.
YOU'RE NO HERO, BLACK ADAM.
YOU'RE A BULLY.
YOU'RE LIKE ALL CHILDREN. UNINTELLIGENTLY DEFIANT.
AND YOU'RE AFRAID OF FIGHTING A KID WITHOUT MAGIC.
MAYBE I DON'T DO SPELLS, BUT I DO KNOW HOW TO FIGHT. SO LET'S FIGHT FAIR.
IF YOU WIN, I GIVE UP THE POWER. IF I WIN?
YOU LEAVE THIS CITY AND NEVER COME BACK.
DEAL?
NO.
THEN KILL ME.
KILL ANOTHER KID AND TELL YOURSELF IT'S FOR THE GOOD OF THE WORLD.
TELL YOURSELF YOU'RE STILL A HERO.
KRAKKAKOOMM
SHAZAM!!

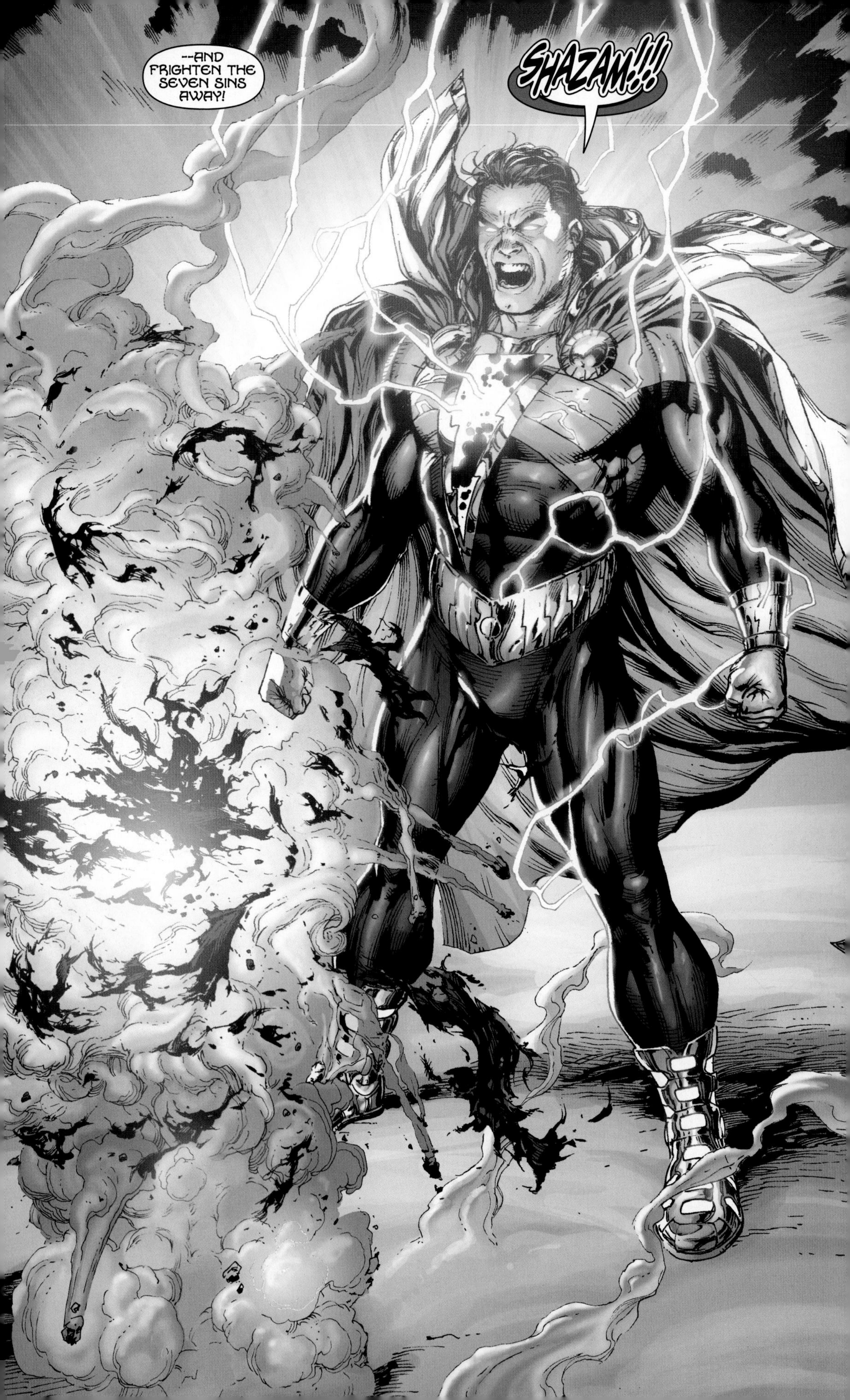
--AND FRIGHTEN THE SEVEN SINS AWAY!
SHAZAM!!!

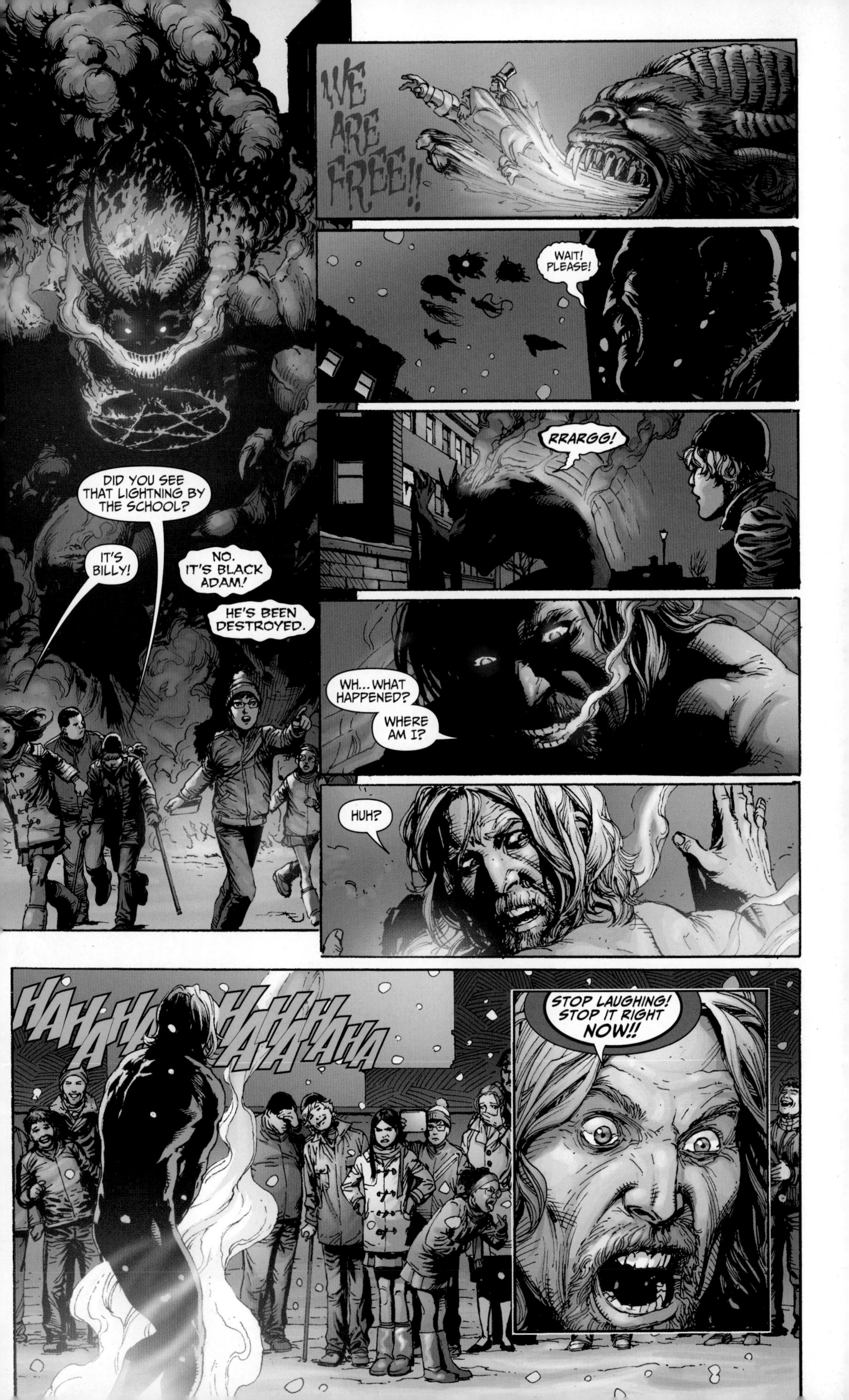
WE ARE FREE!!
WAIT! PLEASE!
RRARGG!
DID YOU SEE THAT LIGHTNING BY THE SCHOOL?
IT'S BILLY!
NO. IT'S BLACK ADAM!
HE'S BEEN DESTROYED.
WH...WHAT HAPPENED?
WHERE AM I?
HUH?
HAHAHAHAHAHAHAHAHA
STOP LAUGHING! STOP IT RIGHT NOW!!

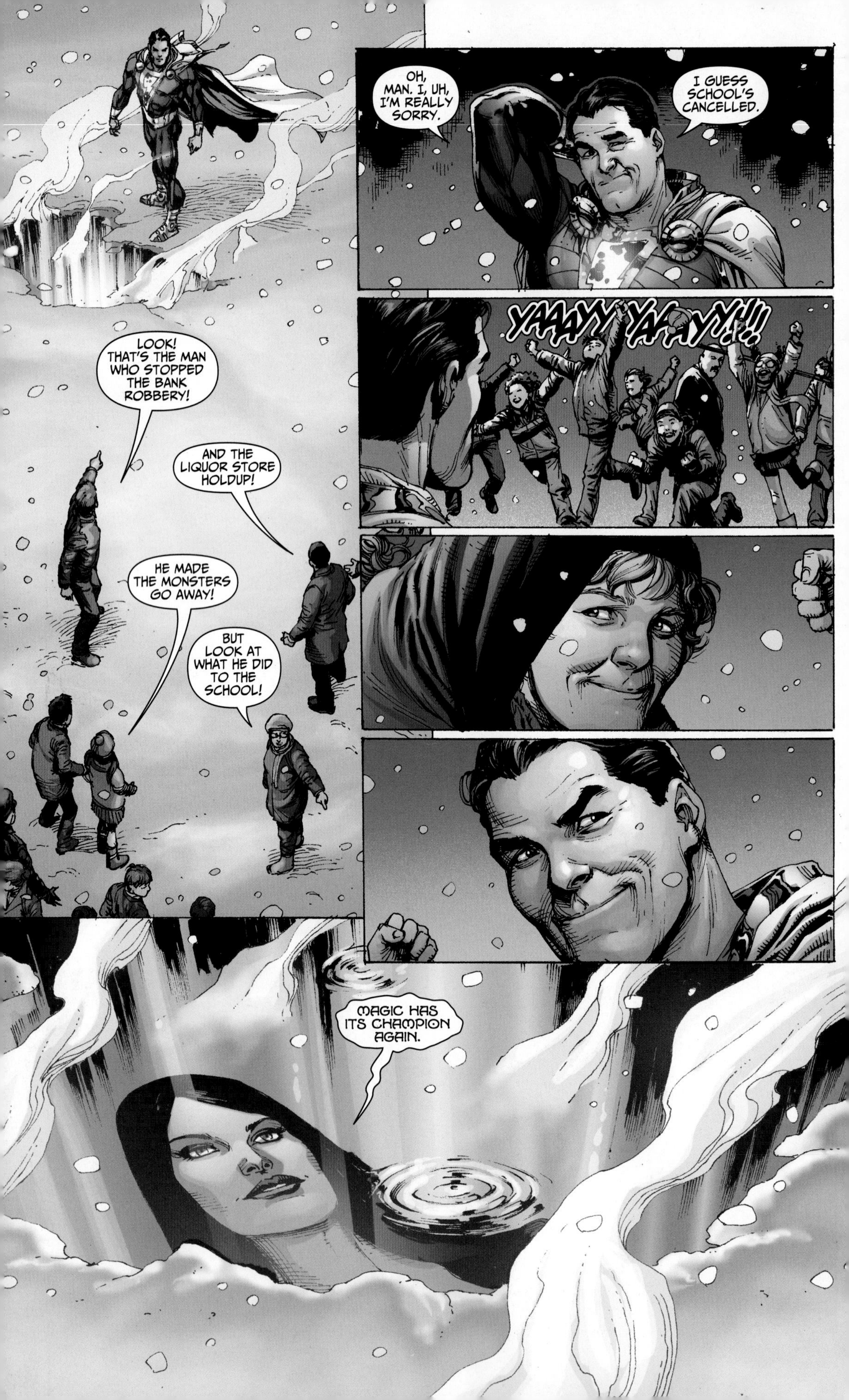
LOOK! THAT'S THE MAN WHO STOPPED THE BANK ROBBERY!
AND THE LIQUOR STORE HOLDUP!
HE MADE THE MONSTERS GO AWAY!
BUT LOOK AT WHAT HE DID TO THE SCHOOL!
OH, MAN. I, UH, I'M REALLY SORRY.
I GUESS SCHOOL'S CANCELLED.
YAAAYY YAAAYY!!!
MAGIC HAS ITS CHAMPION AGAIN.

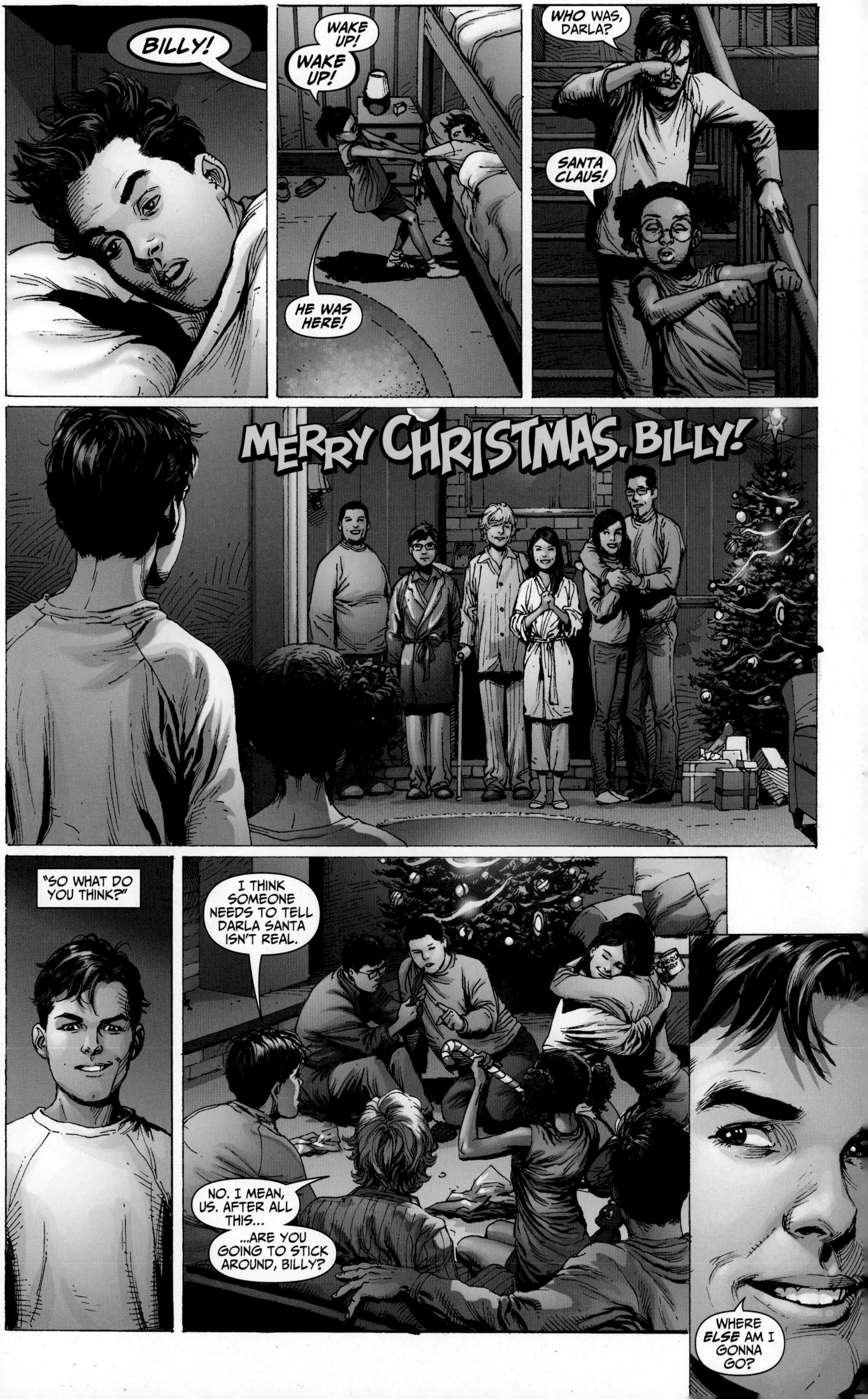
BILLY!
WAKE UP!
WAKE UP!
HE WAS HERE!
WHO WAS, DARLA?
SANTA CLAUS!
MERRY CHRISTMAS, BILLY!
"SO WHAT DO YOU THINK?"
I THINK SOMEONE NEEDS TO TELL DARLA SANTA ISN'T REAL.
NO. I MEAN, US. AFTER ALL THIS...
...ARE YOU GOING TO STICK AROUND, BILLY?
WHERE ELSE AM I GONNA GO?

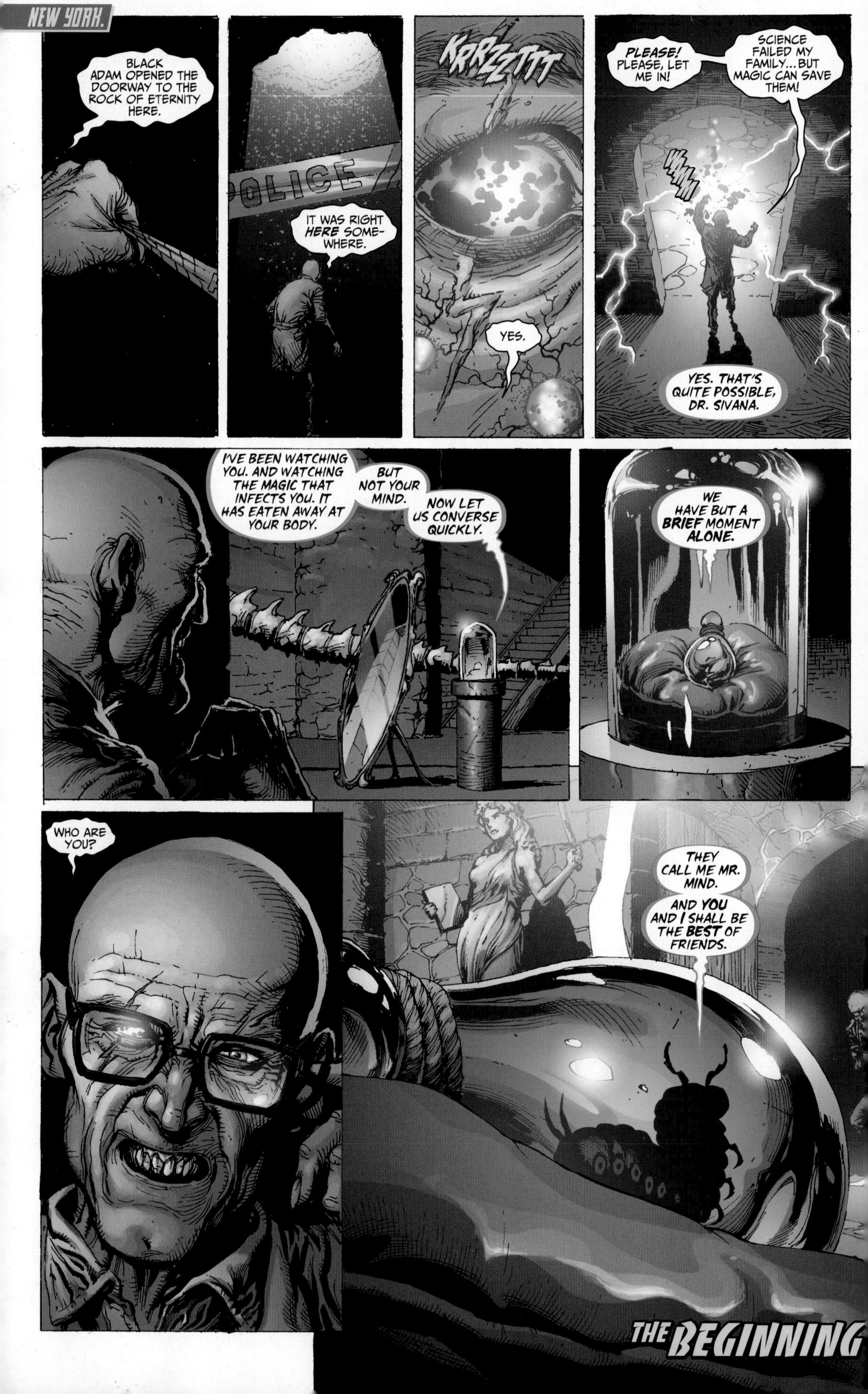
NEW YORK.
BLACK ADAM OPENED THE DOORWAY TO THE ROCK OF ETERNITY HERE.
POLICE
IT WAS RIGHT HERE SOME-WHERE.
KRRZZZTTTT
YES.
PLEASE! PLEASE, LET ME IN!
SCIENCE FAILED MY FAMILY...BUT MAGIC CAN SAVE THEM!
YES. THAT'S QUITE POSSIBLE, DR. SIVANA.
I'VE BEEN WATCHING YOU. AND WATCHING THE MAGIC THAT INFECTS YOU. IT HAS EATEN AWAY AT YOUR BODY.
BUT NOT YOUR MIND.
NOW LET US CONVERSE QUICKLY.
WE HAVE BUT A BRIEF MOMENT ALONE.
WHO ARE YOU?
THEY CALL ME MR. MIND.
AND YOU AND I SHALL BE THE BEST OF FRIENDS.
THE BEGINNING

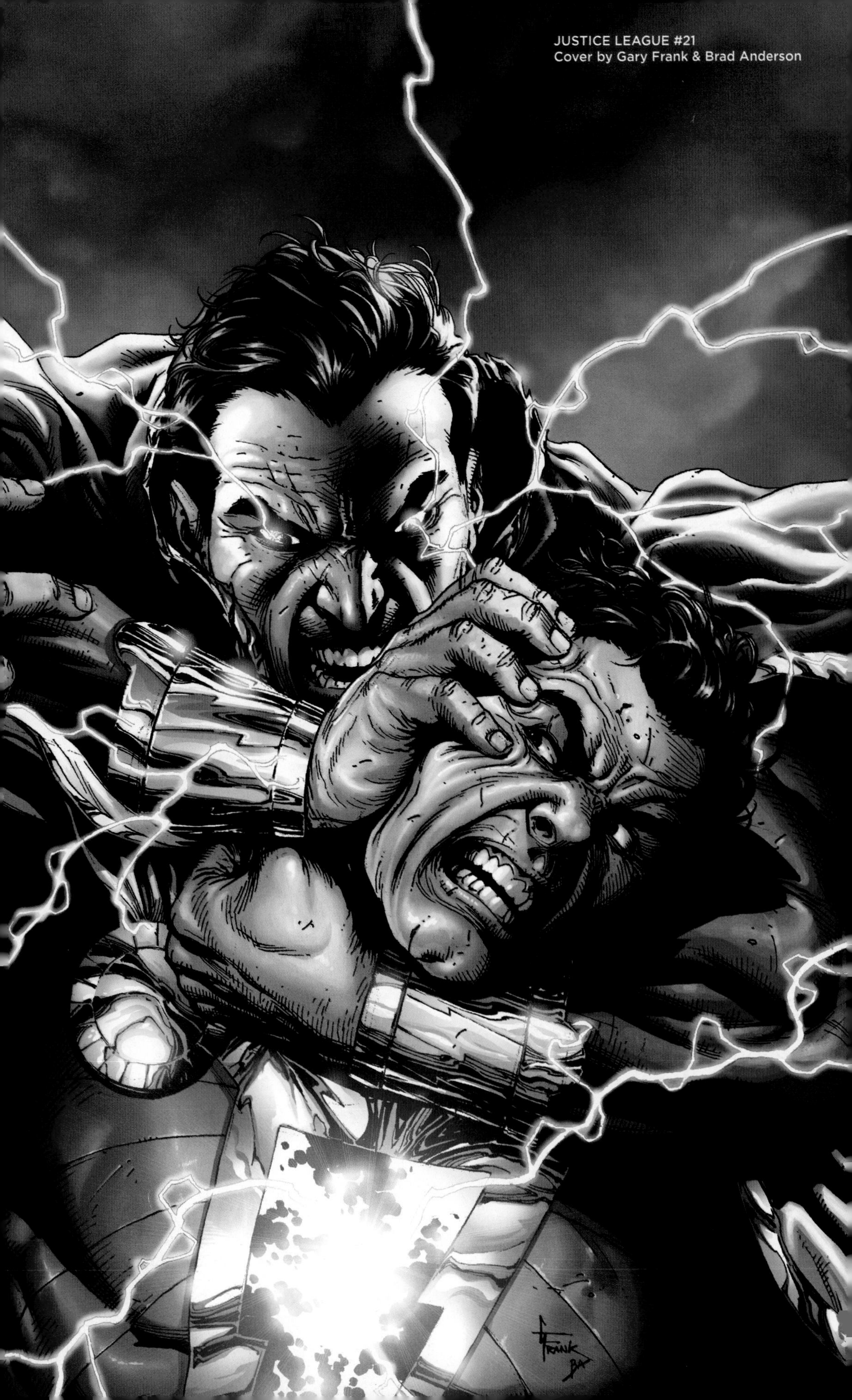

JUSTICE LEAGUE #21
Cover by Gary Frank & Brad Anderson

JUSTICE LEAGUE #21
Variant cover by Shane Davis, Michelle Delecki & Alex Sinclair

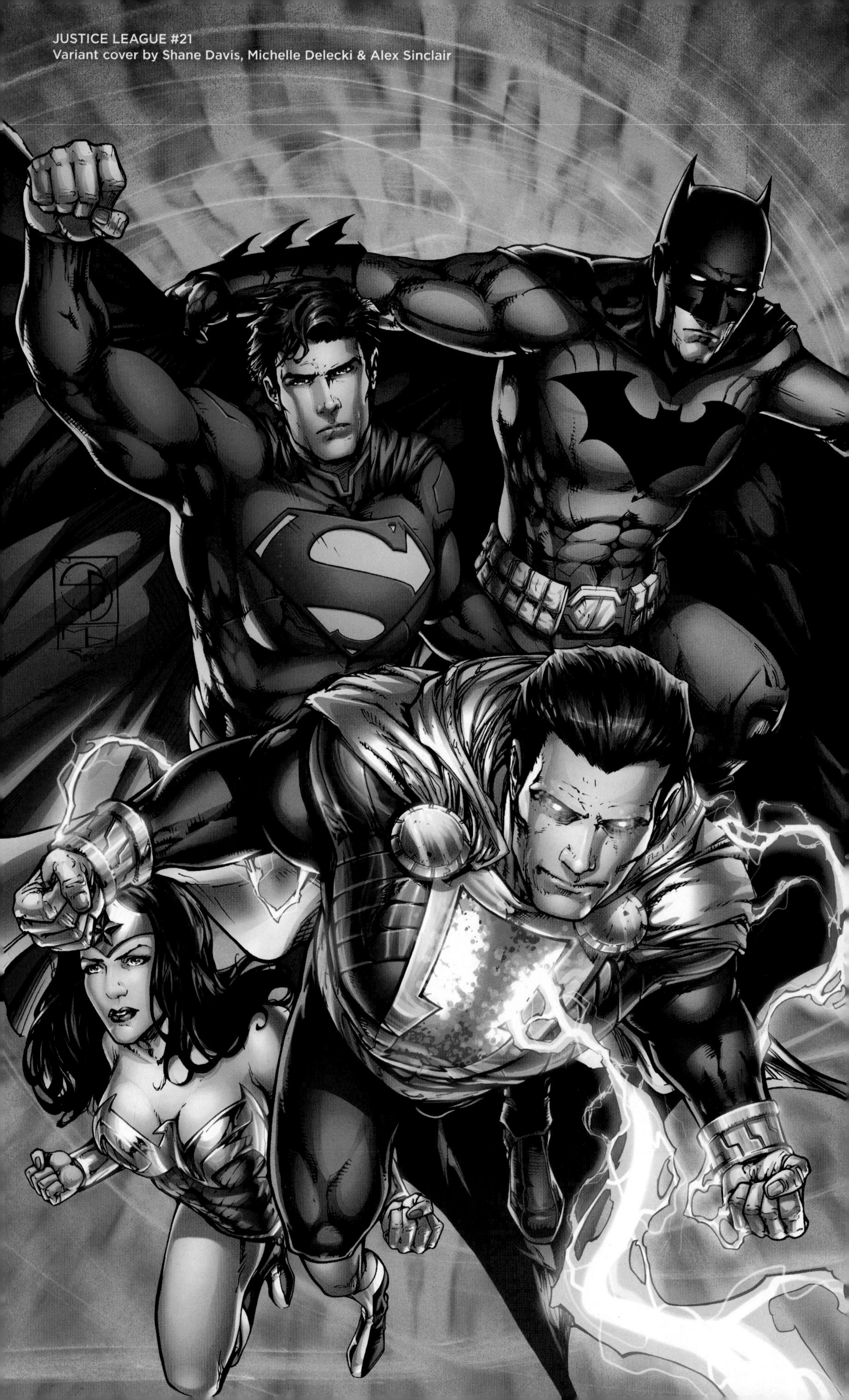

JUSTICE LEAGUE #0
Variant cover by Ivan Reis, Joe Prado & Rod Reis

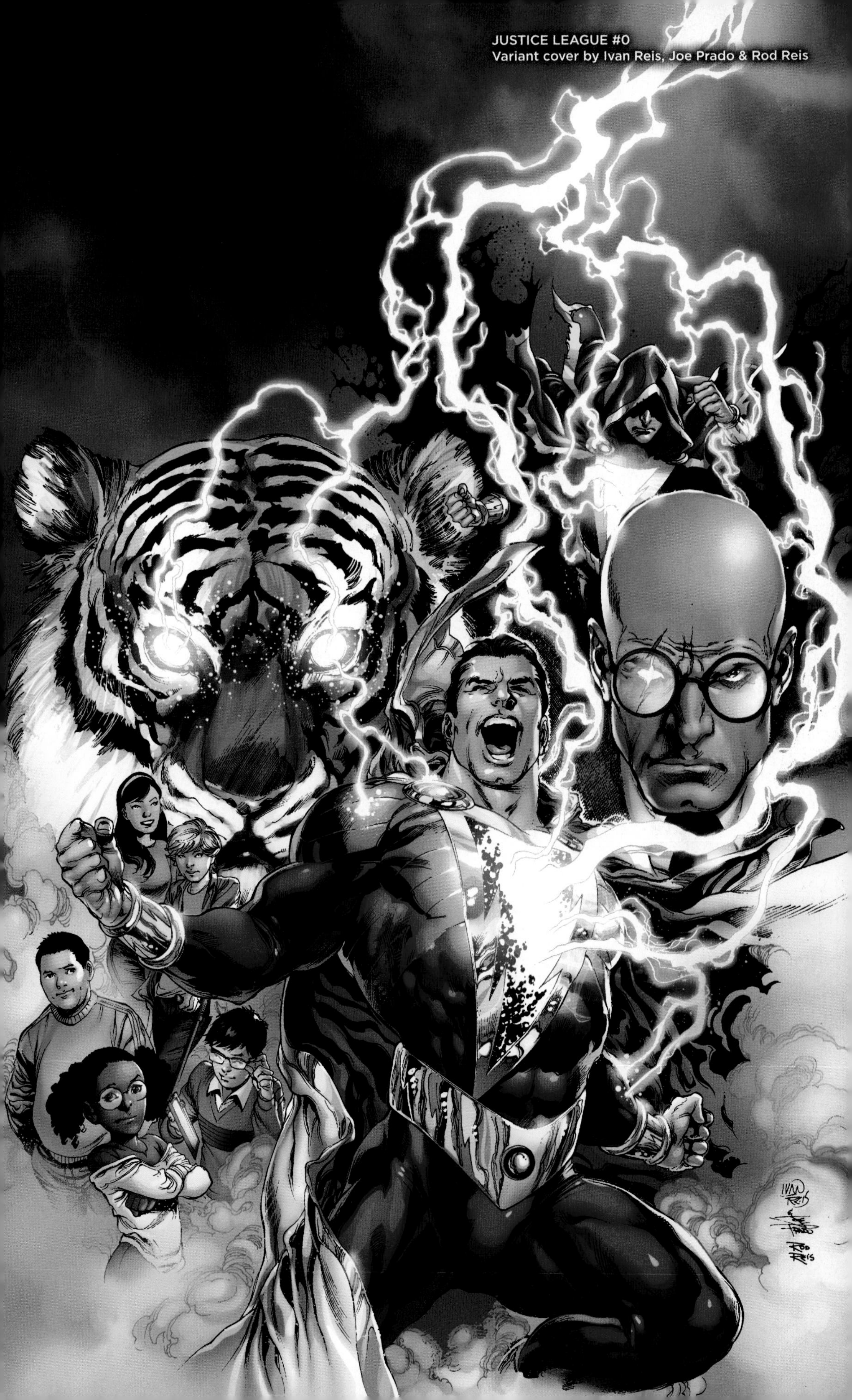

SHAZAM!

CHARACTER DESIGNS BY GARY FRANK

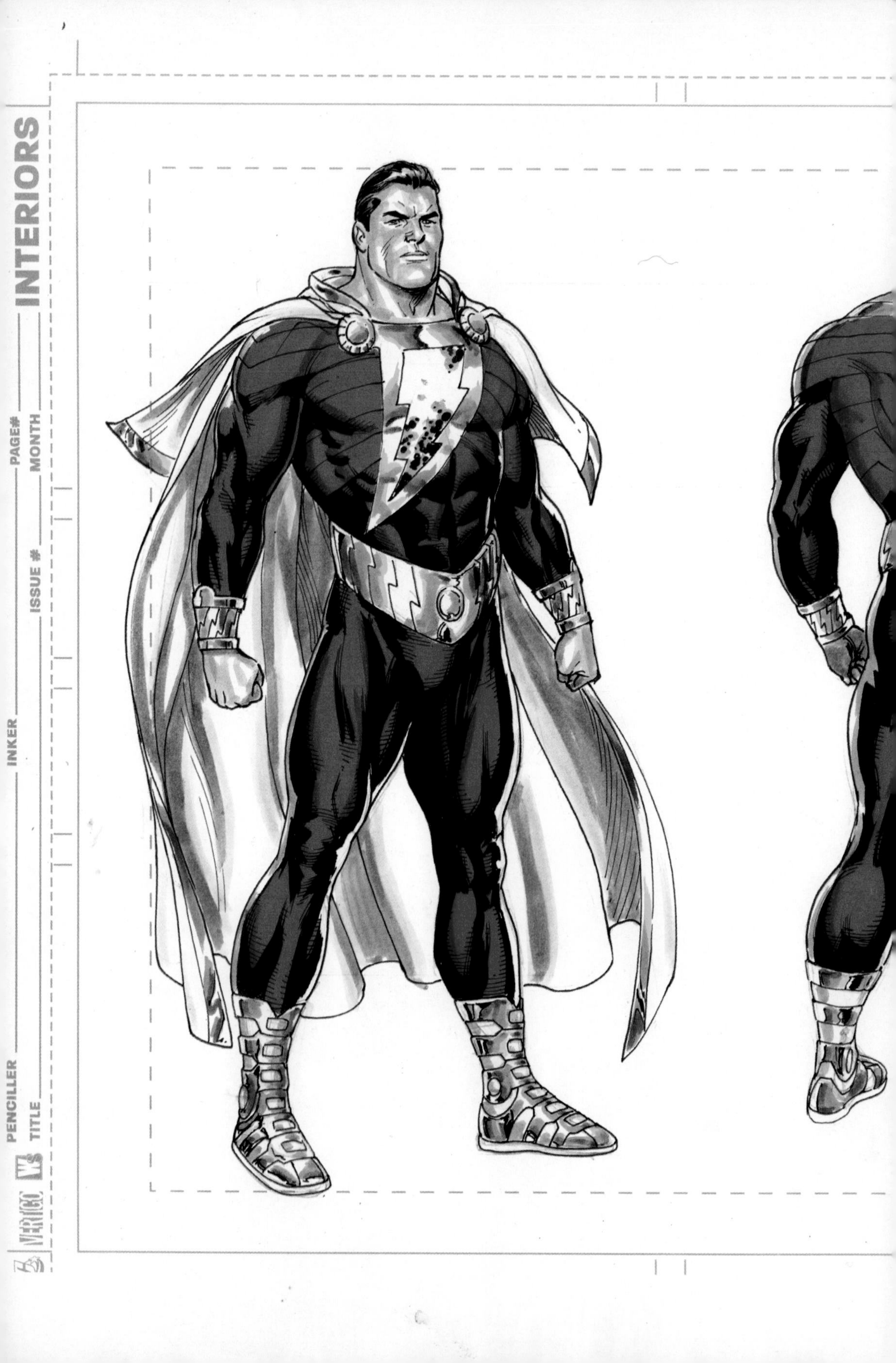
INTERIORS
PAGE#
MONTH
ISSUE #
INKER
PENCILLER
TITLE

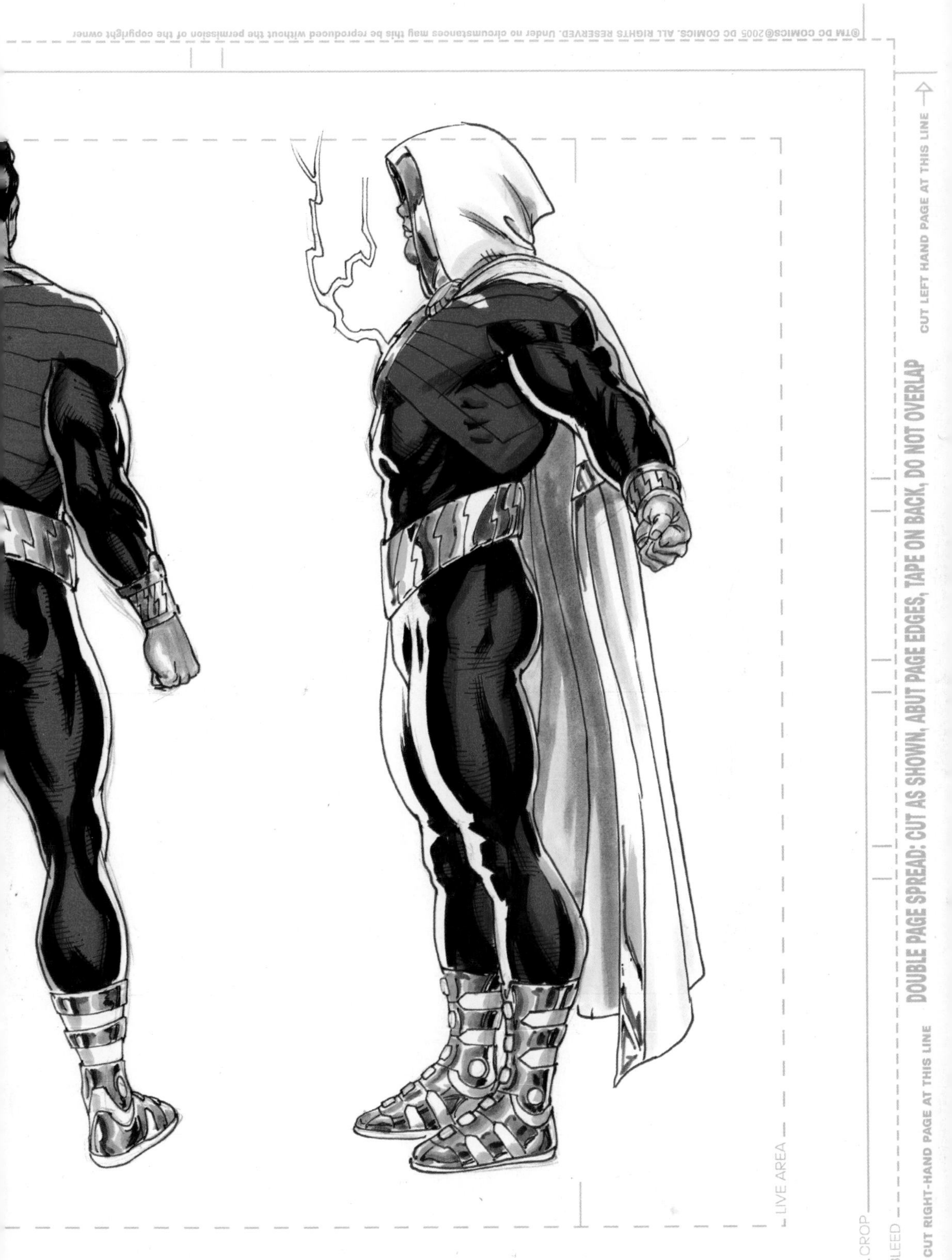
©TM DC COMICS©2005 DC COMICS. ALL RIGHTS RESERVED. Under no circumstances may this be reproduced without the permission of the copyright owner
CUT LEFT HAND PAGE AT THIS LINE
DOUBLE PAGE SPREAD: CUT AS SHOWN, ABUT PAGE EDGES, TAPE ON BACK, DO NOT OVERLAP
CUT RIGHT-HAND PAGE AT THIS LINE
LIVE AREA
CROP
BLEED

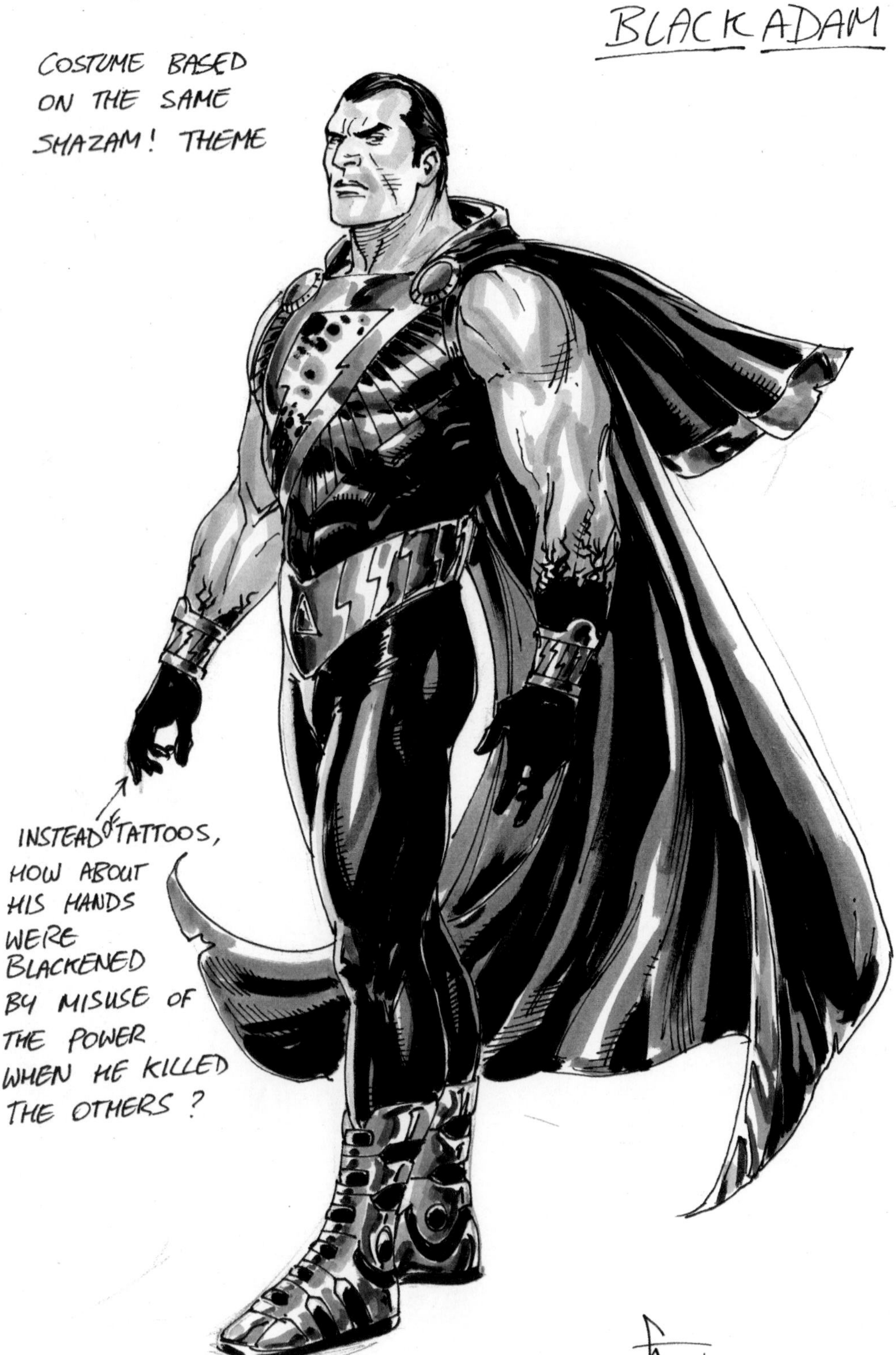
BLACK ADAM
COSTUME BASED ON THE SAME SHAZAM! THEME
INSTEAD of TATTOOS, HOW ABOUT HIS HANDS WERE BLACKENED BY MISUSE OF THE POWER WHEN HE KILLED THE OTHERS ?
FRANK

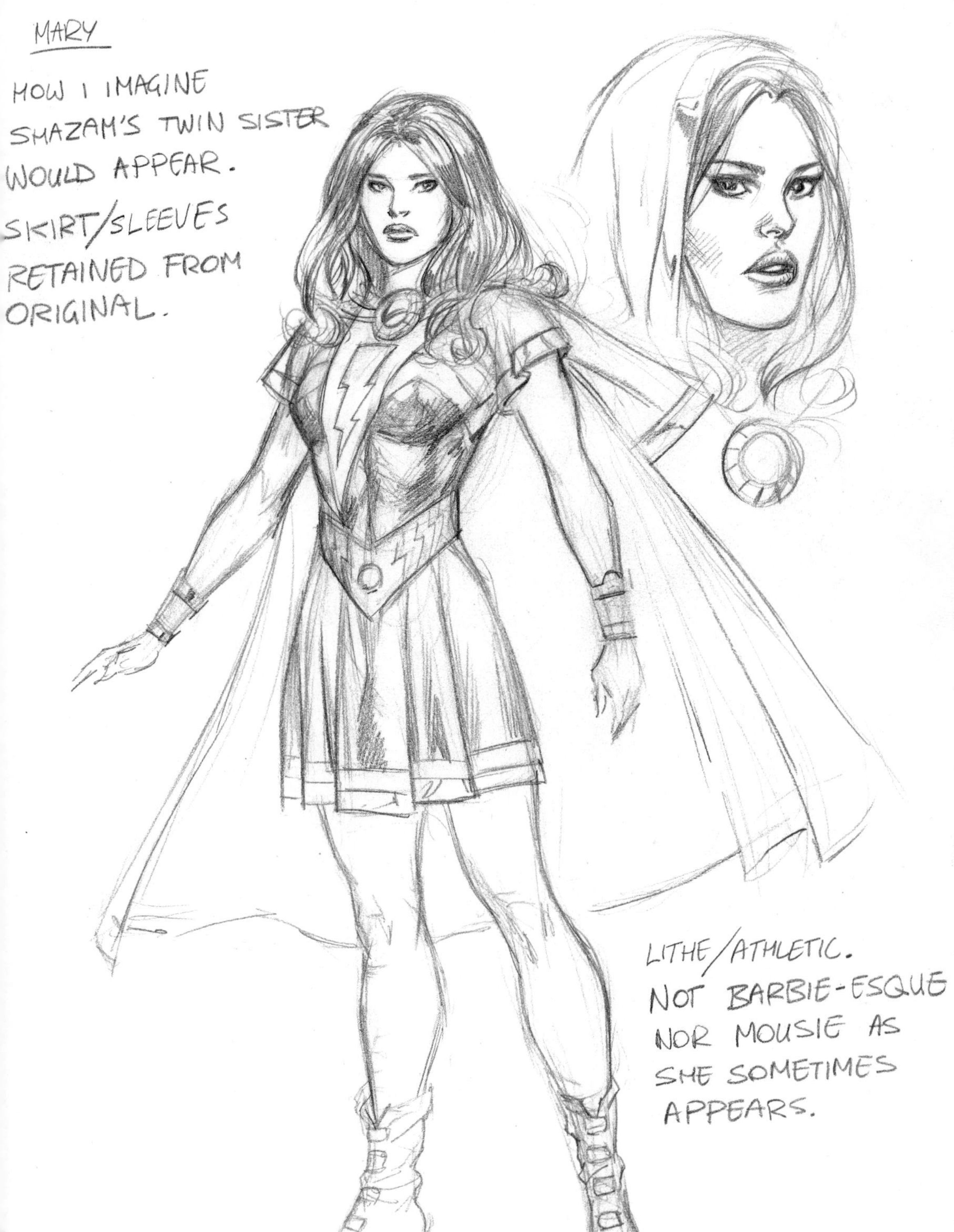
MARY
HOW I IMAGINE SHAZAM'S TWIN SISTER WOULD APPEAR.
SKIRT/SLEEVES RETAINED FROM ORIGINAL.
LITHE/ATHLETIC.
NOT BARBIE-ESQUE NOR MOUSIE AS SHE SOMETIMES APPEARS.

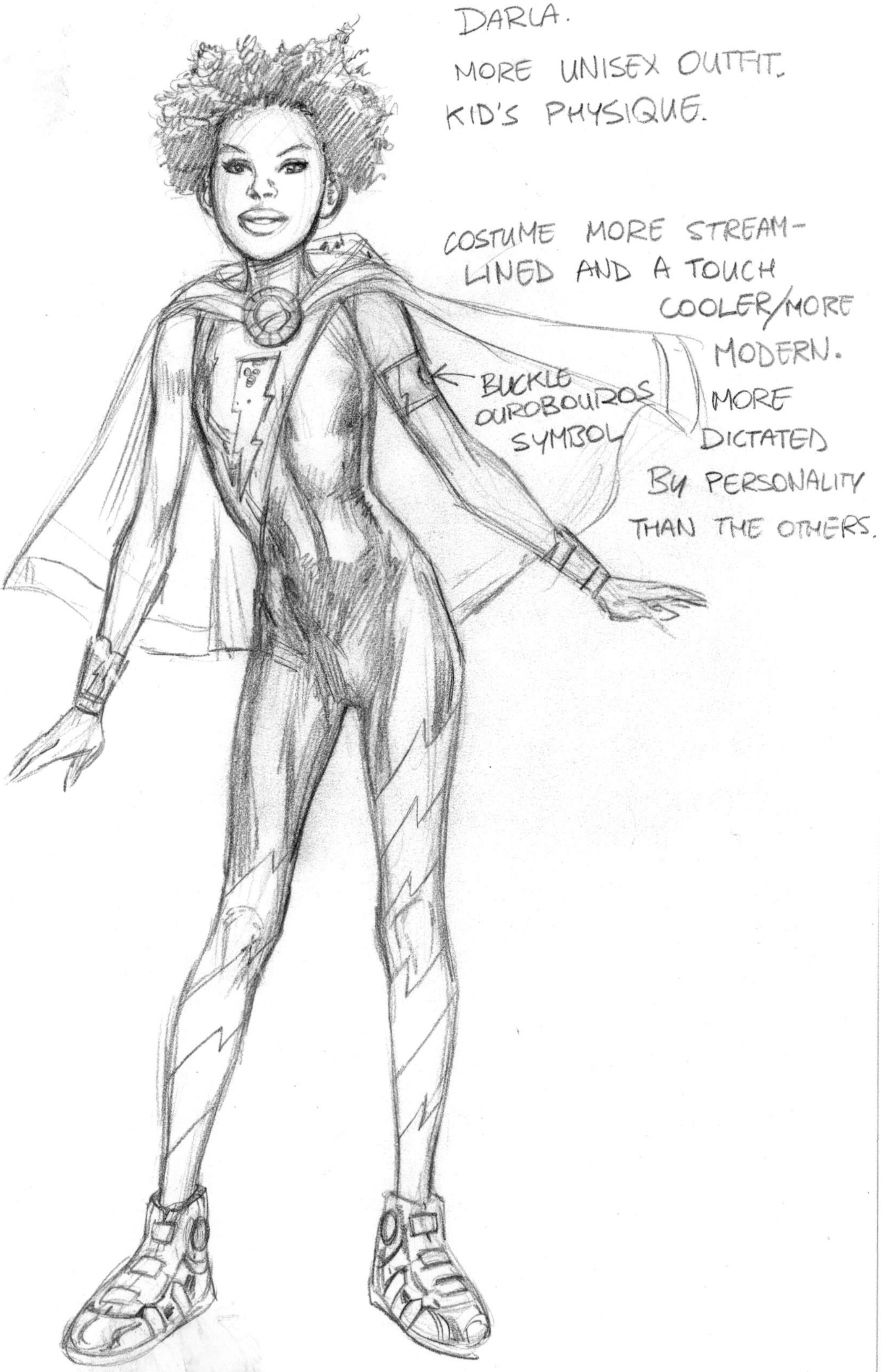
DARLA.
MORE UNISEX OUTFIT.
KID'S PHYSIQUE.
COSTUME MORE STREAM-LINED AND A TOUCH COOLER/MORE MODERN. MORE DICTATED BY PERSONALITY THAN THE OTHERS.
BUCKLE OUROBOUROS SYMBOL

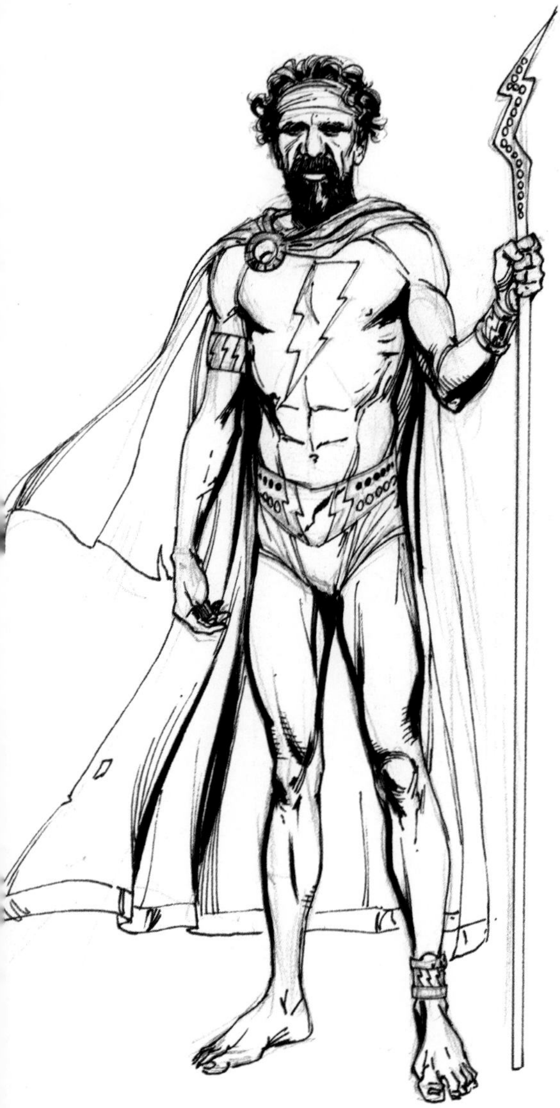

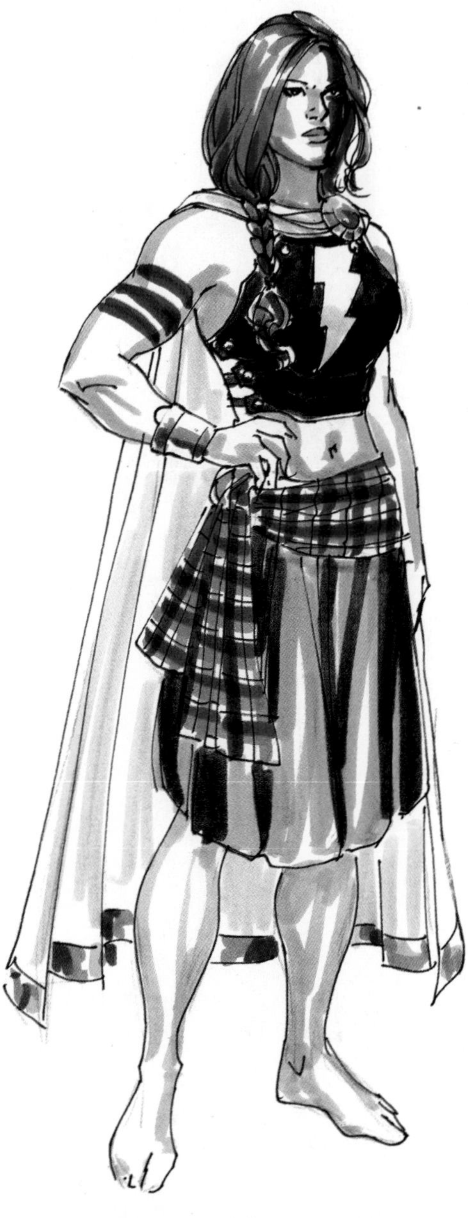

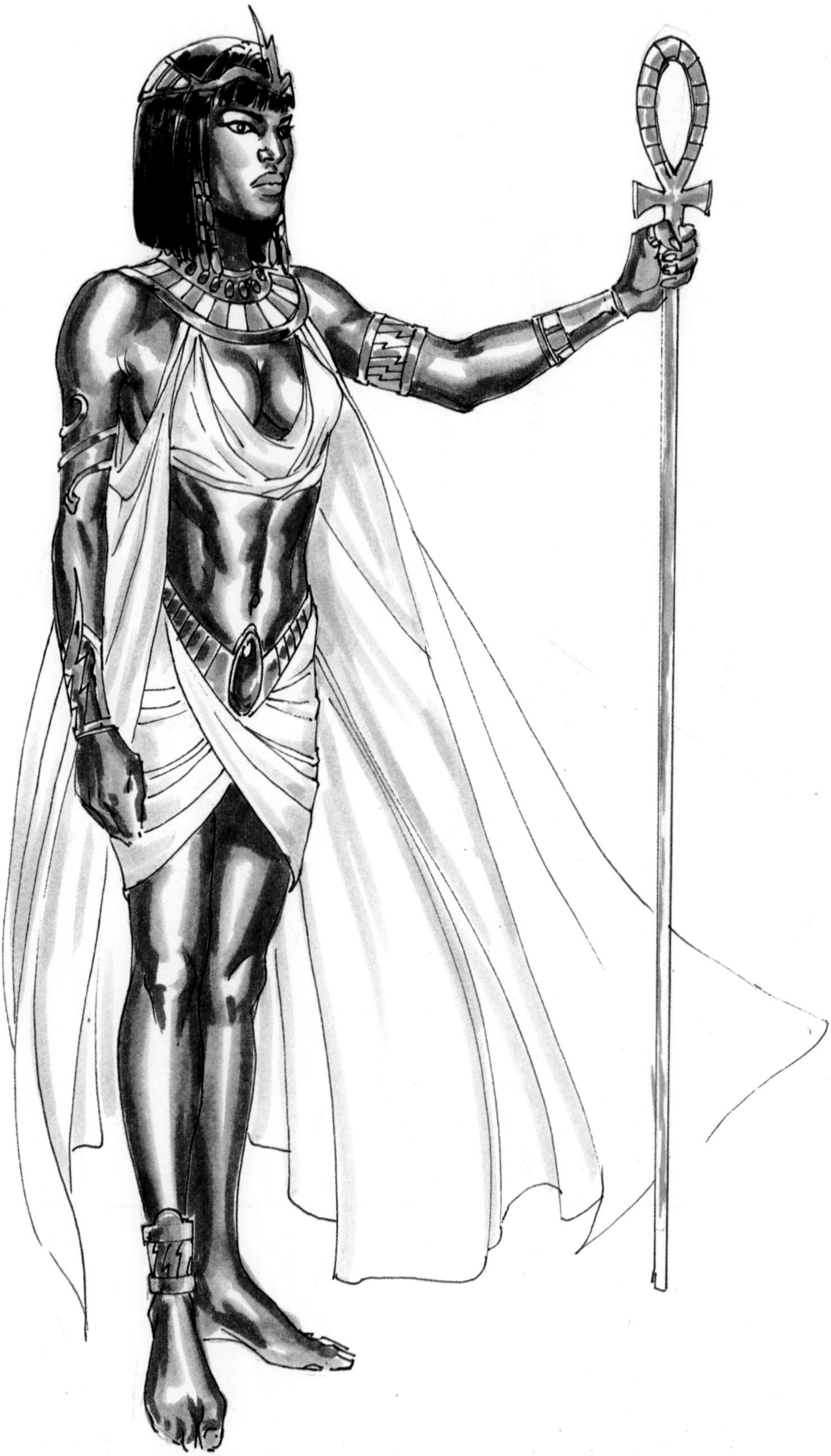

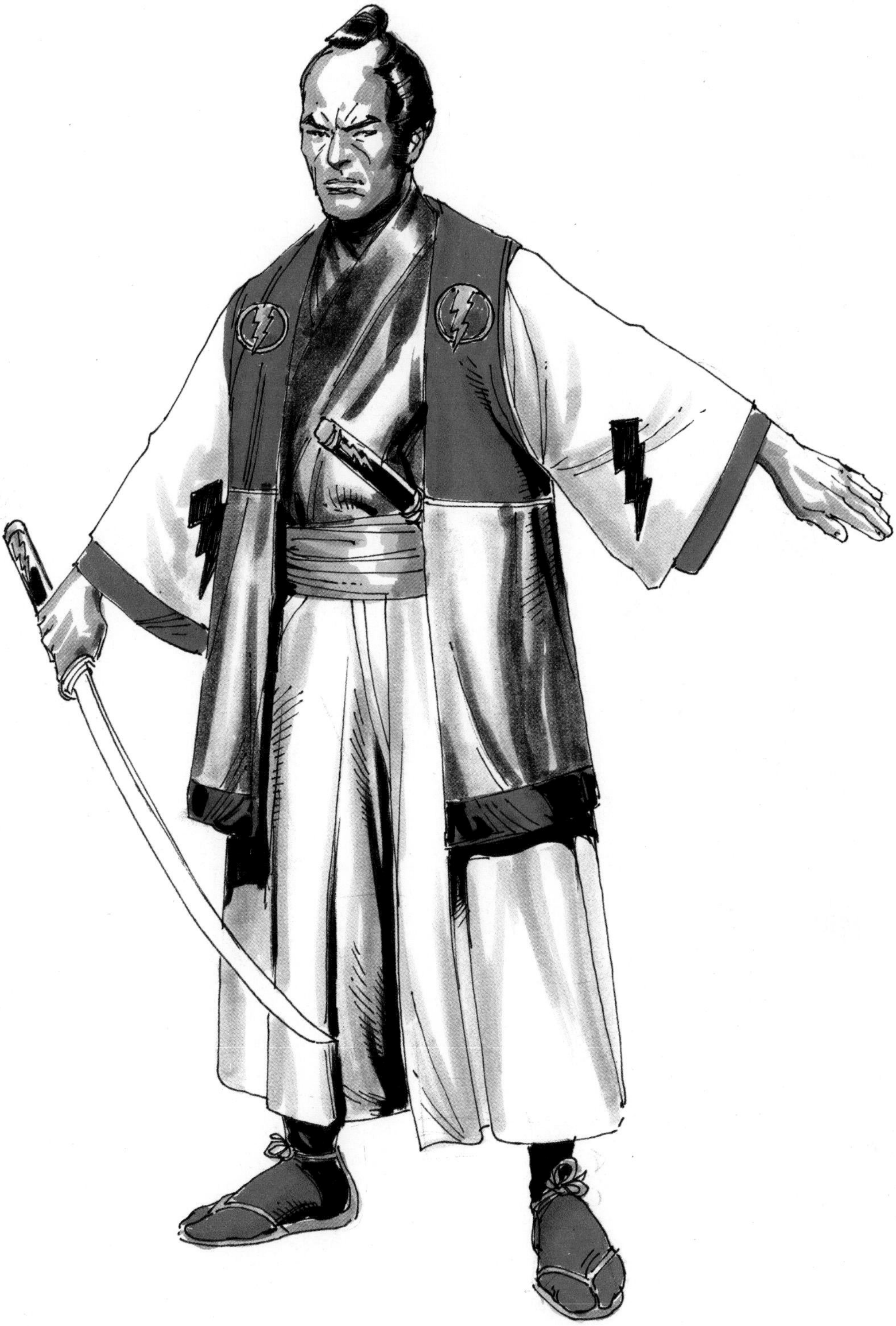

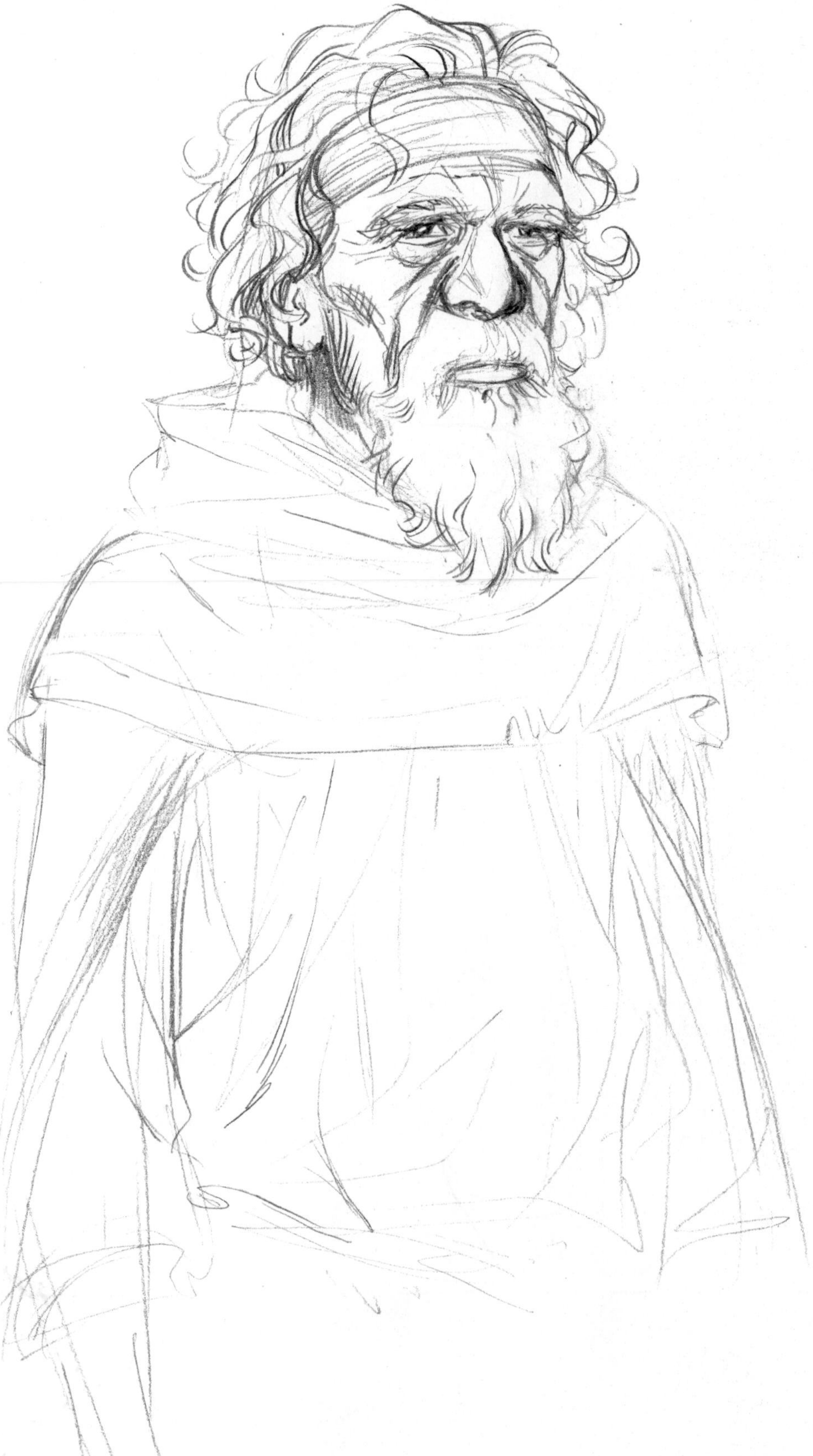

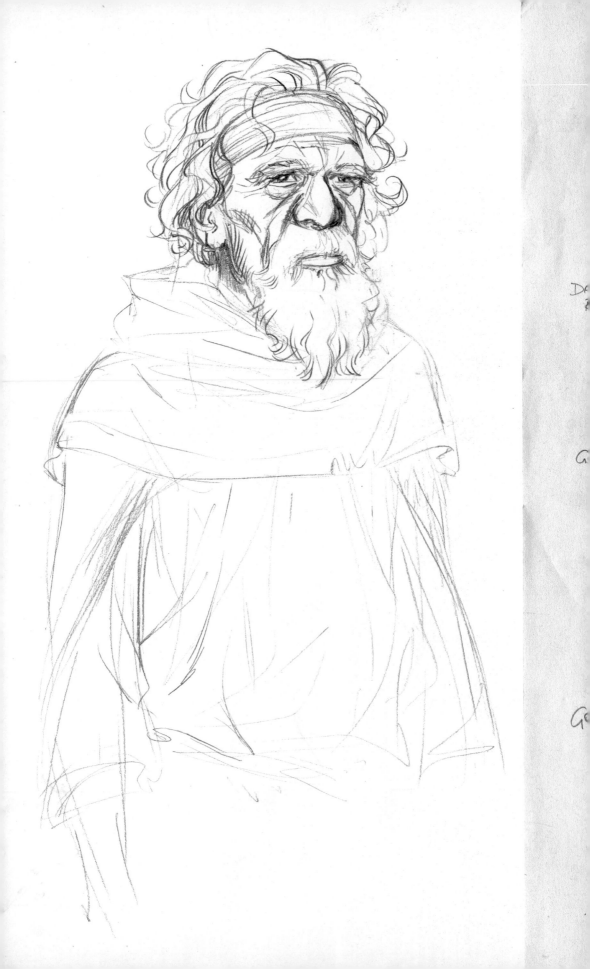

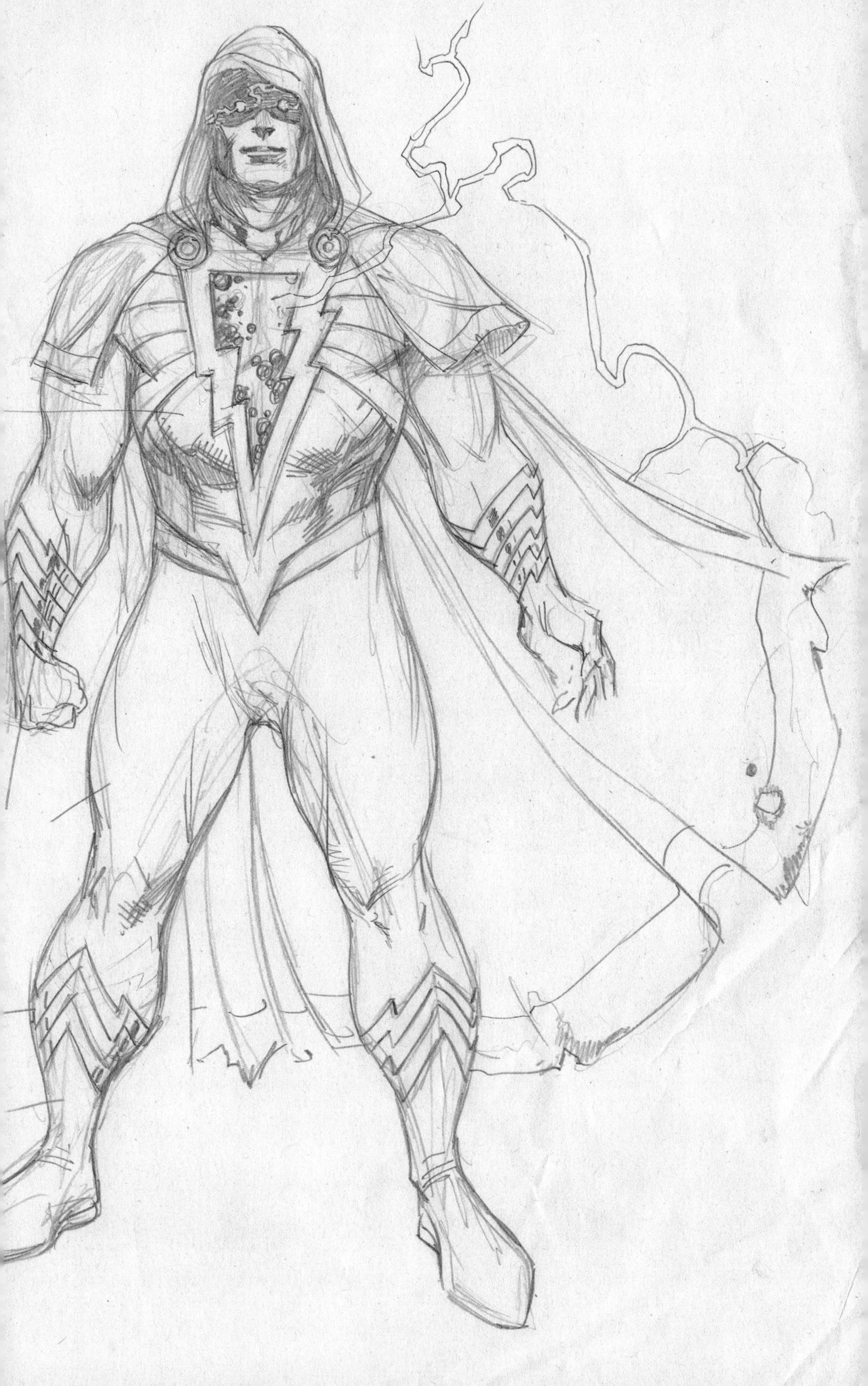

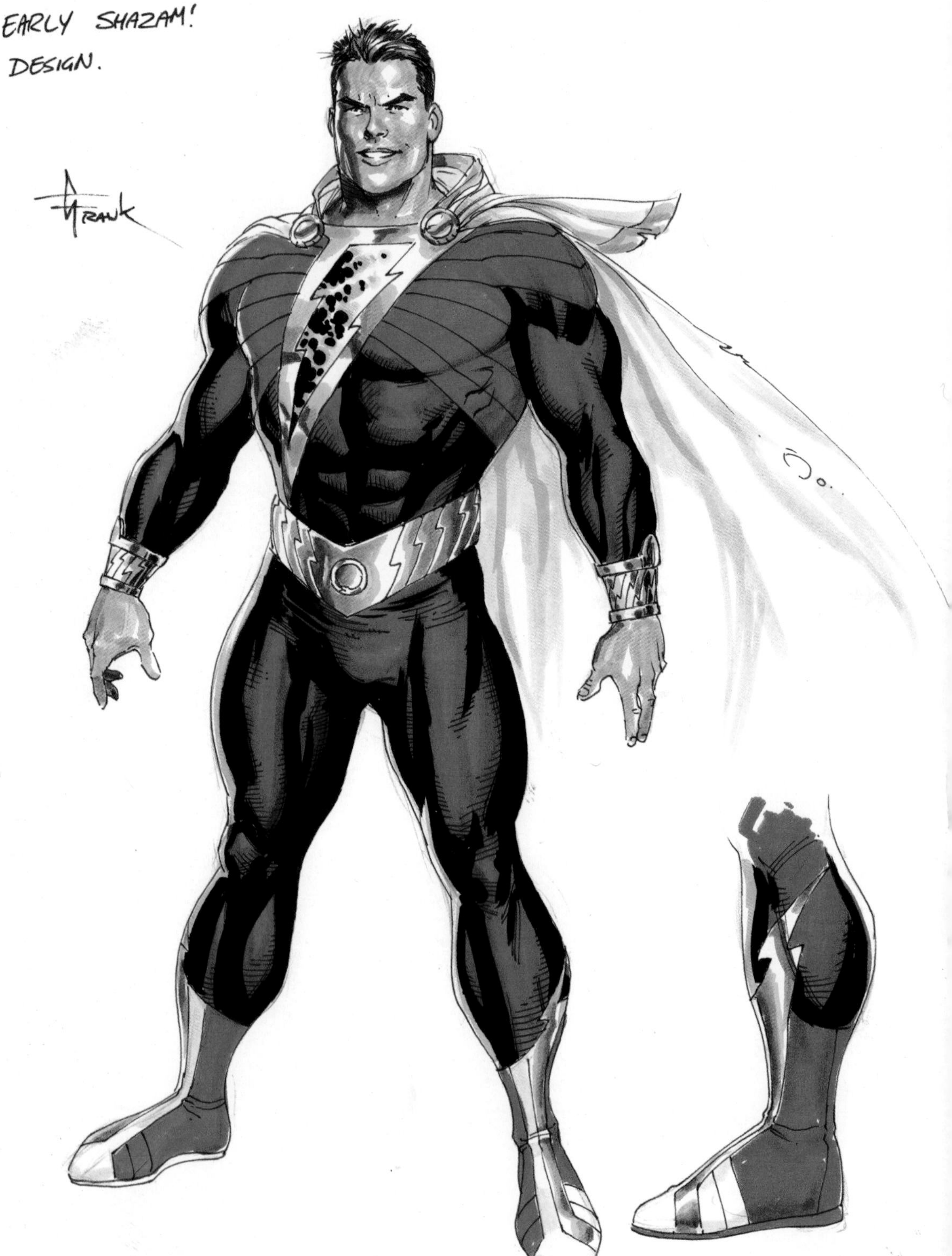
EARLY SHAZAM!
DESIGN.
FRANK